MW01492819

Subversive Seduction

Subversive Seduction

DARWIN, SEXUAL SELECTION,
AND THE SPANISH NOVEL

Travis Landry

A McLellan Book

UNIVERSITY OF WASHINGTON PRESS   *Seattle and London*

the
modern language
initiative

THIS BOOK IS MADE POSSIBLE BY A COLLABORATIVE GRANT
FROM THE ANDREW W. MELLON FOUNDATION.

*This book is published with the assistance of a grant
from the McLellan Endowed Series Fund, established
through the generosity of Martha McCleary
McLellan and Mary McLellan Williams.*

*Publication of this book was also supported in part
by funding from Kenyon College.*

© 2012 by the University of Washington Press
17 16 15 14 13 12   5 4 3 2 1

University of Washington Press
PO Box 50096, Seattle, WA 98145, USA
www.washington.edu/uwpress

Library of Congress Cataloging-in-Publication Data
Landry, Travis.
Subversive seduction : Darwin, sexual selection, and
the Spanish novel / Travis Landry.
p.   cm. — (The modern language initiative)
ISBN 978-0-295-99218-1 (hardback)
ISBN 978-0-295-99219-8 (paperback)
1. Sexual selection in literature. 2. Spanish fiction—
19th century—History and criticism. 3. Spanish
fiction—20th century—History and criticism.
4. Darwin, Charles, 1809–1882—Influence. 5.
Literature and science—Spain. I. Title.
PQ6140.S52L36   2012
863.009'36—dc23   2012025435

CONTENTS

Contents

ACKNOWLEDGMENTS

This book has been several years in the making and would not have been possible without considerable support from a variety of sources. I would first like to thank Anthony Geist and Nil Santiáñez for their committed direction in the early stages of the project and for their enduring friendship over the years. Each has stood by me and repeatedly given invaluable counsel. Likewise, I am also deeply indebted to Marshall Brown and Gary Handwerk, who have been in my corner since day one. Their encouragement and careful readings have had a tremendous impact. David Barash, too, is to be singled out for helping me see the rich complexity of evolutionary science; I still cherish the warm camaraderie we shared talking about life and Darwin so many moons ago. Others along the way who have provided strong backing and suggestions include Francisco Caudet, Edward Baker, and Thomas Glick. I also wish to thank those from my Italian studies, including Giuseppe Leporace and Remo Ceserani. Though their influence on the project is hard to quantify, they nonetheless played a formative role in my broader academic trajectory. By contrast, the involvement of Jerry Hoeg and Kevin Larsen can be easily measured. They took an early interest in my work and were instrumental in my two initial publications to explore the subject that would later become this book. By means of acknowledgment, these were "The Moral Sense of Suitors and Selectors in Jacinto Octavio Picón," *Ometeca* 12 (2008): 137–51, and "Darwin, Sexual Selection, and the Spanish Novel in the Late Nineteenth Century," from *Interdisciplinary Essays on Darwinism in Hispanic Literature and Film: The Intersection of Science and the Humanities,* ed. Jerry Hoeg and Kevin Larsen (New York: Mellen, 2009), 77–99.

Very special words of personal gratitude go, as well, to Dale Pratt and Valerie Hegstrom, who both mean so much to me. Similarly, gifted mentors are rare, and since my undergraduate years at Brown University, I have been fortunate to have grown as a scholar under the warm tutelage of Geoffrey Ribbans, who first introduced me to nine-teenth-century Spanish literature and has followed my progress ever since. And, for Arnold Weinstein, there are no words to express what his vision of life and literature has done for me. He lit a spark, chan-neled my comparative instincts, and has been an anchor for me up to the present. We all need someone to trust along our chosen path, and Arnold has been that person for me. Jacqueline Ettinger, too, has been a most incredible ally, and when it comes to this project, I owe her everything for believing in me from the very beginning. Moreover, I have wonderful colleagues now at Kenyon College and can say that I feel at home among them. Funding from Kenyon, including a Sum-mer Stipend, has been crucial, and the Modern Language Initiative and the University of Washington Press have together made possible the publication of my study, which I am grateful to have included in the University of Washington Press's McLellan Endowed Series. I also want to thank Tim Roberts, for his work as Managing Editor; Jane Lichty, for her excellent copyediting; and those on the design team, including Ashley Saleeba and Sarah Cohen, for making me part of the cover collaboration. Finally, I would like to express my deep love for my family and to close by dedicating the book to Sarah, Sadie, June, and my mom.

Subversive Seduction

Introduction

The Indeterminacy of Natural Law

Charles Darwin was by no means the first to take up the question of sexual selection. A better candidate, in fact, would be Plato. The reproductive practices between men and women concern him time and again as he reflects on how to maximize the common good. In the *Statesman*, for example, he has a young Socrates promote the "weaving together, with regular intertwining" of contrary dispositions as a means to ensure advantageous variation in offices of the State and the populace at large; in *Theages*, the question turns from nature to nurture as Demodocus laments the difficulties of cultivation: "Socrates, all living things tend to follow the same course—particularly man, but also the other animals and the plants that grow in the earth. . . . I found the planting, or procreation—whatever you're supposed to call it—of this son of mine the easiest thing in the world. But his upbringing has been difficult"; in *Laws*, the Athenian counsels Clinias on the importance of making smart choices about parenthood well in advance: "The bride and groom should resolve to present the state with the best and finest children they can produce," which requires due attention to planning at the risk of "deplorable" results; and the most infamous moment, from the *Republic*, treads the dangerous line of selective breeding: "It follows from our previous agreements, first, that the best men must have sex with the best women as frequently as possible, while the opposite is true of the most inferior men and women, and, second, that if our herd is to be of the highest possible quality, the former's offspring must be reared but not the latter's."[1] Of course, this final passage will bring to mind eugenics and all that makes us suspicious about any theory that might control rather than simply explain mating practices among humans, while like fears persist even about the possibility of such an explanation for the unforeseen consequences it might bring.

Now Darwin never advocated for the "sophisticated lotteries" described in Plato, far from it, and neither should eugenics, like so many other ills to come from misguided ideas about evolutionary theory, fall on his shoulders. Still, he brings his fair share of baggage, and the theory of sexual selection as expounded in *The Descent of Man, and Selection in Relation to Sex* (1871) carries with it a cultural legacy colored by patriarchy and women's oppression. With misgivings aside for the moment though, it becomes evident that what Plato and Darwin share is a concern for the social implications of human reproduction. Hence, Plato provides a useful point of departure because his dialogues prove how difficult it is to locate any "zero degree" before Darwin by which the impact of evolutionary theory might be measured with respect to the historical shifts that have come to define the continuance of our lot in terms of sex and everything that surrounds it. Courtship between men and women along with the conventions, uncertainties, and politics existed long before the nineteenth century, and the representation of this dynamic in literature after Darwin was not determined by him. Rather, it absorbs the past in ways so complex that to claim otherwise would be disingenuous.

Consequently, this study is not about the influence Darwin had on a select group of Spanish novelists from the last decades of the nineteenth century. For most of the authors discussed, there is little to no evidence for how much direct knowledge any of them might have had of Darwin's writings, to say nothing of the theory of sexual selection, which in and of itself remains an enigma for its virtual absence from the debates surrounding his science at the time. One may no doubt discover clues that suggest concrete linkages, but these, while they can perhaps enhance certain readings, are insufficient in their own right for an airtight argument of the sort. Moreover, for the exceptional cases where historical records and other supporting documents confirm a particular writer's fascination with Darwin, as with Benito Pérez Galdós and Emilia Pardo Bazán, a recapitulation of this information factors very little in the chapters here devoted to their works, and neither do Darwin's own personal history and letters play a major role. Bert Bender, who offers the only sustained treatment of sexual selection in fiction with his study of American writers from 1871 to 1926, foregrounds influence, but his illustration of how Darwin became appropriated by authors who knew and corresponded about *The Descent*, as useful as it might be, stops short of pushing us to envision why this same fiction might reveal a different Darwin from the one we know.[2] Hence, it is important to admit that the present book breaks with these conventions. Even if sufficient source material were available for the reception of sexual selection among the Spanish novelists, a search for irrefutable ascription of ideas would still remain a one-directional pursuit. To be sure, the intricacies of how a certain figure came to shape another can prove intriguing, as in the case of Bender's exposition and those of others who turn to evolution for Darwinian manifestations of entangled gardens, exquisite manliness, and even love, but this circumscribed attribution of ideas, for the nature of history thus construed, does not discover how time might fold back on itself and redirect understanding of this science in a light other than impact.

In the chapters to come, Darwin's theory of sexual selection acts as a lens for reading literature, and in this respect, the approach shares something comparable with Freudian or Marxist interpretations, which as countless studies have shown need not belabor how much Freud or Marx a particular author might or might not have read. The use of "transcoding" to extend these schools of thought to times and places far removed from the works with which they originated is by now accepted practice,[3] and there is indeed a universal quality to Darwin as well. As chapter 1 points out, an emerging current of "literary Darwinism" applies this broad brush in efforts to explain why characters behave as they do in all literature.[4] Nevertheless, the thinking throughout this study is not Freudian or Marxist or even Darwinian in the purist sense, as David Barash and Nanelle Barash's would be.[5] So, just as readers should be disabused of preconceptions about the anchorage of Darwin's influence, it is also necessary to point out that this exploration of sexual selection goes beyond the analytic optic of a Lacanian approach to contemporary film or a Derridean reading of James Joyce, since the application model, too, is limited by its insistence on "application" for meaningful inquiry. Such methodology would be sufficient if the aim were to draw out what Darwin reveals about a discrete set of Spanish novels or even a much broader set of like novels of the same period beyond Spain, but as it turns out, these novels might just as well be the lens by which we read Darwin, rather than the other way around. This retelling of Darwin through fiction therefore grounds itself in the reciprocity between literature and science.

Since José Ortega y Gasset famously declared that "Darwin sweeps heroes from the face of the earth,"[6] evolutionary theory and determinism have been synonymous in Spanish culture and literary criticism, and in the broader European context the association is no less ingrained. One need only think of the ways Darwin is spoken of in conversations about Émile Zola, Giovanni Verga, or Thomas Hardy, to name but a few, where the traditional, one-dimensional view of naturalism posits an indifferent machine of social circumstance that leads the hapless individual to ruin and despair. In his articulation of an amoral universe, so the story goes, Darwin became the most immoral of demigods, and the literature in his shadow, regardless of those authors who considered themselves "experimental moralists,"[7] to use the nomenclature coined by Zola, caused righteous scandal for showing the ugly underbelly of reality. Such reductionism clouds our appreciation of both Darwin and the novelists.

In truth, indeterminism defines sexual selection, which is arguably Darwin's richest theory for being his most unresolved, and the constant change achieved by the overarching operation of natural selection depends on open-ended variables. The problem is, without literature it proves very difficult to make sense of this aspect of his science in the social sphere, much less to understand it in the context of the late nineteenth century. These are therefore the two guiding aims of this book, and the latter centers in particular on the implications of the representation of sexual selection in the realist novel. Chapter 1 is essential because it sets in motion the theoretical agenda for the project, namely, that the reciprocity between literature and science is about a deeper reconciliation between the two. For far too long, a misconception has persisted that there exists a (humanist) "moral" realm somehow divorced from or other than the (empiricist) "scientific" approach to hard data and experimentation. This was certainly not the case in Darwin's day, and it is untenable to maintain the separation a century and a half later. Ongoing contemporary debates about everything from cloning to global warming, courses and seminars at prestigious universities on the ethics of science, top-selling books on our innate altruism, these are nothing more than a sample of the latest manifestations of a relationship that has been defined by overlap since the outset.

Once in conversation with a renowned expert on evolutionary science during the early stages of my project, I spoke of factors like "love" and "jealousy" inherent in Darwin's views of anthropomorphic sexual selection as "unempirical" and hence less "scientific." His reply was that Darwin would not have understood what I meant. It was then I began to see that when Darwin reflects at length on the "moral sense" in *The Descent* this is not an isolated, "nonscientific" digression, and it is not unimportant (though its absence from discussions of Darwin might lead us to believe so). On the contrary, it is absolutely fundamental to his arguments regarding the origins of humankind and the laws governing sexual selection, which Adrian Desmond and James Moore also make clear in their authoritative biography when discussing Darwin's thought in years leading up to *The Descent*.[8] Neither science nor literature exists in a vacuum. Communal and engaged with each other, they merge, and their assessment in tandem has ethical consequence. The reconciliation does not take place in the moral dimension of Darwin's thought itself, however, because it cannot be perceived or understood in its full social effect absent its representation in real-world encounters, which *realism* of the late nineteenth century in its systematic consideration of material reality and scientific precepts managed to achieve as no other literary movement could. Hence, an articulation of this face of Darwin through attention to the reciprocity between his science and literature does not jettison him as a scientist. In fact, the opposite is true, since in this way we perceive how his writing collapses these distinctions once read through fiction concerned with the social consequence of courtship at the time.

In the wake of the theoretical reconciliation rehearsed in chapter 1, the next step in my argument shows why male-male rivalry and female passive choice, the two principal tenets of Darwinian sexual selection, raise important ethical questions in *The Descent* and the decades since about the subjugation of women, given the gendered power dynamics at play in the social sphere. But being more social in this way does not make sexual selection any less material (or natural) than the historically privileged operation of natural selection, which has always been deemed a more serious (and manly) matter for its concern with survival and self-interest. Yet, as will become clear, sexual and natural selection are not separate and competing theories; the former is simply one of the two mechanisms by which maximum variation is achieved through the latter, the other being environmental pressures. The questions at stake in this study therefore have little to do with what impact Darwin had on transformations in romance

plotlines in the novel in the particular case of Spain after the liberal
Revolution of 1868. Though not to be denied, what transformations
and when, along with whether or not Darwin deserves any of the
credit, is a different argument from the one being proposed here, since
among other reasons it remains confined to the novel itself. Along
with a revisionist approach that shows the indeterminism of Darwin's
thought regarding sexual selection, this study argues that the plotlines themselves of these novels, formally constituted according to
courtship and varied instantiations of the oxymoronic law of female
passive choice in *The Descent*, reveal the crossover between literature
and science to occur on moral grounds by showing the oppression of
women to be wholly antithetical to civilization as Darwin understood
it. Since female agency in the patriarchal social structure is the point
of intersection between literature and science when it comes to sexual selection and its representation, targeted coverage of the feminist
issues across the now well-established field of feminism and science,
from biology to sexual politics in literature and beyond, plays a central role in my larger argument about the social significance of Darwin and the Spanish novel.

In short, the significance is that Darwin, who has long been the
villain for the ways his science presumably proved the natural inferiority of women on evolutionary terms, can also be seen as an advocate for, rather than enemy of, the women's movement once he is
shown to be inconclusive with respect to sexual selection and female
choice. This is what is meant by making sense of the implications
behind this corrective approach to his theories in *The Descent*. However, the argument wants of specificity. As a country known for cultural markers like the legend of Don Juan, the virtuous woman ideal,
honor rites, erotic mysticism, spurious bloodlines, and the temptations of the Church confessional, Spain complicates the theory of
sexual selection and thus provides an ideal model for this investigation. At a pivotal moment in Spanish history, the Revolution of 1868
and the Restoration decades following, womanhood as defined by
patriarchy came under scrutiny as corollary economic, political, and
moral issues concerning the civil status of women, *la cuestión de la
mujer*, began to surface. This was also a moment of nation-building,
when an explosion of cultural production, namely, in the form of the
realist novel, engaged science in unprecedented ways in the name of
progress. It is not surprising, then, that the coetaneous social phenomenon of *el darwinismo*, a nomenclature born from a need to

describe a cultural rather than biological Darwin during those same years, became an ideological powder keg, pitting liberals against conservatives. Where one stood on evolutionary science said much more about where one stood on the future of Spain than about Darwin's works themselves, except, perhaps, as regards the status quo of inequality between men and women. Authoritative histories of Darwin in Spain provide ample evidence of the polemical hot air that characterized debates surrounding popularized catchphrases like *struggle for life* and *survival of the fittest*, as well as the blasphemy that went hand in hand with any view that might have appeared to sympathize with the notion of man's simian descent. For these reasons, chapter 3 contextualizes by painting the historical reception and dissemination of *The Descent* in Spain through close attention to its translations, the ideological agendas of the translators, and the periodical culture. It gives a sense of how much was read, how much was understood, and to what social ends.

In the process, and most important, chapter 3 brings together for the first time in a systematic way *la cuestión de la mujer* and *el darwinismo* by showing sexual selection to be the unnamed crossroads of these two currents of social concern (which were very much in play across Europe and the United States in various analogous forms at the time). The only direct references to the theory appear in the prefaces to the earliest Spanish translations of *The Descent* and a handful of periodical essays in which sexual selection receives passing mention at best. This silence is problematic, because it limits our understanding of the convergence of cultural production and science on this particular front of Darwin in Spain and, more broadly, of the ethical reach of a nebulous theory like sexual selection when it comes to the sexual politics surrounding it. The possible reasons could be many: (1) Spanish intellectuals at the time who were actively engaged in evolutionary theory and the ongoing feuds swirling around *el darwinismo* were unfamiliar with the theory of sexual selection, which seems improbable given that it constitutes more than half of *The Descent*; (2) they knew the theory and found nothing noteworthy about it, which in itself would be telling in light of the arguments Darwin puts forth about female choice; or (3) the theory, however much it was read and understood, passed under the polemical radar and became manifest in the public discourse in previously unrecognized ways. Extensive research has led me to conclude the third, though I would deem any combination of these three to be no less interesting or plausible.

As it happens, the theory of sexual selection was on the mind during the days of *el darwinismo*, but Darwin was not part of the conversation in any real measure, since the topic became subsumed by *la cuestión de la mujer* and often demanded a less than progressive stance from the most progressive Spaniards. In other words, liberal reformers and notorious promoters of Darwin's works in Spain, like Manuel de la Revilla, were able to weigh in on female choice under the enlightened guise of science while upholding the conservatism of the status quo when it came to women's rights. To mention Darwin would have been to undermine the case because of his association with a traditional world turned on its head, but to sound the most problematic instances of his views on men and women proved to be quite persuasive among sympathetic readers of Revilla's liberal circle. Similarly, Leopoldo Alas (Clarín) and Santiago Ramón y Cajal demonstrate a sophisticated understanding of Darwin's preoccupation with female passive choice, but they do not identify the Darwinian thinking behind their own double-edged opinions, nor do they reference his works. Unlike Revilla, though, their respective writings move toward Darwin, rather than away from him, when it comes to the evolutionary mechanics of sexual selection in which women should be free to choose and likewise endowed with equal rights to education, employment, and the political sphere. The problem is that these men, too, waver on the question at every turn in ways akin to Darwin himself, and each brings a host of challenges, from the irony of Clarín to the witty shenanigans of Ramón y Cajal. Darwin frustrates no less, but that is what makes his theory so significant. Sexual selection seeps into the discourse, infiltrates it, so to speak, and thus supports rather than negates change, given that change is a constant inherent in the theory itself.

For Revilla, Clarín, Ramón y Cajal, or any number of other "great (male) minds" to make Darwin explicit in these writings on *la cuestión de la mujer* would have lent a gravity to the subject, keeping in mind the ideological stakes inherent in *el darwinismo* and the intellectual investment in it by these *progresistas*; to do so, though, would have also been at odds with how unserious all these men wanted to appear in their casual interest with the plight of "the weaker sex." Still, as for my argument it matters little how familiar any of these men actually were with Darwin's writings or if they had his theory present when musing on the ethics and variables of female choice in courtship and beyond. What matters is that Darwinian sexual selection, even if silent in name, was anything but absent from the imagination of these writers and, in like ways, the others treated throughout this study. This presence is made visible through unprecedented intimacy with Darwin's own voice at each stage in my argument. The first three chapters together set the stage. Each looks at distinct, yet intertwined, outgrowths of Darwinian sexual selection without losing sight of the indeterminism he engenders with his own vacillations, so that by chapter 4 and its concern with the suitors and selectors in Jacinto Octavio Picón, three things have been made clear. First, an interdisciplinary approach such as mine engages the ethical importance of crossover between science and literature; second, in the particular case of sexual selection, the issue of female choice cannot be divorced from the sexual politics of the social sphere and cultural production; and third, the open-endedness of said crossover and Darwin's views on "passive choice" necessitate a revised understanding of his science and its afterlife, which the particular case of Spain illuminates in unanticipated ways.

Together, these revelations foreground the principal finding of this inquiry into sexual selection and the novel—an indeterminate Darwin and a similarly unresolved preoccupation with choice as it relates to questions of empowerment. To call Darwin an advocate, rather than enemy, of the women's movement is a hard sell, but it is not as impossible as one might think, since I do not mean to herald him as a feminist or champion of the changes that came about or to claim that his science made Spain a more moral nation or alone enabled women's emancipation (which is still very much an ongoing struggle). It is to say, instead, that an indefinite dynamic such as Darwinian sexual selection, with its emphasis on female choice, carries the potential for change within it, and this is enough to cause us to rethink the way we understand Darwin, his revolutionary reputation, and his relationship to literature and social progress in the case of Spain and other countries like it where women were denied the same civil status enjoyed by men.

Consequently, in terms of its engagement with Darwinian sexual selection and the novel, beyond the breadth this book brings to Darwin with the theoretical, the scientific-feminist, and the historical foundations laid out in part 1 ("Origins"), parts 2 ("Adaptations") and 3 ("Speciations") privilege his writing through close readings of The Descent. Many literary studies that aspire to capture what is Darwinian about the works they treat claim to do as much and, instead, never cite Darwin or, worse still, include a couple of recognizable examples of his thought as a way to justify any number of extrapolations no matter how unrelated. In contrast, I show where in Darwin my arguments originate and why Darwin enables my elaborations. For the three chapters included in part 2, "Adaptations," this attention to Darwin's thought provides angles of inquiry that come directly from the factors he sets forth in *The Descent* when discussing sexual selection. Again, whereas we might be tempted to look at elements of literary works like "suitors" or "heredity" in thematic terms, for Darwin's science they are something quite different. Likewise, it may be hard not to suspect that only the most readily "fictional" qualities of Darwin's science are being drawn out of a theory that is otherwise much drier, that is, "scientific," but by the conclusion of this study all sections concerned with anthropomorphic sexual selection in *The Descent* will have been addressed in detail. To clarify the methodology of the three chapters from part 2, then, it is less that sexual selection *is adapted* with conscious intent to accomplish certain ends by any given writer than it is that the plasticity of the theory itself generates advantageous variations, as Darwin would understand adaptation, specific to the role we as readers play in the creation of meaning from the ever-shifting environment both inside and outside the text.

The crossover between Darwinian sexual selection and the novel privileged in part 2 requires an understanding of the basic elements of the theory and where they lead. One of the most problematic and, hence, meaningful aspects of *The Descent* stems from the difficulty Darwin has when trying to reconcile what he sees in nature, where males appear more ornamented and females select, with what he finds in Victorian society, where, when women borrow the plumes of peacocks to adorn themselves, it seems the reverse is true. Much of this trouble is treated in chapter 2 as a means to frame the gendered power dynamics of sexual selection, but the richer details give the basis for chapter 4, which centers on "suitors and selectors" in Jacinto Octavio Picón. For this reason, Picón offers a logical point of departure; his works provide the perfect transition from the inversions traced in chapter 2 and the questions of who does the choosing and why discussed in the essays on *la cuestión de la mujer* in the second half of chapter 3. Plus, Picón is a brilliant novelist, largely forgotten today but beloved during his lifetime, and his fiction has recently inspired a range of important feminist critiques on both sides of the fence about his treatment of women. What is also appealing about Picón when it comes to the suitors and selectors of sexual selection is the way his treatment of Darwin's "complex affair" progresses, always according to the trajectory of the Don Juan figure. He begins with the parody of *Juan Vulgar* (1885), in which a pathetic bourgeois who imagines himself the legendary seducer is bested by his own script of conquest, and then complicates matters with *Dulce y sabrosa* (1891), where an archetypal Don Juan who loves and leaves a young Cristeta later falls prey to her own donjuanesque machinations. Finally, breaking with other writers of the day in Spain and beyond, Picón explores what it means to come full circle with his creation of a female Don Juan in *Juanita Tenorio* (1910), whose private moral code in the first-person psychology of courtship and seduction becomes a question of conscience, of indeterminate choice, or what Darwin calls the catalytic "moral sense" of the social instincts.

The next turn is from the players to the dynamic itself. For years, literary criticism has recognized the importance of fictional rivalries, and groundbreaking scholars from René Girard to Eve Kosofsky Sedgwick have illuminated (and been used to illuminate) what motivates desire in a host of contexts.[9] Consequently, with a theory such as sexual selection, which takes rivalry to be the driving force behind the precept of male-male combat, it would show considerable negligence to pass over the question, since without a foray into this nebulous terrain we cannot adequately appreciate the indeterminacy of Darwin's thinking on attraction. The watershed novel of *La Regenta* (1884–85) by Leopoldo Alas (Clarín), who was in his own right a master of the realist craft, centers on the intense rivalry of Álvaro Mesía, the town playboy, and Fermín de Pas, the perverted priest, in their quest to control the inexperienced and impressionable Ana Ozores. This is only one reason, however, why Clarín fills so well the needs of chapter 5. The other advantage has to do with the finessed irony with which he captures the various ritualized aspects of courtship with ever-greater degrees of complexity. Building on *La Regenta*, I use this quality of Clarín's writing to introduce anthropological studies of ritual and its multifarious forms as a means to deepen what Darwin could only intuit about courtship. Thus, by the chapter's second half it is Clarín's later novel, *Su único hijo* (1890), that manages to best perform the gender blurring and open-endedness that characterizes Darwin's thought. It also shows, like the final analysis on Picón in chapter 4, how choice itself, despite the varied degrees of agency to which we might assign it because of its "passive" qualifier in sexual selection, brings ethical implications when revealed to be indeterminate by its very nature.

From here, the ends of sexual selection emerge as the "heirs and errors" of chapter 6, because in equal measure to the energy Darwin expends on his description of the mechanics of sexual selection he worries over the outcomes. Benito Pérez Galdós, who in many ways defined the course of the Spanish realist novel in the last decades of the nineteenth century, is a central figure in Spain's literary history and can no doubt be placed alongside any of his "better known" contemporaries outside of Spain when it comes to his body of works and achievements. *La desheredada* (1881), often heralded as the first naturalist novel in Spain, is among his greatest contributions, and Isidora Rufete, the disinherited provincial protagonist turned prostitute is the quintessential model for interrogating Darwin's concerns over the "black sheep" of heredity. Her character also raises issues of class and limited mobility that translate directly to the "errors" Galdós takes up in *Fortunata y Jacinta* (1886–87), a monumental novel that tells the tale of "two married women" who in the end attempt to right their own social mismatches in matrimony by reimagining their relationship to each other. As it turns out, the imagination, which Darwin calls "one of the highest prerogatives of man" and Galdós carries to "novel results" in the context of heredity, drives mate preferences, offspring aspirations, and new models of collectivity. The last of these, characterized by the "three mothers" and Fortunata's naming of the child at the novel's conclusion, evidences how Galdós takes Darwin beyond Darwin with a deployment of the mind in response to the matter of marriage in Madrid. Besieged by social impediments that endanger future generations, the female protagonists author a lineage of their own invention that is both maternal and symbolic, as Harriet S. Turner has shown.[10] Thus, inheritance becomes a question of creation, and with a vision of regeneration founded on heterogeneity, Galdós returns to the principle Darwin held most dear. He rewrites community through the characters' own eyes and offers in the final analysis an "evolutionary confusion" of the classes, Madrid, and the *image*nation that moves toward an understanding of the hereditary connection between humanity and its redemptive, Darwinian plasticity.

Together, the three chapters of part 2 inform us about the key elements of sexual selection—the players, the dynamic, and the outcomes.

They are all also essential in many ways to the development of the thesis that guides my study as a whole. What the novels of Picón, Clarín, and Galdós share in their singular representations of sexual selection is the same indeterminacy Darwin falls back on as he grapples with the unknowns of courtship and the suspicion that social constraints, namely, in the form of the subjugation of women through patriarchy and artificially class-based social stratifications, had warped advantageous, natural reproduction by restricting female choice. At the same time, these writers make manifest how loaded an oxymoron like *passive choice* could really be in terms of women's rights. Juanita, Ana, Isidora, and Fortunata are but a few of the cases in which readers find it very difficult to know whether these fallen heroines have actually chosen their respective fates, as decades of scholarship at odds on these novels affirms. This lack of closure is a large part of the appeal, because it forces us to ask ourselves if so, why, and if not, why not. In other words, it would appear that something very serious has gone awry when good women go bad because of social circumstances that exploit their true nature at every turn (and a reading public all too eager to relish every moment of their personal trials). The general understanding of the moral dimension of the naturalist enterprise really is not terribly far off from this synthesis; the critique in these novels could never paint society's best side or credibly employ the transparent didacticism found in earlier works, where poetic justice seemed always to prevail. Consequently, these novelistic performances of Darwinian sexual selection are also more readily about the moral dimension of his science, not what is unscientific about his moralism. Sexual selection aims at change, and this change is brought about through the principal law of choice inherent in its dynamic, which will always be indeterminate and may show varied degrees of agency according to the context of its operation. But neither will it forever be passive, for always being about choice, nor fully active, for being inseparable from circumstances that *circum*scribe said agency.

Still, a full exegesis of sexual selection through the novel, and by extension the novel through sexual selection, demands that we look beyond the constitutive components (suitors, selectors, rivalries, rituals, heirs, and errors) toward what the two in tandem might show us beyond Darwin and literature. That is to say, the chapters on Picón, Clarín, and Galdós stay closer to *The Descent* than the chapters of part 3 do, since the focus of part 2, "Adaptations," is on the specifics of the theory, so to speak, in action. It also foregrounds well the ethical consequence of the relationship between indeterminism and choice in Darwin and the novelists. By contrast, "Speciations" looks at how far this reciprocity between literature and science might be pushed, namely, how it might answer larger questions about genre in a gendered nation, religion and sex, and the marriage contract. This is the moment in the study when sex, science, and culture converge around the latent tensions, like tradition and transformation, in a study of this compass. It looks to answer what more Darwinian sexual selection and its representation might tell us about the social reach of their reciprocity.

Hence, to return to the question of the ever-elusive "zero degree" before Darwin, it is helpful to recall that nineteenth-century realism carries romance within it from the outset. Moreover, as Gillian Beer has argued, Darwin's science was in many ways a product of his readings from Ovid to Charles Dickens.[11] This would seem straightforward enough, until we factor determinism into the equation and the many ways it extends to issues of gender and genre. In the well-established continuum that permeates in one way or another so much literary criticism concerned with the nineteenth century, on the one side we find determinism coupled with realism, science, objectivity, materialism, and all things made "masculine," while on the other are aligned sentimentalism, romance, subjectivity, fancy, and all things presumed "feminine." At the same time, in the particular case of Spain, there exists a contention among many critics that the relationship between nation-building and the realist novel following the 1868 revolution was a masculine enterprise, making both the genre and its desire to reject earlier forms while at the same time absorbing them yet another patriarchal power play during the very years Darwin appeared on the scene. Chapter 7 takes this to task by interrogating the work of Alejandro Sawa, who earned a reputation as one of Spain's most notorious naturalists for his brutal portrayal of women at the hands of lascivious men. In *Noche* (1888), the rape of Lola raises the question of what could ever be moral about the complete erasure of choice in such bleak fatalism and, likewise, how to reconcile such circumstance with the association between Darwin's oft-told determinism and naturalism, in light of the indeterminism of sexual selection as explicated in parts 1 and 2.

No less interesting is the odd couple that sex and the Church make in the Spanish novels of the late nineteenth century. More often than not, the case does not merit scrutiny, since pathological priests in

search of young impressionable maidens conform to ready-made conclusions about the widespread anticlericalism of the day. Sexual selection thus becomes overshadowed by ulterior ideological ambitions of
authors intent on chipping away at the Church. Things are not so
clear cut, however, in the case of Armando Palacio Valdés, whose
novels take the road less traveled in order to yield original insights
on historical deviations that are in every way Darwinian. Centuries
before Darwin in Spain there emerged a curious practice of mystical nuptials by which young women would literally engage in sexual
acts and then wed themselves to Christ. Chapter 8 traces this history
and its transformation in *Marta y María* (1883), where Darwin illuminates why, in matters of limited choice, Christ still makes an ideal
mate at the end of the nineteenth century even in the presence of via-
ble male alternatives more than ready to facilitate real reproduction.
Indeed, through his attempts to understand a perplexing past and
present, Palacio Valdés takes Darwinian sexual selection to lengths
Darwin himself never could have imagined, when robust suitors find
themselves rejected for a Husband not of this world. The other place
is the confessional and its shadowy past of salacious solicitations
since the days of the Inquisition. Only in the case of *La fe* (1892) the
tables are turned, when a young female confessant falls for her confessor and finds that because of his faith she can be neither suitor
nor selector. Foiled after a series of aggressive attempts to sway his
resolve, she accuses him of unspeakable offenses, and he, in turn,
ends up mocked and imprisoned in his laughable defense of a code
higher than man's natural reproductive instinct. Religion, in the realism of Palacio Valdés, has made sexual selection scarcely comprehensible, and yet its indeterminism, even under such distortion, remains
all the more apparent for that very reason, since to confess, that is, to
reveal can mean to hide the moral truth from oneself about choice.

Finally, it is significant that Emilia Pardo Bazán constitutes the
bookend to my thinking, in the same way it matters that she is the
only woman among the novelists I discuss. Her concerns with the
marriage contract reflect many of the same concerns shared by Darwin in *The Descent*, but her telling in *Doña Milagros* (1894) and
Memorias de un solterón (1896), a pair of intertwined novels, shows
much more acutely than he or her contemporaries could both the
harsh realities of reproductive labor and the costs of Duty and Family in the context of sexual selection. What is most fascinating, however, about these two works is how unresolved they appear in the very

realism with which they paint the evolution of Feíta's choice leading up to her decision to marry and renounce her independence at the end of the second work. In other words, it is through the credibility of these novels that we come to best appreciate the implications of Darwinian indeterminism as it relates to the problematic act of passive choice, which is something comprehensible and yet always disquieting for its ideological consequence and apparent self-negation. In her deep engagement with the problems of sexual selection, Pardo Bazán captures this disquiet and the extent of its ethical weight with respect to individual agency, leaving readers to wonder, just as Darwin did, if sexual selection among men and women would be better off without the contracts of sacred and civil unions society has historically sought to impose. Her novels, in effect, confirm that the subversive potential of the theory of sexual selection lies in its inconclusiveness.

At this point, a few additional words about my own choice of Spain are in order before I offer some closing remarks about my conclusion. An old adage runs that Europe ends at the Pyrenees. In truth, the Spanish realists were not minor contributors to the development of the novel in the nineteenth century, and by no means were they incomparable to more "major" novelists beyond the Pyrenees, despite appearances to the contrary in comparative studies. All the Spanish novelists included here were well versed in the intellectual and artistic currents of their day. Most spent considerable time abroad, traveling and studying in a wide range of countries; spoke multiple languages, including English, German, and French; and saw literature as an international enterprise. If, therefore, my elucidations at times give attention to plot, it is not by accident. On the one hand, a study interested in courtship must show how the dynamic of sexual selection unfolds if it is to capture the nuances that escape us when we boil them down to a series of trite formulas. At the same time, any single reader's familiarity with the novels I discuss will surely vary, since I frame the Spanish tradition in an interdisciplinary (science) and international (Darwin) light, thus questioning the country's "outsider" reputation and broadening the audience of my study. So, while these declarations about Spain's claim to inclusion might confuse the already initiated, they are useful in this context. Is every novel discussed a masterpiece? Of course not. In general it is true that many works across periods and national traditions are kept around not for being "great reads" but rather for what they reveal about particular issues or cultural shifts. The texts I have selected all came after

Darwin's science arrived in Spain, and some that are less realized or overly melodramatic serve very specific aims.

Moreover, a Spanish focus should not be confused with a narrow focus, for one, because this study also centers on Darwin, who provides a counterpoint to the Spanish tradition. Many scholars interested in science and literature, and particularly in Darwin, welcome a variety of models, as recent collections of his reach across Europe and the Hispanic world have shown.[12] Plus, more often than not, no one questions the utility of a study on Darwin and Victorian literature, for example, for non-Victorian specialists. The present study also offers an in-depth account of six authors (many of whom are the single subject of numerous monographs) and multiple novels, along with the historical evidence of chapter 3. It reassesses the reciprocity between literature and science and probes at length the science itself. Chapter 2 informs readers of the most problematic aspects of Darwin's theory, while pointing out the feminist issues in play. More than this though, there is considerable engagement with writers outside of Spain from one chapter to the next in an effort to establish a more integrated conversation with the Spanish tradition rather than simply a litany of cardboard analogues overlaid upon it. Plus, my own theorizing, in addition to taking stock of contemporary trends in critical thought from evolutionary psychology to transnational feminism, grants say to influential voices absent until now in discussions on Spain, Darwin, or nineteenth-century realism more broadly.

Could this have been a study about Gabriele d'Annunzio's *Trionfo della morte* (1894), Guy de Maupassant's *Bel-Ami* (1885), and Theodor Fontane's *Effi Briest* (1896)? Would Emily Brontë's *Wuthering Heights* (1847), Ivan Goncharov's *Oblomov* (1859), and Bram Stoker's *Dracula* (1897) have been a better, more problematic mix? The answer is no. Whereas these combinations or any number of like permutations might have captured some of the same truths about the indeterminate operation of sexual selection, they would have lost the historical specificity and cohesion that, with my interest in Spain, orient my readings so as to show a reciprocity premised on what literature is able to illuminate about the social reach of Darwin's science and, conversely, what Darwin's science has to say about literature in a particular setting. Does this mean that such a methodology could not readily be transferred to other traditions in much the same way? Absolutely not. This study aims to tell new truths about Darwin to the extent that literature reveals the ethical implications of

his indeterminism and concern with female choice in the practice of
sexual politics at a moment when novelists took up the task of representing the reality of Darwin's doubts, whether or not they were
conscious of what they were doing with respect to Darwin. This pull
is similar to the way Sedgwick characterizes her own study as a "con-
tinuing negotiation between . . . historicizing and dehistoricizing
motives."[13] The approach to this end is much more about *how* we read
rather than *what* we read. This affirmation might seem contradictory
in light of what I have just said about possible alternative studies until
we realize that much of the *how* has to do with history in the same
way that David Damrosch has theorized on the approach of world
literature today.[14] Though this study cannot be claimed as "world"
enough because of its European parameters, it does share something
with what Damrosch has in mind, given that concerns about influence
remain secondary to conclusions drawn from connections between
texts and between new texts in circulation—without abandoning
their historical context.

Indeed, this book favors confluence over influence. Literature and
science studies are not what they once were. Important works in the
past decade or so by groundbreaking scholars such as Laura Otis,
William Flesch, and others have shown new ways to think about more
complicated questions than who read what when.[15] This study follows
in their wake and maintains as well that there is no need for extremism. In the case of Darwinian sexual selection, the historical milieu
matters if we hope to make perceptible the moral dimension of his science at the level of its social praxis with respect to female choice. The
realist novel, to reiterate, provides a unique cultural artifact to accomplish this end, but not in the abstract. The authors I discuss, all of
whom were writing during the very years *The Descent* made its way
to Spain and into Spanish, converge in their sociopolitical concern
with the gendered power dynamics of courtship; Darwinian sexual
selection reveals why it is such a messy business; and, in tandem, the
two show the ethical dimension of interdisciplinary engagement with
respect to such reciprocity and Darwin's own indeterminism.

The conclusion to my study synthesizes this ethical dimension
around a single word, "conscience," which was paramount to Darwin's thinking about sexual selection in *The Descent*. This term is
first explored toward the end of chapter 4 in conjunction with what
Picón is after with his first-person narration in *Juanita Tenorio*, and
on occasion its resonance is felt in other chapters. It then resurfaces

more fully in a different guise to close my discussion of Pardo Bazán
in chapter 9 and thus frames my six chapters concerned with the novels. My thesis, after all, is about not Darwin's conscience but rather
the indeterminism of Darwinian sexual selection and the change
inherent in choice. This indeterminism is Derridean, to be sure, to the
extent that all language hovers over the abyss of multivalent, decen-
tered meaning; Darwin's writing indeed exemplifies such instability.
Yet what I am after is something more—the uncertainty of his science and how it relates to individual agency and social change. My
focus on the praxis of courtship thus brings with it a threefold objective centered on what Darwin reveals about the novel, what the novel
has to say about Darwin, and what the two together illuminate about
gender as the point of overlap between science and literature at the
end of the nineteenth century.

Hence, the interest in Darwinian "conscience" at various moments
across the chapters and particularly in my closing also has to do
with the way the word itself embeds this overlap, and for this reason in the last instant I introduce the distinction Giambattista Vico
draws between science and conscience with respect to knowledge.
In essence, absent what can be known about reality with absolute
certainty by the intellect (true knowledge / science), our will to act
springs from the truths we already possess (innate knowledge / conscience). My aim is to show that this distinction clouds more than it
consoles, since "con-science" (with knowledge) envelops reason by its
very nature. In this way, the conclusion brings me full circle, back to
the very same questions addressed in chapter 1 concerning the specious dichotomies that engender separate "humanist" and "empiricist" realms, but the moral light now shines much fuller thanks to
the indeterminism of Darwin's own science and the novels I treat. A
careful reading of this final reflection, which acts as a theoretical cre-
scendo of sorts, will show that the forever imperfect "science of conscience" offers a means to tie up loose ends; it should not be misinter-
preted as a catchphrase meant to explain away all the sticky problems
that persist, whether regarding sexual selection or the period or the
works here under discussion. As such, my departing thoughts offer an
ambitious map of the world, figuratively speaking, that contains in its
very conception the *callejuelas* of Madrid. But to see both requires an
eye toward what is transcendent about choice in the context of each.

Here's why. The loosest ends are those concerning agency in a
world of women limited by Nature, as it were, to passive choice in

Darwin's evolutionary model of sexual selection. A paradox defies the laws of logic for being something that at once is and is not, but this quality does not make it any less powerful. On the contrary, paradox means more because of such defiant tension. The same can be said for this conception of choice at a moment in cultural history when the rise of the State and the *civil-yet-uncivil* exclusion of women could not have posed a more acute threat to social progress in terms of certain inalienable rights and equality for all citizens, even those of the "fairer sex" still to be counted. Choice is ethical to the extent that it is indeterminate, as I argue in chapter 5 regarding Bonifacio's defiant act of pluralistic parenting. It only becomes moral, however, at the moment social change for the better becomes not just possible but prefigured by subtle shifts in power relations. Two examples that come to mind are the discourses surrounding *la cuestión de la mujer* and *el darwinismo* that emerged together in Spain during the last decades of the nineteenth century. To debate meant to question, while figurative convergence of these two debates in the courtship plot of the realist novel meant the "moral sense" of sexual selection was in play according to Darwin's own understanding of its evolutionary importance in *The Descent*. Realism took reality to task, and the subjugation of women, once made visible in the most disturbing ways, had a destabilizing effect on the sociopolitical establishment. The reciprocity, then, between literature and science matters only as much as we care to look, and in the particular case of Darwin and the novel, I would hazard that it means more than we have previously thought to imagine.

PART ONE

Origins

CHAPTER ONE

The Very Notion of "Real" Reciprocity between Literature and Science

To say that Charles Darwin is no stranger to controversy is to state the obvious. For the past century and a half divisiveness has come in equal measure to the wonder inspired by his theories of evolution. It would not be surprising, then, if we were to find ourselves desensitized to claims about his overthrow of the world order. The Darwinian Revolution may have indeed run its course. Yet if the widespread celebrations of 2009 proved anything, it is that public interest has not waned, as across the globe people came together to mark the anniversary year of both Darwin's birth (1809) and the publication of *Origin of Species* (1859). In truth, we keep coming back to Darwin because his thought continues to shape our own, and contention no doubt stokes rather than quells interest. Moreover, the discord now inseparable from Darwin in so many circles of debate is often the very thing to capture our attention and, it seems, to provoke allegiance to one side or another. Perhaps a politicized Darwin is therefore inevitable, but in the field of literature and science studies, it is my belief that he should mediate rather than divide in our search for reciprocity.[1]

Hence, this look at Darwinian sexual selection and the Spanish novel in the late nineteenth century does not claim to be new because it is concerned with literature and science; many studies before it have demonstrated how the two together reveal important insights about the development of human consciousness, which is all the more reason to continue on the path. It holds, instead, that Darwin was never a dogmatist; to make of his science a touchstone for polarization says more about us than him. The unforeseen afterlife of evolutionary theory, for its social reach, remains a testament to the indeterminism of Darwin's thought, and the very fact that so much was left to question should tell us something about the theories themselves and the unresolved Nature they treat.

Darwinian sexual selection begs inclusion in the broad, interdisciplinary conversation that literature and science studies offer today, given how readily the sexual politics inherent in it find their way into representation and the discourse surrounding women's rights in the decades after Darwin. Yet a rift that exists in efforts "to bridge the disciplines" complicates this endeavor. Early on, I was surprised to learn that to write on Darwin and the novel would mean to define myself, and no less perplexing was how limited the options were. From one camp, as it turns out, those labeled "humanists" negate traditional distinctions between literature and science on the grounds that each is a cultural discourse, while from the other, self-proclaimed "empiricists" argue that science, albeit a material complement to literature, should never become literature. With respect to Darwin and literature, this posturing then divides "constructivists," who pay close attention to Darwin's language to gauge the interaction between his science and its social context, from "essentialists," who use adaptation precepts of evolutionary theory confirmed by today's science as a means to decipher universals present in all literature.[2]

As it turns out, convinced that literature and science belong together these factions are much more alike than either admits, but an illustration of what they share requires an approach inclusive enough to explain these apparently opposed worldviews and why evolutionary theory tends toward antithetical positions in Darwinian studies of literature. At the same time, it must demonstrate what Darwin's science brings to the study of literature and what literature reveals about his science. Of course, not all of this can be accomplished in chapter 1, especially given the specific ways the Spanish novel factors in my broader inquiry, but building a platform upon which narrative and evolution intersect enables a synthesis that assuages concerns, first, about Darwin and literature in tandem and, second, about the social significance of such an enterprise with respect to sexual selection in the cultural realm. The theoretical adumbration of reciprocity performed in this chapter therefore makes possible a fuller appreciation of the dynamism of Darwinian sexual selection and the novel in anticipation of my larger argument about the two. Indeed, this type of confluence goes hand in hand with how the mechanics of the disciplinary relationship, no matter how arbitrary, between these objects of inquiry are structured. Hence, this first step in my thesis moves from the general to the particular, from abstract propositions about literature and science as complements, to specific Darwinian issues, to questions of human nature and literary history, to those of nineteenth-century realism, of scientific revolutions, and, ultimately, of Spain. In the end, Darwin does not fall on the side of either literature or science but rather collapses the two in a creative unity where our engagement with the material world cannot be separated from responses of representation.

RECONCILABLE DIFFERENCES

From a cultural standpoint, literature and science are separate but not equal when it comes to claims to Truth, given that the latter holds a sacrosanct, albeit specious, relationship to empirical facts and objectivity. Language, as a shared medium of expression, offers one initial means to counter this imbalance through a leveraging of literature to the same status of authority enjoyed by science in the modern era. At the tactical extreme, the distinction between literature and science becomes "a debatable one that deters rather than enhances historical understanding," as together they constitute equal "modes of discourse, neither of which is privileged except by the conventions of the cultures in which they are embedded."[3] Therefore, the tendency is to historicize scientific activity, to make it feel more human, so that it becomes just one more discourse among many, with no more foundation in reality than any other at the level of language. Though sure to bristle some, this reassessment is neither a devaluation of science nor a divorce from its subjects in terms of methodology or findings. Rather, the aim is to emphasize that literature is equally material. Furthermore, a focus on the role of language in science brings to light its figurative dimension: "Scientists need to have recourse to the linguistic dexterity, and . . . the instability of reference, with which literary language recognizes multiple simultaneous levels of event and meaning."[4] By shifting focus in this way, one can begin to see why science, presumed stable because of its empirical base, has over the centuries been so unstable.

It is not enough, however, to call attention to the role of language in science; the argument wants of specificity for its operation. For historians of science tropes function as a foundation that is seldom scientific in its composition, and this recourse to descriptive language, while facilitating the communication of complex ideas, also makes science more vulnerable. In this vein, James Bono calls attention to the importance of metaphor, among several other tropes, as the conduit between science and diverse avenues of cultural production including social, political, and religious texts. A means of transfer, metaphor implicates science in a literary process of meaning negotiation, and as a result it can no longer position itself against literature.[5] No reader of Darwin can fail to appreciate the exchange potential of metaphor in early evolutionary science; from geological formations to historical philology to embryonic growth, examples abound in both *Origin* and *The Descent* of Darwin's recourse to imperfect metaphors to make his theories more palatable. Indeed, both Stephen Alter and Robert M. Young emphasize the ways Darwin borrowed in no small measure from the discourses of his day to great effect and with unforeseen consequences in the reception of his writings, particularly with respect to race and, I would add, gender.[6] Ultimately, with these discussions of tropes a paradox is in play, for figurative language, which always carries an abstract quality within it, serves to make science more concrete. Yet we recognize that it cannot be otherwise because of the centrality of language in the articulation, not just communication, of scientific discovery. Stories offer a means of explanation between us, to be sure, but also a means of understanding for the storytellers themselves. Science therefore enters a "dialogical relationship with literature," as Bono avers, but seldom is the relationship self-evident since neither appears eager to admit as much outright.[7]

Putting "hard facts" aside for the moment in favor of how they come to be shared, the slippages of science with respect to its figurative qualities can be traced to semantic context, which complicates meaning in the same way we recognize the pitfalls inherent in the narrative aspect of literature. That is, since narrative extends to both literature and science, it offers an appealing alternative to what many consider to be capricious distinctions between the two fields maintained on ideological or disciplinary grounds alone. Susan Merrill Squier, for her part, argues that narrative constitutes a site of "mutual imbrication and cogeneration" and to this end sets out to illuminate the "microprocesses" of literature and science "in action," while downplaying "intrinsic qualities" in favor of later cultural transformations and emphasizing that the material foundation of both allows for a flow back and forth.[8] In other words, we should concern ourselves less with the complexity of literature *and* science and focus instead on the constructive dynamism of their coupling. Given that narrative encompasses the communicative efficacy of scientific description, like, for example, Darwin's tale of evolution (a story colored throughout by mythic and romantic undertones without ever becoming "pure fiction" in the eyes of his converts),[9] a scientific text can be read as if it were literature and interpreted on several levels. Of course, Darwin is not representative of all science, neither past nor present, but many of the issues raised about the figurative frame of his nineteenth-century theories still remain relevant today. One need only think of the language used to talk about the Big Bang, cloning, and quantum physics, for example, and conversely, the diverse ways these advances and others have affected the cultural imagination. The advantage of this shift toward the imagination is that science opens itself to new explorations, rather than standing above culture as only and authoritatively "scientific." It becomes, in essence, less determinate to the extent narrative informs our appreciation and appropriation of its claims. This can be true at the level of engagement with the scientific text itself, to be sure, but more important is the possibility of extension to other types of texts and their material circumstance.

Nevertheless, the turn from literature and science to literature and Darwin brings its own baggage, which has distorted the way many perceive this particular interdisciplinary undertaking. For Joseph Carroll, the self-appointed figurehead of "literary Darwinism," there is no middle ground. In his objectionable manifesto *Evolution and Literary Theory*, Carroll demeans scholars of literature and science like George Levine, Gillian Beer, James Bono, and all the others he groups as "semiotic transcendentalists."[10] At the same time, since his position represents an emerging and ever more visible "adaptation" strain of Darwinian studies in the humanities, the tenets of the movement merit consideration in order to establish a necessary distance from its more questionable claims. From the sociobiology of Edward O. Wilson, Carroll reads literature first and foremost as a "biological phenomenon" that, from "physiological structures," reflects "the relationship between the organism and its environment" through "representational activity" determined by adaptive "cognitive mapping." Calling himself an "essentialist," he believes that "innate biological characteristics provide the basis for all individual identity and all social organization." From these precepts, a hermetic "Darwinian paradigm" materializes replete with thematic schemata in a hierarchical arrangement from the cosmos to the individual. Founded on "empirical research," the system, ideal for *all* literature, shows texts to be "the intentional productions of living, individual human beings who are responding to their own particular environmental circumstances" and, in so doing, uncovers "the structure of determinate meaning within the text."[11] In other words, Darwin supplies the absolute Truth with which we might decipher literature from Homer to Italo Calvino and everything in between according to natural laws.

Indeed, Darwinian theories as understood by today's scientific community explain a great deal about human behavior and thus enhance what can be said about a historical (or any other) Darwin and his presence in literature. Carroll, then, rightly advocates for methodological exchange between the sciences and the humanities on this front. Yet his empirical dogmatism clouds this program: "The poststructuralist explanation of things cannot be reconciled with the Darwinian paradigm or modified and assimilated to it. Poststructuralism is an alternative, competing paradigm. It operates on principles that are radically incompatible with those of evolutionary theory. It should, consequently, be rejected."[12] On the contrary, to subjugate literature to the "hard data" and "objective" findings of sociobiology not only alienates potential sympathizers but chokes a critical conversation able to accommodate numerous convergent angles of inquiry. Moreover, through adherence to such doctrine, essentialists like Carroll reduce literature to a mirror (which quickly loses its shine) and Darwinian criticism to a stagnant tautology (i.e., Humans create literature; therefore literature reflects that which is human). As we shall see, Darwin does not show us "the determinate meaning within the text," as if there were such a thing, but rather the opposite, since the meaning of his own text, too, is far from "determinate," whether at the level of language or intention. And what remains unanswered, among other issues, is "that which is human," and no amount of statistics, charts, and empirical chest-thumping can entertain this question without first relinquishing claims on the sole right to truth. For as Benedetto Croce once remarked, "Where everything is real, nothing is real."[13] Hence, "literary Darwinism" promises an enterprise of far greater scope and returns than these hard-line "literary Darwinians" would lead us to believe.

The push for more "empirical" approaches to literature reflects a fear that their inverse, attention to the discursive dimension of science, will somehow erase the reality of its subject and thus transform all scientific analysis and the material world it strives to understand into pure invention. This concern, though overblown, should not be ignored, if for no other reason than what it promises to tell us about the issues at stake. In the case of Darwin, any dismissal of his language in favor of his theories in the abstract fails to grasp how his science lent itself to so much controversy and had such an impact on literature of the period. For example, in the preface to the second edition of *Darwin's Plots*, Gillian Beer answers her skeptics by reaffirming that her intention was never to turn Darwin's writing into fiction. Rather, she hoped to show that "how Darwin said things was a crucial part of his struggle to think things, not a layer that can be skimmed off without loss." The emphasis here falls on the open-endedness of his texts:

> He [Darwin] did not *invent* laws. He *described* them. Indeed, it was essential to his project that it should be accepted not as invention, but description. His work is, therefore, conditional upon the means of description: that is upon language. . . . Though the events of the natural world are language-free, language controls our apprehension of knowledge, and is itself determined by current historical conditions and by the order implicit in syntax, grammar, and other rhetorical properties such as metaphor, as well as by the selective intensity of individual experience.[14]

In other words, now "fixed" Darwinian natural laws (if these exist at all) often bear little resemblance to how Darwin first conveyed them, or, for that matter, how novelists engaged them at various levels, and it is therefore important to note that those critics who choose not to cite Darwin's writings in any real measure (like Carroll and his cadre) often fall far from his thought, despite how well they might know Darwinian science as it lives today. This is not to say, though, that a historical Darwin cannot also be a universal Darwin when it comes to the study of literature. It means, instead, that to achieve better balance we must heed Darwin's voice as much as his verifiable laws for those claims we attribute to him. A landmark biography like Desmond and Moore's can assist us in this, as the letters and debates and personal struggles paint the historical landscape, but *The Descent* provides foothold enough for assessing the indeterminism of its science, which was in no small measure a product of the language used to describe the Nature of its inquiry. But this same Nature and the inquiry itself played an even larger role. Neither the text nor its object was then or is now fixed. In other words, to disregard what Darwin says for what his theories now prove yields only a partial assessment of the interaction between science and literature on this front.

Still, it is by no means easy to unravel Darwin's thought. Lifetimes have been spent in attempts to account for the numerous complicating factors, from his multiple revisions and editions to the plethora of disparate sources to those individuals who popularized his writings. At the level of historical influence, how to know anything with certainty can become a chronic problem indeed, for as Levine points out in his own readings of Darwin and Victorian literature, "to identify purely Darwinian ideas" may very well be a lost cause.[15] This is partly why mine is not an influence study. For his part, Levine seeks an evolutionary "gestalt" by melding Darwin's theories and literature according to specific points of entry, among them, "the human subject," "observation," "change and history," and "chance" (13–20), and after working through these, he concludes in the final analysis that "our way of telling stories, of creating meaning, of distrusting both phenomena and language owe much to Darwin and the writers who absorbed, extended, and reacted to his imagination" (272). This summation allows us to move in a new direction, toward this missing ingredient—Darwin's imagination. Darwin struggled with the uncertainties and complete unknowns that complicated his assumptions. His methodology was first to read and then to interpret the book of Nature. To this end, he observed the perceptible and found causes, with varying degrees of success, in the imperceptible. Therefore, we should begin to ask why Darwin engages us most when we approach a theory like sexual selection as indeterminate in its very essence, rather than as fixed law or in terms of absolutes.

THE ETHICS OF ENGAGEMENT

To return to something I touched on in the introduction, it is wrong to believe that attention to the moral dimension of Darwin's thought is to jettison his science, or likewise to assume that because there is a moral dimension that somehow a reconciliation between the "scientific" and the "unscientific" has already taken place in *The Descent* itself. We cannot understand the workings of sexual selection without attending to sociopolitical questions of female choice and its representation. Still, a conflation of ethics with morality is merely one possible way to understand what is meant by the former of these terms. Whereas morality will always be relative, and therefore both subjective and subject to opposed views, the ethical is transcendent and forever unfinished. Therefore, the ethics of engagement with literature and science has to do with the choices that emerge at every turn. Naturally, there will be an ideological bent once certain choices are made; the affair cannot be otherwise. This study without question conveys as much in its conclusions, but the interdisciplinary approach is different. It is a way of looking at cultural production that does not close itself off to literature or science.

Hence, the ethical aspect of interdisciplinary inquiry matters to the extent that we put the *how* before the *what*. Troubled by competing epistemologies, Ernst Cassirer helps make this clear in his lament that for lack of center we have reached a moment of crisis with respect to self-knowledge in contemporary society. He characterizes the situation as "complete anarchy of thought" in which "theologians, scientists, politicians, sociologists, biologists, psychologists, ethnologists, [and] economists" demand that the world can only be understood on their terms, and as consequence, the question of humankind as the most fundamental interrogation we might aspire to undertake collapses for want of coherence.[16] This antagonism of ideas then threatens cultural life, for facts alone do not bring advancement; there must also be an equal wealth of synthetic *thinking*, as opposed to thought. What is needed is not an abundance of data but rather conceptual unity in the practice of data deployment, which given our unique capacity to create symbolic systems, can only come about from a change in perspective, from a redefining of the individual as an *"animal symbolicum"* (21–26). We are different from other species because of our "symbolic imagination" (33), as opposed to the practical contrivances of other animals. Science may feel distinct from the imagination, but in truth "the facts of science always imply a theoretical, which means a symbolic, element. Many, if not most, of those scientific facts which have changed the whole course of the history of science have been hypothetical facts before they became observable facts" (59). Similarly, the ethical world, in its metaphysical dimension, transcends "the limits of the actual world" and, therefore, "is never given" (60–61). For Cassirer, this hypothetical realm houses all fields of knowledge in a shared way.

Legible contiguity, though, between literature and science requires that their relationship be inscribed within cultural production. Cassirer maintains that "the nature of man is written in capital letters in the nature of the state," a state not limited to the political but inclusive of "all the other activities of man," such as art, religion, language, and science, that "it cannot express or absorb" (63). As such, instead of a unity of effects, synthesis depends on an accord at the level of our shared impulse toward the creative process. This search leads to hope for a universal character to culture, one that will reveal all these other activities to be only variations of a logical continuity. How far Cassirer gets in reaching this destination, however, must be expressed in his own terms. Nearing conclusion, he affirms that the heterogeneous objects of human knowledge, like novels of Spain or scientific treatises of Darwin, belie an inner unity to the forms of that knowledge. He attributes this fundamental harmony to the symbolic content of their messages, adding that no essential difference can be found between the different fields of knowledge at the theoretical level of the human mind (171–76). Thus, Cassirer's recourse to José Ortega y Gasset's dictum, that "*man has no nature, what he has is . . . history*" (from "History as a System," in *Philosophy and History: Essays Presented to Ernst Cassirer*, quoted in Cassirer, 172) is most telling. The hypothetical-symbolic subtends both literature and science, but in the case of literature and Darwin, a reading in time, rather than of timeless Darwinian universals, requires that history be understood as a system of becoming similar to other mediations. Again, this does not mean influence or anything remotely akin to "measuring Darwin's impact" on a select group of novelists. Beyond an elaboration of intersection between epistemologies, Cassirer's work illustrates that whatever reciprocity we might seek between literature and science cannot be outside of history, for the ways such unity works is in accordance with temporal forces at play.

Of course, like literature Darwin belongs to history. History, though, in the very sort of becoming stressed by Cassirer falls prey to the challenges so often leveled against other modes of description, scientific, literary, or otherwise, and, moreover, it is only by taking measure of history as such, following on Cassirer, that the ethical dimension of an intersection between literature and science can materialize in the context of culture. In some sense, this approach to history gets back to the "lost cause" celebrated rather than bemoaned by Levine. First, we must concede that any illusions of stability, of history as fixed entity for objective inquiry for Darwin and literature dissipate as its hermeneutic vulnerability becomes clear. Jacques Rancière explains history as a paradox along these lines: "The distinctive feature of a history is that it may always be either a story or not a story."[17] He terms the mechanism behind this feat of history, that is, being two things at once, a *"poetics of knowledge"* that operates according to "the set of literary procedures by which a discourse escapes literature, gives itself the status of a science, and signifies this status" (8). Beyond what Rancière communicates in terms of the care we must take with any construction of history or reinterpretation of those already written, we should likewise be attentive to what he implies about history as a process of mediation. History appropriates the face of literature, so to speak, in order to wear the mask of science and thus appears in between the two or, rather, in a relationship of commonality similar to what Cassirer describes when speaking on the inner unity of our forms of knowledge.

Yet the status of science, as already shown, cannot free history from this unstable base. For this reason, Hayden White states that the principal problem of historical writing "is not that of the possibility or impossibility of a scientific approach to the study of the past but, rather, that of explaining the persistence of narrative in historiography."[18] Because of such persistence, historical discourse "always means more than it literally says, says something other than what it seems to mean, and reveals something about the world only at the cost of concealing something else" (7). Again, we come back to a plurality of meanings or, rather, the characteristic plasticity that engenders seemingly endless variations within a finite system, much like language itself and, as it turns out, evolution. Hence, for these very obstacles inherent in the discipline, which often work to our advantage, no history goes uncontested, whether we think of Darwinism or anything else. The indeterminacy of history, therefore, highlights what is at stake in using Darwin, who also enjoys the status of science and partakes of narrative, to reimagine the specific case of literary history with tools, like the theory of sexual selection, we might otherwise consider foreign to an understanding of cultural production and the sociopolitical issues involved.

At stake is nothing less than the constitution of a past that delineates the makeup and values of the present, and where one stands on Darwin continues to be almost as value laden today as in the nineteenth century. Yet if, like Tony Bennett, we understand history as a social product and, thus, as a normative process according to what we accept or reject, it is also possible to imagine the discipline of *history making* to be governed by distinctive procedures that oversee the maintenance and transformation of the past as if it were a set of

extant realities.[19] In other words, we must envision the past as part of
the material reality of our present. The pull has nothing to do with
nostalgia; rather, it has to do with the same sort of simultaneity that
Gilles Deleuze and Félix Guattari describe as the rhizomatic nature
of knowledge.[20] With respect to literature, when understood in this
way history ceases to function as an "extra-discursive real" past and
thus provides no "objective anchorage for the meanings of literary
texts—in their own time and, through a continuity of interpretive
horizons guaranteed by history's inherent direction, in the present
also."[21] This observation will be important to keep in mind as we
resist the temptation over the course of this study to ask at every turn
how much direct knowledge the Spanish novelists had of Darwin's
theory of sexual selection; though never losing sight of time, my aim
is not to seek "objective anchorage" for literary meaning in this way.
However, because "regulated" as Bennett describes, history shapes
and is shaped by the present in unforeseen ways, and *literary* history carries with it this same capacity. Neither allows us to foreclose
"interpretive horizons" because as long as there is a tomorrow, the
tale of today will never be finished, given that yesterday continues to
be born anew. The "types of evidences" and "particular zones of the
past" with which literary history deals and from which it produces
knowledge distinguish it from other historical writing.[22] As consequence, to understand these specifics is to move one step closer to the
theoretical platform I seek for my broader illustration of the indeterminate Darwin of sexual selection, Spain, and the novel.

Nevertheless, to extract these "types of evidences" and "particular
zones," much less to make them intelligible, is no simple task, given
that literary history, too, is *in the making*. But Darwin must be part
of literary history rather than something superimposed upon it. To
get at this type of simultaneity, we must begin by thinking through
the social dimension of the historicity of the text, which both exhibits
"the repeated trace of the past order" and, at the same time, "extends
beyond this trace of the past as a constitutive moment of the present,
to the possibility and the particular historical modalities of the text's
assimilation and repetition."[23] Such temporal oneness is what allows
for an unfinished relationship between the text and time, and therefore a theory of literary evolution "must reject the conception of historical movement as an evenly unfolding and integrated continuum,
and stress instead the relatively arbitrary nature of change" in much
the same way Darwin himself understood the term, which, though

seldom used by Darwin, denoted constant change brought about by and effecting parallel changes in the environment.[24] As Stephen Jay Gould has shown, it did not imply progress in the sense of improvement, though slippages and misappropriations by both Darwin and his readers often led to such a conflation.[25]

This unresolved quality of literary history is the very trait that allows for Darwin's integration in Spanish literary history irrespective of influence, given the open-endedness of his science *in time* both at the level of the text and in its social workings. Moreover, in this same vein the process of literary history can be seen to occur in two contradictory ways: "discontinuously, through the production of deviant forms of textuality, and continuously, through the reproduction of the literary norm."[26] The "literary norm" stands in for what John Frow describes as the reductive jockeying that defines literary criticism with respect to either the referential or oppositional positioning from within the text against the authority of the canon. As consequence of this relationship with canonical authority, which makes individual works function as politicized metonyms for what has been included and discarded from our expected reading and why, the text moves outside itself in a sense, extending beyond literature to the domain of the extratextual, where its effects on culture become manifest. And this dynamic also acts as the means by which we discover the inverse, that is, how our own cultural values find their way into the literature we situate in said literary history, as the works (of literature and science) come to stand for principles otherwise unrecognizable in any given ideological context.

In many respects, this turnabout occurs with the Spanish novels I read alongside Darwinian sexual selection, as they foreground the ethical indeterminism of choice and change with respect to the subjugation of women. For the female protagonists of these novels, the acceptance or rejection of suitors, the search for alternatives to the traditional role of submissive wife, and even the most troublesome depictions of specious autonomy, like prostitution, point to the social ills of Spain's patriarchy, while still grounded in evolutionism. Impediments to female agency in the courtship dynamic translate to Darwinian reversions of culture. In *The Descent*, Darwin decries conditions in which women become slaves to men, particularly through the negation of choice in marriage. The Spanish novelists, aware of this at various levels, take a self-conscious lens to their own culture. Hence, the methodological approach by which we compose literary history holds the promise of reconciliation by showing reciprocity between literature and other fields like science, in general, and Darwinian evolutionism, in particular, to be of material consequence. Genre construction plays a central role in our capacity to map intertextuality and crossover between disciplines. As Ralph Cohen contends, we have only just begun to broaden our thinking on these grounds: "Writings that deal with interrelations between literary and nonliterary genres or between genres of different disciplines . . . have led critics and theorists to a reconsideration of genre as a unified kind."[27] When we take up a novel, for example, or better yet a "realist novel," we cannot escape the fact that the "constituents of a text and their multiple relations to political and social aims" (91) shape meaning, and this aspect of genre criticism proves useful in that we find ourselves, to a degree, oriented and in possession of certain hermeneutic tools.

However, writing literary history by genres runs several risks. For example, Bennett cautions against any illusory "sociology of genres," which he believes to be an impediment to literary history for the emphasis placed on a text's origins; such privileging limits the parameters.[28] Instead, he stipulates: "Forms of writing are not active within history once and once only. To the contrary, their very nature as, precisely, writing guarantees their availability to be re-inscribed within new sets of inter-textual co-ordinates and, correlatively, new sets of ideological and political relations" (112–13). Today, interdisciplinary approaches to literature confirm this truth, and genres, like the novel, are no more finished, nor should they be, than the ever-shifting literary history they help explain. Our engagement has ethical consequence, for as Edward Said reminds us, it is the responsibility of literary criticism from within the contested cultural space it inhabits to correct the erroneous view of "literature as an isolated paddock" by promoting "the greater stake in historical and political effectiveness that literary as well as all other texts have had."[29] These are the choices that face us at every turn, the importance of *how* we read. The presupposition, then, of literary history as *simply* "literary" or of Darwin as extraneous to the composition and effects of such history, whether in Spain or other nations where his science took root, dissolves as these governing properties of "real" reciprocity emerge. Interdisciplinary reading practices carry ethical consequence because of the way they foreground the heterogeneity of knowledge in a world of shared humanity, whether between disciplines or from one nation to the next.

NOVEL ABNORMALITIES

For most practitioners of literary history, the nineteenth century
stands apart when it comes to the blurring between literature and
science, and theory of the nineteenth-century novel offers a case in
point. Early cultural historians like Hippolyte Adolphe Taine and Ferdinand Brunetière were among the first to articulate the character
of unprecedented overflow across the two domains—Taine with his
influential tenets of primordial sources, "race, environment, and ep-
och," and Brunetière with proclamations of complementariness, or
"that contemporary pretension to make art with science," and vice
versa.[30] When speaking of Taine and Brunetière with respect to Darwin, Owen Chadwick stresses that "evolution was the key to unlock
all the secrets of literary history,"[31] and Erich Auerbach, a modern
giant of such a history, followed in their footsteps with similar ideas
about nineteenth-century realism. His commentary in *Mimesis*, first
on Honoré de Balzac and later on the brothers Goncourt, underlines
the conceptual rigor of the new scientific outlook that took hold in
the period.[32] Balzac's appropriation of Geoffroy Saint-Hilaire's "principle of typal unity in organization . . . the idea that in the organization of plants (and animals) there is a general plan" (474) allows
for a transfer of biological "milieu" to the realm of the sociological:
"Does not Society make of man, according to the milieux in which
his activity takes place, as many different men as there are varieties in
zoology?" (Balzac, preface to *La comédie humaine*, quoted in Auerbach, *Mimesis*, 475). But Balzac conceives of such translation not just
as analogous but also as revelatory of surplus, of the State as Nature
plus Society. As Auerbach emphasizes, Balzac sees "the far greater
multifariousness of human life and human customs, as well as . . . the
possibility—nonexistent in the animal kingdom—of changing from
one species to another" (476). This excess in which "different species
mate" (476), born from a notion of class-based speciation, engenders
unpredictability, where a pauper can become a prince or a magistrate
can marry a maid, and such transgressions bring a moralism that Auerbach considers foreign to Balzac's project.

Yet one generation later, with Edmond and Jules de Goncourts'
Germinie Lacerteux (1864), this new motif, "the scientific attitude"
alone, morally justifies in Auerbach's view the "right to treat any subject" with an "extreme mixture of styles" (496). After all, in the case
of that particular novel, to use the brothers' own words from their

1865 preface, the tale of Germinie is a "clinical study of love" in which "the Novel is expanding and growing . . . becoming contemporary Moral History . . . [having] undertaken the studies and obligations of science."[33] Hence, a consequential generic shift, ethically grounded in the interface of opposing discourses, namely, romance and scientific empiricism, brings what latent epistemological undercurrents remain from the early efforts of Balzac to the forefront of the realist movement on explicitly moral terms.[34] Indeed, the nineteenth-century realist novel cannot (or at least should not) be divorced from coetaneous advances in science. At the same time and for this very reason, the novel was itself understood by writers of the period to be a science in its own right. Like the brothers Goncourt, their contemporary Émile Zola in "The Experimental Novel" (1880) argues in the shadow of Claude Bernard's writing on medicine that the novel produces "scientific knowledge."[35] Though Spanish writers sought to distinguish themselves in theory from their French contemporaries on certain points, like mechanistic fatalism, science was absolutely integral to the Spanish realist novel in the late nineteenth century as well, whether with respect to Darwin or otherwise. Emilia Pardo Bazán discusses related issues of the Spanish tradition in her famous treatise, La cuestión palpitante (1883), in which she draws a moral distinction between realism and naturalism, body and soul over materialistic determinism, the artist from the scientist.[36] No one, however, much less she herself could deny the importance of science and, in particular, of Darwin for her novels.

It is therefore not only possible but necessary to emphasize in the context of these theoretical postulations that specific features of the nineteenth-century novel can be said to derive from science. A self-conscious genre program on the part of writers of the period imbues their works with newfound uncertainty, leaving readers "to wonder if the human dramas are there to illustrate the scientific principles or if the science merely serves to motivate the human dramas."[37] Mikhail Bakhtin speaks of this type of crossover in Zola, for whom "the activity of coming to know another's word" requires that the "adaptability of the individual" or "testing . . . of the heroes' biological worth" be recognized as the "hybridization" of epic "trial" or "chosenness," of the "image of a language," when placed in dialogic interaction with other discourses.[38] No doubt, these other discourses originate in science particularly during the second half of the nineteenth century, for Bakhtin's characterization of "adaptability" and "biological worth" is, after all, Darwinian. At this point, the surplus as first imagined by Balzac is no longer extraneous to the form but rather so deeply embedded, thinking now of Darwinian sexual selection, as to escape recognition.

At the same time, arguments of "amalgam" or "hybridization" speak to the ways that the novel mediates the distance between "empirical objectivity" and "self-conscious reflexivity," and the subjectivity present in any novel of the late nineteenth century begs the question of what the "real" of realism actually is.[39] How we conceptualize reality offers a point of entry toward the social bedrock of this literary impulse. One way is to think of realism as dependent upon what Marshall Brown describes as a "silhouetting effect," which juxtaposes two modes, the dramatic *coup de theatre* against the atmospheric *tableau*.[40] Here, the significance of dramatic action derives from the "context and representative significance" of a "static background" (231), and writing is "to be realistic . . . whenever and insofar as we perceive ordered silhouetting or embedding effects" (233). The consequence of this dynamic is twofold. First, realism emerges as a structure of consciousness rather than mirroring. Second, individual agency falls under Hegelian terms of historical contingency: "Causality is something imposed on the manifold heterogeneity of real objects; it subjects the freedom of independent being to the imperative of becoming. . . . Understood in this way, reality is a tragic battleground where the active force of the free individual (pure 'possibility') always succumbs to the mastering contingencies of historical destiny ('reality')" (236). What Brown calls the imperative of becoming brings specificity to the social dimension of realism and, thus, shape to the "types of evidences" and "particular zones" we have been after since our consideration of the distinctions Tony Bennett makes between history and literary history. It also recalls much of what we have already said about an indeterminate Darwin and his relationship to such histories.

Moreover, because of the dialectical relationship it highlights between the individual and history, the "silhouetting effect" carries over to questions of community. In this way, Brown complements J. Hillis Miller's claims from thirteen years earlier regarding the social reach of the novel in relation to self-determinism. For Miller, too, the traditional notion of realism as mirroring serves as a catalyst for correction, but not in the way we might suspect. Rather than an objective lens, reflection enables just the opposite: "The mirror image may be a way of bringing into the open the *imaginary* quality of reality. . . . Just as the novel is a verbal structure which creates its own meaning in the play of its elements, so the reality of society is its existence as a linguistic or symbolic game which has the power to create and reveal its own foundation."[41] Indeed, Brown's "structure of consciousness" and "mastering contingencies" together with the generative potential of Miller's "*imaginary* quality of reality," which echoes Cassirer's views on the importance of the hypothetical nature of our collective thinking, liberate realism from the empirically real, subjecting hard facts to the creative mind embedded in community, and in so doing open new space for "real" reciprocity between literature and science. The reality, therefore, that materializes from these theoretical discussions of realism signals ever more complex "patterns of intersubjectivity," as the community, in the face of science, abandons faith in the unified Cartesian self and begins to question the existence of a redemptive Creator.[42] Although never made explicit by Miller, the intersubjective reshaping to which he refers traces back to a proliferation of new forms of knowledge, including science, following the Enlightenment, and in so doing deepens our understanding of the dialectical juxtaposition between "self-conscious reflexivity" (mediation) and "objective empiricism" (distance).[43] Both are enhanced, if not undone, by a plurality of subjects, a community, which makes neither inviolable.

However, despite "the very real importance of knowledge as a new kind of social and cultural currency" in the nineteenth century, knowledge becomes far "less comforting and less secure" after Darwin.[44] As with Cassirer, the abundance of facts undermines what is knowable, but to understand why this proves to be the case beyond the battleground of opposed viewpoints painted by Cassirer we need to get at the question of knowledge itself. Otherwise, though we might find ourselves drawn to the unifying notion of "symbolic knowledge" for what the first of the two terms reveals about the synthetic aspect of our thinking, the latter term of the pairing, as an uncertain "cultural currency," threatens to leave the job of reconciliation between literature and science unfinished. Using a Platonic analogy between perceiving and knowing, Richard Rorty objects to the ancient contention that only that which can be perceived can truly be known. Since "our only usable notion of 'objectivity' is 'agreement' rather than mirroring," knowledge and community are inseparable.[45] In other words, like the realism it fosters, perception itself is a social act and thus nonempirical; reality depends not on what we observe but rather on what we agree we observe. I may see a unicorn in the garden, but to what effect if everyone else finds nothing more than an old nag. This foundation toppling spurs Rorty to characterize science as a "value-based enterprise" (341) and to posit that "the distinction between epistemology and hermeneutics should not be thought of as paralleling a distinction between what is 'out there' and what we 'make up'" (342). His thinking here, a prelude to the sexual politics of science we will take up in chapter 2, shows that the split between epistemology and hermeneutics as "historical and temporary" is not "two areas of inquiry," but instead "inquiry and something which is not inquiry . . . the inchoate questioning out of which inquiries—new normal discourses—may (or may not) emerge" (384). In effect, this conflation of epistemology and hermeneutics complicates the dichotomies of objective and subjective, empiricism and humanism, science and literature, and so forth through an articulation of the truth that, in a "real" sense, to ask is to know.

The inquiry-based knowledge of "inchoate questioning" applies to both literature and science during the nineteenth century, when efforts toward making connections often mattered much more than the answers gleaned. In this light, it is important to clarify that the notion of "normal discourse" is something Rorty takes from Thomas S. Kuhn's reflections on "normal science," which amounts to "paradigm-based research" or "mopping-up operations," while its counterpart, "anomaly," describes the unfamiliar, revolutionary offspring motivating crisis and capable of engendering new, competing paradigms.[46] History places Darwin in the latter of these categories. Still, Kuhn rejects scientific development as a process of accretion, for in his opinion "the same historical research that displays the difficulties in isolating individual inventions and discoveries gives ground for profound doubts about the cumulative process through which these individual contributions to science were thought to have been compounded" (3). In other words, science cannot help but be circumstantial. Kuhn's alternative, aimed at the "historical integrity" of science "in its own time" (3), also holds true for Stephen Jay Gould, who falls somewhere between Rorty and Kuhn in proclaiming that "science is not a heartless pursuit of objective information. It is a creative human activity, its geniuses acting more as artists than as information processors."[47] Here we might recall Cassirer's words on conjecture and likewise what Brown and Miller say about realism as structure of consciousness and community rather than mirror. Going even a step further, I would add that to simplify scientific discoveries to dramatic breaks and abstracted laws erases the most meaningful aspects of what discovery is—a collective experience. Indeed, a pre-packaged Darwin reduced to *struggle for life* or a Spencerian spokesman for *survival of the fittest* or the villain who "sweeps heroes from the face of the earth" gives ample proof of this danger. It is necessary, therefore, to make "abnormal" again that which has become normal through an articulation of the pluralistic facets of Darwin's science.

Yet it must also be admitted, finally, that debate among historians of science continues as to whether or not any "Darwinian Revolution" ever took place at all, and the questions these skeptics ask speak to those who wonder, in the case of Spain and elsewhere, whether Darwin deserves any credit in the first place, given the influences of Jean-Baptiste Lamarck, Herbert Spencer, Ernst Haeckel, Georges Cuvier, Charles Lyell, Armand de Quatrefages, Alfred Russell Wallace, and so many others of the age. In other words, in terms of historical integrity, we must recognize that issues have been raised about the knowledge produced through attributions to Darwin, when in fact he was just one of many voices. Peter J. Bowler, for his part, performs a provocative reinterpretation of nineteenth-century evolutionism to allow fuller appreciation of the role played by non-Darwinian sources and after an exhaustive accounting concludes that it is "unreasonable for historians to claim that the turning point in the emergence of modern culture should be called a 'Darwinian Revolution.'"[48] Yet Ernst Mayr prefers a middle ground: "Although there was a steady, and ever-increasing, groundswell of evolutionary ideas since the beginning of the 18th century, Darwin added so many new ideas . . . that the year 1859 surely deserves the special attention it has received."[49] One way or the other, while "revolution" remains problematic, what is certain is that with Darwin comes a new Kuhnian paradigm, a "cumulative process" to be sure, for understanding the history and behavior of humankind. In Spain, this anomaly came to be called *el darwinismo*.

Still, since this is not a study centered on the attribution of ideas, issues of terminology, like whether or not we can say "revolution," matter less than the consequences of these quibbles, especially given Darwin's place in popular perception. When it comes to questions about the overthrow of the world order, then, the originality of Darwin's voice plays a pivotal role in the reciprocity at issue. It is important, therefore, to add in support of this inquiry, first, that "there is as much 'society' inside . . . and internal to the development of scientific knowledge, as there is óutside," and, second, as Gregory Radick avers, that "making up our minds over the independence or inseparability of Darwin's theory from its history . . . requires us at the same time to make up our minds about Darwin's intellectual legacies. We need to decide not only how best to honour them, but, indeed, what they are."[50] But the search for these "legacies" is further complicated by the fact that "the social power of a theory has never depended on a detailed or correct understanding by its interpreters."[51] And even more problematic still is "science" as a term. Having cataloged a minimum of eight quite different meanings, David C. Lindberg sees no choice but to adopt "a very broad definition of 'science'—one that will permit investigation of the vast range of practices and beliefs that lie behind, and help us to understand, the modern scientific enterprise."[52] Hence, with interdisciplinary engagement one must be mindful of the challenges faced by the disciplines involved. These historians of science remind us that with the potential to mean all things to all parties Darwin's science risks meaninglessness.

In the particular case of Spain, there exists a history in which "science" and "culture" have been made to mean the same thing. Though the origins of this pairing trace back to the 1868 revolution and even beyond, José Ortega y Gasset's pithy formula "Europe = science," from 1908, speaks volumes about the social, political, and ideological implications embedded within this "disinterested" epistemology from the years of Darwin's earliest dissemination into the early twentieth century.[53] Ortega had no doubt about "the need for Europeanization" as the method by which to solve "the Spanish problem" (99); he worried, instead, about the efficacy of the programs in place to achieve such an end. But in a later lecture on Galileo, Ortega better clarifies what he means by science. There, he proclaims: "Science is, in effect, an interpretation of the facts. By themselves they do not give us reality, but, on the contrary, they hide it; that is, they plant the problem of reality."[54] Knowledge, again, is a matter of hermeneutics. Under this premise, Ortega considers science to operate according to two distinct processes: "One purely imaginative, creative, which man enacts from his own free constitution; the other in confrontation with that which is for us man, with that which surrounds him, with actions, with facts. Reality is not a fact, something given, bestowed as if a gift—but instead is a construction that man makes with the material given" (16). This definition of science approximates that of realism, which, as we have seen, is not reality, but nevertheless draws on the tension between "pure possibility" (Ortega's "construction") and "historical contingencies" (Ortega's "material given"). Just like the *imaginary quality of reality*" emphasized by Miller, scientific truth for Ortega is "nothing that we see, but rather precisely what we do not see: the truth of light is not the colors we see, but rather the subtle vibration of the ether that we do not see."[55] And nowhere is this more pronounced than in the "ungraspable" individual: "The reconstruction of personal character will never suffer from guarantees of exactitude" (101–2). As consequence, it has now been shown that science does not mean a negation of self, or humankind as mere matter, or fatalistic determinism, or any of the other charges leveled against Darwin, even if by Ortega himself. Rather, the opposite is true.

Still, should the often referenced anthologist of realist theory George J. Becker be correct when he declares that realism "denied that there was a reality of essences or forms which was not accessible to ordinary sense perception," Ortega's thoughts must fall far from the realist tree, given that from his vantage point, most of "reality" was not "accessible to ordinary sense perception."[56] But Ortega, like Rorty, does not equate perceiving with knowing, and more to the point, it is the combination of Ortega's precepts that makes them relevant to realism, whose practitioners revel in uncertainties like the "vibration of ether" within us all, metaphorically speaking, rather than try to avoid them. In other words, Ortega's definition delineates an imaginative science of the unknowable individual beyond the reach of empiricism, and yet still within the epistemological parameters it establishes for itself. As a result, we must forgive Becker if he understates the scope of the movement. To be sure, the theory of sexual selection exhibits the "abnormal" qualities outlined by Kuhn, yet the revolutionary paradigm shift is nebulous and the problem of female "passive choice" in fiction hardly feels like an "anomaly" after Darwin, if compared to what came before him. Then again, in a world of "pure possibility" and history *in the making* a lot depends on how one looks at what cannot be seen.

CHAPTER TWO

The Power Dynamics
of Sexual Selection

The theoretical articulation of the reciprocity between literature and science rehearsed in chapter 1 yielded several insights. The ethical reach of these fluid domains in the indeterminate enterprise of history making remains inseparable from community, which in its pluralistic, always unfinished composition begs an interdisciplinary approach to knowledge production. Likewise, to the degree that knowledge itself is understood as a collective endeavor concerned more with questions than answers, inquiry supplants influence as a means to make sense of the temporal simultaneity that governs our constructions of the past. Together, these conclusions help us better understand an exploration of Darwin localized to a particular time and place, while abandoning conjectures about his quantifiable impact in favor of the new possibilities brought into being through the union of his science with literature of the same period according to the social concerns both share. The theory of sexual selection as explicated in *The Descent* and the Spanish realist novel framed by the coetaneous currents of *el darwinismo* and *la cuestión de la mujer* converge on the unresolved issue of female "passive" choice in courtship. Through the literary representation of reality, understood not as mirror but instead in terms of the imaginary quality of its ever-changing symbolic constitution, the open-endedness of Darwin, too, comes into view, and as consequence, we must reassess the association of his science and the novel after him with a deterministic worldview, especially with respect to women under conditions of patriarchal subjugation. Otherwise, the moral vision of each is compromised and, with it, our appreciation of a Nature of change in its fullest sociopolitical significance.

None of this carries much bite, however, without a discussion of what Darwin says about female "passive" choice in sexual selection and why it matters in the context of prevailing power structures then and now. As it turns out, many of the same issues central to literature and science studies also pervade debates concerning the conditions under which women experience various degrees of limited mobility in public and private spheres. Faced with a nature-culture dichotomy that has a long history, feminists rightly mistrust arguments of biological determinism, only to then find themselves "empirically" disadvantaged when combating the scientism of sex with arguments of socialization. Some three decades ago, Janet Sayers in her study *Biological Politics* felt it to be "particularly urgent" that "feminists develop a valid analysis of the relationship between biology and women's destiny," given the extremism she found on both sides of this dispute.[1] Yet, despite gains toward a more balanced discourse between science and feminism, Sayers's call remains unanswered with respect to how literature might not only factor in the equation but move us forward. The ideological issues of this rift persist today not for want of attention; studies on gender, after all, have assumed an important place in the humanities and the sciences alike. Rather, little effort has been made to address the biological and cultural facets of sexual inequality on a single front, and Darwin often shoulders much of the blame for making the perpetuation of the politics of patriarchal oppression possible, given the centrality of sexual differentiation to his theory of sexual selection.

The theory of sexual selection indeed brings with it a singular history of power play between the sexes that is born from unresolved tensions of female passive choice and selector role reversals. Nevertheless, these Darwinian principles remain absent from discussions about gender dynamics in the late nineteenth century during a time when the women's movement made measurable gains across Europe and in the United States. It is true that "in the eyes of Darwin's fellow scientists and historians of science alike, *Descent* is stigmatized by its association with sex, and it is thus tacitly agreed that all 'serious' focus should be on *Origin*."[2] Still, more needs to be said about the reasons for and consequences of privileging *Origin* at the expense of *The Descent*. Attention to contributions from interrelated fields, evolutionary biology, rhetoric of science, women's and gender studies among them, reveals that the devaluation traces back, in part, to the complexity of Darwin's conjectures in the second half of *The Descent*. At the same time, the sexual politics must be accounted for, since, as Michel Foucault has shown, sexuality is both an intractable and instrumental element in power relations.[3] As a catalyst for the scientism of sexuality, Darwinian sexual selection extends to more current feminist critiques of patriarchy, exchange, and otherness. Absent this context, Darwin all too easily appears prepackaged as a proponent of women's inferiority, when in fact the situation is nowhere near so clear-cut. In ways similar to the novels to be discussed, his science is complicated by a number of factors, namely, the inversion of suitors and selectors, the degree of active agency that occurs at the moment of selection, and the disconcerting correlation between the savagery and women in conditions of bondage to men. Change, in fact, is what many feminists now choose to privilege as the most liberating constant of evolutionary science, and I follow them with my claim that Darwin's indeterminism should make him an ally, rather than enemy, of women's empowerment.

PASSIVE NO LONGER

Darwin's own account of sexual selection gives rise to more questions than it answers in his two principal works. Saying "a few words" on the subject in *Origin of Species* (1859), he remarks that it "depends, not on a struggle for existence, but on a struggle between the males for possession of the females; the result is not death to the unsuccessful competitor, but few or no offspring."[4] On this basis, he concludes with scant elaboration: "Sexual selection is, therefore, less rigorous than natural selection" (88). Yet, twelve years later in *The Descent of Man, and Selection in Relation to Sex* (1871), he takes up the issue in earnest and speaks at length on male suitors and female selectors.[5] Here, the "eagerness" (1:273) and "power to charm" (1:279) of the male make him "the more active member in the courtship of the sexes," but it is also conceded that "the female, though comparatively passive, generally exerts some choice and accepts one male in preference to others" (1:273). Darwin cites cherished social ideals along gender lines, like "love" and "courage" for males together with "taste" and "will" for females; whereas from a more matter-of-fact tone, we learn that sexual selection "depends on the advantage which certain individuals have over other individuals of the same sex and species, in

exclusive relation to reproduction" (1:256). These things noted, however, Darwin admits that "the precise manner in which sexual selection acts is to a certain extent uncertain" (1:259). The primary question is "how it is that the males which conquer other males, or those
which prove the most attractive to the females, leave a greater number of offspring to inherit their superiority than the beaten and less
attractive males" (1:260). A troublesome answer (from Darwin to the
present, it appears) then surfaces in terms of agency: "The exertion of
some choice on the part of the female seems almost as general a law as
the eagerness of the male" (1:273). As unsettling as it is oxymoronic,
in this way female "passive" choice "almost" becomes *the* "general
law" of sexual selection.

For Evelleen Richards, in her historical treatment of Darwin and
feminism, such "passive" choice gives no real selector agency at all.[6] In
fact, she believes Darwinian sexual selection to be responsible for the
social inequality of the sexes and as proof draws from Darwin's discussion of the differences in mental powers between men and women.
In this section of *The Descent*, Darwin distinguishes between man,
of "a more inventive genius" (2:316), and woman: "The chief distinction in the intellectual powers of the two sexes is shown by man
attaining to a higher eminence, in whatever he takes up, than woman
can attain" (2:327). Using this same passage, Paul Civello explains
that the female, as the passive agent in sexual selection, mirrored the
environmental pressures in natural selection, by choosing or "selecting" those males deemed most advantageous, whether by appearance
or other attributes, for successful reproduction with respect to the
traits of their progeny. More important, however, is what comes next:
"Darwin argued that sexual selection, although significantly altered
in modern society since the male now acted as the 'selector,' played a
major role in the differentiation of the sexes. As a result, man, as the
sex actively involved in the struggle, had become superior to woman
both physically and intellectually."[7] In this light, Civello shows how
feminists of the late nineteenth century, like Eliza Burt Gamble,
appropriated Darwin's "few concessions to woman's worth" (24),
namely, her "maternal instincts" and discriminating "powers of intuition, of rapid perception, and perhaps, imagination" (*The Descent*,
2:326), in an attempt to discount man's superiority, by attributing
"moral sense" to women. Likewise, Lawrence Birken, for whom Darwinian thought "exemplified a contradictory treatment of gender,"
holds that "Darwinism indeed contained the seeds of a conception of

life that threatened to abolish gender itself."[8] And David Garlock, in turn, goes as far as to suggest that "in dealing with issues of sexuality and sex determination, the Darwinian revolution implied an upheaval of the traditional constructs of gender differentiation."[9] In sum, this attenuated overview of the critical history concerned with female choice makes clear that Darwin's unresolved elaboration of sexual selection has much to tell us yet about power dynamics between the sexes.

Nevertheless, in these critiques of Darwin and gender no one mentions the wavering that underlies the final two chapters of *The Descent*. This oversight is problematic, given that only by looking at Darwin's own conclusions can we begin to imagine the extent of the possibilities suggested by his vacillations. Toward the end of the penultimate chapter, Darwin proclaims: "Man is more powerful in body and mind than woman, and in the savage state he keeps her in a far more abject state of bondage than does the male of any other animal; therefore it is not surprising that he should have gained the power of selection" (2:371). But just prior, he observes that there are only "exceptional cases in which the males, instead of having been the selected, have been the selectors. We recognize such cases by the females having been rendered more highly ornamented than the males" (2:371). Throughout *Origin*, Darwin's method is observational; his conclusions derive from what he sees in nature. Yet in *The Descent*, when facing the more complex subject of "Man," he instead extrapolates from nature and assumes that what is true for animals will also be so for humans.[10] Darwin assures his reader that if one accepts his "conclusions," then "he may . . . extend them to mankind" (2:402). Yet the very same Darwin finds himself in a quandary, for he cannot dismiss what he sees in society: "Women are everywhere conscious of the value of their beauty . . . they take more delight in decorating themselves with all sorts of ornaments than do men" (2:372). In anthropomorphic sexual selection, Darwin discovers that behaviors and traits do not always mimic those of animals, and this complicates the continuum between the two he seeks to establish. We indeed prove to be one of those "exceptional cases" he observes, but a discomfort remains over what he paints as an aberrant cultural inversion of the power of selection.

Yet, even as Darwin plays the last card in his "General Summary and Conclusion" (2:385–405), he proffers few unequivocal answers:

> The sexual struggle is of two kinds; in the one it is between individuals of the same sex, generally the male sex, in order to drive away or

kill their rivals, the females remaining passive; whilst in the other, the struggle is likewise between the individuals of the same sex, in order to excite or charm those of the opposite sex, generally the females, which *no longer* [emphasis added] remain passive, but select the more agreeable partners. (2:398)

Here is a grand statement about agency, forgotten in Darwinian studies, that runs counter to his earlier remarks on and the broader social perception about female choice, which in the last instant is "no longer" passive. Moreover, from this bifurcation of the two mechanisms driving sexual selection, male-male combat and female choice, Darwin's language opens up:

Courage, pugnacity, perseverance, strength and size of body, weapons of all kinds, musical organs, both vocal and instrumental, . . . and ornamental appendages, have all been indirectly gained by the one sex or the other, through the influence of love and jealousy, through the appreciation of the beautiful in sound, colour or form, and through the exertion of a choice. (2:402)

With a lexicon far more figurative and emotive than the unfeeling *struggle for life* Darwin familiar to most, he states that "the exertion of a choice" by "the one sex or the other" involves "appreciation of the beautiful," "love," "jealousy," and, later, "mental charms," "virtues," and "intellectual and moral qualities" (2:402–3). Anthropomorphic sexual selection, as such, appears a mutual dynamic, tainted by degrees of power imbalance and inconsistency. Darwin's description is indeterminate throughout, and the sociopolitical reverberations are many.

To summarize, then, in the animal kingdom Darwin finds ornamented males, believes they compete in various ways to gain the favor of the female, and thus defines them as suitors. The females, by contrast, show themselves to be less aggressive and act as selectors to the extent that they "choose" the most attractive male according to certain still nebulous criteria, like fitness or any of the other traits Darwin mentions above. However, confusion takes root as Darwin struggles to make sense of what he sees in society, where men seem to have appropriated the selector status. He is tempted to attribute this to force, to a time when perhaps strong men were "selected" by women who then later found themselves robbed of their selector status, but also fears that such an explanation may lead him down a path of no return, since women in a state of such subjection to men through negation of choice translates, for Darwin, to barbarism. Yet, as far as Darwin's discussion of sexual selection goes, barbarism does not mean "closer to nature" in the way that one might imagine the civilization scale he and others of the day were so often guilty of promulgating, where more "primitive" peoples were deemed less evolved and hence closer to our animal ancestors in subtle and not so subtle ways. On the contrary, though women selectors might have been a baffling (if not fearful) thought, the denial of female choice in the Darwinian model of sexual selection raises even greater discomfort about dangerous reversions of culture. So, while Darwin attempts to wrap everything up neatly at the end, this "complex affair" (*The Descent*, 1:296) is far from a closed case. In fact, Darwin ends *The Descent* by saying that he would rather be descended from apes than from those who make slaves of women through forced marriages and physical subjugation.

The brief synopsis I provide here is meant to clarify some of the basic ways these back-and-forth moments in Darwin's elaboration of sexual selection both stem from and implicate larger questions about the power dynamics between the sexes with respect to courtship and female choice in the context of community. Moreover, these are the very issues that recur again and again in the novels I treat. Nevertheless, to recognize what Darwin's wavering on gender is really all about beyond such anxieties, that is, how it translates to the realm of culture and what steps Darwin and others after him take in their attempts to reconcile the contradictions, requires an exposition of the science itself, followed by the feminist critiques that help us envision more fully what this science shares with literature and the historical context of its production. Only in this way can we perceive the complex interaction of literature and science in the particular case of Spain and, in turn, what those revelations tell us about Darwin.

LIMITLESS CHANGE

With the basic points now evident, a first step to broadening our discussion of Darwinian sexual selection requires that attention be given to the rhetorical dimension of his argument. As noted in chapter 1, Darwin makes frequent recourse to slippery metaphors, whether in terms of evolutionary analogies with language, embryonic growth, geological history, or any of the other discourses of the period from which he borrows. Indeed, in contrasting *Origin* to *The Descent*, George Levine remarks: "That Darwin's evasive and moderate rhetoric was carefully deliberated for the *Origin* is evident in the differences to be found in his handling of the attempt to defamiliarize ordinary experience in the *Descent*."[11] As we have begun to see from the terminology Darwin employs, sexual selection is one such "defamiliarized" experience.

However, to take Levine's assertion one step further, Darwin goes to new lengths in *The Descent* in order to persuade, following the classical aim of rhetoric, and no argument he uses appeals more to his reader's capacity to reason than "the principle of continuity," which he employs to show "as persuasively as possible" a continuum between animals and humankind.[12] As Alan Gross has shown in his writings on the rhetoric of science, empirical distancing in the form of scientific disinterest acts as a ruse that convinces the passions of reason with reasoned argumentation.[13] With his strategy of continuity, Darwin first undermines anthropocentrism by building a case that animals possess, at a primitive level, the capacity for the very qualities which most believe distinguish humankind—tools, reason, and religion. Then, he proceeds to describe man's behavior, like mating rituals, as animalistic. Yet the former of these, which includes an extension of human behaviors to animals in his description of sexual selection, became the most controversial. Of the two mechanisms driving sexual selection, male-male combat appeared an unproblematic extension of natural selection, but the possibility that (female) animals might exercise *choice* in selecting their mates, a process more akin to artificial selection, opened a whole new set of much more uncomfortable questions. Even disregarding the female component of this agency, which most critics did not, choice alone implied that animals might be subject to the whims of taste, the most human of virtues, to say nothing of the exigencies of free will.

Due to Darwin's own account, sexual selection was first thought to be a distinct process from natural selection, with success, in the former, measured by reproduction and, in the latter, by survival. Most modern Darwinists, though, now understand its role not as separate from natural selection but rather as one of the two modes (the other being environmental constraints) by which naturally achieved variation is maximized. For the greater the variation, the greater the chances for variations that will enhance adaptation, and the better adapted an individual, the more likely it is that he or she will live to sexual maturity, to mate, and thus to pass on his or her genes to future generations. However, important distinctions do differentiate natural from sexual selection. Whereas the former may be either inter- or intraspecific when it comes to access to ecological resources, the latter will always occur among members of the same species toward the goal of mating. For this reason, Darwin defines sexual selection as operative according to two dynamics: a competition between two or more members of the same sex (most often males) for the possibility to copulate with one or more members of the opposite sex (most often females) and a struggle between the sexes where a member of one sex (usually a male) engages directly with a member of the opposite sex (usually a female) in an attempt to reproduce. These two processes, referred to as "male-male combat" and "female choice," are by no means as straightforward as the nomenclature implies, and neither are they mutually exclusive.

With regard to female choice, which inevitably spills over into discussions of male-male combat, Darwin to his deathbed held a steadfast conviction not only that it existed but also that an "appreciation of the beautiful" hinged on an aesthetic sensibility in animals and humans alike. In *The Ant and the Peacock*, Helena Cronin treats the biological forces at play in sexual selection together with certain key gender issues implicit in her discussion, which she limits to the animal kingdom.[14] Starting with "Can females shape males?" (165–81), she traces the historical debate between Darwin and Alfred Russell Wallace concerning what, if any, might be the aesthetic standard by which female choice is made. Whereas Wallace rejected such a possibility for animals, Darwin believed that female behavior during elaborate male courtship displays and extravagances like the peacock's tail, which appeared to be of no adaptive advantage whatsoever, constituted sufficient evidence for instances of (often capricious) female preference.

Yet Darwin's theory of sexual selection lacked "any explanation of how female choice itself evolved" (174), which amounted to an oversight at odds with his entire evolutionary platform. He never caved, though, to his detractors, and Cronin attributes such resolution to his faith in the very same principle of continuity between humans and animals we have come to see as the foundation for his postulations in *The Descent*. Moreover, Darwin had the "intuition that there really is something absurd, something indulgent, something blaze-of-glory-ish, about nature's peacocks' tails" (179–80), but, since the scientific community refused to accept an effect without a cause, the question of "why do females choose as they do?" (181) remained. In other words, the most exaggerated effects of sexual selection lacked an evolutionary explanation, and these gaps in the theory spilled over to social anxieties. Given Darwin's conviction about continuity, it did not help women's cause that the modifications effected by females on males among the other animal species were deemed nonsensical. In fact, it caused an unrest that could only be calmed by the reassurance that men had rightfully usurped the power of selection, and it did not seem to cause any consternation that women were borrowing the plumes of peacocks to ornament themselves and attract male suitors.

In 1915, a landmark study by R. A. Fisher proved a genetic, and thus heritable, link between male ornament and female preference; as it turns out, the two evolve in tandem. Cronin makes clear the significance of Fisher's often cited conclusions: "Fisher explained how female choice could be for attractiveness alone, as Darwin claimed, and yet be adaptive, as Wallace insisted it must be. In short, Fisher showed how Darwin's good taste could make surprisingly good sense" (201). That is to say, females had evolved to choose certain traits over others, while males had been shaped to reflect these predilections, and whether female or male the offspring of both together came programmed, so to speak, to repeat and embellish these tendencies. The adaptive aspect was simply a greater likelihood that animals conforming to these tendencies would be more successful in mating and, as consequence, in passing on their genes—a process by which the species as a whole benefits through maximized variations, which the mechanisms of procreation effected without compromise. So, though it might seem that these sorts of predispositions would amount to more of the same, in some respects the opposite proves true. For at the same time, Fisher made evident the reality that good sense does not always equal good taste, as was proven experimentally only much later by M. B. Andersson, who artificially lengthened the tails (a trait preferred by females) of select male widowbirds to demonstrate the reproductive advantage of such an aesthetic exaggeration.[15] Thus, implicit in Fisher's conclusion is the potential for inexhaustible escalation, a Fisherian "runaway" process as it is known, of unchecked male ornamentation under the pressures of female preference.

In *The Descent*, the boundlessness of sexual selection is exactly where Darwin distinguishes it from natural selection, claiming moreover, that the latter will intervene to curb secondary sexual characters once so extreme as to threaten the survival of the species:

> In natural selection, there is in most cases, as long as the conditions
> of life remain the same, a limit to the amount of advantageous modi-
> fication in relation to certain special ends; but in regard to structures
> adapted to make one male victorious over another, there is *no definite
> limit* [emphasis added] to the amount of advantageous modification;
> so that as long as the proper variations arise the work of sexual selec-
> tion will go on. . . . Nevertheless, natural selection will determine
> that characters of this kind shall not be acquired by the victorious
> males, which would be injurious to them in any high degree, either by
> expending too much of their vital powers, or by exposing them to any
> great danger. (1:278–79)

As Cronin makes clear, this notion of natural and sexual selection
at odds ties into the primary, *erroneous* distinction between the two
propounded by classical Darwinism, that is, an "efficient and utilitarian" natural selection as an "asocial" interaction with the environment, in contrast to an intraspecific sexual selection as a "social"
dynamic geared toward mating and reproduction (*The Ant and the
Peacock*, 231). And for Darwin's public, I would add that this bifurcation became a political one, split also along gender lines, with commonsense, pragmatic men pitted against their capricious, irrational
female counterparts, making sexual selection something to be managed by men, given the perception that it had the potential to compromise the "utility" of every *man* for himself. In other words, sexual
selection was an uncomfortable science for the "progressive (male)
minds" of the day, like those Spaniards whom I introduce in chapter
3, who had little to gain by referencing Darwinian evolutionism in
writings on women's rights, since science and patriarchy here were at
odds on the core tenets of the theory. Subversive strategies refracted
Darwin into something he was not and in the process made sexual selection unimportant, as a topic seldom discussed in the same breath
with the gravity of his name and more socially significant advances,
namely, natural selection and man's simian descent.

Modern Darwinism, however, has refined Darwin's original conjectures in significant ways with regard to this manufactured tension
between natural and sexual selection. First, the idea of natural selection as a check to the dangerous extremes of sexually selected traits is
not accurate. As Cronin points out, "although natural selection may
keep sexual selection within bounds, it does not invariably act as the
deus ex machina that Darwin supposed" (234), principally because
sexual selection is a priori subsumed within natural selection. Second,

natural and sexual selection are interdependent, and *both* are social dynamics:

> For modern Darwinism, nothing remains of the traditional idea that the intraspecific and social nature of sexual selection sets it apart from natural selection. . . . It is now routine to regard relations between organisms, particularly members of the same species, as highly significant selective pressures. Mating preferences and intra-sexual competition no longer stand out as atypical. Modern Darwinism can also explain why "selection unlimited" might be expected when female choice is at work. . . . Indeed, it's now standardly recognised that social competition among members of the same species, not merely for mates but for any resource, can be a powerful force for a co-evolutionary spiral. (234)

That is to say, the limitlessness of female choice transcends reproduction, extending to her other survival needs. Furthermore, in terms of gender issues, to marry natural and sexual selection in these ways helps correct the view that female choice is somehow unimportant to species evolution, as a nonadaptive influence, or worse, harmful, by effecting detrimental variations.

Likewise, greater historical context in light of the consensus of today's scientific community on the overlap between the two principles uncovers essential subtleties of "passive choice" that Darwin could not have foreseen. For instance, Cronin by the conclusion of her study opts to distance herself from Darwin's anthropomorphic descriptions like "passive choice," in favor of the genetic foundation that, only in the past two decades, has served to legitimate studies of sexual selection and place them on equal footing with those of natural selection. To this end, she states in the last analysis: "To talk of female choice is only to say that there has been selection for genes that have the effect of making females behave *as if* [emphasis added] they were choosing. . . . It's difficult enough, after all, to work out what constitutes free will in humans; why burden ourselves unnecessarily with the metaphysics of peahen preference?" (246–47). But would Darwin think "the metaphysics of peahen preference" and questions of "what constitutes free will in humans" so different? And in addition, as much as Cronin might like to "by-pass these problems and look at the issue of choice more fruitfully" (246–47), the gene-centered view she adopts, especially when it comes to issues of gender, is far from being the black-and-white panacea of neutrality she imagines it to be. On the contrary, science has a long history of dismissing such questions "in the name of science" without self-questioning the ideology behind these dismissals.

FEMINISM AND AN INDETERMINATE DARWIN

The principal drawback of genetic reductionism stems from the ease with which those schooled in sociobiology use the argument of "programmed behavior" to reinforce the status quo. No doubt, even Cronin's elaboration of the "good taste makes good sense" solution is sure to furrow some brows. Though often refuted on the grounds that bringing scientific awareness of why people act in certain ways (like middle-aged men who, driven by reproductive impulses, cheat on their wives with younger women) does not equate to advocacy of such actions, this charge is not without foundation. In Edward O. Wilson's Pulitzer Prize–winning book *On Human Nature*, an entire chapter deals with the question of "sex." There, after an account of the biological reasons for sexual differentiation in humans, Wilson claims that "the physical and temperamental differences between men and women have been amplified by culture into universal male dominance."[16] It does not take a scientist to infer that having been "amplified," the natural propensity for "male dominance" must have been present all along. Though couched in "value-free assessment" (129), his conclusions, like "universal existence of sexual division of labor is not entirely an accident of cultural evolution" (132) and "even with identical education for men and women and equal access to all professions, men are likely to maintain disproportionate representation in political life, business, and science" (133), call out for scrutiny of how and by whom these "surviving relics of our genetic history" (135) are being excavated. Moreover, when taken to an extreme, as in Richard Dawkins's popular study *The Selfish Gene*, humans become no more than gene machines, and bleak biological inevitabilities come to light: "The female sex is exploited, and the fundamental evolutionary basis for the exploitation is the fact that eggs are larger than sperms."[17] Since eggs show no sign of shrinking to the size of sperm, one might conclude such exploitation to be a cultural given. This type of analysis by Wilson, Dawkins, and others exemplifies a pervasive male bias in sociobiology that, outside their essentialist circle, discredits genetic readings of gendered culture along these lines.

    One strategy to counter androcentrism in the biology of sex with regard to sexual selection is to look to nature for exceptions to Wilson's law of "universal male dominance." For example, Evelyn Shaw and Joan Darling employ this tactic in their scientific study, *Female Strategies*, toward a "shattering" of feminine stereotypes.[18] They contend that sexual differentiation on the basis of gametes alone, eggs and sperm, not only supports the passive-active dichotomy of females and males but also "vastly oversimplifies the evolutionary imagination" (14). Nature, as it happens, resists such generalizations: "Females do not keep tradition if it doesn't work for them; species must adjust to environmental demands, and evolution has provided them with the mechanisms to meet the needs of their ecology" (15). Examples include the aggressive grebe seabird, "an equal participant in a court-ship ritual wherein she bobs about, raises her wings, crosses her bill with the male's, bows, stretches, and vocalizes noisily" (15), and the bigger, more ornamented, more deceptive deep-sea angler fish, who "carries a fringed bait on top of her head that mimics a piece of rot-ting fish" to which males "less than a tenth her length" are attracted only to then be completely stripped of their testis (16–17). From these cases and a litany of others, Shaw and Darling conclude: "So what remains of the feminine stereotype? She is not always drab, meek, and passive" (18). This correction aims to provide greater awareness of female variability and adaptation ability, not to mention agency over passivity in sexual selection. Nevertheless, when it comes to Darwin, literature, and the sociopolitical stakes of the dynamic between men and women, showy seabirds, independent ocean dwellers, oversized spiders, promiscuous perches, and the like, as liberating as they might seem, stop short of exposing the entrenched cultural forces that, once upheld through science, maintain the status quo of sexual inequality between men and women.

In the context of gender discrimination, another response to male bias with regard to biology and sex manifests itself in the now well-established field of feminism and science studies. Within this arena, two principal issues frame the debate: in particular, the construction of femininity through sexual differentiation and, in general, the cor-ollary that science itself operates as an enterprise of masculine "objec-tivity" and power. As for the first of these, Darwin's theory of sexual selection survives today as a key point of reference for the scientism of sex. The theory holds that sexual dimorphism results from the selec-tive pressures brought on by struggle among members of the same sex and between the sexes to pass on their genes through reproduc-tion. The enormous antlers of the roebuck, for use in male-male com-bat, and the pinchers of males in certain species of beetles, used for grasping and possessing the female, are two classic examples of what Darwin called secondary sexual characters, or those traits thought

to have evolved irrespective of (and sometimes contrary to) natural selection forces affecting survival. In *Biology and Feminism: A
Dynamic Interaction*, Sue V. Rosser emphasizes this aspect of sexual
selection and the consequence it carries for gender identity: "In order
to make the differentiation between males and females as strong as
possible, the theory of sexual selection is needed. The theory is the
agent of differentiation, that which assures an ever-increasing separation between the sexes and their operation in two quite distinct
realms that touch only for the purpose of procreation."[19] The behaviors and roles assigned to each sex, in biology and beyond, stem from
their roles in reproduction. Given how little the male invests and his
potential for numerous inseminations, it is in his genetic interest to be
fast and fickle; whereas the female, who must carry the fetus for the
duration of gestation and bear the brunt of the responsibility for its
early (or long-term) nurturing, benefits the success of her gene-car-
rying progeny more when she is coy and discriminating. This is the
explanation so often recited.

For those who know the scientific subtleties and exceptions regarding parental investment in offspring, this characterization of geneti-
cally determined sexual dispositions will appear a gross oversimplification. Yet even those with a sophisticated understanding of sexual
dimorphism have a tendency to fall back on these generalizations,
and for laypeople, little else sticks, given that such "scientific" male-
female attributes confirm age-old perceptions and thus the perpetuation of exploitation. For essentialists, these perceptions provide a
rhetorical safety net; "cultural universals" (a euphemism for stereo-
types or even prejudices) would not, in their minds, exist were they
not founded on underlying natural truths. A contingent of "Darwinian Feminists," though, rather than go the route of other feminist approaches (economic, sociological, cultural) and socialization
defenses (the values assigned to biological differences rather than the
differences themselves), embrace the sociobiological methodology in a
search for "the *origins* of male domination and female oppression."[20]
Instead of rejecting voices like those of Wilson and Dawkins outright,
they engage them on their own terms:

> Feminists using this approach [sociobiology] believe that by under-
> standing the evolutionary origins of male dominance, we will be able
> to formulate more effective responses to counteract female oppres-
> sion. They implicitly assume that human social systems, including
> male-female relationships and societal practices and mores, have a

biological basis and are the end result of organic evolution. Those
who accept such an evolutionary or Darwinian "worldview" believe
that an evolutionary approach can lead to novel insights that may
lead to more efficient strategies aimed at ending the oppression of
women. (118)

Therefore, to understand sexual selection in society (and literature),
one must take measure first of the science of sexual selection as I
have tried to do here or, as Zuleyma Tang-Martínez aptly (though
unwittingly) says in the passage cited above, of "novel insights." In
this regard, a purely historical or cultural reading of Darwin's theory
with respect to the gender dynamics of realism in the late nineteenth
century will remain partial at best. For, as these modern Darwinians
espouse, feminism and biology need not be at odds; at the level of
theory, *evolutionary theory* is not fixed by its patriarchal appropriations, despite a long history to the contrary. Therefore, at the level of
science, to make Darwin a proponent of male dominance is to overlook his indeterminism in the context of the ever-changing Nature
he sought to understand, and literature shows this to be true as well.

Nonetheless, biological determinism, though "overtly rejected"
(119) by Tang-Martínez and other "Darwinian Feminists," still
remains a threat to the advances of the women's movement, while
clouding Darwin's relationship to it. This is one reason my revisionist reading of an indeterminate Darwin matters so much. The fears
connected with biological determinism stem from the fact that in the
cultural realm of humankind a pervasive politicization of "natural
traits" gives rise to a patriarchal power structure that prevents sexual
equality. Kate Millett understands this very real and material phenomenon, absent in the animal kingdom, as the "sexual politics" that
ideologically condition male dominance.[21] Her account details a dangerous transference of "biological truths" from the realm of nature
to that of culture in a patriarchal social structure designed to arrest
female development. Furthermore, this transference puts in question
the foundations of science itself, of empirical objectivity and neutrality, but in ways distinct from, though complementary to, what we saw
in chapter 1. Indeed, the difference here is that the corrective impulse
centers not on the specious separation of literature and science but
rather on exposing the gender bias of an ostensibly impartial epistemology. Enmeshed in the patriarchal system and partisan to it, science cannot escape blame, positioning itself somehow outside these
relations of subjugation.[22] This qualification is important because it

helps us better appreciate the skepticism that any corrective reading of Darwin of the sort I offer with this study is sure to incite. In sum, I do not believe this past should be erased so as to leave no trace of its legacy, which is why I have given so much attention to its adumbration, but there is no question we have yet to hear the full story.

Therefore, it is not surprising that progressive concerns of feminist and science studies, inseparable from the specific issue of the relationship between sexual differentiation and the social construction of womanhood, involve which values science promotes and for whom. Prominent feminists in the field, like Evelyn Fox Keller and Sandra Harding, postulate that science itself, the supposed epistemological beacon of neutrality, is anything but valueless. They contend, instead, that the tenets of science, objectivity, empiricism, reason, and so forth, have since the earliest times (and acutely after the Enlightenment) been culturally aligned with masculinity and steadily counterposed to others, made both inferior and feminine, like subjectivity and sentimentality. Under the umbrella of an inquiry into "the science-gender system," Keller reinforces that "the connections of our subjectivity and our science are . . . crucially mediated (and maintained) by the ideology that denies their existence."[23] Likewise, Harding believes that science "is structured by expressions of gender" and, to this end, shows how a masculine ideology manages, by the same means, to secure "an apparent immunity for the scientific enterprise from the kinds of critical and causal scrutiny that science recommends for all the other regularities of nature and social life."[24] Such "immunity" results in heightened, antagonistic tensions between science and feminist critiques. Sexual differentiation, it turns out, is about much more than scientifically defining what distinguishes males from females, because science remains inextricable from patriarchal power. An operative reciprocity between science and authority, therefore, exists with respect to the structures of power that make the social phenomenon of sexuality central to the mechanics of their pairing, and Darwin, far from escaping the fray, plays a lead role for his writings on sexual dimorphism in *The Descent*.

Indeed, in the wake of important historians of science like Keller and Harding, the "value-laden" dimension of this interdisciplinary study in the context of community, as I defined it in chapter 1, must account for Darwin's dark side as well. Otherwise, my detailed treatment of these feminist issues will feel tenuous at best. In other words, it makes no sense to "revise" our understanding of Darwin, if we fail to grasp the extent of the reputation from which he is meant to be rescued. Ingrained in sexual politics, gender roles, and selector reversals, at the level of praxis sexuality as construed by culture cannot be divorced from Darwin's writing on sexual selection in nature. To get at why, it must be established from the outset that sexuality is a nonscientific category made to appear scientific by a long and complex cultural history, and little is more problematic in the minds of most feminists than the fact that reproduction has come to *biologically* define female sexuality. Speaking against this particular cultural intrusion in evolutionary biology, Elisabeth Anne Lloyd argues that evolutionary explanations which assert a direct link between female sexuality and reproduction "exemplify how social beliefs and social agendas can influence very *basic* biological explanations of fundamental physiological processes."[25] This trend stems from a contradiction in clinical conclusions as they are carried over from animals to humans: "Many researchers, in evolutionary biology, behavior, and physiology, have *deduced* that it must be the case in human females that peak sexual interest and desire occur at the same time as peak fertility. This conclusion is a simple extension of the hormonal determinism model from mice and dogs. While this may have the ring of a reasonable assumption, it is not supported by clinical literature" (94). These researchers take issue with the social construction of female sexuality, which "doesn't *make sense* unless it is in the service of reproduction" (95). The logic behind this assumption, which represents a cultural given in line with tradition but contrary to fact, holds that female desire, to be natural, must only occur at the same time as ovulation and hence in the service of reproduction.

The association between femininity and reproduction holds serious consequence. For one, culture magnifies the contradiction of female sexuality as defined by maternal instinct. To give an example in the context of my own line of inquiry, framed by the public and private spheres, questions of industrialization, domesticity, prostitution, repression, and somatic symptoms all factor into attempts to get at the cultural edifice of sexuality in the nineteenth century.[26] When looked at in these ways, female sexuality reduces to a moral paradox of what it means to be woman, made both the end of male desire and paragon of virtue under capitalist patriarchy. Though more than an impediment to agency, this monster-angel dichotomization of woman in some sense attests to an absence or, rather, a cancellation of anything that might be understood as female sexuality: "Sexually, she [woman] is man's object and falls under his order and authority. In herself, she is outside of the sexual, has no specific sexual being, is untouched by sexual feeling."[27] Indeed, this notion of female sexuality, as only a reproductive vessel and the property of man with respect to his sexual impulse, undermines any possibility to arrive at the very "essence" such a fabrication purports to convey. This conception, woman as an androcentric projection, recalls the difficulties in Darwin regarding the possibility of female selectors, at the same time that it sheds light on his recourse to role reversals, making males the selectors in some of the most memorable moments of his writing: "Man scans with scrupulous care the character and pedigree of his horses . . . but when he comes to his own marriage he rarely, or never, takes any such care" (*The Descent*, 2:402). These were his uncertain attempts to make sense of the gendered power dynamics of his theory in society.

The aberrant unknowns of sexual selection, however, could not be swept away. The fears and hopes of "reversals" inspired everything from Cesare Lombroso's work on women as atavistically inferior and sexually deviant creatures to Charlotte Perkins Gilman's utopian conception of Herland selectors.[28] Some, like the sociologist Lester Frank Ward, even held that primitive women by selecting strength as an attractive male attribute had actually been robbed of their selector status.[29] Such a theory ties back to Darwin's thoughts on bondage as the means by which savage males gained selector status and raises the question: "If . . . human females had selected in some primeval past, what was to prevent them from returning to their unseemly, unfeminine ways? What was to stop Victorian women from snatching the agency of selection back from men, making improper sexual choices, and effectively bringing 'civilization' down with them?"[30] In fact, in Darwin's treatment of avian sexual selection, "a reversal of power characterizes the selection, indicating that agency has been somehow inappropriately or uncomfortably attributed. . . . The female, in the theory of sexual selection, is made a subject and the male an object."[31] But as we have seen, Darwin also ponders the possibilities for such reversals beyond the animal kingdom, or rather, by extension, between men and women, when the power of selection is "gained by the one sex or the other" (2:402). The problem is, these conjectures have been largely passed over or misunderstood.

The implications of sexual selection extend far beyond empirical quantifications of reproductive success. Womanhood itself becomes a question. A line can be drawn directly from woman "made a subject" in Alys Weinbaum's discussion of Darwin to Simone de Beauvoir's concept of woman as "Other" in her influential reading of women's condition from *The Second Sex*, where the issue is raised: "Why is it that women do not dispute male sovereignty? . . . Whence comes this submission in the case of woman?"[32] The cause, in part, can be traced to class-based social stratification, which begins with sex and ends with economics: "A historical development . . . explains their [women's] status as a class and accounts for the membership of *particular individuals* in that class" (xviii). I discuss the problematic leveling that occurs with women made class in chapter 9. For the moment, suffice it to say that for Beauvoir sexual selection far from liberates woman, who lacks the power to choose in her oppression: "In truth woman has not been socially emancipated through man's need—sexual desire and the desire for offspring—which makes the male dependent for satisfaction upon the female" (xx). Male dominance makes woman. This is the radicalism of Beauvoir, her phenomenological inquiry into the very existence of "woman" via her embodiment; the relationship to the world cannot be understood absent the body.

Still, even more radical in the context of the present study is her argument that woman's freedom is a matter of choice. In this way, Beauvoir's focus on real experience bridges her feminism with Darwin, for it calls attention to the erotic ambiguities that confuse subject and object in encounters of desire, in the way we experience each other through our reversals. Sexual selection thus carries already within it a liberating capacity for the woman made Other in Beauvoir's critique of the way sexual difference has been deployed toward oppressive ends. She does not renounce sexual difference but argues instead that "equality," to the extent it means being like man, is to make man the model. Equality should be something else entirely. In her existentialism, which, like Darwin's, is by no means deterministic, the equality she has in mind has much more to do with questioning the experience of the sexual encounter, given that the nebulous intimacy it brings has the potential to blur power structures.

Likewise, Luce Irigaray sees in womanhood man's mirror, that is, the inverse he has created to fill his needs through a social power structure of his design. If she is complicit, this is because, as Beauvoir notes, happiness is conditioned. Entrapped within "the cult of the father," woman has value only insofar as she can be exchanged; she is in effect "the material alibi for the desire relations among men."[33]

This portrayal of male dominance and woman made Object holds Marxist resonance according to the terms of commodification. In one version of Darwin's model, too, "fast and fickle" males have few scruples; they are more than ready to mate with any number of females exchanged among them. Yet as Maria Mies makes clear, uncompensated female reproductive labor lurks behind these "market" practices in the realm of culture:

> The search for the origins of the hierarchical sexual division of labour should not be limited to the search for the moment in history or prehistory when the 'world-historic defeat of the female sex' (Engels) took place. Though studies in primatology, prehistory and archaeology are useful and necessary for our search, we cannot expect them to give an answer to this question unless we are able to develop materialist, historical, non-biologistic concepts of men and women and their relations to nature and history.[34]

In addition to the stress she places on sexual division of labor, which is ever present in Darwin but never made explicit, Mies is useful here for the way she resists an either-or reductionism (i.e., science or society) for what is a far more complex matter because of its dynamic dimension. Even if I would challenge some of the distinctions Mies sets forth, since "archaeology" will always be "historical" and "material," for example, and "relations to nature" can never be "non-biologistic," her point that these explanatory impulses should be complementary reinforces much of what I have tried to show throughout these first two chapters. The sociopolitical consequence of the indeterminate science of sexual selection cannot be understood absent its sociopolitical praxis, and this praxis, in turn, cannot be grasped absent its representation in cultural production at a moment when the two converge during fervent debates about the civil status of women and changes in voting, education, and employment rights.

Darwinian sexual selection and feminist critiques of patriarchy, without question, intersect on many fronts, but it is the engaged, yet unresolved medium of literature that brings them into view in ways neither alone can. Across Europe (and not simply in Victorian England), realism during the late nineteenth century came to reflect and complicate evolutionary science. As consequence, Gillian Beer observes that "topics traditional to the novel—courtship, sensibility, the making of matches, women's beauty, men's dominance, inheritance in all its forms—became charged with new difficulty in the wake of the publication of *The Descent of Man*."[35] Yet in Beer's search to discover if fiction can give the power of selection back to women after Darwin attributes such status to men, it remains questionable, given our close analysis of sexual selection as elaborated in *The Descent*, if Darwin was ever truly convinced that this reversal had in fact occurred. He no doubt suggests as much and at times states so outright. Indeed, as it turns out, Nancy Armstrong is right to contend that "having posited a biological basis for differentiating the roles of the sexes, then, Darwin's theory turns around on itself and roots sexuality entirely in culture."[36] She points out the paradox that "in selecting 'the more agreeable partners,' the female of the species quite literally creates the male in the image of her desires" (222), which returns us to Cronin's earlier inquiry into whether or not females shape males. Armstrong, then, sees what was dismissed as mere peahen preference; "primitive culture" for Darwin is "not a culture at all because it suppresses female authority" (224).

To conclude *The Descent*, Darwin recalls his repulsion upon seeing the Fuegians while a young man aboard the *Beagle* and explains in his own words: "I would as soon be descended from that heroic little monkey . . . as from a savage who . . . treats his wives like slaves" (2:404–5). No doubt, his science has come to mean many things to many people, as is evidenced in responses to the gender divide that permeates culture, past and present. With regard to courtship in the novel, I understand female choice in the Aristotelian sense of plot, that is, a "serious" and "complete" action, because of its socially problematic "passive" dimension as well as for the pathos it evokes.[37] In this light, I would suggest that our responses to female choice, the pathos we feel at the limited options for female protagonists in novels of the late nineteenth century who find themselves in unhappy marriages, abandoned, thrown to the street, or worse, trace back to the ethical aspect of Darwin's conjectures on sexual selection, a theory that gets reified as deterministic and patriarchal in the back-and-forth of sexual politics. Again, this pathos is born from concerns about our own humanity, about what it means to be civilized, in Darwin's mind and our own. Indeed, just as in his own day, Darwin all too often becomes a mere ideological placeholder for one position or another without sufficient attention given to the complexity of his thought. We saw a more plastic Darwin in chapter 1 when establishing the reciprocity between literature and science once each is shown to be fluid and, here, in chapter 2 with respect to the indeterminate space his writing opens for women and new forms of questioning.

It is, in fact, quite meaningful that Darwin ends his magnum opus on humankind by proclaiming that he would rather be of simian descent, where female choice remains intact, than find himself, that is, his lineage, in those who treat their wives like slaves, which stands in his view as an overthrow of the natural order through brutish oppression. Of course, one could take issue with Darwin's characterization of the Fuegians or argue that the distinction he makes between himself and them reflects a twisted contradiction of his theory of descent in its very essence, but to do so would only deter rather than enhance our understanding of his position on the power dynamics of sexual selection. To be sure, it is easy to become distracted by all that makes us uncomfortable about Darwin, but at the same time, we should not forget that, as Cynthia Eagle Russett avers, the most striking quality of his science and the "one that set him apart from the majority of commentators on male and female nature—was the tentativeness of his conclusions and the cautiousness of his recommendations. Darwin was not a dogmatist."[38] He remains an open book, and as we have seen, feminists enjoy an uncomfortable marriage with Darwin, for having to confront his theory of sexual selection they come to profit from it: "Darwinian Feminists assume that behavior is plastic, perhaps to facilitate individual success in a variety of changing social environments so that the best 'cure' for many diseases is changing the environments rather than the individuals."[39] In the end, this approach grants us the reassurance that change is not just possible; it is a certainty: "Culture can be understood as part of the ongoing evolution of the natural, the variable spirals and complications of a nature that is always already rich in potentiality to be developed in unexpected ways."[40] This vision defines the "Darwinian feminism" of today, and this feminism reflects the "potentiality" of choice in sexual selection and illuminates the empowering indeterminism that makes Darwinian "determinism" a misnomer.

CHAPTER THREE

Translations, Translators, and the Sexual Politics of Sexual Selection in Spain

Part 1 of this study centers on "origins" according to the theoretical, scientific-feminist, and historical components necessary for a reassessment of Darwin's indeterminism through the novelistic representation of sexual selection in the late nineteenth century. Chapters 1 and 2 were by no means tangential to this aim, nor were they digressive lead-ins to a book that is otherwise concerned solely with Spain. The argument does not start now but rather began, naturally enough, with the beginning, since original insights about Darwin matter in equal measure, if not more so, to those about the Spanish context and novels I treat. Chapter 1 made clear how we might read Darwin in history, without asking that always imperfect affirmations about his reach rewrite that history in a one-directional way. It showed the relationship between knowledge and inquiry to be ethical, given the choices that surround the pluralistic subjects we engage, and communal, given their collective, unfinished nature. Chapter 2 lent specificity to the particular case of Darwinian sexual selection in light of these criteria by showing the indeterminism of the theory itself and its sociopolitical implications with respect to a set of select feminist issues. Following both chapters, then, it would be surprising if in a country like Spain, which found itself consumed by Darwin and "the woman question" during the last decades of the nineteenth century, science and society did not converge in unprecedented polemics about the merit of sexual selection.

Yet sexual selection remains absent from histories of *el darwinismo* in Spain, and what connection does exist between the theory and coetaneous issues of women's rights, *la cuestión de la mujer*, is not self-evident.[1] Accounts describe Darwin in the context of the liberal Revolution of 1868, a climate characterized by institutional reform, a nascent free press, and urban modernization. Made synonymous with determinism, that is, with an indifferent Nature of fixed laws, his theories became a polemical powder keg between reformists and conservatives, and the period remains defined along these lines, with the social consequences (ethical and economic) of natural selection from *Origin* center stage during a series of early debates (1868–76), followed by reaction (mostly religious) against man's simian origin in the wake of *The Descent* in Spanish (1877–88). This chapter, therefore, has two important aims—first, to write the unwritten history of Darwinian sexual selection in Spain and, second, to show how that history, through influential voices of those in Spain who supported Darwin and promoted his science, intersects with political writings on the women's movement.

The silence that looms over sexual selection in Spain is problematic. It limits our appreciation of Darwin by obfuscating the crossover between sexual politics and his science at a moment when the very citizenship of women was in question. Today, accounts of the historical reception of Darwin in Spain speak of the "utter banality" of political hot air and tend toward generalizations: "It is as if the entire cultural atmosphere, full of historicist and scientistic ingredients, needed, for its complete self-affirmation, the work of Darwin."[2] The landscape, thus, lacks depth. Nevertheless, these claims signal an awareness that there is more to be said, for it is true that "the biological impact" of Darwin "invades all schools of art and thought, as well as moral and political conduct" in Spain during the period.[3] In this respect, one important difference between *el darwinismo* and "Darwinism" lies in the social dimension of the former, as a nomenclature born from a need to describe Darwin as filtered through the popular imagination. The problem is, we do not know precisely how or in what ways proclamations about biological impact and invasion might mean something more than a relatively limited number of concrete, demonstrable linkages of correspondence and intent between Darwin's works and the society he has been characterized to have shaped in these pervasive ways. The material set forth in this chapter, therefore, encompasses both the approach of traditional reception studies and the possibility that the influence of sexual selection, no matter how murky, was nevertheless real.

As a result, there needs to be more specificity about the other faces of Darwin in "all schools of art and thought, as well as moral and political conduct." With regard to sexual selection, the evidence shows that *The Descent* was accessible, and even if questions of by whom and to what extent persist, there can be little doubt that many in Spain at the time knew of this work and its importance. It also makes clear the indeterminate overlap between his theory and sexual politics of the day as promoted by prominent *darwinistas*. Together, these findings illuminate how the unresolved contradictions of Darwin's science, as discussed in chapter 2, extend to the gendered power dynamics of a particular time and place. This extension is the sociopolitical praxis of Darwinian sexual selection, while the spectrum of responses in the writings here presented will show the effect of Darwin's uncertain conclusions about choice. Only in these ways can we begin to give novel shape to *el darwinismo*—Darwin in the imagination—where he is no less meaningful or material, simply unfamiliar to those who know him only as deterministic.

The first task, therefore, becomes one of documentation. That is, *what* did Spaniards read? To this end, the earliest French and Spanish translations of Darwin, namely, of *The Descent*, offer insights into how his language crossed over. Next, *who* made it possible? Here background on the translators illuminates the interdisciplinary agenda that propelled his dissemination. Finally, *where* did it end up? The Spanish press, to be sure, provided a forum for somewhat sundry references in contributions to major journals like *Revista Europea* and *Revista Contemporánea*, but to uncover sexual selection and its overlap with sexual politics in Spain also necessitates attention to lesser known writings, which at first glance seem disconnected from Darwin. Reflections published on women, love, and economics by Manuel de la Revilla, Leopoldo Alas (Clarín), and Santiago Ramón y Cajal, who were all prominent intellectuals immersed in *el darwinismo*, provide a representative sample of the unexpected and often troublesome ways sexual selection took shape in the public discourse. Whereas natural selection acted as an ideological catalyst for polarization under the guise of science, fueled by empty rhetoric and blind convictions swirling around a politicized Darwin, sexual selection escaped this fate and instead, without being identified as such, fused with the "social musings" of the period concerned with women's rights. This alternative history, of sexual selection in translation and its curious transposition to the question of women's emancipation, rescues Darwin from dry polemics and situates him in the realm of science imbedded in Spanish culture, in those moments when gender relations, questions of female agency, and preoccupations with social mobility converge.

THE TRANSLATIONS

An analysis of the earliest translations of Darwin in Spain serves two principal purposes. From a practical standpoint, what is propounded about Darwin's works as they first surfaced in Spain, namely, *The Descent*, remains incomplete and removed from the translations as historical documents. As corollary, it is also therefore important to take to task, first, the popularized notion that Spaniards only read Darwin in inferior French translations and, second, that Spanish translations were either unknown at the time or distortions of Darwin's original text. Although Spanish translations of Darwin lagged behind those of other European countries (though not as much as has been assumed in some cases), complete and reliable French translations were available to the Spanish public soon after Darwin's works were released in English. Furthermore, when Spanish translations did come out, they were published and distributed by key figures in the intellectual community of the day, and records, though scarce, indicate healthy circulation of the texts. In other words, those Spaniards intent on reading Darwin could find him in reliable translations following the Revolution of 1868, and contrary to the idea that Spaniards knew little about his actual works, many *darwinistas* demonstrate considerable investment in the study of his science, whether through their own writings, participation in conferences, or promulgation of Darwin's texts.

A pivotal moment in Darwin's Spanish history came with the earliest French translation of *Origin* by Clémence Royer in 1862. This edition, bearing the title *De l'origine des espèces, ou des lois du progrès chez les êtres organisés* (widely available in Spain by the third edition in 1870, by which time a significant change had been made to the title, from "*du progrès chez les*" to "*de la transformation des*"), set the stage for the popular Spanish perception of Darwin then and, it might be argued, up to the present.[4] Though Royer's translation offered a complete reproduction of the 1859 English edition, including Darwin's chapter summary headings, footnotes (occasionally with Royer's own flamboyant insertions, which were reduced by the second edition in 1866, and virtually eliminated by the third edition in 1870), index, and illustrations, it also contained a lengthy, loaded preface that made Darwin synonymous with progress in a way that threw down an ideological gauntlet between political factions.

Writing on Darwin's history in France, Robert E. Stebbins remarks that "the idea of progress was more important to Royer than the idea of natural selection" and notes Darwin's misgivings about Royer's introduction, which Darwin believed had damaged his scientific reputation and "injured the book in France."[5] However, Royer's preface goes far beyond a misguided emphasis on progress and Malthusian principles; it underscores the hypothetical-unproven aspects of evolutionary science, makes Darwin a messenger of revelations (in line with the likes of the ancient Greeks, Jesus, Dante, and John Locke), and draws a polemical line in the sand between science and religion, which Darwin himself would have rejected. Royer also intersperses bold pronunciations about the originality of Darwin's science, a quality that remained in doubt in the context of French scientific history and, especially, because of persistent challenges to Jean-Baptiste Lamarck's transformism. The translator's claims became a catalyst for polarization in Spain; for in France as in other countries, "when opponents of the Darwinian views wanted to object to the social and moral implications of his ideas, they could refer to Royer's introduction to see just what those implications were."[6] Regarding these implications, it should therefore be noted that any moral objections would come in response to the amoral (and hence immoral) platform of evolutionism. As I hope to show over the course of my study as a whole, this has been the pervasive and enduring misunderstanding of Darwin's science, even with Royer long since absent from the conversation. Intelligent design would be the most visible vestige today of distorted attempts to mitigate the damage Darwin has been deemed to have done to our moral fabric. In any case, without losing sight of the present argument, Darwin's arrival in revolutionary Spain through the voice of Royer threatened the foundations of the conservative worldview and tradition. Consequently, Spaniards took sides from the beginning, believing that where one fell on the question of el darwinismo was a political rather than scientific declaration.

The authoritative French translation of The Descent appeared in 1872, only a year after the first English edition, with the title La descendance de l'homme et la sélection sexuelle.[7] Disgruntled by the preface added to Origin in French, Darwin rejected Royer as his translator for subsequent editions of Origin and, likewise, for The

Descent. In the case of the latter, he chose instead Jean-Jacques Moulinié, who provided a comprehensive and accurate translation, complete with Darwin's chapter summary headings, footnotes, index, and
illustrations. This authorized translation also included, with Darwin's
permission, a preface by the controversial naturalist Carl Vogt, whom
Darwin cites on occasion in the original 1871 English edition. However, Vogt's preface, which was a direct transcription of an address he
had given in 1869, appears far less ideological than Royer's introduction in her translation of *Origin*, even though Vogt was considered by
his contemporaries to be equally antireligious and as much an advocate of science as the only road to progress. Vogt's message concerns
the novelty and significance of Darwin's contributions:

> Darwin takes man as he finds him today; he examines his physi-
> cal, moral and intellectual qualities and investigates the causes that
> must have converged in the formation of these qualities, so diverse
> and complicated. He studies the effects that these same causes have
> produced acting on other organisms and finding analogous effects
> produced in man, he concludes that analogous causes have been in
> play. The final conclusion of his investigations, conducted with rare
> sagacity equaled only by his uncommon erudition, is that, man as
> we see him today is the result of a series of transformations brought
> about since the earliest geological times. Undoubtedly, these conclu-
> sions will find plenty of detractors. That is not a bad thing, though,
> for truth is born from a clash of intellects.[8]

This homage, in the context of Spain, reveals in part why Darwin
had such a dramatic reception; his science was perceived from the
outset as radical for its disquieting claims to truth. Moreover, as for
the quality of the translation, Darwin's theories in this earliest French
edition of *The Descent* remain intact. Vogt's preface and a selection
of excerpts comparing Moulinié's translation with Darwin's original
give evidence against the popular perception that Spaniards who read
Darwin in French could not have appreciated or understood his theories.[9] Perhaps anything coming from France at the time ran the risk
of being discredited out of hand by Spanish liberals and conservatives alike, given the historical tension between the two nations, but a
case can be made for why the opposite would be true as well in light
of France's cultural influence in Spain and across Europe. If, in any
event, the earliest contact most Spaniards had with *The Descent* was
through the Moulinié translation, there is nothing to indicate that the
edition, simply because in French, would alter Darwin's science beyond recognition.

In terms of Spanish translations, the story offers enough intrigue to capture the imagination and, at the same time, reveals the inter-disciplinary agenda of Darwin's translators, whose identities have remained obscure and whose humanistic project has been overshadowed by the popularized polemics of *el darwinismo*. Since J. A. Zabalbeascoa's discoveries in 1968, the consensus has been that a Catalan poet, Joaquim Bartrina, was the first to translate Darwin into Spanish with his 1876 unauthorized edition of *The Descent*, which predated by a year the earliest translation of *Origin* in Spanish.[10] Historical evidence, however, sheds some doubt over Zabalbeascoa's claims (and, as it happens, Bartrina's as well). The Biblioteca Nacional in Madrid has among its holdings a twenty-eight-page document, cut short because of suspended publication, titled *Origen de las especies por selección natural: O resumen de las leyes de transformación de los seres organizados (con dos prefacios de Madame Clemencia Royer)*, published in 1872.[11] This "edition" was released in Madrid by Jacobo María Luengo as a serial publication in the Biblioteca social, histórica y filosófica without reference to the translator. Although these pages contain little to nothing from Darwin, it is significant that his first appearance in Spanish originated from the French translation with Royer's controversial preface. Similarly, another enigmatic Spanish edition of *Origin* exists, bearing the title, *Origen de las especies: Por medio de la selección natural ó la conservación de las razas favorecidas en la lucha por la existencia*.[12] Documented as published in 1873 in Madrid by José de Rojas and translated by Enrique Godínez, the same translator of the official, authorized *Origin* released in 1877 by José del Perojo, this translation, if authentic and accurately dated (which is questionable), would make Godínez, not Bartrina, the first translator of Darwin in Spain and place the first complete Spanish translation of Darwin's *Origin* ahead of that of *The Descent* and four years earlier than the 1877 *Origin* edition, believed to be its first translation in Spanish.[13]

What is certain, however, is that the 1877 translation of *Origin*, carried out by Enrique Godínez and published by José del Perojo as *Origen de las especies por medio de la selección natural ó la conservación de las razas favorecidas en la lucha por la existencia*, merits attention for being the first complete and authorized translation of Darwin in Spanish.[14] This edition, often referenced by historians of Darwin in Spain, has yet to be discussed in terms of its quality or composition. In effect, a comparison with the 1859 English edition shows the translation to be accurate, with a faithful transference of Darwin's original notes and illustrations. The text opens with Darwin's own words, without a translator's preface, and closes with a useful glossary of scientific terms, presumably to assist Spanish readers unfamiliar with Darwin's terminology. Other additions include a brief note immediately following the title page and detailing the status of international translations of the sixth English edition, from which the Spanish was taken. This account of Darwin in international translation might have been intended to signal Spain's delayed recognition of an already well-established science, especially in the shadow of more "advanced" European neighbors, or as a means to impress upon the Spanish public the legitimacy of Darwin's work. The other inclusion in these opening pages is a transcription in English and Spanish of a correspondence between Perojo and Darwin in which the latter gives his permission and expresses pleasure regarding this "first" Spanish translation.[15]

Yet it is agreed that Joaquim Bartrina trumped Godínez and Perojo with *El origen del hombre: La selección natural y la sexual (primera versión española)*, released by Renaixensa publishing house of Barcelona in 1876.[16] Because this pirate edition was anonymous, Bartrina's role in Darwin's debut in Spanish remained a mystery until Zabalbeascoa unearthed excerpts from the translator's preface in an unpublished volume of Bartrina's collected works. Commenting on the translation, Zabalbeascoa notes "numerous discrepancies" and laments: "Bartrina set himself to omitting fragments here and there, following who knows what criteria; ultimately the selection seems to us very arbitrary."[17] Moreover, Zabalbeascoa questions "if Bartrina realized his version of *The Descent of Man* directly from the original" (272), suggesting instead, with stylistic similarities, that it may have come from a French translation. And finally, there is the issue of the translator's desire to remain anonymous, which Zabalbeascoa attributes to the unauthorized aspect of the project, concluding that "the nervous and incomplete character of Bartrina's edition" shows "a book put together with a certain degree of urgency" (275). In these ways, Zabalbeascoa performs a considerable service by bringing Bartrina's role to light.

Nevertheless, Zabalbeascoa undershoots the scope of Bartrina's enterprise and contribution. Nothing about this first edition of Darwin in Spanish indicates disingenuous intentions. The translation is not complete, but neither does it pretend to be. On the contrary,

Bartrina's efforts come across as an earnest attempt to offer the Spanish public a representative, abridged version of Darwin's principal theories. The text, composed of the first seven chapters of *The Descent*, seeks to simplify Darwin's thought and to clarify his theory of natural selection, presumably for readers unfamiliar with the content of *Origin*, which had yet to be translated to Spanish. A colorful preface by Bartrina opens the translation, and after the seven-chapter body, two short appendixes, one on sexual selection and the other from Darwin's writings on the expression of emotions in man and animals, close the work. Although the preface contains no explicit commentary on the theory of sexual selection, it gives unique insight into Bartrina's cultural agenda while at the same time painting a picture of what could be understood of evolution at the time by a Spanish poet, without scientific training, who taught himself English so as to read Darwin in the original.

In contrast to Royer in her French introduction to *Origin*, Bartrina states his objectives concerning *The Descent* with more humility: "In undertaking its translation, we do not seek to impose it upon intelligent minds, by granting it the character of an absolute truth, but rather to present it for open examination so that without prejudices either for or against, it may be examined and judged."[18] He also reveals, in clarifying his approach, what would likely have been the opinion of Spaniards interested in evolutionary theory when Darwin's works were beginning to circulate in the early 1870s:

> In order to explain satisfactorily the origin of man the theory of natural selection is sufficient; therefore, we have translated some entire selections, and elsewhere included excerpts, of the section of the work in which Darwin develops this theory with great attention to facts and observations. The new hypothesis of sexual selection, like the even more recent theory of the expression of emotions, are useful complements for the confirmation of the primary theory; for this reason, we are offering from them an extract as complete and concise as possible, achieving in this way a summary of all the major works of Darwin in a single volume. (viii)

This passage from Bartrina's 1876 preface, in addition to showing knowledge of Darwin's original English publications to be quite current in Spain, supports the idea that the theory of sexual selection was understood as secondary to and in service of natural selection.

Though Bartrina subsumes sexual selection under natural selection, calling it and the expression of emotions "useful complements," his explication of natural selection suggests how comparable he found the two theories. When it comes to the subject of man, natural selection for Bartrina, as for most of his contemporaries, though encapsulated in the bilingual catchphrase of "lucha para [por] la vida (*struggle for life*)" (x), boils down to questions of heredity. When speaking of natural selection among humans, Bartrina echoes important moments from Darwin's description of sexual selection:

> In this continual struggle [for life], aimed entirely at personal advantage, no matter how small, individual superiority in all its forms can allow the possessor to triumph over his rivals, and while these perish more or less soon thereafter without leaving heirs, those alone survive and eventually are able to reproduce. From this most natural occurrence, from which the individuals favored in the struggle for life become the only ones to have descendents, one may deduce that the second generation will differ from the first. In this second generation, some individuals, if not all, will possess, by means of inheritance, the advantage that allowed their parents to triumph. But even more, and this is one of the most important laws of heredity, when an attribute has been passed down during a series of generations, it is not transmitted then simply as it was in its origin, but rather it is accentuated and augmented without limit, having in the end, in the last generation, acquired such degree of force, that it differs in essential ways from the primitive state. (xi–xii)

Here Bartrina conflates natural and sexual selection by speaking of the former in terms of inherited traits "without limit"; Darwin, though, attributed the capacity for "no definite limit" (*The Descent*, 1:278) to the latter. As I make clear in the section "Limitless Change" from chapter 2, of natural selection Darwin states: "In natural selection, there is in most cases . . . a limit to the amount of advantageous modification" (1:278). Hence, Bartrina's emphasis on heredity, that is, reproductive success as a mediator with respect to maximized variation, constitutes an important conceptual bridge between natural and sexual selection that resurfaces time and again in writings, fictional or otherwise, of the period. Most significant, however, is Bartrina's acumen on modifications "without limit" through sexual selection. So, though there does exist in Bartrina's preface a tendency to reduce Darwin, as had been the case in most of the French translations, to a naturalist recapitulation of Thomas Malthus—"The theory of Darwin is an application to Nature in its totality, of the principle set forth by Malthus" (Bartrina, xi)—which was a perception of Darwin's science that had significant economic and ideological repercussions in

Spain as in England and elsewhere, it should be emphasized that in the last decades of the nineteenth century, and particularly in Spanish translations, the boundary between natural and sexual selection blurs. That is to say, since one could not be understood without the other, we should question the accepted notion that the former made the latter simply an afterthought.

In the seven chapters that compose the body of the translation, Bartrina condenses Darwin's writing by limiting the number of examples and the verbosity of technical explanations contained in the original. He maintains Darwin's principle of continuity throughout and manages to capture the main ideas in often lengthy passages that appear to have been taken directly from the English in a manner accurate enough to feel like an actual translation rather than merely a paraphrase. Nevertheless, it is not until the first appendix, an addendum of only thirty pages in its entirety (as opposed to the more than three hundred making up the second half of *The Descent*), that Bartrina treats the theory of sexual selection.[19] This appendix, though, is not a direct translation of Darwin at all in parts, and on occasion Bartrina even refers to him in the third person. However, many passages do resemble Darwin's own language to a considerable degree, and even in light of drastic differences with the original, namely, the sweeping omissions and paraphrases, Bartrina succeeds in relaying to his Spanish public (however large or small) some of the richest subtleties of sexual selection.

For example, Bartrina captures Darwin's principal dilemma in sexual selection, that is, exaggerated modifications deemed disadvantageous to survival, and gives an acceptable definition: "How can the magnificent plumage of the peacock contribute to his security, or to that of the nightingale his melodious voice? In order to explain the acquisition of such traits it is inevitably necessary to have recourse to another process [i.e., other than to *struggle for life*]. Darwin finds it in sexual selection, which, in its essence, is only a form of natural selection" (282). Whether regarding ornamentation, female choice, or anthropomorphism, Bartrina touches on the most unresolved and significant assertions in Darwin without tempering the implications:

> The characters whose origin one must attempt to discover are precisely those whose principal object appears to be the perfection, to some degree, aesthetic, of animals. . . . Thus the males display their ornaments before the females, to the point of neglecting their own security in order to cause them to fall in love. Does it not seem

natural that when the moment arrives for the female to choose from among her suitors that she will give herself over to the one among them whom she believes to be the most beautiful and best endowed? Is it not also probable that the females might have developed in their own fashion some aesthetic sense that makes them prefer some ornaments over others, or unexpected adornments over those which are familiar? Choosing always the most attractive males the females would be the *cause* [emphasis added] of their perfection, or simply of the variety in their species. (282–83)

While Bartrina's appendix on sexual selection may be only a tenth of Darwin's original in terms of length, and often not in direct translation, it is far from watered down. Indeed, Bartrina conveys here that the presumed perfection of men, or at least their claims to superiority, could actually be traced back to female choice.

Likewise, in his treatment of the origin of language, Bartrina paraphrases moments in Darwin with imaginative acuity:

The primitive use of the vocal organs of animals was and is united with the propagation of the species. The indefinable sensation that song produces in us, and many other singular acts intertwined with the effects of music, become completely explicable if we admit that musical sounds and rhythm were employed by the simian-human ancestors of man, during the time of reproduction, in that all animals find themselves subject to the influence of the strongest passions. And if this were to be true, following the profound principle of inherited associations, musical sounds could awake in us, in a vague and indeterminate manner, the internal emotions of a most remote age. (306)

Recognized as the first translator of Darwin in Spain, Bartrina also stands as the first Spaniard to identify passages of paramount social and creative implication in *The Descent*. His text, despite its shortcomings, allows us to appreciate one of the earliest documents of *el darwinismo*, and one that escaped the moralistic polemics and fashionable attention surrounding *Origin* at the time.

Less mysterious (historically speaking) than Bartrina's translation, but by no means less important, is the comprehensive, authorized translation of *The Descent* by José del Perojo and Enrique Camps in 1885.[20] Published in Madrid by the Administración de la Revista de Medicina y Cirugía Prácticas (Rivadeneyra) and complete with Darwin's chapter headings, notes, and illustrations, this edition carried the literally translated title *La descendencia del hombre y la selección en relación al sexo*, which holds particular significance in light of the fact that subsequent Spanish translations have all been titled *El*

origen del hombre (which is the title familiar to most who know *The
Descent* in Spanish).[21] The Perojo-Camps translation begins with a
two-page preface from the translators that sheds light on a misunderstood Darwin in Spain:

> The inexact idea that one ordinarily has of Darwinist theory, the
> translation to our rich language of a work that has deserved the
> acclaim and acceptance in all civilized countries, and the enrichment
> of our natural understanding with the immense sum of facts accumu-
> lated by the inexhaustible erudition of Darwin in the present work
> have been the principal motives that have propelled us to undertake
> this work.[22]

The translators also make clear that of all the major works of Darwin,
and eleven are listed with titles given in Spanish, "only *On the Origin
of Species* has been translated to Castilian." In other words, no mention is made of either Bartrina's edition of *The Descent* or the other
possible earlier versions noted above. Moreover, the preface shifts attention from natural to sexual selection, while redefining Darwin as
philosopher, as opposed to naturalist, in an effort to elevate his intellectual prowess: "A profound spirit of observation was responsible for
the discovery of the laws of sexual [listed first] and natural selection
that have given him [Darwin] so much importance as a philosopher."
Finally, Perojo and Camps do not fail to recognize (or applaud) the
challenge of their own enterprise: "If we have faithfully interpreted
the clarity of style and the solid foundations of the illustrious author,
our efforts and care will be compensated in the interpretation of such
thorny material." These clues from the translators' preface speak to
the Spanish perception of Darwin's complexity and make *The Descent* in Spanish appear a cultural necessity, which it was, rather than
a threat to the social order (which was also the case).

THE TRANSLATORS

As important as these various translations are as historical documentation of Darwin's arrival in Spain, no less telling are the lives of the
translators, particularly Bartrina and Perojo, whose interdisciplinary cultural agendas concerning Darwin's dissemination in Spain
beg resurrection. Indeed, who these individuals were reveals a great
deal about what they believed Darwin could accomplish in Spanish
translation. Other than Zabalbeascoa's article on the first Spanish
translation of Darwin, Bartrina enjoys little recognition outside of

Catalonia, remembered there for his 1874 collection of poems titled *Algo*, rather than for his efforts with Darwin. Two obscure sources exist for information about Bartrina, Zabalbeascoa's 1968 dissertation and a memoir published by Josep Roca i Roca in 1916. While the former of these contains a certain wealth of facts, it is the latter that best captures the brief life of a young man who dedicated himself to the pursuit of finding common ground between literature and science.

Born in Reus on April 26, 1850, Joaquim Bartrina died just thirty years later of consumption in Barcelona on August 4, 1880, shortly after his 1876 translation of *The Descent*. Roca i Roca considers Bartrina's days in Barcelona after 1874 to be the most representative of his character:

> His six years of Barcelona life were like an orgy and an intoxication, nurtured by a continual fever of mental labors, that unfortunately, as brilliant as they were disordered, were to find a tragic end in a premature and cruel death. The day did not have enough hours for him, and the tempting superabundance of human connections left him unable to find limits or to open guided paths. He wanted to know and scrutinize everything at the moment. On the wings of his astonishing intuitive faculties, in all things he discovered novel aspects, illuminating all of them, and in him their splendors made of his spirit a live flame. Simultaneously he immersed himself in physics, natural history, paleontology, prehistory, biology, philology, geography and travels, history and biography, art and literary criticism, and it must be noted that he fled from generalities, as safe as looking to the sun for light, and instead attended to concrete and definite aspects of all of those disciplines. . . . Of no one with greater cause may it be said that Bartrina gave scientific value to Poetry and poetic value to Science.[23]

I quote this description at length to underscore that, as much as from the polemical debates of Madrid, Darwin arrived in Spain through the eyes of a poet who saw the potential for crossover between evolutionary science and literature.[24] Put in this context, Darwin in Spain transcends the liberal versus conservative polarization that for so long has packaged his reception and *el darwinismo* becomes something more than an ideological placeholder of the day. Bartrina's work exemplifies an early initiative to show how and why Darwin's science was thought to matter in Spanish culture, emphasizing the interaction of evolutionary theory with other disciplines to be an imaginative enterprise of the utmost social consequence. For Bartrina, such was the poetry of science.

Like Bartrina, José del Perojo also took cultural production to be pluralistic and to this end believed that Darwin needed a voice at this turning point in Spanish history. The difference between Bartrina and Perojo, however, is that the latter stood at the apex of *el darwinismo* and was a vocal figure in the most progressive circles of Madrid following the Revolution of 1868.[25] Born in Cuba on January 19, 1850, Perojo later moved to Spain as a young man and with inheritance from his father's death traveled throughout Europe, where he studied at several prestigious institutions without obtaining a degree. While in France during the early 1870s, he published and spent time in the circles of prominent French intellectuals, like Paul Janet, Hippolyte Adolphe Taine, and Claude Bernard. He then went to Germany and, at the University of Heidelberg, befriended a group of neo-Kantians, among them, Hermann von Helmholtz, Friedrich Albert Lange, Otto Liebmann, and Kuno Fischer. Convinced that neo-Kantian philosophy would open an intellectual path for the modernization of Spain, Perojo returned to "Europeanize" Spain and spoke out against the Krausist idealism in vogue at the time. To this end, he published a series of seven articles in the *Revista de España* and *El Tiempo* in 1875. He also, in that same year, took up the writings of Herbert Spencer, whom he saw as a bridge between the material and philosophical sciences, and at the Ateneo of Madrid from 1875 to 1876 argued with passion on his behalf.

Shortly thereafter, Perojo made a bid to purchase the *Revista Europea*, which was a leading publication in Spain at the time, but unsuccessful in his attempts, instead founded the *Revista Contemporánea*, which became the principal transnational scientific and cultural serial in Spain. And in 1877, he opened his own publishing house, Editorial Perojo, which was "of a markedly philosophical and scientific orientation, dedicated to offering the Spanish public works by Spanish authors and, above all, direct translations of works by foreign authors, in line with his [Perojo's] project of promoting European modernity in Spain and of strengthening and invigorating the national culture in the context of European culture."[26] The works released by the Editorial Perojo constituted the Biblioteca Perojo, which in addition to Enrique Godínez's 1877 translation of *Origin*, also published Spanish translations of René Descartes, Benedict de Spinoza, Voltaire, and Herbert Spencer. In 1883, after financial problems resulted in the sale of the *Revista Contemporánea*, Perojo independently published the first Spanish translation of Immanuel Kant.

Yet after the early 1880s, Perojo's attention turned from philosophical to political questions, and especially to issues of colonization, Cuba, and Spain's foreign policy there. It is in the colonial context that, in 1884, Perojo took part in a contentious political debate
with a Cuban politician named Gualberto Gómez. They exchanged
a series of insults in which Perojo adopted a racist attitude of social
Darwinism "very much in vogue at the time,"[27] declaring Gómez to
be an inferior mulatto and himself superior for being white and European. This episode is telling, for only one year later, in 1885, Perojo
translated and disseminated *The Descent* with Enrique Camps, the
brother of Elvira Camps de Rochas, a Cuban woman whom he married in the late 1870s.[28] In the years following the translation, Perojo
wrote numerous commentaries colored by social Darwinism in *La
Opinión* under the pseudonym "Germanus." He lived through the
Revolution of 1868, fought against the conservative pressures of the
Restoration, and after the crisis of 1898 felt his efforts at a Spanish transformation to have been in vain. His legacy, only now being
understood, reveals a commitment to the interdisciplinary exchange
of knowledge, from translations to editorials to public debates, in the
interest of giving birth to a more modern Spain through cultural production and by means of transnational dialogue.

Still, much about Perojo remains to be said. It is curious that not
a single one of his sixty articles makes reference to sexual selection
or to the question of women's rights, a topic of considerable public
interest at the time. Perojo either found nothing controversial about
sexual selection and ignored *la cuestión de la mujer* all together or
saw no connection between the two, or perhaps both, perhaps neither. The point is that, given his involvement with Darwin's works, he
appears an ideal candidate for mention of sexual selection in the context of the broader political climate (or at all) in Spain, yet the theory
does not surface in his cultural writings, other than in the translation of *The Descent*. In addition, the historians of Perojo here mentioned often downplay the ferocity of Perojo's views on race, which
are troublesome appropriations of ideas from *The Descent* by one of
Spain's most "progressive" thinkers. Whether social Darwinism was
"in vogue" or not, it is significant that Perojo, the self-proclaimed liberal, public figure, and translator of Darwin, not only believed slavery to be natural but also denigrated the black race as a retrograde
manifestation of the human species.[29] Perojo, therefore, evidences a
problematic oversimplification one finds across the wider spectrum

of studies on nineteenth-century Spain—that of the polarized classification of liberals and conservatives, the dichotomization of free-
thinking progressives and closed-minded traditionalists. The ideological landscape was far more complex, as "revolutionary" figures like
Perojo took "dangerous" ideas like those of Darwin and, depending
on the issue, used them to reinforce a conservative political agenda
and the status quo.

SEXUAL SELECTION IN SPANISH PERIODICALS

Only in recent years, as a wealth of early Spanish periodicals have increasingly become available in digital form thanks to the Biblioteca
Virtual de Prensa Histórica project led by Spain's Ministry of Culture,
have keyword searches enabled a more accurate assessment of the reception of Darwin's theory of sexual selection in the Spanish press.
Without this tool, given that sexual selection does not figure explicitly
in any article title of the period or bibliography on Darwin in Spain
or even in the writings of attractive candidates like Perojo, identification of where and when the theory first began to appear in the public
discourse has been a serious obstacle. As it happens, sexual selection
first surfaced on the Peninsula as early as 1874 with a short piece by
Antonio María Fabié in the *Revista Europea* titled "Exámen del materialismo moderno," and then about a dozen times after that in articles through 1885 in this same periodical as well as in the equally
important *Revista Contemporánea*. Still, despite the short span (curi-
ously, the decade before rather than following the 1885 Perojo-Camps
authorized translation of *The Descent*) and limited number of references, several insights can be gleaned about how Darwinian sexual
selection made its way to Spain through these publications.[30]
    In many cases, the contributions of the *Revista Europea* were
simply Spanish translations (or recapitulations) of articles that had
originally appeared in foreign publications. These include an 1875
piece on democracy by Elme Marie Caro from the *Revue des Deux
Mondes*, an 1876 contribution on Ernst Haeckel by Eduard von Hartmann from *Deutsche Rundschau*, another that same year on Hartmann's own philosophical system as framed by Darwinism and first
published in 1874 in the *Westminster Review*, a handful of 1878
contributions by Haeckel himself in lectures translated to Spanish
by Claudio Cuveiro, and an 1876 translation from the *Edinburgh
Review* by Armando Palacio Valdés of Caro's own work concerning

morality. Along with the range of international sources in play with the dissemination of Darwin's theory, what this abbreviated list and particularly the last example provide is documentation for links to Spanish authors. Leopoldo Alas (Clarín), for instance, published an 1878 article in the *Revista Europea* that concludes on the same page where an essay by Haeckel about Darwinian sexual selection and the dispersion of organisms begins. In other words, it can be assumed that in Spain's circle of novelists these highly visible publications were responsible, at least in part, for bringing sexual selection to the attention of the literary community.

Moreover, this reception history via the periodical culture yields telling clues about which editions of *The Descent* were being read by the Spanish intellectual elite and the sorts of positions that were being formed vis-à-vis the most often privileged components of the theory of sexual selection in the context of the ideological uproar over fears of an atheistic universe. In cases of original reflections by Spanish authors (A. Torres-Solanot, 1876; Pedro Estassen, 1878; L. Carrau, 1879; Joaquín Sánchez de Toca, 1879), as opposed to pieces like those above by foreign authors previously published elsewhere and inserted in translation, it is not uncommon to find lengthy citations of Darwin from *The Descent* provided in Spanish with the title of his work given as a footnote either first in French and then in Spanish, as *La descendencia del hombre*, or simply in Spanish from the outset. However, the pagination indicated plus the supporting fact that there was no accessible Spanish edition of the text until 1885 makes it clear that the authors of these essays in the *Revista Europea* and the *Revista Contemporánea* were working from either the 1872 Moulinié translation or its second edition as released in 1873 and revised by Edmond Barbier.[31]

Spanish contributors to these periodicals were carrying out their own translations of *The Descent* from the French, and more often than not, this was not something that they took great pains to clarify. At times, targeted remarks suggest an intimacy with the English original that is suspect to say the least. In his moralistic refutation of Darwin's position on language and conscience with respect to sexual selection, Sánchez de Toca, for example, inserts this footnote following a quotation from *The Descent*: "The reader will perceive the difficulty of a translation of these lines to Spanish, but I must say in my defense that Darwin's thought must be so profound that not even he could express it in good English, nor has his French translator J.

J. Moulinié known how to interpret it without abusing the gram-
mar. . . . [T]he wise naturalist found it necessary to enshroud [his lan-
guage] under so mysterious and impenetrable a formula that only the
angelic organisms of the final evolution will be able to decipher it."[32]
The passage in question concerns Darwin's discussion of the social
instincts, where he says: "Man will then feel dissatisfied with himself, and will resolve with more or less force to act differently for the
future. This is conscience; for conscience looks backwards and judges
past actions, inducing that kind of dissatisfaction, which if weak we
call regret, and if severe remorse" (*The Descent*, 1:91). What Sánchez
de Toca provides, though, is a jumbled paraphrase of Darwin's ideas.
His use throughout the essay of the Moulinié translation, together
with his virulent references to Darwin "made Messiah" in *La Créa-
tion du monde organisé d'après les naturalistes anglais et allemands
de la nouvelle école* as published by Charles Martins in the *Revue
des Deux Monde* in 1871, sheds doubt on how well he knew "good
English" or whether he was working from the English original at all.

Yet, while the example of Sánchez de Toca might be typical of
other cases of Spaniards writing on sexual selection as far as French
sources are concerned, his dismissal of Darwin on spiritual grounds is
only one reaction in a much richer constellation of published writings
on the topic, even if scant in number. In other words, there is nothing
systematic or predictable about the appearance of sexual selection in
Spanish periodicals from these years. At times, the theory is merely
tangential to articles otherwise concerned with prominent European
figures of the scientific-philosophic community like Hartmann (1876)
and Haeckel (1878); in other instances, it is of interest regarding matters of marriage and public policy, that is, in what ways, if at all,
reproduction should fall under the domain of legislation (Caro, 1875);
and there are moments when it is purely scientific, as in "Coloración
de los insectos y las flores" ([R.A.S.], 1885), or useful for conjectures
on the origins of religion, as in "La religiosidad en los animales"
(Pedro Estassen, 1878), or simply tongue in cheek, as in a piece on
Samuel Butler called "Un adversario de la evolución" (Cran Allen,
1879). Therefore, it is important to point out that although the periodical reception of the theory, as these many manifestations show,
might have been a mixed bag of foreign sources, language issues,
polemics, and passing mentions, the evidence is there to affirm that it
indeed had a history.

THE SEXUAL POLITICS OF SEXUAL SELECTION

Still, the translations, translators, and periodical dissemination of sexual selection tell only part of the story, and nowhere are the sort of contradictions we saw in Perojo more pronounced than in the ways influential men who were for all intents and purposes *darwinistas* appropriated, whether consciously or not, (r)evolutionary ideas to form "progressive" opinions about the "inferior" sex. It was not at all uncommon, in fact, to find Darwin deployed in various guises by Spain's most "enlightened" thinkers when it came to the question of greater social rights for women. But of course, assuming they did know what they were doing, in this context to mention Darwin, who was a virtual figurehead for anarchistic liberalism, would have meant risking that their messages might be undermined through the very association. Indeed, Darwin's theory of sexual selection, without being named, also emerges in Spanish cultural discourse during the years of *el darwinismo* as the scientific lens by which Nature comes to mediate between the political and economic issues surrounding women's place in what Jo Labanyi has called the nation's burgeoning "civil society."[33] In this vein, I have selected three documents as exemplary of the intersection between Darwinian sexual selection and *la cuestión de la mujer*.[34] It will not be argued, however, that the presence of Darwinian sexual selection in these essays and the omission of Darwin's name were intentional strategies on the part of the authors. Again, it is not known with any certainty how well, if at all, these men knew the theory. To the extent those connections are perceived, they are interesting, but nonetheless arbitrary. What is not arbitrary is the "science" of this "social" concern with female choice and the consequence such an overlap held for the broader community.

The first document, "La emancipación de la mujer" (*Revista Contemporánea*, 1878–79), comes from Manuel de la Revilla—an early advocate and first reviewer of Darwin's work in Spain, the subject of a recent seven-volume study/collection of his complete works, and a "supporter of progress and open to all new schools of thought."[35] As the title might suggest, Revilla's article opens with a "progressive" enough tone: "The betterment of the social condition of women is one of the concerns of this century, without a doubt the most humanitarian of all" (pt. 1:447). Expectations rise as it seems enlightened reason and science will intercede in this struggle for reform: "Therefore, it is necessary that calm and cool reason, taught by a close examination of the facts, take the word in this debate, where until now imagination and feeling have reigned. Sociology must be today a more positive science, and positive and practical must be, therefore, the solutions that are given to the social problems" (pt. 1:448–49). To this end, Revilla begins by questioning if women really need to "emancipate" themselves, which he believes would necessitate a preexisting condition of "servitude." In his honest opinion, despite being "only . . . deprived of political rights, of access to the majority of public positions and professions of scientific and literary character" and affected by a law that imposes "certain obstacles and limitations [that] place her in a certain relation of inequality with her husband," women suffer not under material conditions of servitude, rather just from "an inferior social position" (pt. 1:449). There are, of course, reasons to worry about situations of moral servitude, with prostitution, for example, but for Revilla, "the supporters of the emancipation of women" (pt. 1:450) misunderstand the issue. The real question should be asked in the following terms: "The inequalities that exist between the sexes, are they the work of nature or society, or can they be attributed to both causes? If the second is true, which come only from society, and from these, which must be abolished for being unjust and erroneously founded?" (pt. 1:450). His responses evidence a Darwinian sexual selection that is anything but what might be expected from the "revolutionary" Revilla.

As it turns out, Revilla maintains that "inequality is a fundamental law of nature" (pt. 1:450). Natural forces determine sexual roles, and because the human organism is subordinated to the reproduction of the species, "the destiny of both sexes is as diverse as their organization" (pt. 1:451). Here we see the sexual politics of Darwin's views on sexual dimorphism in play as elaborated in chapter 2 with respect to prevailing power structures. To support his case, Revilla proffers a litany of "empirical facts" regarding sexual differentiation. He includes many of the usual suspects from the nineteenth century (smaller female brains, weaker female bodies, more hysterical female dispositions, etc.), from which Darwin himself was not immune, but other passages bring to mind Darwin's own language from *The Descent*. Women show themselves to be "passive by nature," and their minds "comprehend quickly all that is not abstract; but rarely do they make deep connections and reflect, except in cases where it concerns their personal interest or practical life" (pt. 1:452). In these ways, Revilla posits that instinct subsumes female intelligence, and "instinct" here facilitates a turn in his argument: "The life of a woman centers on the family and has as its only end reproduction" (pt. 1:452–53). Any woman who renounces her natural maternal role, according to Revilla, "deserves only aversion and scorn" (pt. 1:454). For men, however, reproduction remains just one more pursuit, like any other. All female traits are in the service of motherhood, and if woman is "weak and passive in everything, it is because in the act of reproduction it has been her luck to take the passive role. If she is modest and man is not, that is due to the fact that modesty, instead of a check, is a spur to the masculine appetite" (pt. 1:454). In these instances, the point is not that Revilla sounds Darwin verbatim but rather that the sociopolitical stakes of certain facets of sexual selection, like the association between femininity and reproduction, come into full view. Without being attributed to Darwin (whose name went hand in hand with liberalism), Revilla is able to use an indeterminate evolutionism to bolster a fixed and very conservative science of repression.

Along the very same lines of our discussion of the possible social implications of Darwin's thinking in the previous chapter, here we see firsthand how Revilla's position provides an alarming example of the sexual politics of sexual selection in practice. Turning from science to the social, Revilla laments the misinformed notion that sexual inequality is a question of women's limited access to education; instead, he argues, if inequality exists at all, it originates in the "psycho-physical organization" of women (pt. 1:455). Historians like Carlos García Barrón and those who, along with Fernando Hermida de Blas, have recently brought to light Revilla's complete works never fail to characterize him as the model reformer, and often because of his role in the promotion of Darwin's works. Yet the case of Revilla is similar to that of Perojo, where the line between progressive and traditionalist blurs, ironically, with respect to "Darwinian" ideas. As it happens, Darwin believed just the opposite about women and education, as Desmond and Moore's biography confirms and attention to *The Descent* shows: "In order that woman should reach the same standard as man, she ought . . . to have her reason and imagination exercised to the highest point" (2:329). Hence, coverage of Revilla's lesser known writings on gender, like "La emancipación de la mujer," reveals a dangerous conflation within his political agenda, grounded in progressive knowledge of evolutionary science, but far from faithful to it.

As chapter 1 made clear, the *progressive* dimension of evolutionary science (preferably toward social betterment, but, in the abstract,
simply what moves society forward over time) is the change inherent
in it, but change was the furthest thing from Revilla's mind when it
came to *la cuestión de la mujer.* At one point in "La emancipación de
la mujer," he even chastises the "reformists," among whom he by no
means numbers himself:

> They want women to have access to professional and higher-learning
> studies and entrance into all the professions and careers of the State.
> They want to make them philosophers and writers, attorneys and
> economists, doctors and pharmacists, engineers and veterinarians,
> physicists, chemists, mathematicians, and naturalists. What a grave
> error, which only proves in those who sponsor such ideas the most
> complete ignorance, not only of the nature of woman, but of human
> nature! (Pt. 1:456)

Revilla's ideology, centered on the premise that "the life of men
is purely exterior and has a more public nature than private" (pt.
1:456), exemplifies a principal sector of the "cultural" engine driving
the public-private divide that came to define the civil status of wom-
en. Revilla reiterates that "[nature] made men and women, not only
distinct, but opposites" (pt. 1:458). In this light, what Labanyi calls
the "outside-inside" status of women in Spain's civil society,[36] Revilla
makes patent: "Public and private life are incompatible" (pt. 1:458).
Women's "incapacity" for public life is "notorious" (pt. 1:460), and
therefore "political life is incompatible with women's destiny" (pt.
2:163) and, by extension, women's suffrage in Spain.

  Therefore, as for *el darwinismo,* Revilla's essay complicates what
can be asserted about the role of evolutionary science in Spanish
polemics in the late nineteenth century, namely, with respect to generalizations about the reformist agenda of *darwinistas* when it came
to women's rights. Again, traditional characterizations of a demar-
cated liberal-conservative polarization at this moment in Spanish history show serious shortcomings when it comes to discourse on gender.
Furthermore, Revilla provides evidence of one way the indeterminate
science of Darwinian sexual selection entered the public discourse via
la cuestión de la mujer, so as to promote the "material servitude" of
uneducated women and the image of a modern, civil Spain built on
notions of "the inequalities of nature" (pt. 1:450). But lest we forget, Darwin never advocated for relations of subservience between
the sexes; on the contrary, he would rather have been descended from

monkeys than from those who make slaves of women through negation of choice.

Though no less colored by Darwinian sexual selection, the message of Leopoldo Alas (Clarín) in his article "El amor y la economía"
(*Revista de Asturias*, 1879) differs to a large extent from that of
Revilla on the issue of women's emancipation.[37] Clarín says at the
outset: "This article, although it is quasi-scientific, is quasi-dedicated
to women" (126). The foundation of his argument, that "economics should be the total opposite of love" (126), introduces the social
problem: "The suitor that you, beautiful reader, choose for yourself,
is a suitor in the true sense of the word. The suitor that your father
chooses for you is the *economic suitor*. I'm sorry to say that the *economic suitor* tends to be older and uglier than the other. But you,
kind readers, usually marry for economics" (127). And a marriage
of this sort represents self-interest in that the selection of the *economic suitor* amounts to a privileging of the individual over the species, which would demand the opposite choice, the suitor of true love,
what Clarín calls "the suitor of the *unconscious*" (128).[38]

However, the choice of the older, uglier economic suitor is comprehensible given the state of "roguish necessity" in which women find
themselves; though their selection be unnaturally natural, that is, premised on self-interest, it is not malicious: "It is not that you are trying
to end the world, nor that you have ill will toward the species; nothing
of the sort; if you do not marry for love it is because the most important thing is to live, and woman does not live on bread alone, but
rather also on chignons, gems, plenty of lingerie, etc., etc." (128). The
consequence, for Clarín, appears inevitable: "On the contrary, the
economic husband, although he might not be the one that nature had
prepared for you, although he might do less for the species than two
cents worth, makes the life of the individual possible" (128). Typical
of Clarín, the argument unfolds with no shortage of cynicism, making it difficult to know what he believes from one moment to the next,
but as the causes of this selection process come into view, a degree of
distress, too, becomes evident.

Searching for origins, Clarín finds that history deserves much
of the blame for women's decision to favor the economic husband
over that of the unconscious in Spain of the late nineteenth century. The history he pinpoints, however, is not a political history,
or even economic, but rather sardonically, literary: "If over the generations that have preceded us the empty hours had not been spent

in song about the disdains of thankless women, the problem of love and economics might have been resolved, [and] at this time women, instead of being slaves to their necessities . . . would live in the purest atmosphere of idealism" (128–29). That is to say, literature has never been "in the hands of the *economic suitors*" (129), and therefore it is not surprising that the idle dreamers, poets unable to make a buck to save their lives (to paraphrase Clarín), the suitors of the unconscious (or, perhaps more aptly termed here, "the unconscious suitors"), should fill their verses full of scorn after having been rejected by pragmatic women. Clarín calls such words "pure calumny" (129). The true character of woman being the opposite of her composition, not only has she been misrepresented, but she has been driven to the state that inspires their rebukes by the oppressive conditions of her existence:

> Women live in full reality; so far from the gross materialism that is the degradation of humanity, as much as of the romantic and abstract idealism that nourishes with spiritual mushrooms and roots . . . held by emotions. Women want love; they know that woman is born for love, her heart asks for it, the body begs for it . . . she is disposed . . . to perpetuate the species that depends on her. But as much as she might want true love, with real desire, not with some fantastical aspiration to satisfy the instincts of her human nature, not for the pleasure of pure aesthetic representation . . . she procures love on conditions of viability. If she unites with the *non-economic* suitor, who is so poor that he doesn't even have a place to fall dead, she already knows that her love will be hunger for today and hunger for tomorrow. For as much as she wants love, she wants it in conditions in which she can live. (129)

With this elaboration, Clarín depicts a circumstance in which, in his eyes, natural selection, that is, *struggle for life*, guided by the self-interest of the individual, wins over true, species-oriented sexual selection as the determinative factor of female choice.[39] Today's sociobiologists would have no trouble justifying the natural motives for such selection: women understand "instinctually" that their genes have a better chance at being passed on to future generations if nurtured in the nest of the economic husband, though not necessarily if he is "older and uglier," since their offspring (assuming the husband's age does not make him impotent) will be less physically attractive (but perhaps more so if rich). Be that as it may, Clarín perceives the unnatural pressures placed on women in modern culture, even while he rationalizes the selection outcome in terms of natural forces.

Troubled by the selection process he sees, Clarín ponders two possible solutions to the problem: "Either we must make all men rich so that women can choose, not according to economics, but rather for love, or . . . and this is my thesis [i.e., Clarín's own] . . . we put woman in conditions in which she can earn a living, of being economically free, independent, so that if her heart demands it she can load herself down with one of numerous lovers without a job or income" (129). Though never making mention of Darwin, Clarín reflects on sexual selection, on passive choice, and on the conditions needed for the freedom of female selectors, a requisite for civilized society that appears in several passages from the second half of *The Descent*, and he arrives at the following conclusion: "I believe that woman, protected by laws and customs, would do wonders of activity in order to obtain this glorious emancipation to which principally she must aspire" (129). Clarín holds that the "woman question" is a "purely economic question" and, therefore, explains her conditions in terms "even a man can understand":

> The woman of today is a slave to the home, because she has her heart pinned inside an account book of bread. Love is for women what work is for man, a career. For a woman just as for a student failure is a very serious matter, and hence, as there are students who commit suicide for not passing, countless women throw themselves from balconies for *a year lost* in the career of their loves . . . her entire future depends on trapping a husband; the struggle for existence is determined in this sense. . . . Human miseries! Why can't a woman work who does not have anything? Why must she reduce all of her industrial ability to doing business with her heart, to giving herself over to fishing for the *economic husband*? Single women, victims of the social concern that denies you the right to work, reveal yourselves, emancipate yourselves; the reward of your efforts will be the most dear to you alone; you will be able to *choose* [emphasis added] a husband instead of waiting, like the hen of the seraglio, whom the sultan, the cock of the harem, deigns to give a look. Yes: demand economic freedom, make yourselves independent, earn a living for yourselves with your own activity; run to work, to careers, to occupations. (130–31)

Indeed, Clarín's views change over time, and his position on women, marriage, and civil rights grows increasingly conservative as he ages. Blanket revisionism of his outlook on *la cuestión de la mujer* is therefore sure to remain unconvincing, given what we know from other writings about his thoughts on women.[40] In this instance, however, he speaks with certain conviction on women's rights, on the symbiotic relationship between free will and human nature. Darwin's theory of sexual selection pervades the discourse, and there is little doubt about women as the rightful selectors in the power dynamics between the sexes. At the same time, there is wavering, just as in Darwin, between passive and active choice, and a notion that sexual dimorphism, especially in the context of aptitude for employment and education, amounts to a cultural construct rather than natural necessity.

Though most remembered today for his scientific contributions in the twentieth century, Santiago Ramón y Cajal was a product of the nineteenth century in very concrete ways. He was also a prodigious writer of nonscientific literature, including works of fiction and social musings. In a series of reflections organized in chapters and grouped together under the title *Charlas de café* (1908), the second chapter, "Sobre el amor y las mujeres," offers a peculiar instance of intersection between sexual selection and *la cuestión de la mujer* that, although premised on the issue of women's emancipation, departs from Revilla and Clarín as only a scientist well versed in Darwin's theories could.[41] Indeed, Ramón y Cajal opens by righting any idealized, anthropomorphic notions of human relations: "We believe ourselves to be the protagonists of the grand comedy of life, when in reality we play only the most humble and minor roles. Even in the spirited duo of love we are mere delegates of the species, which, when it comes right down to it, is the great beloved. She [the species] makes use of us as a brewer uses yeast to stay in business and prosper" (954). We might rightly smirk at the language here, but digressive as the thoughts of Ramón y Cajal might be, they do show serious purpose.

First, he seeks to erase any illusions: "In a woman's dictionary, 'to love' doesn't exist, in the majority of cases, more to the letter would be 'to speculate,' that is, to appraise. In like circumstances, the ugly or beautiful female will always prefer the male who has greater financial credit or more plentiful funds, with the sole condition of satisfying the maternal instinct, the most profound and sacred of life. The supreme end of children sanctifies all of her selfishness" (956). Second, he offers words of counsel: "The discreet suitor should pay more attention to the content than to the form. The happiness of a husband does not depend on the color of female hair, but rather on the structure of her mind and its emotional and cultural composition, that is to say, of an organ whose color is the same in blonds or brunettes. Less dermatology and more psychology: that should be the motto of the man who aspires to matrimony" (962). And finally, his position on female choice emerges: "*All misfortunes of marriage are born from the fact that the woman does not choose, but rather is chosen* [emphasis added]. Fortunately, in the majority of cases, the wife grows accustomed to her husband in the same way that he habituates himself to beer and tobacco" (965). Without question, the genre employed by Ramón y Cajal presents a number of challenges, namely, that the science gets lost in his popular tongue and often offensive witticisms, but in some sense this very aspect of the text, rather than undermine, enhances what can be asserted about sexual selection in its discursive manifestations in Spain. In essence, Ramón y Cajal's fragments move from a biological explanation of why wealth factors into female preference, to cautions against appearance alone in advocacy of the moral virtue Darwin describes in *The Descent*, to the recognition of the unnatural gender dynamics in a society where women are unable to act as selectors.

He obfuscates these affirmations, though, to such an extent that the theory of sexual selection becomes almost unrecognizable. Part of the problem with an unclouded discussion of sexual selection for Ramón y Cajal stems from a difficulty reconciling certainties he has about women's need for emancipation, for natural rights, when faced with a cultural background and readership steeped in sexism. For example, at one point Ramón y Cajal states:

> Where will we stop with this wretched phenomenon of sexual dis-differentiation? I really fear that, in the future, the domestic angel will become a mean mannish woman, and that love, the supreme delight of life, will become an onerous charge. . . . If it weren't for intelligent single women unable to marry and unemployed widows, I would dare say that, upon obtaining all the political and professional privileges of man, that women, without knowing it, will also obtain the right to ugliness and premature old age. (969)

Yet only two pages later, he calls out for greater equality: "The ancient ideal of joining in one individual the pleasures of friendship and love . . . only has one honorable biological solution: to elevate women's culture" (971). These contradictions recall those we have seen in Darwin's own reversals and uncertainties.

In the argument's final turn, Ramón y Cajal attempts to redress social ills, to a degree. He refutes at length the common belief at the time that women possess smaller brains and proffers a list of the biological reasons why women should categorically renounce the practice of taking the last name of the husband as their own and for their children. Nevertheless, this "activism," on the whole, remains tepid:

"A woman should be married, have a broken leg, and stay at home."
Here's a saying, perhaps of Arabic origin, which, taken too much to
the letter, has had the unfortunate effect of converting the majority of
Spanish females, from the age of thirty on and sometimes earlier, into
an ocean of fat, where grace, beauty, and healthy activity sink without remedy. And cosmetics are worthless because there is nothing
more insatiable than a pathologically distended stomach or anything
less elegant and deformed than a wrinkled balloon. (972)

To say the least, point of view acts as an obstacle for Ramón y Cajal,
and myopia weakens his assertions: "What extremists of feminism
call 'women's emancipation' is often nothing but the imposition of
the formidable yoke of exhausting work, without the consoling com-
pensation of love and family" (989). Nevertheless, in his mind, he
speaks with the best of intentions: "Without denying the existence of
frustrated and even pathological females, I still think that the normal
woman is the salt of life. Supreme stimulation of civilization and heroism, in her converge all the refinements of art and progress. For and
because of her, as has been said many times, one invents, one fights,
and one dies" (992). More than Ramón y Cajal's own limitations,
however, this finale speaks to the principal impediment to increased
women's rights in Spain—the discourse, because controlled so often
by men during the decades of the Restoration, returns to male concerns. The challenge, therefore, becomes one of transformation, to
remake these impediments as opportunities, or rather windows into
the emerging consciousness in an age of change, of moments when
science and society converge in consideration of female choice.

Darwinian sexual selection, absent explicit mention, shadows
voices like those of Revilla, Clarín, and Ramón y Cajal as they pre-
sume a status of liberal, progressive ideological orientation regardless
of the content of their messages. At the same time, however, when
used as an analytic tool for the critical evaluation of these and other
comparable works, sexual selection shows itself to permeate the ideas
and descriptive language upon which these writings depart (and often
go astray). As such, it merges with how *la cuestión de la mujer* was
discussed within and toward the realization of a civil society. Yet this
truth is by no means self-evident. As distinct from the theories of
natural selection and man's simian ancestry, which generated a body
of polemics impressive for its quantity but not always its quality,[42]
the theory of sexual selection does not appear on the bibliographical map. This silence, though, speaks volumes about sexual selection

in Spain. The theory reached the Peninsula, to be sure, but rather than cause a revolution or act as a one-dimensional touchstone for controversy, its indeterminate discussion of female choice infiltrated the culture without ever being acknowledged. This phenomenon, in turn, says as much about sexual selection as a theory as it does about Spain at the time. Neither is unequivocal. Thus, the unwritten history of sexual politics and Darwinian sexual selection in Spain reveals the complex ambiguity and material potentiality of a theory that was anything but absent from the Spanish imagination.

PART TWO

Adaptations

CHAPTER FOUR

Suitors and Selectors— Jacinto Octavio Picón

Now in place, the interrelated "origins" of part 1 have provided the conceptual tools for a study of this compass. The previous chapter, in particular, transposed the theoretical and socio-scientific insights from the first two chapters to the case of Spain during the years of *el darwinismo*. There, the translations and cultural agendas of the translators were framed by issues of community and its fate. Just as knowledge relates to "inchoate questioning" in a world that is both pluralistic and never static,[1] the arrival of Darwin's works in Spain entailed a collective inquiry into the role of science in the progress of a nation and its people. In the praxis of sexual politics, the theory of sexual selection assumed a curious, unspecified presence in writings on *la cuestión de la mujer* by men knowledgeable about Darwinian evolutionism and with a reputation for being reformers. Yet the inconsistency of their positions on female choice came to highlight the unforeseen effects latent in the open-endedness and contradictions of Darwin's own writing. The coetaneous currents of *el darwinismo* and *la cuestión de la mujer*, in this way, meet at the crossroads of sexual selection, which, as it happens, was very much on the mind even if absent in name. The indeterminism of the theory itself underwrites such an outcome, since its unfinished character translates to new types of questioning in the social sphere.

In terms of cultural production, it is no less the case that Darwinian sexual selection ghosts the imagination of Spain's novelists in unforeseen ways. Realism made of representation a laboratory, and the individual enmeshed in social circumstance was the experimental subject of its works. In principle and in practice, the novel took part in the inquiry model I theorized on in part 1 and have just reiterated here. The three chapters of part 2, "Adaptations," deliver the specifics of this claim at an elemental level, that is, with a focus on the operative mechanics of the theory and the constitutive elements themselves set in realist representation. Again, the basic premise of these chapters is not so much that Picón, Clarín, and Galdós adapted (i.e., "appropriated") Darwinian sexual selection with conscious intent, although they may well have. Rather, the plasticity of the theory generates important variations, as Darwin would understand adaptation, in literary portrayals that shed fresh light on the key factors involved. Through an interdisciplinary approach, we must recognize that temporal simultaneity, as outlined in chapter 1, destabilizes the text, given that its own historical context and interim up to the present infuse often treated topics with new resonance to the degree that something deemed foreign to its accepted purview, like Darwinian sexual selection, shapes our reading in unanticipated ways in the present.

   In the chapter at hand, this approach opens with an original assessment of the participants—the suitors and selectors—of sexual selection and, in the two chapters to follow, continues with the mechanics and their outcome. It assumes as a given that Darwin's theory complicates the much-discussed phenomenon of *donjuanismo* in Spanish literature, to the extent this same *donjuanismo* forces us to rethink his science. In other words, we cannot get to the true indeterminism of sexual selection in the social sphere and with respect to feminist issues of the day without an appreciation for concurrent modifications in the indefinite makeup of the archetypal seducer, who transforms over the novels of Picón from a parodic bourgeois imposter to an authentic Juanita of moral character. Consequently, though this chapter has a lot to say about Don Juan and Picón's trajectory as a writer, it is every bit as much about Darwin, whose own voice serves as a point of departure and return in the context of my larger argument about the reciprocity between literature and science.

   Indeed, there is no better place to begin my own inquiry into Darwinian sexual selection and the Spanish novel in the years of *el darwinismo* than with the mythic figure of Don Juan. This libertine's legacy extends beyond Spain's borders, with a singular presence in works by Molière, Mozart, Søren Kierkegaard, Lord Byron, and so many others. Yet in light of Tirso de Molina's original seventeenth-century *burlador*, later Romantic sensations like José Zorrilla's *Don*

Juan Tenorio (1844), and the writings of Miguel de Unamuno and José Ortega y Gasset into the twentieth century, the place of Don Juan in Spanish cultural history remains unparalleled by any other European tradition. To be sure, Don Juan has played a complex role in efforts to construct and reconstruct Spain's national identity, and countless Spanish writers have engaged his character in one form or another up to the present. I have chosen to focus on Jacinto Octavio Picón (1851–1923), for whom Don Juan borders on an obsession, for several reasons. Far from a household name today, Picón was widely read during his lifetime, and recent scholarly attention to his works has shed new light on their importance. In large part, the interest stems from his ambivalent treatment of women, but I would also suggest, as complement, that this quality of his fiction, which is grounded in unresolved questions about female choice, remains inextricable from a webbing of Don Juan, evolutionary science, and the country's direction at the time.

The movement for social equality between the sexes serves as a catalyst for Picón's exploration of a courtship dynamic that had become tainted by questions of class, domestic idealism, and romantic disillusionment at this turning point in the nation's history following the Revolution of 1868. However, though these may be common themes for literature of the day, in the company of other Spanish realists Picón's approach to suitor-selector role reversals brings together Darwin and Don Juan in a way that exploits this component of sexual selection. At the same time, Picón's representation of women, clouded by Pyrrhic victories, reflects the imprecise science behind Darwin's principle of female "passive" choice. Yet Picón's writing, noted for its ambivalence with respect to women's issues, also shows stability, for true conquest in matters of the heart depends on the "social instincts" Darwin understood as "conscience." Moving beyond the carnal to the psychological, Picón posits the ultimate seduction, of Don Juan himself by his female counterpart, to be inseparable from Darwinian "moral sense," that is, the ability to reflect on past actions with dissatisfaction and feel remorse. Thus, we witness still another historical shift in the formation, or rather reformation, of Don Juan, who can no longer live according to the ideal of unscrupulous conquest in the abstract. In his place, comes *her* story, and with it an individualism born from trial and oriented toward what Darwin calls the "highest stage in moral culture" (*The Descent*, 1:86), a civil State (in the Darwinian sense) of sexual equality in matters of choice.

Picón's treatment of suitors and selectors wavers to such an extent that readers struggle to know whether his fiction supports or seeks to undercut the patriarchal power structure that prevailed during his day. Noël Valis, who has written a large portion of what little criticism there is on Picón, considers his corpus to be representative of writing in the late nineteenth century in general, which is in her words "a verbal *striptease*, in which the artist makes a fetish out of the feminine, converting it into a trope of ambivalent values."[2] Likewise, in the context of Picón's reputation during his lifetime as a supporter of "individual freedom," Hazel Gold observes with acumen that such notoriety gave him "the legitimacy . . . of eroticism in literature"; that is, by challenging sexual taboos he asserted his right to self-expression. Gold questions "to what extent Picón carries the liberal position in his fictions" and concludes that "it is possible to trace a progression in the direction of greater personal emancipation in the heroine figure despite the miserable role that has been defined for her by society."[3] Finally, Ángeles Ezama Gil postulates a "feminine prototype" in Picón's fiction that promotes women's emancipation through a problematic intersection of "the expression of the sexual instinct" and "the moral consideration of women."[4] Together, these commentaries provide important insights on Picón and reflect the critical conversation that surrounds his female protagonists, who stand as both masculine objectifications and progressive steps toward reform.

The tensions one finds in Picón, however, recall similar difficulties in our appreciation of Darwin's treatment of the power dynamics in sexual selection. Yet it is the trajectory of Don Juan in Picón's novels that reveals what we might not otherwise imagine with respect to suitor-selector reversals in Darwin. As we shall see over the course of this chapter, Don Juan begins as a laughable puppet of what he once was, unable to separate reality from fiction, to then find himself beaten at his own game in a plot of seductive inversions, only to come full circle and end, literally, as Juanita Tenorio in Picón's last novel. In this way, the eternal Don Juan disappears, losing his universality, as we perceive the effects of time and how history has made repetition, the ethic of his formula of conflict and of his 1,003 victims and beyond, an anachronism. George Bernard Shaw in his preface to *Man and Superman* (1903) calls attention to the plasticity of Don Juan and contends that by the nineteenth century, at the hands of writers like Henrik Ibsen and Lev Tolstoy, "Don Juan had changed his sex and become Doña Juana, breaking herself out of the Doll's

House and asserting herself as an individual."⁵ Indeed, at this point,
"Man is no longer, like Don Juan, victor in the duel of sex" (14); he
finds himself "the quarry instead of the huntsman" (18). In his own
drama, Shaw deploys Miss Ann Whitefield as the "Nonconformist
Conscience" in her initiatives to bring the revolutionary John Tanner,
M.I.R.C. (Member of the Idle Rich Class), under her hand, leading
him to "renounce freedom . . . for the cares of a household and a family" (208). Picón follows suit, to be sure, but his ultimate vision moves
beyond what Shaw presages, for not only does he call his Don Juan by
a new name (in the diminutive), Juanita, but he also shows how the
biological underpinnings of love need not place Darwinian "family
ties" in opposition to self-determination. For as Albert Camus once
said of Don Juan, loving is "his way of knowing,"⁶ and in Picón we
discover that this means letting *her* voice be heard in what is nothing less than an overthrow of this god among men, and nothing other
than a Darwinian inversion of an accepted cultural practice of callous
conquest.

THE COMPLEX AFFAIR

As we have seen from our discussion of sexual selection in *The Descent*, Darwin contrasts males as suitors to females as selectors. However, the gender traits at play in courtship are not immutable, and
roles are reversed as Darwin struggles to transpose to society what
he finds in nature. This much has already been made clear. The process, though, by which it occurs, is more complicated at the level of
assigned traits than my targeted explanation in chapter 2 could adequately convey. Through the nuances of his thought as it extends to
the players involved, the power dynamics are predicated, foremost, on
which attributes these suitors and selectors introduce into the mix, but
constitution should not be confused with fixity. The qualities themselves tend to be open in their design, that is, adaptive, and the mating chess match more often than not leads to elaborate displays and
dissemblance of their true makeup. Hence, an important first piece
toward a more indeterminate Darwin, whether for literature, the science itself, or the social praxis of sexual selection, is to understand
the plasticity of the participants according to their sexual makeup on
Darwin's own terms. It is also impossible, moreover, to see why Don
Juan might cause us to rethink our assumptions about the laws of
courtship absent this emphasis on the composition of those involved.

Darwin sets the board for Don Juan, and Don Juan, in his gender morphing, reveals where Darwin locates change with respect to female choice in the realm of culture.

Concerned with the "secondary sexual characters," or those "not directly connected with the act of reproduction," Darwin first stipulates that the male possesses "certain organs of sense or locomotion, of which the female is quite destitute" and has "them more highly-developed, in order that he may readily find or reach her" (*The Descent*, 1:253). The male begins as a suitor who has evolved according to reproductive impulses that compel him to pursue the female. Males show "greater size, strength, and pugnacity" in relation to the female, as well as "weapons of offence or means of defence against rivals . . . gaudy colouring . . . various ornaments [and] power of song" (1:254).[7] These and other sexual "structures" serve one end: "to allure or excite the female" (1:258). Furthermore, males have "stronger passions" than females, and because the law of nature dictates that the male "shall seek the female," it follows that he is "the more active member in the courtship of the sexes" (1:272). The "coy" female, by contrast, appears "less eager than the male" and "may often be seen endeavouring for a long time to escape from the male" (1:273). She is, then, the selector: "choice on the part of the female seems almost as general a law as the eagerness of the male" (1:273), which is a tepid way of introducing what in actuality becomes *the* constant in Darwin's model as it unfolds. In sum, the active male suitor in competition with rivals seeks to win the passive female selector who tests his character.

Because "the great eagerness of the male has . . . led to the much more frequent development of secondary sexual characters in the male than in the female," males are "more liable to vary" (1:275). As corollary, males adapt and progress under the exigencies of courtship, while females remain retrograde. In addition, with "no definite limit to the amount of advantageous modification" (1:278), sexual selection results in variations equal to or even exceeding those of natural selection, which is now known as the Fisherian "runaway" process.[8] Victory in courtship optimizes male evolution: "The advantages which favored males have derived from conquering other males in battle or courtship, and thus leaving a numerous progeny, have been in the long run greater than those derived from rather more perfect adaptation to the external conditions of life" (1:279). Here again, we find Darwin hedging on natural selection as the principle mechanism for evolution, when placed in comparison with the dramatic effects of sexual selection. Moreover, as "could never have been anticipated," the male's ability to win the female plays a most crucial role: "The power to charm the female has been . . . more important than the power to conquer other males in battle" (1:279). And this affirmation, alluded to in the previous paragraph, gets us back to the question of female choice as the general law of courtship, rather than being "almost as general a law" as eagerness or competition among males. Still, while the attributes and consequences may be apparent to Darwin, sexual selection depends (obscurely) in the last instance: "on ardor in love, courage, and the rivalry of the males, and on the powers of perception, taste, and will of the female" (1:296). What began as a straightforward active-passive dichotomization becomes a mutual courtship dynamic between men and women fueled by "love" and "taste" and other open-ended factors scarcely understood then or now.

With no shortage of quandaries then, Darwin anthropomorphizes the sexual dimorphism he observes in nature while maintaining a "principle of continuity" between animals and humans.[9] Males continue to be much more varied than females, for "it is the male which has been chiefly modified" (*The Descent*, 2:321); woman's disposition differs from man's, "chiefly in her greater tenderness and less selfishness," which does not surprise Darwin given maternal instincts; and those abilities granted to females such as "powers of intuition" and "perhaps of imitation" remain faculties "of the lower races, and therefore of a past and lower state of civilisation" (2:326). Sexual differentiation then follows, as Darwin shows his less enlightened side: "The chief distinction in the intellectual powers of the two sexes is shown by man attaining to a higher eminence, in whatever he takes up, than woman can attain—whether requiring deep thought, reason, or imagination, or merely the use of the senses and hands" (2:327). Carried out in full, the sexual dimorphism between superior men and inferior women inverts their suitor-selector roles: "In civilised life man is . . . influenced in the choice of his wife by external appearance" (2:338). Men become selectors, and women exhibit greater modification:

> The men of each race prefer what they are accustomed to behold; they
> cannot endure any great change; but they like variety, and admire
> each characteristic point carried to a moderate extreme. . . . Hence
> a perfect beauty, which implies many characters modified in a

particular manner, will in every race be a prodigy. . . . If all our
women were to become as beautiful as the Venus de Medici, we
should for a time be charmed; but we should soon wish for variety;
and as soon as we had obtained variety, we should wish to see certain
characters in our women a little exaggerated beyond the then existing
common standard. (2:354)

Female traits vary according to the mercurial tastes of *choosy* males,
and thus the reversal from nonhuman to human sexual selection appears complete.

This reversal should not, though, be seen as some sort of parallel to
a rhetorical reversal in Darwin, from "savage" to "civilised" humans.
When Darwin says "civilised life" in this instance, he means to establish a distinction between humankind and the animal kingdom according to selector status. His thought process here is clear from what he
says just following about "every race." All of this, of course, enhances
the contradictions of the text and its indefinite conclusions, given my
earlier example in chapter 2 of Darwin's position with respect to the
Fuegians. The difference is one of degree rather than of kind. Simian
descent is preferable to a lineage traceable to those "savage" tribes who
keep their women in a state of bondage. Yet the appropriation of choice
on the part of men seems to extend to both, leaving us much to ponder.
Either Darwin understood his own culture to be guilty of the socially
concealed and condoned enslavement of women through unequal
access to education and employment, in which case the final words of
The Descent can be read as a self-critical line of comparison between
Victorian society and the Fuegians, or he recognized that in both the
male selects, without managing to equate the two types of servitude as
analogous. My inclination would be toward the former, that is, a cagey
caution on the part of Darwin against ongoing practices in his immediate sphere, if it were not for the fact that he appears so enamored in passages like the one above characterized by a latent idealization of male
selector status and evolved superiority.

No doubt, Darwin senses as much and wants to answer himself.
How well he succeeds, though, is another question. He stops short of
describing a total role inversion between the sexes because, while men
may be granted selector status, women never fully become suitors.
Instead, what occurs in the final two chapters of *The Descent* can best
be defined as a pervasive wavering on Darwin's part with regard to
suitor and selector behaviors. At times, his explicit vacillations make
it impossible to know which sex controls courtship:

Civilised men are largely attracted by the mental charms of women, by their wealth, and especially by their social position; for men rarely marry into a much lower rank of life. . . . With respect to the opposite form of selection, namely of the more attractive men by the women, although in civilised nations women have free or almost free choice, which is not the case with barbarous races, yet their choice is largely influenced by the social position and wealth of the men. (2:355–56)

In addition to these considerations of class and capital, Darwin further compounds his earlier inconsistencies with outright waffling. In what he terms "civilised nations," women are believed to enjoy "free choice"; however, man has acquired and maintained his selector privilege through force: "Man is more powerful in body and mind than woman, and in the savage state he keeps her in a far more abject state of bondage than does the male of any other animal; therefore it is not surprising that he should have gained the power of selection" (2:371). Plus, "social position" and the "wealth of men," both patriarchal outgrowths, condition female choice in the "civilised nations" he describes.

The problem is that Darwin cannot reconcile what he sees in nature with observations of his society: "Women are everywhere conscious of the value of their beauty; and when they have the means, they take more delight in decorating themselves with all sorts of ornaments than do men. They borrow the plumes of male birds, with which nature decked this sex in order to charm the females" (2:372). In other words, women allure men with male attributes, which become twisted to the point of becoming synonymous with feminine frivolity. Furthermore, though never in explicit terms, Darwin suggests that in this social environment male (passive) selectors act as the objects of female (active) suitors, who show modification through ornamentation. Though Darwin's public may accept these conclusions and "safely extend them to mankind," the suitor-selector bifurcation remains unresolved to the very end: "Courage, pugnacity, perseverance, strength and size of body, weapons of all kinds . . . and ornamental appendages, have all been indirectly gained by *the one sex or the other* [emphasis added], through the influence of love and jealousy . . . and through the exertion of a choice" (2:402). The assumption here is that he means for both humans and nonhumans. Indeed, sexual selection proves an "extremely complex affair" (1:296) because it is so confusing. Sexual dimorphism, that is, the differentiation between men and women, allows for transformations that appear anything but natural, and it is hard to know from one passage to the next whom Darwin believes to be the rightful selector of a "civilised" society. Case in point: "in civilised life man is . . . influenced in the choice of his wife by external appearance" (2:338) in comparison with "in civilised nations women have free or almost free choice . . . largely influenced by the social position and wealth of the men" (2:356). These vacillations exemplify an important feature of the Darwinian indeterminism I have in mind for this study as a whole, since qualifications like "almost free choice" and flip-flops toward eager, ornamented females and the prowess of passive male selectors amount to unsuccessful attempts to reconcile the tension already inherent in an oxymoron like "passive choice," which forces us to wonder what sort of choice it is at all. These, it seems, are questions of evolutionary science better answered by the laboratory of literature in its equally material concern with reality.

VULGAR SELECTION

As the quintessential seducer, Don Juan personifies the primordial male suitor described by Darwin in his discussion of sexual selection. This legendary rake—active, attractive, and fickle—embodies evolutionary virility, for to woo women constitutes his raison d'être. Yet other than Gregorio Marañón's "biological study," which misses the mark for its ideological bent on marriage, scant correlation has been made between Don Juan and Darwin.[10] Coverage, instead, concerns the features (and limitations) of Don Juan's mythical constitution. Noting several historical transformations, Mercedes Sáenz-Alonso sees not a single, archetypal Don Juan but rather a plurality of figures who share one constant end: woman.[11] That is to say, although his representation might vary, his aim remains unchanged, and victory awaits him because of his innate ability to adapt to the circumstances of his conquests. Moreover, as a vital force subject to carnal impulses, Don Juan projects Nature, rather than pertain to the spirit or intellect.[12] Kierkegaard, who finds Don Juan most true to form only in music, or what Darwin might term the language of the "love-call" (*The Descent*, 1:332), would characterize him as sensuous, as opposed to psychical, for being forever unfaithful and never finished, "about whose history one cannot learn except by listening to the noise of the waves."[13] This gesture toward endless return gets at what Camus says of Don Juan's "profound quest" in the moment, which removes him from illusions for the future and reservations about the past, "whence each woman hopes to give him what no one has ever given him" and "each time they are utterly wrong and merely manage to make him feel the need of that repetition."[14] As such, Don Juan is the seducer we associate with "once more" instead of "at last." And, as Shaw points out, Don Juan's beginnings as "the enemy of God" in sixteenth-century Spain have placed him "in mortal conflict with existing institutions" ever since.[15]

Indeed, from unrepentant sinner banished to hell for his pride to idealized Promethean rebel to indifferent dandy, Don Juan bears the stamp of the age that claims his soul as its own, while at the same time an emerging social consciousness in him unmasks his humanity as his depiction moves from legend to parody, verse to prose. Without shame, he infiltrates walled convents in the face of his Creator; without explanation, he ceases to be indiscriminate and acts the part of a Don Quixote in search of his Dulcinea; without Faust as his mirror and longings for salvation, he falls far from tragedy; without recourse he becomes a bourgeois anarchist fated to marry and procreate. A man of his word, subject to the chivalric code of honor, he is no less deceiver, trickster, impersonator, pure language, and beyond language. Vigilant fathers and inferior rivals inspire disdain in the blood of Don Juan, for equipped with boundless passion and unmatched courage, he "shall seek the female" (*The Descent*, 1:272), and virgins no less. He is at once their salvation and ruin. Woman operates within him, for his narcissism pulls him toward her, and outside of him, for selected by her "appreciation of the beautiful" (*The Descent*, 2:402), he takes shape in her image. A cultural icon and Spain's most infamous expatriate, Don Juan thrives because of the contradiction innate to his character. In this way, Don Juan, too, is indeterminate.

Juan Vulgar, in comparison, believes himself to be all of these things and winds up being none of them. To be sure, Picón's early novel, *Juan Vulgar* (1885), could not be more aptly titled.[16] A naive young man from the country travels to Madrid in search of fame and fortune, lands a low-level civil job, and finds that he is too poor to compete for the wealthy María, his first and only true (idealized) love. What is worse, this hapless suitor discovers not only that a now married María has had an affair with a lesser rival from his town, Pipierno, but also that he himself, Juan Vulgar, has fallen prey to a savvy father and been hitched to the compliant daughter Pilar, with whom he must live out the rest of his days in utter bourgeois tedium. The

story concludes as Juan discovers that his domestic angel has fallen
into a deep slumber while reading, in an effort to please him, the literary manuscript that holds his most intimate aspirations for a life
other than the one he has. At the same moment, the calendar reminds
Juan that that very day is his thirtieth birthday, and with the final
words of the novel, he exclaims: "My God! Thirty years, thirty years!
My youth wasted!" (352). Given his marriage, Juan consoles himself
with despair—"Here there is no victim other than me!" (340)—and
in this way, his character stands as an antithesis to the Don Juan upon
whom he models himself.

In reality, Picón could not be more interested in Don Juan, and his
message, transmitted through Juan Vulgar, has much to do with the
same contradictions of sexual selection Darwin struggled to articulate. Picón's protagonist lives according to the Don Juan ideal, and
parody illustrates the social obstacles that have come to confuse the
"exertion of a choice" by one sex or the other. A careful reader of
Picón knows him to be well versed in Don Juan's history; keen allusions to many of his predecessors' representations abound in both
his novels and short stories. It is only fitting, therefore, that Señor
Balduque, the father of Pilar, should be the one to outwit and slay,
in the figurative sense of betrothal to his daughter, the intrepid Juan
Vulgar. In Tirso de Molina's *El burlador de Sevilla y convidado de
piedra* (1630) the fates are reversed, with Don Juan Tenorio killing
Don Gonzalo de Ulloa, the father of a young woman, Ana, whom he
has seduced. Picón's version, however, gives us a different take. Meeting the bachelor Juan by chance and finding him gainfully employed,
Balduque knows a good opportunity when he sees one. He positions
his daughter within the sights of the sentimental suitor, surprises
them in a compromising moment, and appeals to the code of honor
synonymous with the idol of this vulgar copy: "You sir, Don Tenorio,
should have been more loyal to me" (311). Since Juan, who fancies
himself a budding writer, understands his life as a fiction, he is "far
from thinking that he had been caught in a trap" (312) and instead
tells himself: "This has no other arrangement than the clear, legitimate, and honorable solution . . . duty is an upright line. (Great sentence! I'll make a note of it for the drama!)" (312). Juan and Pilar then
marry in a most depressing, perfunctory ceremony, and it is only a
matter of months before Juan feels suffocated. He thinks to himself,
"I wish that she knew how to understand me better," and laments,
"For her, what isn't of the house isn't of the world" (322–23). Much to

Juan's chagrin, Pilar is the right woman not for his adventurous spirit but rather for the home.

On the topic of choice among nonhumans in sexual selection, Darwin remarks that female birds, "by having long selected the more attractive males, have added to their beauty" (*The Descent*, 1:259). He implies with this assertion that "powers of discrimination and taste on the part of the female" (1:259) have shaped the male according to the image of her desires. When Darwin then feels compelled to reverse selector privilege in the anthropomorphic realm, the explanation involves a history of unnatural male domination over women who, kept in a state of bondage, have lost their selector status. The inverse corollary then translates to a female molded by male preference, and to maintain his control and undermine her political will in the nineteenth century, the companion of Spanish male choice becomes *el ángel del hogar*, the domestic angel. Passive and maternal, this feminine figurehead of the home stands at the opposite end of the suitor-selector continuum from Don Juan. In 1862, María del Pilar Sinués de Marco explained the natural disposition of this angel: "Woman is born loving, and loving she dies."[17] Yet part of becoming a woman, continues Sinués de Marco, requires a coming to terms with the fact that "woman is constantly the victim of man" (256). Just one in a long line of nineteenth-century manuals on feminine virtues, Sinués de Marco's text conditions her readers on moral terms to feel inferior, born to be wives who understand their place to be the private sphere alone.

Bridget Aldaraca, using Fray Luis de León's conception of *la perfecta casada* (the perfect wife) as her point of departure, explains the syllogism along Darwinian terms of sexual dimorphism and in the context of sexual politics: woman is different from man, and therefore home is her place; woman's place is in the home, and therefore she is different from man.[18] Likewise, Geraldine Scanlon, for her part, elucidates the logic that came to justify a complacent social acceptance of female machinations toward self-domestication: "The slavery [of wives] was attractively disguised; the capture of a rich husband implied a life of luxury and leisure, while emancipation offered few attractions for those who were conditioned to be dependent."[19] Women "select" by entrapping, or they "choose" the man who chooses them first, or else the father makes the call based on what is in "her best interest." This brings us back to what Beauvoir, in chapter 2, was shown to posit in terms of conditioned happiness, that is, woman made complicit in her own subjugation. Moreover, Bram Dijkstra speaks of a translation from "Mary, the Mother of God" to "virgin, mother, and wife," in which the passive selector, the savior of fallen Man, provides the spiritual balance to the carnal suitor, who for his part, confronted by her virtuous reluctance, has no alternative but "to play Ghenghis Khan, or some other barbarian conqueror on the home front."[20] Sacrifice is a natural extension to the sex known for "her greater tenderness and less selfishness" (*The Descent*, 2:326). So, though the domestic angel might carry the double within her, Charles Baudelaire's *fleur du mal* or the *femme fatale* lurking in the shadows of male desire, prostitutes and Don Juan negate each other. An idealized being born to be violated, a material reality made to symbolize disillusionment after consummation, the *ángel del hogar* is no less a contradiction than Don Juan, and no less indeterminate despite her fixed appearance.

Picón's Juan Vulgar, as selector, discovers these contradictions firsthand. Like Victor Frankenstein, he finds that his creature has taken on a life of her own, one that could not be more foreign, and yet more of his making. She represents the effect of the patriarchal power structure he seeks to uphold; as selector, he has molded her in his image, just as Cronin and Armstrong ask if female selectors shape males.[21] All Pilar knows how to do is "take care of the house, feed him well, always keep the linens meticulously ironed . . . be organized, clean, [and] economical" (*Juan Vulgar*, 342). Confronted by *la perfecta casada* incarnate, Juan literally finds himself in a state of self-alienation. She senses his disappointment and grows troubled by the growing distance between them. In a desperate attempt to regain his affections, Pilar decides one evening while Juan is out to stage herself reading his play in his study as a way to show her love when he returns and finds her there devoted to careful consideration of his innermost thoughts. But things do not go as planned, and when Juan enters: "Everything in the study was hushed, silent, without the least sign of life, as if nobody were there" (350). He approaches on tiptoes and "all of a sudden stood still, with his eyes immeasurably open, and an expression of painful astonishment drawn on his face that would have made him afraid of himself were he to see his own image in the mirror" (351). The fact is, though, Juan does see himself as if in a mirror. Pilar lounges there sound asleep, while her husband's precious manuscript lies in pieces, having slid from her lap to the floor in a heap.

At this early stage in Picón's fiction, the two main characters in some ways conform to the most straightforward articulation of Darwin's model of suitors and selectors in nature and as understood by today's science. Juan Vulgar is eager and active, while Pilar remains discriminating and coy, complicit in the machinations to beat Juan at his own game. She is passive to the extent that she lets him come to her and only "chooses" after the choice has been made. Though somewhat distorted, male-male combat still occurs between Don Juan and the father, Balduque, if we can imagine the latter to be as interested in passing on his genes as the former. Still, in the context of sexual selection, agency surfaces as a thorny issue. Juan Vulgar, after all, fashions himself suitor and selector. He is suitor for the role he scripts for himself as born seducer, upholding the legacy of the quintessential virile male forever fast and fickle, while his perceived charge as selector seeks to validate the same world Darwin confronts when trying to reconcile what he sees in society with the continuum of secondary sexual traits between humans and nonhumans necessary for his science of descent to be persuasive. The result is that Juan Vulgar finds himself in a conundrum brought to life by his own contradictions, and while the parody might bring some laughs, it also brings concern. Picón wants to hold the mirror to his reader as well, in the imaginary quality of its symbolic constitution. In this way, though the character types appear fixed, the message about choice is far less so. Who has it, how it is being used, and to what ends are questions that carry sociopolitical consequence. In this most legible example, then, *Juan Vulgar* gestures toward the unfinished faces of the suitors and selectors we once thought we knew. The bleakly sardonic outcome shows these elemental components of the dynamic to be far from elementary and hence the unique capacity of realist representation to capture the sexual politics at stake in the praxis of sexual selection. In "civilised nations" where women have "free or almost free choice," men do the "choosing" in accordance with the inferior "second sex" they desire and detest. The ultimate surprise of Juan Vulgar when confronted with the mate of his making is meant to tell us something about the indeterminacy of sexual selection in the cultural realm; this "extremely complex affair" baffles Darwin for the ideological forces his science of society downplays and yet cannot ignore.

ORNAMENTAL INVERSIONS

With his most acclaimed novel, *Dulce y sabrosa* (1891), Picón probes the irreconcilable issues of Darwinian sexual selection through an inversion of gender roles.[22] As a means to signal the cultural forces at play in moments of choice, ornamentation captures with concision Picón's reversal of the Don Juan scenario, which begins with his predictable victimizing and ends with him molded by his female counterpart to be the ready victim. Indeed, from the outset the affable, yet villainous, Don Juan de Todellas, of "all women" (todellas = todas ellas), appears the suitor-seducer who knows how to adapt to the objects of his affections:

> Don Juan possesses the enviable trait of being able to speak and make requests of each according to who she is, and with adjustment to the moment in which he solicits and implores. She that denies repeatedly for timidity, finds him daring, and she that distrusts his boldness, restrained . . . some he only attempts to seduce with looks and words; others he persuades at once that a man's arms were made for embracing lovely waists.[23]

However, because Don Juan must also be selector, Picón limits his adornment. Though he would like to dress in the manner of his forefathers, as if it were "carnival all year round" (77), he has "resigned himself to using prosaic cotton pants, tricot frock coats, and cheviot jackets, keeping as the only practical element from earlier times the gold coins that he carries in his vest pocket" (78). Hence, Picón contrasts a past age of antiquated male extravagance with his own nineteenth-century present of progressive and always economical pragmatism and, in so doing, refracts evolutionary science and Darwin's notion of "civilised" culture, which shuns flamboyant masculine attire. Don Juan's dress camouflages him and thus facilitates a tactic of surveillance with his inspections of the feminine quality of his possible conquests: "Perhaps he was too meticulous and rigorous in these examinations; but he excused them, saying that if a racehorse requires innumerable traits in order to be judged beautiful, many more should be wished for collected in woman" (80). To be sure, this passage recalls Darwin at his lowest: "Man scans with scrupulous care the character and pedigree of his horses . . . but when he comes to his own marriage he rarely, or never, takes any such care" (*The Descent*, 2:402). In sum, from his modest ornamentation to his scrupulous evaluations, Don Juan de Todellas takes the culturally

usurped role as selector in earnest, that is, the powers of discrimination and taste with which Darwin finds females endowed in nature,
while as a born suitor he has the necessary attributes, including the
lack of conscience of his virile ancestors, to spread his seed with un-
rivaled efficacy.

In contrast to Picón's treatment of Don Juan, however, the adornments of the novel's female protagonist, Cristeta, act as a determinative factor in the sexual selection process. The work opens with a temporal play, placing readers in the narrative present and denying them
the history of Cristeta's earlier victimization at the hands of Don
Juan, and thus her first appearance in chapter 2, as seen through his
eyes in the Retiro park after more than two years apart, introduces a
dramatic descriptive motif that proves central to the text: "The outfit
could not have been more elegant. It was put together by a black skirt
folded in tiny pleats with exquisite artistry, a short coat of rich gray
fabric with lots of embroidery, which fit her bewitching body perfectly,
and a big hat, also black, embellished by ruffled feathers, and a veil of
tulle with polka-dots that, simulating burls, softly shaded her face"
(*Dulce y sabrosa*, 81). As Picón moves back in time, his account of a
previous encounter between Don Juan and Cristeta in the backstreet
theater where she performed runs with comparable detail: "dressed
as a gypsy, with a full percale skirt, flowing scarf around her waist,
curls on her temples and a low chignon, made to look like a garden
of pure flowers" (106). Indeed, the relationship between Cristeta and
her manner of dress, as developed in the first half of the novel, serves
to characterize her malleability as a female subject to the male gaze,
his desires, and "gold coins." Don Juan wins her over in the dress-
ing room by saying, "There is no similarity between you and that
attire" (106), and blinds her before their first romantic adventure with
the purchase of "a magnificent gray coat, long and very fitted at the
waist; a wide-brimmed hat, adorned with black bows [and] a sachet
of Russian leather" (124). In the chapters leading up to her seduction
and abandonment, therefore, ornamentation works against Cristeta's
character as an instrument of Don Juan's manipulations. Her agency
as suitor remains questionable, and if selector, hers appears a "passive choice" at best. Hence, descriptions of dress and appearance in
Picón function at a deeper level than what one might associate with
the stock prolixity of the realist pen, and there is little here that shares
the same concern with emerging consumerism that a novel like Zola's
Au Bonheur des Dames (1883) takes up.

Yet, in the second half of the novel, Cristeta uses the experience of having fallen victim to Don Juan as a foundation for reclaiming him as her own. With a turnabout, she goes for broke and uses the money he "generously" left her in his getaway as her means to win him back. To be sure, after painful hesitation, he took his plume and on that check "wrote in bold letters *five thousand pesetas*" (182), which the narrator, from the consciousness of Don Juan, is quick to qualify for readers who might imagine this to be too much: "If the Venus from antiquity, maimed and dismembered, meant only to please our eyes and unwilling to come down from her pedestal, is priceless, how much should a twenty-year-old woman who is a living and loving statue be worth?" (182). Nevertheless, ornamentation, Cristeta's weapon for the conquest of such a rogue, becomes an attribute that she controls, rather than one that exercises power over her as if she were nothing more than "a statue," as was the case in the first half. From a location unbeknownst to Don Juan, she arms herself with all of the necessary fineries, hires a luxury coach, and one day in the Retiro makes her debut: "She wore a plain skirt of gray fabric, forming large pleats, cut so as to show off her feet, which wore black stockings and petite shoes of the latest French style, a very dark coat, drawn to her waist with cords of silk that hung to the ground, and a plush red lining that one discovered with each step; a small ash-colored velvet hat with a little veil and crimson bows" (250). Wooed by the display, Don Juan grows certain, now in his suitor mentality, that a rival must be the bankroll behind her transformation and even suspects that the child-ornament at Cristeta's side might be his own. Her appearance renders the once all-powerful Don Juan de Todellas debilitated, and a crisis ensues that causes him to question everything he once was as self-assured selector. Cristeta, along with her suitor modifications, retakes the selector status in a move that mirrors Darwin's own turnabouts. Nevertheless, at the moment of an "exertion of choice," she invites Don Juan in the last chapter to her spartan room and presents herself to him with the utmost modesty: "She was dressed and combed with adorable simplicity; the outfit, of dark wool without adornments" (344). Don Juan begs her hand in marriage, but she responds in defiance: "That . . . never!" (348). Still, he assures himself, "She will be my wife," as she thinks, "If I marry, I'll lose him" (349). Thus, Picón delivers a tale of Darwinian inversions, in which a passive female selector becomes an ornamented active suitor, only to turn in the last instant, unadorned selector anew on her own terms. This is the "moral consideration of women" Picón draws from the indeterminism of sexual selection in the social sphere according to Darwin's precepts.[24]

CONSCIENTIOUS SEDUCTION

From domestic angels, parody, and reversals of conquest emerges a full-fledged female Don Juan in Picón's last, longest, and most intricate novel, *Juanita Tenorio* (1910).[25] The plot, though, offers little indication that this title is anything more than an ironic play on the fate of the protagonist, Juanita, who could not be more unlucky in love. As a female bildungsroman of sexual selection built out of Juanita's psychologically imbued first-person narration, the tale moves forward with her amorous trials from one heartless suitor to the next. She suffers a lonely childhood under the cold hand of a father left bitter after the death of his much younger wife, whom he suspects mothered Juanita from an affair with another man. Juanita is then shipped off to a boarding school, and when her father dies and leaves her his bookshop, she returns at the age of eighteen as the legal inheritor of the business. Not long after, Juanita gives herself to Ángel, a clerk at the store, but the affair comes to a painful end as she discovers that he is anything but angelic. Righteous but ruined, Juanita sells the bookstore and is taken in as the personal assistant of an ailing wealthy woman, where she is vulnerable to the advances of two contrasting suitors, Gonzalo, a handsome young relation of her boss, and Blancas, a distasteful older gentleman who manages the estate finances. Gonzalo pursues Juanita with the sort of "stronger passions" Darwin describes for the "more eager male" and seduces her, only to leave her destitute when his mother discovers their tryst.

With little chance for survival, Juanita sells herself to Blancas as his concubine and instrument of revenge against Gonzalo's mother. Blancas marries a rich widow a few months later, but he nevertheless passes a sum of cash to Juanita sufficient to keep her comfortable. She falls ill and admits herself to a sanatorium, where she meets Irene, a childhood friend eager to acquire a title of nobility for her son by any means necessary. To this end, Irene wants Sancho, the Marqués del Ajalvir, a relative of her husband, and true Don Juan, dead without any heirs. Hating all men by this time, Juanita agrees to make him fall for her, only to crush him when he is most vulnerable, with the idea that he will spiral toward death from a broken heart. Just the opposite happens, however, and Juanita finds herself not only in love but beaten for the affections of the marquis by a younger virgin rival named Niní. Exiled to a dilapidated house owned by Sancho outside Madrid, Juanita withers away in isolation, as he and Niní marry and move to Paris. True to her colors, Niní cheats on Sancho and makes him the object of public scandal. He returns to Spain a broken man and, close to death, is rescued in the final scene by an ever-faithful (and disinterested) Juanita.

These two paragraphs of plot summary condense a five hundred–page tour de force of suitor-selector intrigues and bring to light the problematic irony of Picón's title. Victimized by Ángel, Gonzalo, Blancas, and Sancho, Juanita writes an autobiography that appears anything but the traditional Don Juan story. In this light, critics like Elena Soriano and Osvaldo Orico have used Picón's novel as a model for the impossibility of a female (suitor) Tenorio. Soriano argues that "Juanita Tenorio is actually anti-donjuanesque, [that her character] shows once again the feminine characteristics that prevent her from being a true Doña Juana: sentimentalism, zeal for one eternal love, and a certain degree of erotic tepidness."[26] And Orico, for his part, maintains that "while in Don Juan there is a sentimental democracy that brings him to exercise his passions without greater compromises on the part of the other, in Juanita Tenorio one finds proof of a tyranny of instinct, imposed by her will. . . . The essential difference between the two is that Don Juan courts love; Juanita Tenorio no: she demands it."[27] One alternative to these readings would be to focus on those instances in the novel that illustrate Darwinian sexual selection in action, like chapter 13, when Juanita drops her clip to allure Sancho, or chapter 17, when she adorns herself and goes on the attack against the overt displays of Niní. However, the problem with this identification approach of isolated examples is that it fails to account for the protagonist over the entire novel.

In other words, can a "Juanita Tenorio" be reconciled with a woman who not only suffers the abuses of numerous seducers but who delivers herself to the worst of them all in a gesture of idealized domestic salvation? In truth, she does live up to her name, but only in the context of a paradigm shift that has taken place in the figure of Don Juan by the end of the nineteenth century. A transformation indeed occurs through the centuries from "appalling villain" to "tragic idealist," and still the most useful (and neglected) interpretation of a less obvious "evolution" of Don Juan comes from the psychoanalyst Otto Rank, whose writings overlap with Darwin's in curious ways.[28] The "Stone Guest," the supernatural representation of the dead father in Tirso de Molina's play, is Rank's point of entry for contending that "the characteristic fantasy of conquering countless women . . . is ultimately based on the unattainability of the mother and the compensatory substitute for her."[29] The desire originates in libidinal drives: "This unattainability does not refer to sexual possession, to which there is certainly no barrier in primitive times and character. Rather, it involves the deeply-rooted biological wish for the exclusive and complete possession of the mother" (95). However, for Don Juan sexual conquest of multiple women, as a partial regression, leaves him only "partially fulfilled" (95). Therefore, according to Rank, poet-writers of Don Juan return again and again to "the death complex," because such a representation "offers the unconscious a much fuller satisfaction" of the "primal tendency" (96). Rank writes of the manifestations:

> The devouring animals of the underworld, the grave, and the coffin are clearly unambiguous mother symbols; thus in the punishment that overtakes Don Juan we have not only the expression of the deepest wish fulfillment—to behold the path of return to the mother—but also a particularly heroic fantasy portrait: the father figure, who otherwise bars access to the mother, now shows the way directly. In the figure of the Stone Guest, who also represents the coffin, appears the mother herself, coming to fetch the son. (96)

The historical trajectory of Don Juan confirms the operation of this primal image. Reflecting on portrayals of Don Juan either without family or as the bastard of an unfaithful mother, Rank sees a gradual "devaluation of the Don Juan type" that "forces the bold conquering hero to capitulate before a host of sentimental memories of love that distress his conscience" (119). The representations of Don Juan across more than three centuries evidence a penetration of the psychological impulses, the maternal longings that define the seducer's behavior.

Yet Rank's reading is ripe for a Darwinian reversal. Of all Picón's works, *Juanita Tenorio* stands out as the most psychological. In addition to the intimate first-person narration given by Juanita, the story begins with an extended exposition of her childhood and, particularly, of her attempts to come to grips with the death of her mother. As a young girl, she never understood the distance between her parents or the frequent visits of a kind gentleman to their house. She does recall, however, that one day her mother had a physical collapse, and the visits came to an end with this gentleman's revelation that he planned to marry another woman. From such a memory, Juanita reflects: "I think that man was to blame for the death of my mother."[30] Let it be supposed then that Juanita is an illegitimate child who, more than yearn like Don Juan for a lost mother, struggles as his female reflection to reconcile her absent father in an inversion of Rank's theory. Toward the end of the novel, Juanita finds herself recuperating at the ramshackle property of Sancho after he has run away with the younger Niní. The house there comes with a story. Called the Farm of the Duchess, it is the place where a beautiful noblewoman caught her husband in an affair; seeing him through the window at dinner with his lover, she called his attention and then drowned herself in the garden pond.

One afternoon during the convalescence, Juanita finds herself mesmerized by the same garden pool. It takes on the appearance of glass, "as if it were crystal" (376), and all of a sudden, she says, "The rectangle formed by the pool was a black and terrifying stain: it looked like a large tomb from which the lid had been snatched away. . . . I, fixed on the balcony, continued looking, without wanting to look, at the site where I knew the water was, even though I could not see her [presumably, the deceased duchess]" (376). As Juanita explains, "Something mysterious and ill-fated pulled me," and after recovering from a faint, only a strange force of "alienation" (377) remained from the experience. Perhaps, as some have suggested, during these minutes she contemplated suicide or, perhaps, she sought her own dead mother. But it is also possible that, being a Juanita Tenorio, she looked through her mother, the crystal water-tomb stain that "otherwise bars access," in search of her father. Days later, she visits the grave of her mother, and as she approaches who should appear but Blancas, the unsavory father figure who left her just like the gentleman who left her mother (and whose name, like Ángel's, plays on a character who is not "white" [blanco] but rather the dark "stain" of her past). She tells him sometime later: "I am free in the sense that no man has a right to me; but more so I want to be free out of respect to my own ideas, to my own feelings, to that which I have sworn to myself" (397). She has found her "moral self" (401), and upon learning that Sancho has fallen ill, she returns to aid him, as if he were the dying father she had sought. Figuratively, he represents the now ghostly "cult of the father," debilitated and vulnerable, in the passing of the times Picón perceived.[31] Symbolized by Sancho as the broken archetype, the institution no longer stands unassailable, for she has left the Doll's House just as Shaw described.

Hence, whatever the limitations of Rank's psychoanalysis, namely, that it can ever be disproven, his theory is useful for mapping Don Juan in the context of Darwinian sexual selection. The historical trajectory shows an ever more psychological Don Juan of distressed conscience and unconscious concern for family ties. To make of Juanita Tenorio the antithesis of Don Juan in the manner attempted by Soriano and Orico fails because, given the plasticity inherent in Don Juan, by the end of the nineteenth century suitor-selector traits reflect Darwinian theories of sexual dimorphism in which attraction in courtship depends, literally, on questions of lineage. But there is also an indeterminate, moral component to heredity, even if "inherited traits" bring to mind all that is deterministic about evolutionism. In truth, Darwin begins chapter 3 of *The Descent*, titled "Moral Sense," with the premise that "any animal," and above all humankind, endowed with "social instincts" will "acquire a moral sense or conscience" (1:71). The definition he repeats throughout the text specifies that "a moral being is one who is capable of comparing his past and future actions or motives, and of approving or disapproving of them" (1:88). Conscience stems directly from such an ability, "for conscience looks backwards and judges past actions, inducing that kind of dissatisfaction, which if weak we call regret, and if severe remorse" (1:91). Both the "social instincts" and "moral sense" relate "exclusively to the community" (1:97), and the "highest stage in moral culture" comes about when we recognize that how we think, our "mutual love and sympathy" (1:86) correlates to the welfare of others. In his final discussion of sexual selection between men and women, Darwin comes to the conclusion that the "social instincts" themselves spring from "family ties" (2:391), and even, in the material sense, from those dissolute fathers who act the Don Juan. To reclaim the past then in Picón's *Juanita Tenorio*, this past must be rewritten by Juanita's "moral self" (401) and unfinished future.

Yet the operation of an evolved moral capacity from social instincts to conscience to community requires human volition in Darwin's account:

> Owing to this [moral] condition of mind, man cannot avoid looking backwards and comparing the impressions of past events and actions. He also continually looks forward. Hence after some temporary desire or passion has mastered his social instincts, he will reflect

and compare the now weakened impression of such past impulses,
with the ever present social instinct; and he will then feel that sense
of dissatisfaction which all unsatisfied instincts leave behind them.
Consequently *he resolves* [emphasis added] to act differently for the
future—and this is conscience. (*The Descent*, 2:393)

At this stage, "conscience" becomes the "supreme judge and monitor" (2:394) of man (and woman). By *Juanita Tenorio*, Picón's vision
reflects a science of "moral culture" in which the "conscience" of his
central character spurs the remorse felt from past actions. True to his
progressive reputation, Picón arrives in this late novel at a union of
ethical commitment according to Juanita's resolve and in the interest
of the welfare of the community.

No doubt, the social dimension of Picón's fiction draws meaning
from an ambivalent marriage of morality and individualism. From his
major novels to short stories, a Darwinian "dissatisfaction" with the
enforced gender relations of suitors and selectors in Spanish culture
calls attention to an "extremely complex affair" made unnatural by
the patriarchal limitations placed on female choice. James Mandrell,
who holds an antifeminist line on Picón's fiction, asserts that "seduction must stand in some positive relationship to individual honor as
it is constituted in language."[32] Though Mandrell uses this premise
to argue that Picón's own tongue seduces as a means to maintain the
status quo, tricking women readers so that "they might better understand how to please men" (191), the principle of "individual honor
as it is constituted in language" risks exposing the opposite of what
Mandrell aims to prove. Without question, a maternal Tenorio is not
the "rebellious angel" described by Américo Castro when speaking of
Don Juan,[33] but neither is she the domestic angel one finds in the passive Pilar of Picón's earlier *Juan Vulgar*. On the subject of language
and Juanita's narration, Noël Valis states that "words are the only
thing women, in Picón's view, possess."[34] Possession opens the path
to individualism, but along with these words, Picón's female selectors
also possess "conscience" in the Darwinian sense.

While the traditional male Don Juan figure represents "an anti-
social element . . . a baneful individualism . . . an exaltation of the
self dangerous for the rest of humanity,"[35] the individualism of Picón's
Don Juan–Juanita Tenorio breaks this mold, for "the rest of humanity" is exactly what motivates her, biologically. She courts on different grounds. Founded on economics and appearances, public morality matters little to Juanita; her "individual honor" defers to a private

(written) code, "to that which I have sworn to myself," as she says to Blancas (*Juanita Tenorio*, 397). José Ortega y Gasset postulates that "Don Juan turns against morality, because morality had revolted first against life. Only when an ethic exists that is constituted . . . on vital plenitude, will Don Juan be able to yield. But that means a new culture: the biological culture."[36] Indeed, Don Juan need not be "incompatible with the emancipation of women," as José Lasaga Medina argues,[37] because a new Don Juan, which Picón literally engenders through a Juanita Tenorio, considers the species foremost in her choice as selector. Arthur Schopenhauer in his essay on the metaphysics of sexual love pointed out to Darwin and his contemporaries that amorous individualism, which appears to be working against the species, is actually doing just the opposite; the individual, unlike Nature, is capable of finding the moral in matter out of a will to live in generations to come.[38] He also said that it "lies in the nature of women to regard everything merely as a means to win the man" (620). This unsettling adage returns us to Shaw and the suitor-selector reversals where we began, but more important, to the consequences that Schopenhauer's distasteful views might otherwise cause us to overlook. For just as he says that "woman by nature is meant to obey" (626), he fancies to himself what women must be thinking: "The constitution, and consequently the welfare, of the species are placed in our [women's] hands and entrusted to our [women's] care by means of the next generation coming from us; we [women] will conscientiously carry this out" (618). There is the obvious obstacle of the "femininity = reproduction" bind as I introduced it in chapter 2, but here it also seems that Schopenhauer does not suspect that to "conscientiously carry this out" might not mean "to obey."

So, what can we attach to the idea that Juanita courts "conscientiously" and selects according to her own moral code? From our reading of Darwin, there is a moral dimension, to be sure, but Juanita as Sancho's salvation defines herself, by extension, in reference to him, as another *mujer virtuosa* one step away from the good wife and mother. As a result, though "family ties" and "social instincts" do deepen our appreciation of the indeterminism of Darwinian sexual selection in the case of Juanita, these facets of its operation stop short of explaining, on her terms, the "conscience" Darwin had in mind. Moreover, to position her character against Sancho, that is, to measure her worth according to the good she does him upon her return, runs counter to her individualism and the disobedient movement at the end of the nineteenth century for women's liberation. It is hard to

see, though, precisely how she disobeys or where the rebellion lies. As
a result, we cannot help but wonder if Juanita Tenorio projects the
author's "proto-feminismo," as Gonzalo Sobejano describes Picón's
stance in his introduction to *Dulce y sabrosa* (27), or, better yet, if she
is still in any sense an enemy of the gods for taking an emancipatory
torch from her Tenorio forefathers.

The answer is yes on both accounts, for as both Valis and Mandrell
agree despite their opposed views on *Juanita Tenorio*, when it comes
to Don Juan we must take account of language. Indeed, to shift attention away from Juanita Tenorio's tale to how it is told foregrounds
her agency, which sets her "in mortal conflict with existing institutions" as Shaw defined Don Juan. The endless conquests of the archetypal libertine obfuscate the repeated victimization of the women he
desires, for Don Juan himself is nothing less than a cultural institution in Spain across the centuries, and his overthrow, a symbolic sub-
stitution in the form of a Darwinian suitor-selector reversal, cannot
be complete without the voice of a Juanita Tenorio, made diminutive
and nonthreatening so as to be all the more effective in her subtle
subversion of the patriarchal power structure. She assumes the suitor
role in order to appropriate her selector status through a power play
enabled by the material plasticity already intrinsic to the dynamic.

In this light, it will be remembered that Giacomo Casanova, too,
wrote an autobiography, *Histoire de ma vie* (1794), in which the truth
about seduction was revealed.[39] Though his aims differ from those of
both Picón as author and Juanita as narrator, what they share is a first-
person perspective predicated on self-reflection. For this reason, Casanova's life story represents a turning point in the historical trajectory of
Don Juan, from the purely sensual to the psychical, even if the author
claims at the outset a life devoted to sensual pleasure. Casanova writes
as "a free agent" (25) who is quick to admit a seduction of another sort,
from writer to reader: "To win your confidence, I had to portray myself
with all my faults, just as I am, or have come to know myself" (31).
This is not false humility in Casanova but rather something much more
akin to a Juanita Tenorio who finds herself seduced and abandoned by
every man she meets. The humanity we associate with this imperfec-
tion draws us in, along with the way Casanova describes his past as a
"thinking being" (44) with the understanding that "thought . . . cannot precede the existence of memory" (29). These are the "stains" of
Juanita's past, her lineage, and the Don Juan who was her unknown
yet ever-present father now transcended and hence embraced according

to her own conscientious yet defiant code. In this way, it is important that Casanova emphasizes another curious inversion: "Feeling that I was born for the opposite sex of mine, I have always loved it and done all that I could to make myself loved by it" (32). This vision of virility contrasts earlier claims about women's nature, which Schopenhauer, for one, belittles for being consumed by the opposite sex. Therefore, no matter how unconscionable the exploits recounted might be, the auto- biographical narrative makes the once universal seducer a self-reflective individual selector who no longer lives in the abstract and, in this way, provokes a hard look at a reality of evolutionary contradictions.

That is to say, as long as Don Juan remains timeless, beyond lan- guage, we can revel in his existence as pure play. This was the Don Juan that Kierkegaard held most sacrosanct:

> In the Middle Ages, much was told about a mountain that is not found on any map; it is called Mount Venus. There sensuousness has its home; there it has its wild pleasures, for it is a kingdom, a state. In this kingdom, language has no home, nor the collectedness of thought, nor the laborious achievements of reflection; there is heard only the elemental voice of passion, the play of desires, the wild noise of intoxication. There everything is only one giddy round of pleasure. The firstborn of this kingdom is Don Juan.[40]

The attraction of this image lies in the absence of transgression, for where there is no reflection there are no social instincts in Darwin's model of "civilised life" (*The Descent*, 2:338). For this reason, Ki- erkegaard believes that Don Juan in the ideal can only be found in music, the "proper medium" where the seducer "hovers between be- ing idea . . . and an individual" (*Either/Or*, 1:92). As long as Don Juan maintains this in-between privilege, he outwits history, for out- side of history reflection is not possible. But when Don Juan speaks, "everything is changed" (1:106); he becomes an individual and "is *eo ipso* in conflict with the world about him" (1:107). The recourse then to his reflection entails a reversal of epic proportion: "As soon as Don Juan is interpreted as a reflective individual, an ideality corresponding to the musical ideality can be attained only when the matter is shifted to the psychological realm" (1:108). Juanita Tenorio speaks, and with her words, the psychical supplants the sensual in a direction other than Rank might take us, as we find ourselves both inside history, in its very *making*, and in "moral consideration of women," as Ezama Gil states, in a world where sexual selection cannot be separated from sexual politics.

These fruits of psychological reflection have a Darwinian "moral sense" because they allow us to see the "complex affair" of suitors and selectors in Picón's realism and with respect to the question of female choice. Marxist feminists recognize the material forces of subjugation, and Juanita Tenorio, whose class and gender negate her "free or almost free choice" (*The Descent*, 2:356), finds herself vulnerable to the unscrupulous Don Juans of her reality. Picón, thus, makes sexual selection in the last instance a choice of her "moral self," as she looks back on past actions and resolves to act in accordance with what she has sworn to herself, regardless of social conventions and public approbation. Agency relocates itself, though, in her telling, and with her imperfections on display, she shows culture to be the culprit and catalyst of reversals that have left her no other choice at all. What is most persuasive, however, is that in the larger body of Picón's writing this social critique is a constant, rather than an aberration.

Hence, I will close with two additional examples to make this point clear, Picón's short stories "La prudente" and "Divorcio moral." The women protagonists of both find themselves deceived, the first for having once been engaged to a man who had fathered a child with another woman and abandoned both penniless, the second for having married a crook guilty of robbing an innocent man, since dead, to pay for their wedding, while leaving his victim's widow to starve. Neither of these women accepts such behavior, and the matches are dissolved despite (rather than because of) social outcry. Manolita, "the prudent woman," opens up to an empathetic narrator as they chat about "how risky the selection of a husband is for the woman," and she explains to him in the shadow of the misfortune that has left her single for life: "Let me be clear . . . men flee from us [women] when they see that we are capable of thinking and the firm assertion of our own will."[41] To be sure, she was condemned "to live among lepers" (22), as the narrator cannot help but lament. And Rosa, for her part, finds herself the talk of the town after demanding to be "divorced" for all intents and purposes from her dishonest husband; having given up all the comforts of marriage and social standing, she declares that "neither honor nor conscience has a sex."[42] Though Casanova stipulates that "man . . . is not free if he does not believe it,"[43] the unresolved reversals of Darwinian sexual selection in the context of Picón's fiction and the principle of choice at issue should leave no doubt that the conditions of *her* freedom are no different.

CHAPTER FIVE

Rivalries and Rituals— Leopoldo Alas (Clarín)

The "suitors and selectors" of the previous chapter opened a broader, tripartite discussion of the constitutive components of Darwinian sexual selection by bringing into focus the concomitant reversals in evolutionary science and realist literature with respect to the players involved. Darwin's inconsistencies and outright contradictions about the power dynamics were shown to mirror comparable tensions in Picón's novels concerned with Spanish society in the decades following *The Descent*. In the process, Picón's own "moral consideration of women," in its open-endedness, gave sufficient cause for reflection on the status quo of gender relations in a way that in Darwin's discussion of "conscience" and the "social instincts" remains much more abstract. As consequence, the trajectory of Don Juan toward its unforeseen end in Picón's last novel, an introspective Juanita Tenorio intent on being true to herself, took the inversions of sexual selection into the realm of culture through the representation of their praxis in the social sphere. The indeterminacy that enabled this literary translation and subsequent elaboration of Darwin, moreover, is central to the operative mechanics and outcomes of the theory as well. These issues form the conceptual base of the remaining two chapters of part 2, "Adaptations," and reveal the "complex affair" of sexual selection to be the axis of interest in both Darwin and the Spanish novelists to be discussed. In fact, female choice proves *the* constant in the reciprocity between the two and cannot be separated from questions of community, as exposure of the empty conventions of traditional marriage practices signals a progressive shift toward unions sanctified by self rather than by accepted norms.

Darwin is not a writer we usually think of as ironic, though history has at times revealed certain ironies behind his theories. The same, however, cannot be said of Leopoldo Alas (Clarín), who employed irony to great effect in his fiction and critical essays. This approach is especially evident in his two major novels, *La Regenta* (1884–85) and *Su único hijo* (1890), where role-playing and gender blurring constitute key issues encompassed by irony.[1] Darwinian sexual selection illuminates the mechanics that govern the interdependence of these three components of Clarín's fiction and, as corollary, a purpose for irony beyond its customary effect of destabilization in his literary production. To conceive of irony in Clarín as an interaction, rather than a narrative technique aimed at self-referential negation, moves us closer to the ethical dimension of its operation. Never static, Clarín's irony entails a process of negotiation that becomes increasingly more open-ended in his representation of courtship practices among men and women from one novel to the next. Darwinian sexual selection, as a dynamic in its own right, thus provides a formal structure well suited to discovery of the interplay among irony, performance, and gender in the reproductive impulses that infuse Clarín's plots.[2]

At the same time, in the case of Clarín, literature again helps us read Darwin anew. In the novels here discussed, sexual selection would not be possible without desire and invention, which drive the rivalries and rituals central to the way Darwin understands mating mechanics in *The Descent*. In using Darwin as a point of departure for the dynamism of his theory in its broader socio-anthropological reach, we are able to raise new questions about the relationship between irony and ethics in Clarín's endings—Ana's memorable collapse on the cathedral floor in *La Regenta* and Bonifacio's final declaration of paternity in *Su único hijo*—as well as the events that precede them. Often seen as an odd pair because of their marked differences, these two novels in truth complement each other, rather than stand in opposition according to the customary realism-modernism bifurcation that has come to define them. Irony absorbs female choice through Ana's downfall so as to censure the conventions behind her fate, which in turn clears the way for the plurality of the unfinished individual one finds in the relational ambivalence of Bonifacio's heir. Herein resides the continuity that brings us back to Darwin. Indicative of Clarín's ever more nuanced representation of its operation, Darwinian sexual selection proves ethical to the extent that its own irony is its "Comic Spirit," which is both unfinished and intersubjective. Like the language they engender, mating games mask the playfulness inherent in our always ongoing reproductions, for to procreate depends as much on the mind as on the body. Indeed, in a social world where indeterminate difference defines sex, connective thinking trumps connected thought, given that the former is never closed. We understand one another in terms of our relations, but the multiplicity confuses identity, just as the branches and blanks of a family tree complicate notions of a unified self. This process of articulation, even in the act of naming the next generation, remains permeable because of the indefinite permutations programmed into sexual selection through its performance.

RIVALRIES REWRITTEN

As is my approach in all three chapters of part 2, the first step is direct engagement with Darwin's writing, as a means to tease out the implications of his ideas. Of the two fundamental laws of sexual selection, the competition built into male-male combat gives rise to ample discussion in *The Descent* concerning the causes and consequences of rivalry. Speaking of sexual differentiation, Darwin posits that "weapons of offence and the means of defence possessed by the males for fighting with and driving away their rivals" (1:257–58) were born out of the pressures applied by sexual rather than natural selection. It is not insignificant, as shall be shown over the course of this chapter, that at an earlier point in the text Darwin counts language among these developments: "When we treat of sexual selection we shall see that . . . this power [voice] would have been especially exerted during the courtship of the sexes, serving to express various emotions, as love, jealousy, triumph, and serving as a challenge to their [male] rivals" (1:56), and later, "The vocal organs were primarily used and perfected in relation to the propagation of the species" (2:330). Interested in Darwin and the origin of language, Elizabeth Grosz points out that "the facility of vocalization . . . primarily functions as a sexual lure," and it is the case that music and the universality of song are very much related to attraction.[3]

Still, according to Darwin these secondary sexual characters, such as the vocal organs, "depend on . . . rivalry," for "when we behold two males fighting for the possession of the female . . . and performing the strangest antics . . . we cannot doubt that, though led by instinct, they know what they are about, and consciously exert their

mental and bodily powers" (*The Descent*, 1:258). A reciprocal relationship materializes between male rivalry and "stronger passions,"
and of the resultant modifications, the male becomes "the more active
member in the courtship of the sexes" (1:272). In fact, for Darwin
rivalry defines the male constitution in culture as well: "Man is the
rival of other men; he delights in competition, and this leads to ambition which passes too easily into selfishness" (2:326). Moreover, only
when unchecked will rivalry be most effective in sexual selection:
"There should be open competition for all men; and the most able
should not be prevented by laws or customs from succeeding" (2:403)
in procreation. This is an important point more generally; according
to Darwin, social convention should not impede the natural operation of sexual selection. Should it do so, just as in the case of the
"barbarous" tribes who use force to repress female choice, reversions
can occur contrary to the "civilised life" Darwin aims to promote
through his exposition of natural laws. Therefore, at this point it can
be said with certainty of *The Descent* (1) that sexual selection generates rivalries between males and (2) that these competitions involve
the passions, antics, and language that originate and evolve because
of contested females.

No doubt, there is a fundamental relationship between rivalries
and sexual selection, and in *La Regenta* competition among males
for possession of the female protagonist, Ana Ozores, predominates.
The daughter of a respected aristocratic family, Ana is also the tar-
nish on the family line, despite her legendary beauty, for having
been born from a scandalous marriage between her free-thinking
father and a lowly Italian dressmaker who died in childbirth. She
grows up under the rigid hand of a tutor and later the protection
of her controlling aunts, who marry her off to the much older Víctor Quintanar, the town's former regent. Her upbringing and passion for reading inspire an education in the imagination, which in
turn fosters romantic fantasies and mystical yearnings under her
oppressive conditions. One might recall here the free-spirited Effi
Briest of Theodor Fontane's novel by the same title and her arranged
union to the much senior Geert Innstetten, whose pedantry and out-
dated views stifle the heart of his child-wife until her affair with
Crampas brings the plot to a tragic end. Yet, though adultery is central to both novels, in *La Regenta* Ana becomes the object of conquest for two opposed suitors—Álvaro Mesía, the local Don Juan,
and Fermín de Pas, her perverse confessor—who seek to take her

from her husband. Caught between the two and confused by enigmatic desires, she yields to the temptations of Mesía, the "Messiah" who has come to save her, literally, in the flesh. The priest takes his revenge, and when Ana's husband learns of the affair, he challenges Álvaro to a duel, much like the by now anachronistic honor rite performed between Innstetten and Crampas in Fontane's novel. For Clarín, however, these honor rites are as pathetic as the degenerative world that clings to them. Hence, far from being the victor his name implies, Quintanar dies a pitiable death, Mesía leaves town, and Ana finds herself ruined.

Throughout the novel, Clarín showcases man's proclivity to measure himself against and feel challenged by his fellow man. While there are occasions when Álvaro Mesía appears the superior specimen when set in relief against those of his circle, like Pepe Ronzal (alias Trabuco), who "had to confess to himself that he was inferior to his beautiful ideal [Mesía]," or Paco Vegallana, who "endeavored to imitate the ideas and tastes of his idol [Mesía]," or even all of those anonymous onlookers of the theater who "envied him [Mesía] as much as they admired his good fortune and handsome appearance," the featured rivalry of La Regenta is that between Mesía and Fermín de Pas, the power-hungry priest whose spiritual relationship with Ana presents a very material threat.[4] When De Pas, who for his feminized frock is also the focus of gender blurring in the text, shows up for lunch at Paco's house near the end of the first half of the novel, Mesía finds himself seated at the same table face-to-face with his rival in the presence of Ana (and, rather unimportantly, her husband, Víctor Quintanar, so old and impotent as to be nothing more than a nuisance or, when necessary, a strategic tool for these two suitors). Alarmed by Ana's reaction of disappointment upon learning that De Pas does not plan to join them in the gardens after the meal, Mesía experiences what feels like a sharp sting, which makes him angry, and judging her sentiment, he thinks to himself: "It meant that that woman was in fact really more interested than he had thought; and that there were obstacles, and of such a type! a priest! a good-looking priest, he had to admit" (1:598). The stage has been set for a "homosocial" confrontation between these two men, to use the language Eve Kosofsky Sedgwick has employed to describe this type of male-male desire made patent through the undesired woman,[5] which Darwin for his part would simply call the "law of battle" between rival males (The Descent, 2:323).

The actual altercation in Clarín's novel, however, yields no bloodshed. Instead, in a suggestive encounter, these two men become aware at this unexpected moment of the union latent in their opposition:

> And then, the dimmed eyes of the elegant Mesía lit up as they became fixed on the Magistrate [De Pas], who felt the jolt of the look and resisted it with his own, projecting his pupils like daggers out of all that effeminacy. Don Fermín was frightened by the impression that it made on him, more than the words, or even the gesture of Ana; he felt a sweet pleasure, a hot sensation, completely new, in his innermost regions; there, it was no longer that of vanity gently gratified, but rather of some heartstrings that sounded in a way he had never known . . . and it was precisely at that moment when he found himself under the eyes of Don Álvaro; it was a look that transformed itself, upon impact, into a challenge. . . . They were both standing, close to each other, both arrogant, lithe; the tight jacket of Mesía, fitted, severe, displayed his gravity with lines no less dignified and elegant . . . than those of the pompous, hieratic skirt of the cleric that shone like the sun, falling to the earth. (*La Regenta*, 1:598)

Clarín makes clear that behind rivalry lurks desire. Ana does not fuel the "stronger passions" of these two males; for Mesía and De Pas she exists as object. Instead, the rivalry itself subsumes the desire each suitor believes he experiences for her, and thus the attraction between the two men. Moreover, it is not by chance that the very next episode involves the novel's most memorable test of strength, in which Don Fermín rescues Obdulia, the town's mischievous coquette, from a dislodged swing with a superhuman show of force, causing Mesía to see the priest as "an athlete, a man very capable of killing him with a single blow" (1:604). These moments show a sizing up between the two men, both psychological and physical, as a significant stage in the law of male-male combat.

As a relationship of mediation, the rivalry of sexual selection (whether in Clarín or Darwin) hides the dark secret of desire, or what René Girard has called the "double bind" predicament.[6] Girard writes that "rivalry does not arise because of the fortuitous convergence of two desires on a single object; rather, the subject desires the object because the rival desires it. . . . The rival, then, serves as a model for the subject . . . in regard to desires" (145). This "unchanneled mimetic impulse" causes conflict in that "it invites its own rebuffs" as it gyrates toward "the signifier of ultimate desire . . . whose beauty depends on its being inaccessible and impenetrable" (148). The structural model for this theory, "triangular desire," defines novelistic discourse; it is "the desire which transfigures its object" and denounces the "illusion of autonomy to which modern man is passionately devoted."[7] That is to say, mediated desire can only be transcended through death, since death by triangulation, so to speak, brings about the heightened awareness that being, because mediated, is social, and every such recognition, in turn, delivers the same ontological rebirth, as in the novels of Miguel de Cervantes and Marcel Proust, for what it sows—an end to desire, now made empty, and hence to social *being*.

This schematization interests a critic like Sedgwick in particular for the way it shows that "the bond that links the two rivals is as intense and potent as the bond that links either of the rivals to the beloved."[8] What Sedgwick is right to point out, however, are the diachronic, "hidden obliquities" of the synchronic, "hidden symmetries" Girard lays out (22). In other words, boundary drawing for male bonds is never arbitrary when it comes to the sexual/nonsexual power determinants from one historical period and place to the next, given that such boundaries mask asymmetrical distributions of power in the gendered configuration of such rivalries. Girard "perceives no discontinuity in the homosocial continuum" (24), but the continuum, in fact, shows considerable disruption over time with respect to what is and is not permissible when it comes to male-male bonds and the role of women in these. Therefore, only by getting at these "hidden obliquities" can we begin to understand "*men's* relations to male power" (24). These structures, the battles for instance, exclude woman even as they appear to draw her in by being "about her" from the very beginning. In other words, there really is no "beloved" in the scenario Sedgwick describes. Power relationships between men and women, in this sense, are really power relationships between men. The "homosocial" then is patriarchal, and need not be heteronormative, per se, in the ways most often associated with heterosexual desire, though the structure itself never admits as much. This is why the exchange potential of women, as mates, matters and is also why Sedgwick draws on the anthropological studies of Claude Lévi-Strauss involving the traffic of women. Much more is in play: "What *counts* as the sexual is . . . variable and itself political" (15). Removing sex from the "homosocial" bond hides a complex past and an ideology, and together these rename the object and exploit her to the extent that she marshals the masquerade. Her political oppression cannot be divorced from her sexual alienation, and neither is it ahistorical.

Indeed, relationships of "homosocial" and "triangular" desire infuse *La Regenta*. In the pull between De Pas and Mesía, these two figures, as ideological placeholders in narrative, disguise what is in actuality a false dichotomy of the sacred (De Pas) and the secular (Mesía), in that the sacred is always transgressive and the secular always idolatrous. This "violent opposition" remains "transparent yet opaque."[9] It is little wonder then that on the early spring morning when the two men find themselves alone walking in opposite directions, as their paths cross unavoidably, "each continued on his side, but the next morning neither returned to the Paseo Grande . . . they feared another encounter" (*La Regenta*, 2:399). With no Ana in sight, their trepidation is not without cause, for at some level the rivalry tells them that to desire is to find oneself in the other, to discover *being* in a mirror. At the point of zero separation, according to Girard, death awaits, and this intuition frightens Mesía and De Pas. An erasure of distance means an end to mediation and, in Sedgwick's model, a collapse of the sexual power structure. That morning, so close to each other, they both sense the rivalry itself to be threatened and fear the consequences of the union.

Yet mediated desire focused in this way on its end of consummation does not reach the other face of rivalry in *La Regenta*. When it comes to sexual selection in the cultural context, Clarín shows the most pivotal moments of male-male combat to occur not between Mesía and De Pas but rather in the mind of their selector. The power of the written word over Ana, whether from her readings of Romantic literature, the mysticism of Santa Teresa, or the letters from her confessor, represents a central theme in the novel and one that spills over to questions of Ana as an author of her own self-seduction.[10] Often, in those instances of interior monologue when Ana carries out comparative judgments of her two suitors, reflections on fiction, poetry, and drama frame her imaginative musings. At Paco's, before Álvaro and Fermín experience the above confrontation between each other, Ana evaluates them according to discrete selector criteria. Her thoughts come across in free indirect discourse: "Ana saw them together, both tall, Mesía a bit taller, both smart and elegant, each in his own way; more robust the Magistrate, more nobly formed Don Álvaro, more intelligent for his gestures and look the cleric, more graceful features the elegant one" (1:582). She weaves these two men together in her consciousness and then thinks of her conscience and earlier confession with Fermín, of his seductive voice filled with "promises of enlightenment and of poetry," and of the books in which "a few times she had read of something like this" (1:582).[11] Though confused, Ana was clear on one thing: "In Don Fermín lay salvation, the promise of a virtuous life . . . that at the same time gave dignity and purpose to the dead, brutish, unbearable existence that [the town of] Vetusta had offered her to that day. For the same reason she was certain of saving herself from the blatantly criminal temptation of Don Álvaro; giving herself to Don Fermín, she wanted to defy the danger" (1:583). In this way, she scripts the rivalry, even while an authorial cynicism lurks throughout.

Indeed, we might recall from earlier discussions of sexual selection alongside feminism and science studies that Darwin's "law of battle" extends to an array of questions about female taste. There I showed how his remarks on the "appreciation of the beautiful" (*The Descent*, 2:402) underwrite the assumption that the selected variations behind male refinements, which serve no other purpose than to charm the female, have led scientists like Helena Cronin to ask if females can shape males. The data tell us they do. But I would add that novelists, Clarín among them, were probing these same possibilities in the years following Darwin's debate with Alfred Russell Wallace over "good taste" versus "good sense." With respect to *The Descent* and sexual dimorphism, that is, the appearance of secondary traits that distinguish males from females, the two central scientific issues were (and continue to be) (1) the relationship between the apparent boundlessness of sexual selection under the pressures of female preference and (2) whether or not such preference is harmful when it reaches extremes so extravagant that the effected variations become detrimental to both sexes. I do not believe literature in the late nineteenth century can be excluded from this fascination and am certain in the case of *La Regenta* that Ana's place in male-male combat complicates the degree of direct agency that can be attributed to the rivals who fight for her possession in their "homosocial" power play. Far from being a passive spectator as Darwin's other law of female "passive" choice suggests, Clarín's selector-protagonist actively assigns meaning to the roles of her respective suitors so as to guide her actions and theirs.

Writing on love as "civilization's miracle," Stendhal avows that "desire is what leads to deeds."[12] He sees women's modesty at once as the engine of shame, but always in conjunction with the imagination, which protects love so as to give it "the chance to survive" (83). As we have seen, Ana indeed feels shameful for her thoughts and often pulls back or feels attracted toward De Pas rather than Mesía because of her Catholic indoctrination and the allure of salvation. Yet Stendhal's musings also illuminate the chivalric hue that colors Ana's fantasies, because the imaginative feats of Mesía and De Pas both confirm and measure, for her, the ardor she inspires in them. That is to say, she marries desires and deeds in her mind, while also using the imagination to check herself, as Stendhal would have it, with interjections about the risks to her honor and virtue. At no point is this more the case than in that moment after the meal when she sees the stare down between her two suitors and formulates its significance:

> Both seemed beautiful and interesting to her . . . both were thinking about her, that was for sure; Don Fermín like a protector friend, the other as an enemy of her virtue, but lover of her beauty; she would grant victory to the one who deserved it, to the good angel, who was a little less tall, who did not have the mustache (that always looked good), but who was valiant, handsome in his own way, as much as possible from under a cassock. . . . And above all, those two men looking at each other in that way for her, each claiming victory with a different end, the conquest of her will. . . . Honor, that mysterious thing that was always present in the verses her husband recited, was in no danger; it went without saying that there was no need to think about that; but it could be good that a man as intelligent as the Magistrate might defend her against the more or less fearsome attacks of that good young man, who was no frog either, who was showing plenty of tact, great care, and what was worse, a true interest in her.
> (La Regenta, 1:599)

Without question, an ironic disconnect resonates from her thoughts, especially given that the two men are actually thinking not about her but about each other, and Ana's own vanity or insecurities or unhappiness might be all that is needed to explain the comical surface of her ideas. It might also be, as Tony Tanner avers, that "just as one could say that by entering into an adulterous relationship, a person introduces a new element of narrative into his or her life, initiates a new living 'story,' so for the novelist it is often not really marriage that initiates and inspires his narrative, but adultery."[13] These avenues might indeed give sufficient clarification for why Ana should *desire* desire, or why the author should need her to do so, in the same way that Girard's writing on external mediation might illustrate Ana's yearnings to be modeled on those of fictional heroines or religious martyrs far removed from her "real life" situation.

However, I think it more useful, especially in terms of the indeterminacy of Darwinian sexual selection, to move from these questions of *what* to the *why* of narrative. Does the reason Ana plots the rivalry that engulfs her also compel Álvaro to write himself into a role of the Don Juan figure or her husband Víctor to cast himself in his own Calderonian intrigues? Is desire behind the laughable, yet lamentable, duel at the novel's end? Peter Brooks talks about these issues in terms of narrative desire: "We can . . . conceive of the reading of plot as a form of desire that carries us forward, onward, through the text. Narratives both tell of desire . . . and arouse and make use of desire as dynamic of signification."[14] His notion of "reading for the plot" resonates with respect to *La Regenta* if the characters themselves, rather than just the reader of the novel, are seen to desire narrative, for, as Sedgwick, too, points out, "ideology . . . is always implicitly narrative."[15] Brooks is right then to surmise that "desire as narrative thematic, desire as narrative motor, and desire as the very intention of narrative language and the act of telling all seem to stand in close interrelation," for it is true that narratives "lay bare the nature of narration as a form of human desire."[16] This theory sheds light on Ana's literary comparisons of Mesía and De Pas, as well as other manifestations of her narrative desire, such as when the theatrical production of Zorrilla's play prompts her to transpose Fermín to her Tenorio (*La Regenta*, 1:131) or the mass procession induces her to read her body in the mirror as if a textual image of the Virgin (2:350). She is complicit in trafficking herself through these mediations of the "homosocial" rivalry that conditions the sexual politics responsible for her alienated repression.

The risks of reading rivalry for plot, though, do not fully take shape until Fermín tells Ana of his humiliation at the hands of Álvaro and his cronies, who have passed by his residence at three in the morning, drunk, shouting, "Álvaro! Álvaro! here lives . . . your rival . . ." (2:358). At that moment, for Ana, narrative desire collides with what has become a distasteful reality: "Ana looked frightened at the Magistrate. . . . It appeared she did not understand his words" (2:358). His speech, however, brings everything to the surface: "It was the first time the Magistrate had spoken in that way . . . he had said: *your rival*, with force" (2:358). Unable to make intelligible to herself the "homosocial" dimension even when confronted with such language, she now must either face the possibility of this "repugnant absurdity" (2:396), that is, that De Pas wants to have sex with her (and, by extension, with

Mesía), or else allow her desire to resolve through narration an imagined rivalry that has become actual. She chooses the latter.

In a Darwinian rewrite of the earlier scripted sexual selection, she tells herself that consummation with Álvaro, as opposed to Fermín, would be perfectly "within the natural laws" (2:488). Then, she inverts the ending of her previous scenario, by inventing an inversion of roles between the angel (Mesía) and enemy (De Pas): "The passion, which now gratified her with its new life, conquering, close to exploding, suggested to her with sophism after sophism that she should find the Magistrate's conduct to be repugnant, despicable, criminal, and that of Mesía, noble and chivalric" (2:488). Considerable theoretical writing has been done on desire, much of it applicable to La Regenta, but none weds desire and invention as well as Brooks's work on narrative when it comes to why Ana chooses to read and revise the male-male rivalry of the sexual selection that engulfs her.[17] The reason Brooks is so useful is that he brings us back to Darwin via the indefinite mechanics of the dynamic in the social sphere as represented by Clarín. But we must not lose sight of Sedgwick either, in that her theorizing bridges Ana's narrative desire to the ideological operation of invention in this instance of female choice: "The exact, contingent space of indeterminacy—the place of shifting over time—of the mutual boundaries between the political and the sexual is, in fact, the most fertile space of ideological formation."[18] The relation of sex to power will always be volatile and hence unstable. In other words, it is Ana's sexual alienation, her exclusion from the rivalry rather than inclusion, that enables her response. The Virgin of the mass procession, the verses of Santa Teresa, the performance of Zorrilla's play, these symbolic imaginings have a cultural history, "shifting over time," and blended together in the protagonist's curious reconciliation. Darwin could not have been more right when he wrote: "When we behold two males fighting for the possession of the female . . . and performing the strangest antics . . . we cannot doubt that . . . they know what they are about" (The Descent, 1:258). The possession of her is paramount to the power of men's relations, but these sociopolitical stakes and the "hidden obliquities" inherent in them, the boundaries, woman made conduit, the trafficking, the masking of a continuum, and the indeterminacy of rivalry itself cannot be perceived in Darwinian sexual selection absent their representation. The realism of Clarín's novel thus serves to decode Darwin.

RITUALS OF REGENERATION

Nevertheless, though rivalry is essential to Darwinian sexual selection and *La Regenta*, it can only take us so far. It no doubt brings Darwin and Clarín together, while introducing desire and invention into their pairing, but the triangular relationship among Mesía, De Pas, and Ana, albeit driven by constructions of narrative, stops short of exposing the true extent of the open-ended dynamism of sexual selection. In other words, these rivalries in many ways remain scripted, and hence legible, especially in light of how much theorizing has been done on rivalry. It is, as I said in the introduction, where scholars of literature have felt most comfortable in the past several decades. Irony, moreover, remains something we must superimpose on rivalry in Clarín's first novel, rather than draw out as internal to it—for example, that Ana assumes the men are thinking of her, when in fact they are thinking of each other. Likewise, with these discussions of rivalry in *La Regenta*, we can only approximate the other key elements of gender blurring and performance on a surface level, and their relationship to an interactive irony is far from clear. In truth, despite holding clues to the sociopolitical consequence of "the law of battle" among men, whether between Mesía and De Pas or in Ana's imagination, rivalry serves a less evident but more important purpose by leading us to ritual, the organizing force behind the operative mechanics of Darwinian sexual selection. The courtship ritual assumes uncommon complexity in Clarín's later novel, *Su único hijo*, and its unfinished quality reflects the workings of the fundamental law of female choice in Darwinian sexual selection to be ethical in the continual, indeterminate *becoming* of its intersubjective playfulness.

Though Clarín implicates Ana in the rivalry between Mesía and De Pas, via her fantasies and fictions, female participation within male rivalry is not included in Darwin's model as such. Plus, as we have come to see, women are already implicated in male-male rivalries, paradoxically, through their exclusion. We might imagine, therefore, from the terminology that what Darwin calls female "passive" choice can come only after the rivalry has been decided, which would be the case in Ana's selection of Víctor (a man whom she does not desire, except perhaps as surrogate father) after he had already "won" out over Don Frutos Redondo (*La Regenta*, 1:313–17). Furthermore, the degree to which male-male combat becomes manifest in sexual selection remains highly variable, though it is always present as long as one male is selected from among other males, and sexual selection, as Darwin notes, would not have the same effects, especially in terms of sexual dimorphism, were it not for rivalry.

However, according to Darwin, since sexual selection cannot function without female choice, or else is greatly impeded, such choice alone remains the theory's absolute constant. Conversely, after the "law of battle" plays out, as with Mesía and De Pas, at the moment of choosing in sexual selection desire on the part of the female has run its course (if she ever desired the male to begin with, which may not be the case), because at this point the female selector understands, given the circumstances surrounding her choice, that consummation is a certainty. Without checks, real or fictitious, the appetite of desire is no longer spurred by obstacles in Darwinian sexual selection at the moment of choice. Rivalry thus stands subordinate to the circumstances of selection, that is, the interaction of events or what Darwin in *The Descent* calls "courtship" on so many occasions. As process, courtship demands the participation of both sexes, and rivalry, with all that it entails, remains a secondary component often between the males alone in nature (where the ideological dimension of the "homosocial" bond does not exist), even if also occurring in the mind of a female selector like Ana. Invention is important because, as shall be shown, it feeds and is fed by ritual, which structures courtship and shows why the ethics of irony in Clarín explain a great deal about an indeterminate Darwin. Hence, rivalry taken through the theories of Girard and Sedgwick on mediated desire up to Brooks on reading for plot paves the way for ritual in *Su único hijo*, where sexual selection shows how we might imagine each individual as unfinished according to choice in reproduction, whether real or not.

To speak of the "courtship ritual" is commonplace today, but Darwin never pairs the two terms as such in *The Descent*. Instead, in most instances, he describes courtship as a "complex affair" (1:296) or else emphasizes aspects like "display" (2:399). The absence of the word "ritual" from Darwin's text, however, does not mean that courtship is not a ritual; it simply requires that the connection be made with a historical and theoretical context for ritual.[19] In its analytic usage, "ritual" first came to be employed in the nineteenth century "to identify what was believed to be a universal category of human experience," as fundamental to culture, and generally, "as action" rather than as a conceptual construct, like myth.[20] Roy A. Rappaport defines ritual as "the performance of more or less invariant sequences of formal acts and utterances not entirely encoded by the performers" and goes as far as to maintain that "unless there is a performance there is no ritual."[21] In addition to the stress he places on the fundamental inseparability between ritual and performance, a claim many anthropologists would acknowledge but question, Rappaport makes the important distinction that ritual should be conceived of as formal rather than functional (26–27); it is, in this way, a unique medium: "Ritual is not simply an alternative way to express any manner of thing . . . certain meanings and effects can best, or even *only* [italics original], be expressed or achieved in ritual" (30). In sum, from these selected postulations, ritual should be understood in terms of action, performance, and form. Ritual reduced to symbolic representation, or by extension to an attempt to make sense or control one's environment, misses its dynamic character.

Toward an articulation of the purpose of ritual, Claude Lévi-Strauss contends that rituals conjoin by taking "asymmetry" to "equilibrium."[22] He sees them as different from games, which tend to move toward indications of inequality, winners and losers, premised on established rules in which the structure produces events. Rituals, by contrast, "take to pieces and reconstruct sets of events" (33) using their structural patterns to varying ends. We might pause here to wonder if "mating games" is an apt way to describe courtship; though this nomenclature may denote the importance of play, it seems to miss the sort of always unfolding "bricolage" (33) quality Lévi-Strauss and, I think, Darwin would use to characterize sexual selection. In any case, for now, it is enough to point out that "thought, merely by being thought, creates an ever-increasing gap between the intellect and life. Ritual is not a reaction to life; it is a reaction to what thought has made of life. It is not a direct response to the world, or even to experience of the world; it is a response to the way man thinks of the world."[23] Thus, ritual counteracts the "resistance of man's thought to man himself" (681). Without ritual, according to Lévi-Strauss, we might overthink ourselves right out of life, into a state of intellectual inaction.[24] In such stasis, there could be no reproduction.

Picking up where Lévi-Strauss leaves off, Don Handelman therefore pushes ritual toward reproduction, as a phenomenon of self-organization whose integrity comes from within rather than from the social surround. As such, ritual ceases to be a static solution to social relations and instead constitutes pure form, prone to curve in on itself toward self-closure, into self-reference in ever-greater complexity, until "the most complex kind of agency a ritual can have built into its design is that of making radical change through its own interior dynamics."[25] Handelman's theorizing on ritual offers a corrective to what Rappaport reduces to "invariant sequences" and the popular perception of ritual simply as mindless repetition. Instead, in its most developed composition ritual undergoes internal transformations wrought by the participants according to their interrelationships and hence because subject to continuous differentiation can itself be transformative in nature.

This transformative quality is the first stage in this brief exposition of the depth of ritual as it pertains to Darwinian sexual selection and Clarín. The second starts from Bruce Kapferer's assertion that ritual is best understood as an aesthetic domain in which "human beings invent, or through the imagination construct, their realities into existence."[26] In other words, it is transformative according to the caprices that emerge contingent on circumstance. He calls this ritual space "a habitus that, as part of its vital dynamic, is orienting and reorienting the bodies of participants, directing them into meanings that they are frequently made to produce and enjoined to bring before their conscious awareness" (42).[27] Ultimately, ritual's intrinsic capacity to deconstruct and reconstruct thought complicates its association with performance. Though disinclined to negate the coupling, Kapferer views ritual not as the staged representation but rather as "closer to what goes on behind the scenes in theatrical performance" (50–51). In sum, through ritual, "social realities are forged anew" (51), and courtship in this context enables a departure from transparent mannerisms, and even the bare bones of sexual selection, to those moments when Darwinian laws on dimorphism, as uncertain as they may be, break down even further only to resurface under an unfamiliar guise, which once depicted proves to originate, in a curious return, from the very ambivalence of the claims Darwin makes in *The Descent* about gender differentiation.

Since ritual acts as a "generative force" of new social relations, writes Kapferer (38), the approach to courtship in Clarín as ritual promises to illustrate unforeseen implications of Darwinian sexual selection in its novelistic expression, especially with regard to role-playing and ambivalence about sexual dimorphism. In addition to the selector reversals characteristic of Darwin's theory, like those treated in the previous chapters, at times Darwin blurs the gender distinctions he takes such pains to establish. Along these lines, John Tyler Bonner

and Robert M. May in their introduction to *The Descent* make a provocative qualification regarding the validity of its scientific contributions: "The discussion of sexual selection in *The Descent* is greatly
hindered by Darwin's lack of understanding of the specific biological mechanisms producing differences between males and females"
(xxxi). For the purposes of our analysis of Clarín's novels, two claims
by Darwin on this subject suffice for an illustration of this scientific
shortcoming. First, Darwin lets it be known that "in the dim obscu-
rity of the past we can see . . . the two sexes united in the same individual" (2:389); second, he qualifies his doubts on the power dynamics between men and women with a vague remark much earlier about
"a few exceptional cases" in which there has been "a complete transposition of the ordinary characters proper to each sex" (1:276), with
the females acquiring male traits and vice versa. For nineteenth-century men preoccupied by the "woman question," the former of these
statements suggests a descent potentially more troublesome than that
of simian ancestry, while the latter questions the outcome of gender
differentiation all together.

Speaking on characters from Spanish novels at the end of the nineteenth century, including Fermín de Pas from *La Regenta*, Ricardo
Krauel notes the "destabilization of the certainties of masculine and
feminine" that attests to a "crisis of indifferentiation."[28] Also concerned with *La Regenta*, Jo Labanyi argues that Clarín's efforts to
cross gender codes signal a critique of cultural regression in contrast
to the Darwinian "notion that females are incomplete males, whose
development has been arrested at a lower evolutionary stage," and
that he (Clarín) "insist[s] that both men and women have evolved out
of an original indifferentiation."[29] While she does well to bring attention to Clarín's transgression of masculine and feminine, Labanyi
overlooks what Darwin says about the "two sexes united in the same
individual" and hence mischaracterizes the relationship of his science to Clarín when it comes to issues of gender. For Clarín does not
in fact differ from Darwin here. The problem is that Darwin's own
uncertainty, coupled with the legacy of his association with sexual
differentiation, does not make it any easier to know this. In other
words, Labanyi's reading is not to be faulted but rather showcased as
an example of why the indeterminism inherent in Darwin's writing
causes such difficulty.

Still, the best case for gender ambivalence in Clarín is not *La
Regenta* but instead his second novel, *Su único hijo*. In the context

of this work, Noël Valis describes the "inner androgyne that exists in Bonifacio," the patriarchal protagonist made maternal; Abigail Lee Six states that "questions are raised throughout the novel about gender identities"; Beth Wietelmann Bauer finds pervasive travesty via "cross-dressing and gender confusion," which open the text to "plural meanings and perspectives"; and Roberto G. Sánchez affirms that "gender roles are confused and with them, the traditional notions of masculine and feminine."[30] All of the aforementioned critics agree on gender blurring in Clarín, with particular accord in the case of *Su único hijo*, and they share a tendency to identify gender as a theme and reflect on its implications as such. Consequently, it makes sense to turn to Darwin for some answers to why the constitutive relationship of courtship in these novels involves this confusion of the sexes and what its dynamic interaction has to do with irony, which Carolyn Richmond has called the "saving grace" of Clarín's fiction.[31]

The ritual of sexual selection, now understood as a formal medium for altering the constitution of social relations, allows for the reconsideration of gender ambiguities in Clarín and Darwin. No doubt, courtship permeates *La Regenta*, and, to use Handelman's model, varied degrees of self-referential curvature exist. The straightforwardness of the arranged union between Ana and Víctor, who to a degree "competed" with Don Frutos, exemplifies a linear track or "minimal self-closure,"[32] following a classic storyline, while Ana's eventual adultery with Mesía folds in on itself multiple times from, listing the more memorable turns, the theater experience at the Zorrilla play to readings of Santa Teresa to the Holy Week procession to the Carnival dance to the country excursion and storm to the garden wall Mesía climbs to reach Ana in her own bed. Yet while gender crossover does factor in *La Regenta*, namely, in the characters of Fermín and his domineering mother, the blurring remains tangential and at times contrived. Moreover, ritual in *La Regenta* literally collapses on itself with Ana's fall and the duel between Mesía and Víctor, for Clarín exhausts the conventions of the adultery plot. The work's trajectory and outcome are indicative of what Handelman might categorize under his second degree of self-closure. His example is a dance that begins spontaneously only to gyrate round and round in ever more complex elaborations, until the form peaks and participants can no longer sustain the movement.[33] Sexual selection in Clarín's first novel runs just such a course, as an unconscious Ana on the cathedral floor at the conclusion confirms.

Yet what is latent in *La Regenta*, the courtship ritual as performance, Clarín explodes in *Su único hijo* by insisting that sexual selection occurs in the theater both of the text and of the mind of its idealistic protagonist, Bonifacio (Bonis) Reyes, whom the author parodies as a sentimental romantic. More important, in this novel ritual arrives at reproduction, the catalyst and end of sexual selection, via a dramatic, imaginative reconfiguration of social relations toward gendered inversions of choice. In effect, Clarín dispenses with the formalities of the "selection" history between Bonifacio and his bride, Emma Valcárcel, in the first few pages of the text. Working as a clerk for Emma's father, Bonifacio attracts her attention. An only child, the juvenile, spoiled, and headstrong Emma "dragged him by force" in an attempted lovers' runaway, and once caught by her father, she spends some time in a convent until he dies.[34] When Bonis disappears from the town, unable to find him Emma marries an aged and ailing American who not long afterward leaves her a widow. Lineage, honor, and lost youth then drive her to entreat a lovesick cousin, Sebastián, to track Bonifacio down; they marry, and eight days later she "understood that he was not the same Bonifacio she had dreamed of" (7). Although his good looks never disappoint her, Emma takes melancholic pleasure in seeing herself as a "resigned victim" (20) of poor choice.

Dominant, prodigal, and of violent temper, Emma treats Bonifacio as a "miserable plebian," and yearning for "emancipation," he experiences acute sadness and annoyance after his wife's first failed pregnancy, foremost, for being denied a son and, second, for having to endure "incessant persecution" under her rule and never-ending maladies (22–23). He becomes her "slave" (27), and the only escapes are his nostalgic conversations with a circle of "ex-Romantics" (33) and the theater, especially rehearsals, where he succumbs to the beauty and voice of the exotic soprano Serafina Gorgheggi, whose voice is in and of itself an inversion of the prowess Darwin attributes to male songbirds. From here, Clarín carries his reader through a series of humorous scenes, taking aim at illicit love and Flaubertian devices, in which the hapless Bonifacio seeks salvation through his overactive imagination. The ritual form, however, even under the pressures of parody and slapstick that play on Bonifacio's manliness, maintains stability through the transgressions we recognize in the conventions of the adultery plot. Included among these are "the dangerous operation of the *declaration* [italics original]" of unfaithful love (55), the

passions born as if from a novel (56, 85, 92), the "catastrophe" of his
wife and lover together (144), the moment when Emma discovers the
amorous escapades, and the point at which Bonis must lie to her "like
a hero" despite the risks (153).

At the same time, however, a distinct "complexification" of ritual begins to emerge in the gender ambivalence and role-playing that
materializes "behind the scenes,"[35] internal to Bonifacio and other
characters, rather than assigned to them from the outside by a cynical
narrator, as tends to be the case in *La Regenta*. That is, the ritual of
sexual selection becomes self-referential as it organizes itself in a way
that "would not occur without the erasure of boundaries," the third
and final degree of ritual self-closure.[36] This shift arises when Emma
smells the scent of a rival on her husband and forces him to resume
"the intimacy of intimacies" (*Su único hijo*, 111). In order to fulfill
"his most rudimentary duties as husband" (111), Bonis pictures himself as his wife's lover, though his wife's bestial display and orgasm
horrify him, and after he opens his *"eyes to reality"* (113; italics original), he cannot help but characterize Emma as "a magnificent man
of action" (114), in what Peter Gay would describe as the *femme-
homme* that became "a specter for terrified men to conjure with" in
the nineteenth century.[37] She, for her part, after learning of Bonifacio's affair manhandles him by the neck in a scene of burlesque eroticism and with the boot that led her to Serafina now in his face proclaims: "Look, look, I am *la Gorgheggi* " (*Su único hijo*, 161). And
when it comes to pass from these revivals of "the intimacy of intimacies," or more likely from Emma's own suggested infidelities, that
she is pregnant, Bonifacio hears the "mystery of the Annunciation"
from Serafina's lips and thinks to himself: "I am going to be a sort of
virgin mother . . . that is, a father . . . mother; I am going to have a
son, legitimate of course, that although delivered to me by you [con-
flation of Serafina and Emma], *materially*, he will be *entirely* mine"
(200; italics original). For Bonifacio, a Darwinian case of "the two
sexes united in the same individual" (*The Descent*, 2:389), descent is
duplication, and ritual creation, the "coronation" of "another Reyes
[Kings]" (*Su único hijo*, 291), amounts to the reproductive end of sexual selection.

The reproduction of ritual appears, then, to function as repetition,
yet like all copies, simulacrum here is at once the same and different.
After all, Bonis declares: "A son, a son of my soul! That is the avatar
that I need. A being who will be me, but beginning anew, outside of

me, with blood from my blood!" (228). Clarín does not disappoint; this son is born. Indeed, in certain respects his image points to the father, for Emma, now forty, is made to reflect on the choice she made so long ago: "That *was* [italics original] him, yes, him, the son that was there, that announced with the pain of the mother, with that sad and mysterious solemnity, grave and sublime in its uncertainty, all the great moments of natural life" (283). The birth brings the revelation that the child *was* (most uncertainly) Bonis. Yet female choice for the maternal father is a different matter all together, as we gather from the exclamation he makes to himself: "He was going to be a father!" (287). Repetition, through ritual, becomes pure invention as he lays individual claim over its operation. He perceives in the child "the living image of his own face, as he had seen it at times in a mirror, at night, when he cried alone out of humiliation, out of misfortune" (292), the very same mirror that reminded him of the night when his mother had died, and it matters not that "others could not see the likeness" (293). There is, so it happens, a second and final Annunciation from Serafina: "Bonis, you always were an imbecile. Your son . . . is not your son" (323), but her words fall on deaf ears. Bonis reads fatherhood in the ritual itself, he interprets signs, he re-embeds indeterminate Darwinian sexual selection in the gaps he fills with his own maternal desire: "Serafina . . . I forgive you . . . my son is my son . . . I have faith in my son . . . I am sure . . . my son . . . he is my son . . . he is my son! . . . I have not had time to explain to you what now passes through me: what it is to be a father" (324). What passes through him, "what it is to be a father," is a defiant certainty in the face of biological uncertainty, but it is also what conjoins gender asymmetry through ritual, as Lévi-Strauss might explain it. Certainty in paternity is an appropriation of a natural maternal privilege. Hence, Bonifacio's final declaration brings an end to this self-organizing, ritualistic sexual selection, which generates new social relations in the aesthetic habitus of its Darwinian form.

Yet the irony is that there is no closure, at least not in the ways we tend to associate a conclusion of the sort Bonis gives with his own self-fashioned resolution. To show why requires that irony be understood as an interaction in its relationship to the transformative capacity of ritual, for this, in turn, will reveal the particular ways Clarín and Darwin intertwine, each bringing to light new insights about the other. The writings of Kierkegaard begin best the work of achieving this synthesis between literature and science, in that his conception of irony comes closest to the way it has traditionally been attributed to Clarín, though no connection, to my knowledge, has ever been drawn between the two. Kierkegaard starts from the premise that all irony is characterized by "saying the opposite of what is meant," which makes the phenomenon of irony "not the essence but the opposite of the essence."[38] In this way, irony acts as a "negation" (248) of the truth value of the literal statement. Whether it be something communicated "earnestly that is not meant in earnest" or else jestingly "that is meant in earnest" (248), irony cancels the face value of meaning. For Kierkegaard, this cancellation shows everything to be vain, except for the ironic subject itself. Hence, in irony, "everything becomes nothing," but only if this nothingness remains "full of content," like the silence of the night (258). The content behind the cardboard world created by Clarín's irony in *La Regenta* reads as a straightforward social critique; it interests the reader for what it says, in particular, about the history of Restoration Spain and its moral corruption and, more generally, for what it reveals about the ugliness that haunts humanity in circumstances of hypocrisy and oppression. Nevertheless, this negation, howsoever it might be construed, remains ironically transparent.

However, when Clarín sets himself to compose *Su único hijo*, irony emerges closer to what George Meredith calls the Comic Spirit, which "conceives a definite situation for a number of characters, and rejects all accessories in the exclusive pursuit of them and their speech."[39] Meredith aligns the Comic Spirit with Art and sets it against the Science, to blame for the realistic method, that "introduced us to our o'er-hoary ancestry . . . whereupon we set up a primeval chattering to rival the Amazon forest nigh nightfall, cured, we fancied. And before daybreak our disease was hanging on to us again, with the extension of a tail. . . . That is all we got from Science" (4). Science versus Art here in Meredith's view, and Darwinian Science at that, could very well define much of the critical discourse that treats *La Regenta* and *Su único hijo*, as the former conforms to the deterministic exigencies of high realism and the latter awakens us to the fragmented dawn of modernism. Such a separation, though, obfuscates a deeper continuity. Where opposition, union, where negation, sameness, but it takes Darwin within literature and, conversely, literature within Darwin to show these dynamics of convergence between Science and Art, *La Regenta* and *Su único hijo*, and thus the specious nature of these dichotomies.

If George Bernard Shaw is right to say that "in our novels . . . we see the most beautiful of all the masks: those devised to disguise the

brutalities of the sexual instinct in the earlier stages of its development,"[40] then we might say that Clarín indeed unmasks. The rivalries and rituals of his two novels examine these brutalities of sexual
selection under a microscope, and still, the author cannot do without masks in either work, for his irony covers an ethics of idealism
intrinsic to female choice. In other words, through the rivalries and
rituals of sexual selection, Clarín's masking of meaning moves from
one of negation (*La Regenta*) to that of the self-consciousness of intersubjectivity (*Su único hijo*). In the former, the mask appears real, as
the author believes in his deception, whereas in the latter, all parties
recognize the mask as a mask and accept it as such. This trajectory
brings Clarín to what Gary Handwerk calls "ethical irony."[41] In irony
at this stage, "an incompatibility in discourse suspends the question
of identity by frustrating any immediate coherence of the subject,"
and this suspension results in "a certain undecidability between alternatives" (2). The individual in this conception of irony becomes "con-
stitutively unfinished and incoherent" because the ethical makeup
undermines "the integrity of the subject it seemed to imply existed"
(3). Bonifacio represents just such an "unfinished" individual, as he
flows between male and female and hence exhibits the "intersubjective consciousness" Handwerk finds in irony painted with irony (43).
This heightened awareness of the interdependence of subjects yields a
"condition of being between," where the ironic conscience functions
as "an Absolute irreducible to specification that can still serve as a
basis for human interaction" (53). Ethical irony operates as interactive dynamic in *Su único hijo*, rather than as negation, through the in-
between ambivalence of gender, reproduction, and choice. Meredith's
Comic Spirit, for Handwerk, binds "individuals together in a community of reinterpretations" (94), in that the interface is both plural,
"a number of characters," and language based, tied to "their speech"
(95). In this context, Bonifacio's declaration at the culmination of his
relational ritual, at the threshold of repetition, shows the intersubjective reach of sexual selection.

   The Art of ethical irony, therefore, allows Clarín to realize the Science of alternative endings, but because Darwinian sexual selection
already weds the two, they cannot be divided as Meredith would have
it. In tandem, *La Regenta* and *Su único hijo* uncover what is behind
Darwin's clouded awareness of the operative mechanics that fuel the
"complex affair" of courtship, the generative forces of its rivalries and
rituals. Both works turn on oppositions, which merge and reemerge

out of the invention of individuals who take part in the creation of the environment they inherit, and Darwinian "strange antics" and "display" shape the indeterminism of its unfolding. Likewise, language is always in motion and, by extension, speech and music, for these means of expression originate in the competition and mating games of sexual selection. It is also always self-referential, promoting reconfigurations of meaning out of the relational nature of its own internal structure. Indeed, to return to Elizabeth Grosz's summation of Darwin and sexual selection with respect to language, it is quite powerful to imagine that origin is "a function of language,"[42] as an indicator of where we choose to differentiate according to resemblance, preexistence, or proximity. What we call origin amounts to the "discernable but noncalculable measure of degrees of difference" (23). We are, in other words, quite literally our relations when it comes to descent.

Hence, sexual selection in Clarín is a matter of play. Mating games, as it turns out, are less about what Lévi-Strauss defines against ritual in terms of controlled outcomes than they are about the possibility of infinite substitutions within a finite structure as understood by figures like Ferdinand de Saussure and Jacques Derrida. The ludic nature of language is something Nil Santiáñez explains to great effect in his treatment of La incógnita (1889) by Benito Pérez Galdós, where the literary act itself takes part in the fun.[43] Together, games and literature, as Santiáñez reminds us, have a long history, and with respect to language, the former were understood by Ludwig Wittgenstein, whose work on "family resemblances" frames Santiáñez's own study of modern Spain's literary history, to depend, first, on a self-consciousness that language games constitute our reality and, second, on those situations in which speakers play with the message of their speech.[44] Hence, the ethical as that which is moral, that is, in the common usage of being directed at the "good," makes "ethical irony" appear redundant, given that irony in the Kierkegaardian sense of negation aims at critique and implies judgment. The ethical half of this coupling, however, must be aligned not with morality but rather more broadly with Aesthetics. Wittgenstein uses such a repositioning to argue that events can never be ethical because, like facts, they can at best only ever have relative value. Since no experience has absolute value, the existence of language alone is ethical, and anything expressed to be ethical by means of language will remain nonsensical, though perfectly comprehensible and laudable. In this way, as I use the term, the "ethical" of "ethical irony" has little to do with subjective moral judgment and everything to do with what Wittgenstein calls the "miracle" of language.[45] Irony, though constructed with language, specifies a particular way language is used, whether toward negation or (as in this chapter) alternative meanings. So though "ethical irony" can be redundant, it need not have to be, so long as we go beyond "the boundaries of language," or what Emmanuel Lévinas characterizes as thinking rather than thought.[46]

The continuity, therefore, between Clarín's two novels runs from rivalries to rituals according to the desire, invention, and open-endedness of courtship in Darwinian sexual selection. Still, in the final scene of *La Regenta* an indifferent Nature overpowers language, once language has made palpable, through a perverse kiss, "the cold and viscous underbelly" (2:598) of its own destructive potential. Only acerbic silence remains after this testimony to Darwin's caution against the mating "ambition which passes too easily into selfishness" (*The Descent*, 2:326). With *Su único hijo*, however, Clarín sings a curious sequel to this tale, as he plays with reproduction, the unfinished individual, and a language that has rewritten sexual selection by the choice of "the two sexes united in the same individual" (*The Descent*, 2:389) through speech. As if the progeny were pure language, Bonifacio orchestrates his final lines in the third person, declaring to Serafina in self-referential syntax: "Bonifacio Reyes firmly believes that Antonio Reyes y Valcárcel is his/her/their [open third-person possessive pronoun] son. He is his/her/their only son. . . . He is his/her/their only son!" (*Su único hijo*, 324). Indeed, Antonio is *su único hijo*, at once plural, singular, and thus uniquely *único*, for in literature where choosing is ethical, decisions matter less than deciding. Sexual selection among humans is bound up with their language—it is playful, self-referential, and indeterminate; literature, as a language-based art, carries this capacity within it. In this way, Clarín shows how blurry such clarity on Darwinian laws can be.

CHAPTER SIX

Heirs and Errors—
Benito Pérez Galdós

With this, the final chapter of part 2, the outcomes, or "heirs and errors," of Darwinian sexual selection become the focus. As nebulous as it is troublesome for Darwin, heredity raises unique concerns in *The Descent*. Without genetic science, he must conjecture on a wide range of potential problems, from degenerative reversions to disadvantageous reproductive practices among the various social classes, and at one point even resorts to the "hypothesis of pangenesis, whether or not it be true" to explain the transmission of traits from one generation to the next according to which "every unit or cell of the body throws off gemmules or undeveloped atoms" to the offspring of both sexes (*The Descent*, 1:280).[1] Such imaginative imprecision mirrors analogous liberties in literature during the same period, and in the case of Benito Pérez Galdós, Spain's most iconic realist, the enigmatic laws of inheritance reflect the indeterminate course of a nation, its people, and the novel itself.

Given the title of Galdós's *La desheredada* (1881), interest in the novel's use of heredity is to be expected, whether as a tableau for characterization, a key to the social stratification of nineteenth-century Spain, or any number of like readings.[2] Yet there is also unique synergy between this work by Galdós and *The Descent*, and neither evolutionary science nor Galdosian realism is clear-cut with respect to the overlap between the two. Indeed, no feature of the realist novel enjoys the infamous reputation of heredity in equal measure, since the representation of characters *determined* by birth undercuts free will to the extent that their behavior is shown to be conditioned by the family line rather than personal volition. Nevertheless, unresolved issues of agency in Galdós's fiction, particularly with respect to his female protagonists, reflect Darwin's own ambivalent appeals to the imagination for his substantiation of the laws of inheritance. The theory of sexual selection, in addition, brings to the fore social anxieties about heredity, namely, that reproductive errors resulting from unfavorable matches will have far-reaching consequences for the welfare of the community. Darwinian sexual selection thus points to why Galdós, from a cultural standpoint, would take up disinheritance as a central problem; the plight of Spain, in moral and political disarray during the Restoration, cannot be divorced from the patriarchal limitations placed on female choice as Darwin understood it in evolutionary terms.

By the same token, Darwin's own preoccupations about heredity remain only partially intelligible absent the type of reformist ideology promoted by Galdós in fiction concerned with the ugly realities of the day. His writing is charged with political significance that operates in tandem with his push toward the novelistic innovations one finds in *La desheredada*, which delivers a host of destabilizing narrative approaches, including dramatic dialogue, second-person framing, and free indirect discourse. Moreover, the ambiguities of *The Descent* regarding heredity make Darwin's evolutionism a real question mark, and Galdós therefore constructs and later erases the identity of Isidora Rufete, the hapless protagonist of *La desheredada*, with an understanding that heredity of the sort is an inexact science. Her life is a tale of disillusionment, as she believes herself to have been orphaned and denied an aristocratic bloodline by mysterious circumstance. Rather than take an "inferior" husband, even if hardworking, she falls for a rake, endures abuse as the courtesan of a brutal politician, and ultimately turns to prostitution.

However, her tragic flaw, the heredity hubris she never overcomes, does not translate to tragedy without difficulty; the novel warns in the end not to fly with the "false wings" of empty ambition and envy.[3] In other words, since Isidora refuses to relinquish claims of noble birth, her rejection of multiple suitors and corresponding fall represent a critique of romantic idealism. Darwinian sexual selection thus at once underwrites the sentimentalism of Isidora and frames the fatalism behind her abject end. Extended to questions of genre, this tension illuminates unforeseen implications; the condemnation of illusion on the part of Galdós hides the attraction of an illusory reality. With her final renunciation of name, Isidora abolishes patriarchal lineage dependent upon the law, because *pater semper incertus*, and reconfigures maternal heritage on figurative terms, as her illegitimacy signals an indeterminate material transmission in the form of inherited inequalities born from her class and gender. Galdós, in this way, illuminates an otherwise obscure crossover in *The Descent* between uncertain heredity and the tenet of female choice in the sociopolitical praxis of their intersection at this moment in history.

In addition, heredity for Darwin, complicated by the complexities of sexual selection, exhibits a plasticity that foils predictable outcomes. The environment both shapes and is shaped by unexpected variations that alter it in some measure with each successive generation. To understand Darwin in this way is to posit that adaptation functions as a response and a catalyst. It is not simply appropriation or conformity, even if it involves recasting the old in new forms. In this sense, adaptation naturalizes the process of change through inherited traits by showing the process to be organic rather than oppositional, while making "progress" signify modifications in time. Though it need not have to, this constant flux can bring advances. I would offer as a case in point the Spanish reforms that favored women during these very decades, like the Civil Marriage Law and the Association for the Education of Women. In this vein, with his later novel *Fortunata y Jacinta* (1886–87) Galdós presents "two stories of married women" to show how the imagination, so central to Darwin's own thinking, begets the regenerative authorship of a nation and its symbolic heir.[4] He takes Darwinian heredity beyond the questions of free will raised by *La desheredada* toward humankind's creative capacity for change even in a world presumably defined by unchanging natural laws. Again, however, female choice proves to be of paramount importance. Though Galdós's novel begins with Juanito Santa Cruz, it ends with Fortunata and Jacinta, the women who manage to rewrite the ending through reproduction. The plot draws meaning from mismatches in sexual selection, that is, Darwinian "errors," and the characters craft their own corrections. The birth at the novel's conclusion therefore reshapes relations through new "family ties" and the interconnectedness of shared humanity enabled by enigmatic heredity.

HEIRS OF DISINHERITANCE

For its puzzling operation and effects, heredity confounds Darwin, but not so as to silence him. Rather, in *The Descent* he addresses the subject with sustained attention and often preoccupies himself with possible outcomes at the expense of sound explanations about how personal traits carry over from one generation to the next. In the first half of the text, Darwin makes inferences about heredity from his observations and personal experience. He opens with a hierarchical model of intelligence: "We may trace a perfect gradation from the mind of an utter idiot, lower than that of the lowest animal, to the mind of a Newton" (1:106); then, he speaks about inherited attributes: "With man . . . it is too certain that insanity and deteriorated mental powers . . . run in the same families" (1:110–11); and shortly thereafter, he introduces the little-understood phenomenon of reversions, "the reappearance of long-lost characters" (1:113), which can cause arrested development or even deformations (1:121–27). Darwin also pauses at one point to give an account of the formative role of environment: "There can . . . be no doubt that changed conditions induce [in the individual] an almost indefinite amount of fluctuating variability, by which the whole organisation is rendered in some degree plastic" (1:114). Thus, change, a constant in the Darwinian model, results from a process of adaptation in which reproductive success depends on the use or disuse of certain faculties, and the entire operation *might* effectuate corresponding modifications in offspring: "Whether . . . modifications would become hereditary, if the same habits of life were followed during many generations, is not known, but is probable" (1:117). In sum, from disquieting hierarchies to open-ended questions about nature versus nurture, Darwin's initial presentation of heredity teems with ambiguities. He recognizes that differences in mental capacity and tendencies toward psychological instability do not depend on environment alone and yet concedes the shaping powers of circumstance. Likewise, the undeniable occurrence of latent traits that surface without warning makes him wary of our reproductive choices, which can never be fully informed when it comes to what our progeny might or might not inherit from generations past. In the end, Darwin can only be sure about endless variation, which brings about a plasticity as dangerous as it is necessary for survival.

Out of these vacillations and uncertainties about the mechanics of heredity emerge concrete concerns regarding the broader social implications for the community. Evocative of Galdós's own fascination with the state mental institution of Leganés, pathology, and the repercussions of public deviance, Darwin worries about degeneration, given that civilized nations impede natural selection with their exaggerated compassion: "With savages, the weak in body or mind are soon eliminated. . . . We civilised men, on the other hand, do our utmost to check the process of elimination; we build asylums for the imbecile, the maimed, and the sick; we institute poor-laws; and our medical men exert their utmost skill to save the life of every one to the last moment" (1:168).[5] However, though it might seem anti-Darwinian, that is, a transgression of the code of self-preservation, failure to fulfill such humanitarian responsibilities, according to Darwin, would be catastrophic for all: "If we were intentionally to neglect the weak and helpless, it could only be for a contingent benefit, with a certain and great present evil" (1:169). More than mere documentation of Darwin's reflections, the slippages of these passages suggest something unnatural, even potentially injurious, about altruism in the short term, while the language reveals how these issues of the welfare of the State were discussed in the move toward modernization across Europe. In fact, Darwin explains the social instincts in *The Descent* according to an inborn "mutual love and sympathy" for our "fellow-men" (1:86), which Peter Kropotkin would later develop more fully in his theory of mutual aid some decades after Darwin's death.[6] Yet, in the shadow of Malthus, Darwin hopes that inferior individuals will not marry, a trend already maintained in his model by the economic disadvantages of the lower classes. Most troublesome are the "black sheep" (1:173), society's perfidious members. No check, though, to their propagation need be instituted, for "in regard to the moral qualities, some elimination of the worst dispositions is always in progress. . . . Malefactors are executed, or imprisoned . . . so that they cannot freely transmit their bad qualities. Melancholic and insane persons are confined, or commit suicide. Violent and quarrelsome men often come to a bloody end" (1:172). Indeed, the checks to heredity extend to the organic well-being of the State: "progress is no invariable rule," for without these balances, "the nation will retrograde" (1:177).

Galdós understood this correlation between heredity and the state. As T. E. Bell demonstrates in his study *Galdós and Darwin*, evolutionism supports Galdós's novelistic scrutiny and censure of Spanish society.[7] Nevertheless, Bell's analysis of influence never goes beyond an identification of Darwinian elements in Galdós and, focused on the better-known *Origin*, makes slight mention of *The Descent*. In *La desheredada*, critical shortcomings of this sort amount to a reductive association of Darwin with determinism and a corresponding preference for natural over sexual selection. This trend waters down natural selection to a *struggle for life* polemic, while disregarding the operative mechanics of courtship as the engine of gender relations, procreation, and what Darwin sees as the moral imperative of "family ties" (*The Descent*, 2:391). That Galdós knew Darwin's works certainly matters, but not necessarily for the purposes of this study, which aims in this particular chapter at reading both Galdós *and* Darwin anew via their overlap on particular issues. Heredity constitutes Isidora's identity, at the same time that it exposes the imaginative space opened by Darwinian speculations on inheritance and humanity in *The Descent*. This reciprocity displays the dynamism of such coupling, rather than the deterministic fixity that Darwin shoulders when aligned with Galdós on the subject of transmitted traits. In other words, Isidora "was not who she appeared to be" because her blood, as she maintains, belongs to the aristocratic house of Aransis.[8] However, she ends up disinherited, since her noble parentage was a ruse of her demented father. In Isidora's own mind, one need only look to literature: "I've read my own story so many times . . . !" (171); her life, a family romance, has meaning as long as she believes herself to be caught in a foundling plot, superior to the masses.[9]

Hence, while heredity albeit a paternal concoction provides Isidora with a material foundation for the creation of her identity, it also gives her the social norms, which she herself construes, for her behavior and self-image. Like the numerous occasions when Isidora aspires to reform her wayward brother Mariano, a product of the dire conditions that surround him, she prepares for the first visit to her presumed, noble grandmother, the marchioness of Aransis, according to her own model of the upper class: "It was essential that her unassuming, modest, virtuous, and reserved appearance reveal the dignity with which she passed from her miserable state to one of splendor. As such, she would show herself to be worthy of her new standing, making clear that she had not dishonored her origin in conditions of lowliness" (261). Here, two worldviews on the constitution of the individual collide—on one hand, identity as authentic and autonomous (idealism) and, on the other, as susceptible to environmental contamination (materialism). Mariano stands as a one-dimensional cutout of the latter and thus has a tendency to be misread as the most

"Darwinian" character of the novel, while Isidora is far more complex because she displays the unresolved tensions of character construed in these two polarized directions. Again, it was Darwin who said: "There can . . . be no doubt that changed conditions induce [in the individual] an almost indefinite amount of fluctuating variability, by which the whole organisation is rendered in some degree plastic" (*The Descent*, 1:114). Nothing in Galdós's novel should lead us to believe that Mariano deserves more consideration than Isidora in this respect; on the contrary, she is the character who best exemplifies the indeterminism that provides the bookend to Darwin's reflections.

Isidora admires herself in mirrors throughout the novel, not solely out of the author's own voyeurism or as a critique of the burgeoning consumerism of the day but also to confirm her heredity with empirical observation. Upon hearing "the voice of her blood" (*La desheredada*, 265), Isidora knows herself, and her physiognomy, a "stamp of distinction and goodness" (265), makes being just another face in the crowd, "a nobody" (458), impossible. In fact, heredity replaces God as a naturalist divinity, no less imperceptible than the Creator, which Isidora reveres in hopes of salvation from her prosaic life: "The faith in her high origin burned in her like the faith of a Christian giving light to her mind, strength to her will, and a solid base to her conscience" (266). Conscience here, again, is innate knowledge, *con-scientia*. This unshakable conviction induces her to proclaim: "I swear that I am who I am" (266); her sense of self depends on an honorable lineage that remains intact as an internal and external safeguard against transgression: "I am virtuous, I want to be virtuous, so very virtuous, out of respect to my name, to my family" (312). Her character anchors itself in an idealized past so as not to be swept away by the ugliness of the reality in which she finds herself.

Yet, when hard facts mount against Isidora, the courts deny her deliverance, and "the idea of not being who she thought she was" (461) begins to haunt her. The musings of Hamlet—*to be or not to be*—take on new resonance as Isidora asks herself in the shadow of nineteenth-century science concerned with heredity, degeneration, and other mysterious forces of nature: "Am I or am I not?" (462). For Hamlet, as Arnold Weinstein suggests, "*self is dying* . . . this devastating view that time undoes self, that all our notions as to who we are and what we would are quaint fictions";[10] for Isidora, the existential amalgam of the physical and metaphysical in heredity, that which she assumes to be real but cannot prove empirically, leads her to wonder if *self* ever was at all. The laws of inheritance, instead of liberating, now incarcerate her both literally and figuratively; a fallen woman jailed in Madrid for possessing false documents, Isidora "one night, finding herself alone, ran to the bars, throwing herself against them, wanting to break them to pieces, and with screams that excited the street, said, . . . 'Don't rob me of my nobility, because it is my essence, and I cannot be without it'" (464). The narrator observes with an irony made possible by the plasticity (rather than fixity) of heredity: "All the laws had conspired against her, and they would condemn her and would wall her in a prison" (475). A short time later, Isidora carries out this presentiment in an act of self-annihilation, of symbolic suicide: "I am an anonymous person, I do not exist . . . I am another . . . I have died. That Isidora no longer exists except in your imagination. This whom you see, no longer preserves of that other even the name . . . I am no longer Isidora" (487, 490, 498). The shouts of the populace upon taking to the street with the proclamation of the Republic, that "We're all equal!" (272), amount to a double entendre, if not a bitter lie. The state laws based on the inheritance of capital in Spain in the late nineteenth century, like the laws behind the democratic ideals of personal liberty during the Enlightenment and the Darwinian natural laws for heredity and class, turn on obfuscated relations of inequality. In sum, the account Darwin gives in *The Descent* of the possible ends of the individual upon inheriting the qualities of ancestors, be they close or distant, shows how Isidora dissolves under the pressures of scientific classification that makes her, because of heredity, an inferior gradation, a "black sheep," in the Darwinian model.

Darwin's theory of sexual selection, as it intertwines with his views on heredity, helps us make sense of how female choice in the courtship dynamic figures in Isidora's rejection of suitors. Isidora shields herself with her inheritance, that is, with her pretensions to nobility, in an effort to protect herself once she realizes what little importance love has in the industrialized, self-interested society of Spain at this moment in history. There is no doubt about the impression that Augusto Miquis, a medical student from Isidora's hometown, inspires in her at their first encounter in Leganés after so many years: "That pale and brown face, so brown and so pale that it looked like a big olive; that snubbed nose, contrasting with the bestowed grandeur of the mouth, whose gleaming white teeth were always on display; that wide eyebrow, so black and thick that it looked like a strip of velvet, and those blue eyes . . . that comic ugliness" (*La desheredada*, 92). During their stroll through the Retiro park, Isidora responds to the insinuations of the love-struck and persistent Miquis, who could not be more different from her, by saying to him: "No one will impose a husband on me who is not to my liking" (131); but he does not back down: "Your liking, Madame, will be molded to my liking. . . . You will be married by force. I will compel you. Forget learning. You'll sew, iron, and make the stew-pot froth" (136). In the end, however, Isidora's answer between laughs, "I do not love you" (136), shows her resolve on matters of taste.

Overshadowed by countless trials and a tragic end, choice in courtship on the part of Isidora does, in fact, remain a constant throughout the novel. She refuses the marriage proposal of the brutish yet hardworking Juan Bou (John Ox), whose "gallantries . . . were like those of a bear that wanted to show affection to his master by killing a mosquito on his forehead" (377); she rejects her tyrant lover Don Alejandro Sánchez Botín after he evicts her and then offers to buy her off: "I'm willing to assist you, giving you a tobacco shop" (362); and even in the case of Joaquín Pez, once her beloved, she prefers to be "Single! Free!" (419) after his deceptions and unwillingness to recognize the child he gave her, the deformed *Riquín*, "the antichrist" (424), as his own. Isidora's final break with Joaquín, and his from her in his farewell letter of empty regrets ("*Riquín*, my son . . . I will recognize him" [424]), calls attention to her greatest wish, that he complete the civil paperwork needed to legitimize his paternity under the law; his failure to do so is not only the last straw for Isidora but, as such, puts in question the patriarchy he represents, which is premised on a broken State. In this way, a conflation of the natural and civil laws emerges, a wry construction of the same turnabout evident in Isidora's pleas during her imprisonment. With the parallel Galdós establishes between the morally and fiscally bankrupt Joaquín and all that is wrong with Spain at the time, disinheritance threatens the social bedrock. Moved by an acute disenchantment with the options, Isidora's will, rather than her ambitious pride, inspires her courtship choices in the face of hard facts. She is thus not as unsympathetic a character as she once was. She refuses to belong to any of these men in the role each might assign her, whether domestic servant or kept woman or illegitimate spouse, and hence, despite uncertainties (or because of them), *willed* heredity acts as a romantic defense against societal expectations in the cultural context of sexual selection.

Furthermore, in Darwin's discussion of heredity and sexual selection, he does not limit himself to reflections on the inferior classes; he also theorizes on the nobility. In a curious moment, the outcomes of marriages caused by aristocratic avarice take center stage in his observations:

> The evil consequences . . . of the continued preservation of the same line of descent, without any selection, are checked by men of rank always wishing to increase their wealth by marrying heiresses. But the daughters of parents who have produced single children, are themselves . . . apt to be sterile; and thus noble families are continually cut off in the direct line, and their wealth flows into some side channel. (*The Descent*, 1:170)

It is true that deceased Virginia de Aransis, whom Isidora fashioned as an idealized, aristocratic mother, had two children before her death— a daughter who perished at birth and the young son who now spends ten hours a day at the piano playing Beethoven in the company of his grandmother. Nevertheless, the figurative sterility of Virginia, "apt to be sterile," beyond these symbolic destinies of her actual progeny, can be seen in the mute, sepulchral palace of her widowed mother as it continues to haunt the conscience.

Hence, the "side channel" suggested by Darwin, in the figurative dimension of *La desheredada*, is best understood in terms of the adaptation of genre in Spain to its historical circumstance, from the sentimental Isidora to the anonymous prostitute, from the *folletín* to the naturalist novel. But again, let me be clear, I use the term "adaptation" here as Darwin intended it, that is, with respect to variation rather than progress toward *perfeccionamiento*. Galdós's text is a response to its cultural context, neither superior nor inferior to the romances from which it draws meaning, simply altered in its dire depiction. In other words, to use Darwinian language, the "wealth" of romantic idealism, which allows for Isidora's ineffectual escapism from the reality she inherits, "flows into" a hybrid form aimed at showing how social conditions in Spain after the 1868 revolution continue to thwart the self-determination of women. The oppression of women, therefore, encapsulates the contradictions of Spain's "civil society" in its transition to "civilised life" (*The Descent*, 2:338),[11] just as Isidora lives a contradiction by seeking the very privilege that holds her in check, as a victim of the class-based structure she holds most sacred.

Elizabeth Amann, in her analysis of the last hieroglyphic respirations of Isidora's father in Leganés ("My children . . . , the marchioness . . . " [*La desheredada*, 91]), juxtaposes metaphoric-paternal lineage to metonymic-maternal lineage.[12] Using the work of Roman Jakobson, she extends her model to the origin of the patriarchal system—the uncertainty of fatherhood—which depends on a legal system of names and titles in order to counter the alternative, namely, suppositions about physical similarities that so often offer specious proof of legitimate paternity. Evolutionary biologists, too, have drawn like conclusions from the phenomenon of *pater semper incertus*, which provokes the practice of multiple wives in some cultures but not the reverse. The patriarchal imagination, which prompts Isidora to envision herself to be a "living portrait" of Virginia de Aransis at her first meeting with the widow marchioness, provides unconvincing evidence, as the widow's dubious reaction drives home. With respect to maternity, in contrast, material contiguity via the birth defines motherhood independent of uncertain resemblances and civil codes. Amann directs this dichotomy toward a political reading of *La desheredada* framed by France's role in the history of the Restoration, but her gendered differentiation of heredity also allows for a "Darwinian" reconstruction of the relationship between the *folletín* and the naturalist novel.

That is to say, while some, such as Catherine Jaffe and Eamonn Rodgers, find a clash of paradigms in *La desheredada* where realism triumphs over romanticism, others describe a dialectical relationship between the two.[13] Frank Durand, for example, propounds "the real world of imagination," emphasizing that for Isidora the mind and its fantasies have far-reaching material effects.[14] Stephanie Sieburth, by contrast, takes this line of thought in the opposite direction, toward reality as illusory, in order to postulate under Marxist theories of fetishism that Isidora, as an object of art, is an article of consumption.[15] Understanding Isidora's identity to be a manifestation of the authorial fear that authentic art risks extinction at the hands of mechanical reproduction, Sieburth maintains that "the conclusions to be drawn from the plot of *La desheredada* are apocalyptic";[16] the tragic end of the protagonist signals the conservative ideology of the author.

Without taking anything away from the case Sieburth puts forth, it is just as plausible that Isidora's renunciation of name and her decision to prostitute herself, together, erase heredity or, more to the point, paternal heredity. At the level of plot, it is true that Galdós mocks Isidora's claims to noble parentage; the "facts" prove that she is not the daughter of the deceased Virginia de Aransis. However, as G. W. F. Hegel might say, so much worse for the facts, for at the structural level, the story ends quite differently, in that a lineage between the two can be affirmed. Naturalism's prostitute, who at one time called herself Isidora (now the sentimental shadow of the past), remains the contiguous, metonymic daughter of the marchioness of the *folletín*, because the generic relationship is one of origin and cause.

When Isidora visits Miquis out of desperation in the last days before her ultimate fall, she shudders to find a skeleton in his office and asks: "Whose poor bones might those be?" (*La desheredada*, 394). He replies: "They're of a woman. Maybe one as beautiful as you. . . . Look at yourself in that mirror." To which she adds: "Your mirrors are very peculiar" (394). Hence, the "moral" (503) of *La desheredada* need reside not in the narrator's final chastisement of those who aspire to fly with "false wings" (503), where Sieburth and others sound a Galdosian allegiance to the status quo, but rather in the romantic, Darwinian constitution of the protagonist, in "the reappearance of long-lost characters" (*The Descent*, 1:113). The (maternal) heiress to (paternal) disinheritance, Isidora shivers at the sight of her paradoxical bones, which like those of the naturalist novel are a "very peculiar" mirror indeed. The idealism decried by Galdós has come to support its transgression, as this skeleton in the realist closet, so to speak, reflects novel heredity in *The Descent* as no other. And this reciprocity between the two, Darwin and Galdós, provides one of the "types of evidences" for the indeterminate operation of literary history as first described in chapter 1,[17] whereby evolutionary theory and, particularly, the oxymoronic precept of female passive choice open the "interpretive horizons" for unforeseen interdisciplinary, intertextual relationships across time.

ERRORS OF UNDERSTANDING

For all his doubts about the mechanics of heredity, Darwin never wavers in his conviction that heirs and errors go together when it comes to sexual selection. In *Fortunata y Jacinta*, errors in the pursuit of progeny define the plot, as Juanito Santa Cruz ends up with the infertile Jacinta only to have a child out of wedlock with Fortunata, who endures a loveless marriage to the impotent Maximiliano Rubín. One way to read these errors is to pit Nature against Culture. The characters themselves, including the narrator, warn against the dangers of custom when it becomes a barrier to sexual impulse, and the birth of the real *Pituso*, Juan Evaristo Segismundo, at the work's conclusion stands as the "natural" solution to a "cultural" quandary created by divisions of social class. These errors originate from sexual selection and related hereditary motivations in the context of nineteenth-century Madrid. However, characters' responses to such errors and the significance of their resolutions, absent consideration of *The Descent*, expose troubling contradictions in Galdós's magnum opus from an ideological standpoint, given that with Fortunata's death her more righteous and wealthy double, Jacinta, becomes the child's legitimate mother. This outcome, so powerful after so many hundreds of pages, leads us to suspect that Culture plays the last card, with the bourgeois order restored and patriarchy intact.

As it turns out, the imagination, which Darwin introduces and Galdós carries to its end in the context of heredity, drives mate preferences, offspring aspirations, and new models of family ties. The last of these, characterized by the "three mothers" (*Fortunata y Jacinta*, 987) and Fortunata's naming of the child at the novel's conclusion, evidences how Galdós circles back on Darwin with a deployment of the mind in response to matter. Besieged by social impediments that endanger future generations, the female protagonists of *Fortunata y Jacinta* author a lineage of their own invention which is both maternal and symbolic. Thus, inheritance becomes a question of creation, and with a vision of regeneration founded on heterogeneity Galdós returns to "the indefinite amount of fluctuating variability" (*The Descent*, 1:114) Darwin privileged. He rewrites community through the characters' own eyes and offers in the final analysis an "evolutionary confusion" of the classes, Madrid, and the nation.[18] In these ways, *Fortunata y Jacinta* moves us closer to understanding the hereditary connection between humanity and its redemptive, Darwinian plasticity.

The two marriages that structure the plot of *Fortunata y Jacinta* amount to the sort of misguided matrimonies that would trouble Darwin. With respect to Juanito and Jacinta, an arranged union between cousins, Galdós makes their bond, described as both fraternal and as mother to son, the barrier to their intimacy.[19] Harriet S. Turner in her pivotal essay "Family Ties and Tyrannies: A Reassessment of Jacinta" demonstrates Jacinta's sterility to be the consequence of her incestuous circumstances, rather than proof of any biological flaw that would make her "naturally" inferior to Fortunata in terms of female reproductive ability—the critical criterion by which Jacinta's worth has traditionally been measured in a culture where fertility defines womanhood.[20] As for Maximiliano and Fortunata, their match is literally a mismatch; Fortunata, as everyone in the novel knows (including Maxi), is far too much woman for her husband. In contrast to the robust, beautiful Fortunata, synonymous with the *pueblo* and "the essence of Humanity" (*Fortunata y Jacinta*, 518), Maxi exhibits a "small body, not well formed, so feeble that it looked like the wind was going to carry it away, a flat head, and lank, sparse hair" (295). He is a "mollusk" beset by premature baldness and plagued by migraines, who has "glossy, delicate, skin of a childlike complexion with signs similar to those of a sickly, chlorotic woman" (296). To convey how "disfavored by Nature" Maxi is, the narrator recounts: "He had a sunken, snubbed nose, as if made of some flabby substance that had received a punch, resulting not only in ugliness, but also obstructions of nasal respiration that were without a doubt to blame for his mouth always being open. His teeth had come out with such irregularity that each piece was, we might say, wherever it pleased" (296). In effect, Maxi's physical and mental "inferiority" (298), compounded by his separation from the world as "a man who was all spirit" (307), prefigures trouble for any mate.

Yet, for Fortunata a specimen as disagreeable as Maxi spells disaster, all the more so because her heart belongs to Juanito from the outset. In a pivotal domestic moment with her future husband, Fortunata looks across the table at Maxi and thinks to herself that "he's nothing like a man . . . he even smells bad" (348). When Doña Lupe, Maxi's no-nonsense aunt, learns of her nephew's matrimonial intentions with Fortunata, she foresees the inevitable: "This cannot be, she's too much woman for half a man" (417). But after Fortunata's reformative stay in the convent of Las Micaelas and subsequent marriage to Maxi (a sour remedy to her dire situation, exacerbated by social pressures that she be a model wife), reality sets in: "When they went on a walk together, everyone stared at Fortunata, admiring her beauty; then they looked at him. Maxi guessed that they all made the observation that he was no man for such a woman" (525). Indeed, theirs was "the farce of an impossible marriage" (540), and yet Maxi

. . . desired ardently to have children, for two reasons: first, to burden his better half with another bond and new ties; second, so that maternity might spoil some of that splendid beauty. . . . The disproportion between their two statures and the overall impression of their personal appearance together mortified the poor boy to such an extent

that he made impossible and, at times, ridiculous attempts to lessen
that lack of harmony. . . . Unfortunately, although Fortunata barely
put herself together, the disproportion was always visible. (686)

It is important to point out that Maxi's aspirations for an heir, that
is, "to burden his better half with another bond," signal the ways heredity can also be manipulated as an instrument of control, toward
patriarchal subjugation here and, later, for subversion in the case of
Fortunata's determination to have Juanito's son. With Maxi's efforts
to offset the imbalance, in the end Doña Lupe's worst fears come true:
"So much woman for so little man . . . naturally, the poor boy had to
either die or lose his mind" (895). He does lose his mind, suffering
psychological attacks until ultimately admitted to Leganés. Hence,
Galdós describes Maxi's pairing with Fortunata throughout the novel
as an affront to the laws of sexual selection, an offense to Nature confirmed by the popular gaze and culminating in Maxi's final insanity.

Insight into the Darwinian errors of *Fortunata y Jacinta* comes
through Evaristo Feijoo's counsel to Fortunata during the days when
she finds herself under his protection. Feijoo is a friend of Fortunata's
brother-in-law, Juan Pablo Rubín, and his role in the novel is that of
"an *ex*-liberal" with too much experience of political hypocrisy to
have any illusions about the Restoration or the moral makeup of his
fellow man.[21] Instead, as Geoffrey Ribbans explains, "in a world of
solemn farce which masks self-interests and degraded values he seeks
to salvage individuals who interest him, subverting it by adopting its
methods for his own purposes" (109). Ousted from the Rubín home
for her transgressions, Fortunata becomes one such individual for the
aging Feijoo, whose years cast him as a father figure rather than lover
or husband, and his message to her centers on a worldview in which
Nature and Culture stand in opposition:

> What they call infidelity is nothing more than Nature's authority,
> which wants to impose itself against social despotism. . . . Love is
> the reclamation of the species that wants to perpetuate itself, and
> as a stimulus to this necessity, as much a means to self-preservation
> as eating, the sexes search each other out and unions occur through
> inevitable choice, which remains superior and foreign to all the arti-
> fices of society. A man and woman look at each other. What is it? The
> exigency of the species that requests a new being, and this new being
> demands of his probable parents that they give him life. Everything
> else is fine talk, inanity, the hot air of those who have wanted to actu-
> alize society in their sitting rooms, removed from the immortal foun-
> dations of Nature. (637–38)

This tension latent in Darwinian sexual selection, as understood by the progressively pragmatic Feijoo, derives from the paradoxical conclusion that Culture is unnatural; that is to say, the worst enemy (and best ally) of humankind is humankind. Nature can be frustrated, but it cannot be suppressed. Demetrio Estébanez Calderón describes Galdós's conception here as one of "an innate nature or set of tendencies and qualities that mark the vocation and destiny of the individual. To contradict this innate nature is an error that leads to the existential failure of the individual."[22] With respect to his marriage to Fortunata, Maxi himself articulates in his final thoughts before being institutionalized at Leganés: "We overlooked Nature, who is the great mother and teacher that rectifies the errors of her wayward children. We make a thousand mistakes, and Nature corrects them for us" (*Fortunata y Jacinta*, 1036). A restorative force, Nature hides its own mysterious teleology, and Darwinian sexual selection operates as its engine, toward an end of "advantageous" reproduction through the open-ended operation of a dynamic that "should not be prevented by laws or customs" (*The Descent*, 2:403) in the cultural realm.

Still, to understand what constitutes "advantageous reproduction" as described at the outset of this chapter with respect to adaptation and progress necessitates that the Darwinian significance of Nature's solution, Fortunata's child, be established within the Galdosian model. With the erroneous marriages now outlined against the novel's ideology as elaborated by Feijoo, it becomes important to show where this ideology collapses on itself. The Nature-Culture dichotomy manifest in the cynicism of Feijoo represents a moment of fallacious reductionism, and hence disingenuousness on the part of Galdós, given that "Nature's corrections" in *Fortunata y Jacinta* depend on the imaginative responses of its characters to the societal barriers in which they find themselves. Yet the mind, the locus of the imagination and hence of these responses, is neither "natural" nor "cultural" but instead shows the very impossibility of such a bifurcation, which is a dichotomy that has plagued the discourse from the Enlightenment up to the present. Though both Darwin and Galdós took issue with the conventions they thought to be opposed to human nature, I think that both would concede that human nature is behind those very same conventions. In other words, the problem stems from the very unity, rather than a separation. For this reason, the fact that the creative energies of so many characters center on heredity is not by accident, for in the given environment, their errors require solutions of their own invention. Whether in terms of Jacinta's yearnings for the false *Pitusín* that "could or could not be" (*Fortunata y Jacinta*, 222) of her husband's blood, or the "villainous imagination" (284) that compels Juanito to behave as a "hunter" (285) in search of Fortunata, or Maxi's chivalric fantasies about "virtuous women" (299), or Fortunata's "so very ardent desire to look like Jacinta, to be like her" (453), the mind bridges life's physical limitations with its own fanciful realities.

Where Darwinian sexual selection is concerned, heredity bends to the caprices of the imagination, or rather its defenses, with uncommon plasticity in the cases of Fortunata's *"fixed idea"* and the characters' own construction of familial relationships. If we recall, Darwin states that "there can . . . be no doubt that changed conditions induce an almost indefinite amount of fluctuating variability, by which the whole organisation is rendered in some degree plastic" (*The Descent*, 1:114). With her own convictions, Fortunata overturns cultural mores through an assertion of her right to be Juanito's natural, legitimate wife, given her ability to bear him an heir. Reproduction, in effect, justifies this rationale. As such, Galdós does not advocate for the opposition between nature and culture but rather shows our tendency to create such a hierarchy in our appeals for justice and corrective restitution. Moreover, in Fortunata's plan, we can again see the ways heredity becomes instrumental in social ties, as an insurance of codependence and material arm that can serve to subvert just as much as to uphold the status quo.

Discussing Jacinta's "mania for children" in the context of "the pain that her sterility causes her" (*Fortunata y Jacinta*, 522), Fortunata explains her idea to Juanito with the utmost sincerity: "I will cede your son to her, and she will cede her husband to me" (523). Later, in the company of the "saintly" Guillermina Pacheco (and an out-of-sight Jacinta), Fortunata reiterates: "It is my idea, it is my very own idea. And I'll say it again: the wife who cannot give children is worthless. . . . Without us, those of us who do give children to them, the world would come to an end" (762). Heredity is her salvation. And when Fortunata finally does become "the mother of the heir" (956) to the line of Santa Cruz, her reversal of the laws that govern the species comes full circle: "I am the mother of the only *son of the house*, I am the mother. . . . Will there be anyone who might deny it? I'm not to blame if the law requires one or the other. If the laws are huge mistakes, I have nothing to do with them. Why were they made that way? The true law is that of blood, or . . . Nature, and I, through Nature, have taken from *Heaven's darling girl* [Jacinta] the place that she had taken from me" (956). Sexual selection, the dynamic that enables heredity, in the face of arbitrary social norms provides Fortunata with the authorization she needs to recodify culture in natural terms. Her response to obstacles of class and caste amounts to an *idealized* mediation, an *idea fija* rooted in the imagination and nourished by the tangible, empirical proof of a living being whom she brings into this world.

In the end, characters rewrite reality through the conceptual fabrication of family ties in response to those imposed on them. Beyond Fortunata's claims to Juanito, other invented relationships unfold in defiance to a morally bankrupt society. A destitute Fortunata and a lonely, empathic Feijoo maintain what amounts to an unspoken marriage, despite talk on the streets (636), until Feijoo's failing health and concerns about social decorum cause the bond to become filial: "Everything is finished . . . Fortunata, I'm nothing more for you than a father. . . . The man that loved you as a husband loves his wife no longer exists. . . . You are my daughter" (660). Likewise, a disillusioned Jacinta and Manuel Moreno-Isla, a family friend whose experiences of the world yield an uncommon sensitivity Juanito will never have, form a union of the heart, an "if only" romance of soul mates foiled by circumstance, to the point where Jacinta upon accepting Fortunata's child, "remade his features, giving him her very own, mixed and confounded with those of an ideal being, that very well could have the face of Santa Cruz, but whose heart was surely that of Moreno . . . that heart that adored her and that died for her. . . . Because Moreno certainly could have been her husband. . . . Ah! then the world would be as it should" (1031). A sociobiologist today would understand Jacinta's preferences about appearance concerning the child's face and her promise to marry Moreno even without Juanito's good looks as genetic input regarding her chances of having grandchildren (even if Fortunata's child, ironically enough, shares none of Jacinta's own genes). More than likely though, Darwin would simply attribute such sentiments to "love," one of the principal variables in his theory of sexual selection among men and women. For my part, I would call Jacinta's personal inflection of hereditary laws one more example of the reach of evolutionary indeterminacy.

Still, there remains much to reconcile when it comes to the ways Galdós fills the gaps left by Darwin. For one, evolutionism appears to explain little about Maxi's *intervalos lúcidos* with regard to the "Messiah" he divines in Fortunata's womb, fathered by *"pure Thought"* (908). The imaginative, metaphysical dimension of Fortunata's child in Maxi's mind and within the narrative itself, like the other constructed family ties of the novel, cannot be understood outside the creative capacity of the individual. The first level of creation along these lines entails the ratification of maternal privilege where patriarchy fails. Close to death and unable to nurse the baby, Fortunata tells Guillermina: "This blessed child, this glorious creature is going to have three mothers: I, who am the first mother, she [Jacinta], the second mother, and you, the third mother" (987). Turner rightly calls this "a new 'feminist' family . . . a radically new, 'holy' and 'Trinitarian' family of women. It is an inclusive family."[23] Indeed, Juanito never enters those final scenes of Fortunata's labor, childbirth, and death. Nevertheless, the actual terms of exchange complicate this "feminist" vision, for in Fortunata's dictation of the heredity decree to Plácido Estupiñá, the man who embodies Madrid for his intimate connection to its people, places, and history, she states: "This son is not false; he is legitimate and *natural*, as you will see in his face. . . . I beg you to look at him as a son and that you hold him to be *natural* to you and the father" (*Fortunata y Jacinta*, 1018). That is to say, proof of the child's legitimacy, in Fortunata's eyes, returns to the physical resemblance he bears to his father. We might see this declaration as an inversion of Isidora's own unanswered appeals to the higher authority of shared maternal traits and the theme of *pater semper incertus* in the case of *Riquín*, which can only be resolved by the civil paperwork Joaquín Pez never completes. Isidora's imagination, though, never manages to resolve her disinherited plight; the turn to prostitution reminds us of this material consequence.

By contrast, *Fortunata y Jacinta* takes a step closer, if not beyond, Darwin's presentation of the potential for change inherent in heredity. Jacinta assumes a new "power" once in possession of the heir; she "dispatched with her husband as she pleased" (1029), telling him after the truth comes out with Fortunata's letter: "You are as free as the air" (1030). In this way, Jacinta liberates herself from the child's father as rightful custodian of his lineage and, at the same time, erases him:

> Alone with him [the child], the gentlewoman [Jacinta] entertained
> herself fabricating in her daring mind castles of sand with towers of
> air and even more fragile cupolas, for being made of pure fancy. The
> features of the inherited child were not those of the other [Fortunata]:

they were hers. And so much was the imagination capable of, that
the putative mother reached the point of being enraptured by the art-
ful memory of having carried in her womb that precious son, and of
trembling with the supposed pains suffered upon bringing him into
the world. And through these games of mischievous fantasy she came
to reflect on how out of order things of the world go. She also had
an idea with respect to the ties established by the Law, and she broke
them with the mind, realizing the impossible feat of turning back
time, of changing and touching up the traits of individuals . . . making, in the end, some corrections so extravagant to the entire work of
the world, that God would laugh to himself were he to know of them.
(1030)

Whereas the imagination in Galdós is often understood as the cause
of errors, as in Isidora's conviction in *La desheredada*, in the conclusion of *Fortunata y Jacinta* it remedies them. Jacinta adjusts the
"Law" of heredity with her mind; she fixes with "fantasy" those moments of selection when a higher authority went astray.

Finally, it is important to also clarify that Fortunata's maternal
Trinity, this "feminist family" as Turner describes it, appears to contrast with the name bestowed on the child through Fortunata's own
creative act of constructed heredity— "Juan Evaristo Segismundo and
some others" (959). This name, in truth, hides a parallel, masculine
Trinity, which retains the name of the father, Juan, at its head. Hence,
in addition to Fortunata's claims of a natural legitimacy on the basis
of shared paternal features, the son's identity remains a literal mirror
of his father's, and as John W. Kronik postulates, by adding (Evaristo)
Feijoo to the equation Fortunata allows "Juan Evaristo" to stand as
"the fusion of passion and reason, of rebellion and submission, of
the failure and the success of creation . . . of the biological [and of
the] most practical act."[24] Theresa Ann Smith, in her reflections on
the emerging female citizen in Spain,[25] might characterize Kronik's
thoughts on this "fusion" as a way Fortunata negotiates her environment in accordance with her own desires, not as passion versus reason, but rather women's participation in the expression of ideas, for
"Juan Evaristo" pulls traits from both passion and reason. From the
joining together of these perspectives, it can be argued that this adaptive variation on the part of Fortunata in her choice of names initiates a movement from the imaginary to the symbolic.[26] When taken
alone, "Juan Evaristo," as a symbolic naming, retains the patriarchal, for just as Juan is the father of the child, Evaristo was a father
to Fortunata.

However, the tripartite name, even with this meaning attributed to these two male figures of Fortunata's life (as Kronik would have it), moves beyond the established paternal order, for the threefold "Juan Evaristo Segismundo" actually projects the mind of the mother in its fullest realization. Like Jacinta, Fortunata has recombined the traits of certain individuals from her vantage point, for it is Segismundo Ballester, her compassionate confidant, who *names* her "an angel" (*Fortunata y Jacinta*, 1037) at her grave. Hence, through the choice of such a name for her son, Fortunata not only dictates a new lineage for him, out of her own idealized past, but she also prefigures a hereditary, angelic salvation both for herself and the society that buried her "*de Rubín*" (1037), the wife who *belonged to* Maximiliano, as was etched on her tombstone. Moreover, I do not think it a coincidence that Pedro Calderón de la Barca's own Segismundo once said, "Weighed down by these shackles . . . I saw myself in another more gratifying state."[27] Through naming, Fortunata portends her own redemption in foreshadowing Segismundo's prophetic pronunciation. The novel's antiheroine becomes its "angel" through her Darwinian family ties, which capture heredity through the permutations of its built-in variability, that is, "Juan Evaristo Segismundo and some others" (*Fortunata y Jacinta*, 959).

Early in *The Descent*, Darwin proclaims: "The *Imagination* is one of the highest prerogatives of man. By this faculty he unites, independently of the will, former images and ideas, and thus creates brilliant and novel results" (1:45). It is in the context of these words that "Juan Evaristo Segismundo" should be seen to point back to the opening of *Fortunata y Jacinta*, where Galdós taps heredity as a metaphor for Madrid and its community. To say, "We're all one" (*Fortunata y Jacinta*, 22), to wed the Jacinta's family line of Isabel Cordero de Arnáiz with Spain's political history (43–44), to ask of commerce in the capital, "But who will be able to discover its mysterious link with the disordered and crossed shoots of this colossal blindweed?" (113), together speak of the sublime interconnectedness of humanity in the relational heredity of the city: "The surest mind is unable to follow in its labyrinthine entanglement the directions of the offspring of this colossal tree of Madrid's families" (114). This description can only call to mind Darwin's own conclusion to *Origin*, in which he pauses "to contemplate an entangled bank . . . and to reflect that these elaborately constructed forms, so different from each other, and dependent on each other in so complex a manner, have all been produced by laws acting around us."[28] The first among the laws he lists is "Growth with Reproduction" and the second, "Inheritance which is almost implied by reproduction" (489). In *The Descent*, where he achieves his fullest account of reproduction with the theory of sexual selection and, particularly, as it extends to humankind, we find inheritance not only "implied by reproduction," as suggested in *Origin*, but also what the possible implications are. Like Darwin's, our curiosity about uncertain heredity stems from the social growth that occurs, which cannot be doubted, while the real fascination lies in the fact that no one can predict its direction. Here, we find the face of sexual selection overlooked in both Darwin and Galdós.

Yet, if the above image of an "entangled" Madrid is Darwinian, the *image*nation needed to "unite" these "disordered and crossed shoots" belongs to Galdós, for his is a genealogical representation of Spain as a nation, of its capital as a "family tree"—past, present, and future. Indeed, one of his most enduring ideas goes back to the "leveling" of the classes he discusses in "La sociedad presente como materia novelable," his address to the Real Academia from 1897. He declares there that

> the so-called middle class, which still has no real existence, is merely an inchoate conglomeration of individuals who come from the superior and inferior categories, the product, so to speak, of the decomposition of both families. . . . This enormous mass without its own character that absorbs and monopolizes all of life, subjecting it to endless regulations, legislating outrageously over everything, without excluding those things spiritual, the exclusive dominion of the soul, will end by absorbing even the feeble remains of the classes at the extremes, the depositories of the most elemental feelings.[29]

Art, says Galdós in this address, must adapt to these changes by changing itself, from the inside out, toward more "plastic representation," able to take on "new forms" that will "serve to announce future ideals" (164–65). The conclusion to *Fortunata y Jacinta* should be seen in just such a light, as the author brings to fruition "the decomposition of both families" according to the heredity imagined by the two women it most concerns.

However, Galdós's most profound truth, which is also his most Darwinian, depends on Fortunata alone, for she is the one character without a family line in a novel that goes to great length (literally) in its accounts of lineage. The narrator makes clear that "this story would not have been written" (*Fortunata y Jacinta*, 60) if Juanito

Santa Cruz were not to have made a visit to "primitive Madrid" (61) on one particular day, for there he found himself face-to-face with Fortunata, her mouth full of raw egg, in the most explicit display of sexual selection in all of Galdós's fiction:

> [She] had the clear blue scarf over her head and a shawl over her shoulders, and in the moment of seeing the Delfín [Juanito], puffed herself up with it . . . so as to make that characteristic arching of arms and rising of the shoulders with which Madrid girls from the *pueblo* offer a welcome from within the shawl, a movement that makes them look like a hen that fluffs up her plumage and gives herself airs only to return then to her natural size. (62)

Primordial in these respects, Fortunata answers Darwin's own perplexities about heredity. As a Darwinian contradiction incarnate, a being outside of history and at the same time reflective of its formative power, she offers a tabula rasa much like the one upon which the *always already* story of evolution continues to be written. In a telling sentence (to a large extent, of the critical destiny that awaits Fortunata in Galdós studies), Feijoo reveals the plasticity inherent in her character: "She will always be whatever those who get involved with her want to make of her" (659). Advantageous reproduction then, for Darwin, is not Nature's teleology, and neither is it so for Galdós; the paradoxical "end" of Nature is variation, constant change, out of which some forms thrive, in certain spans, for being better suited to concurrent conditions. In this light, Galdós takes Juanito from "smelling like the people" (10) to procreating with their "angel." In the context of genre development, both *La desheredada* and *Fortunata y Jacinta* exemplify this approach to art and life on the part of Galdós, even if in different ways. In the latter, he breaks down the social stratification of Madrid through sexual selection and, in a political tour de force, makes Juanito worthy of his democratic name (13), once it comes to be bestowed on his son along with "some others" (959). At the same time, however, Fortunata carries not only the child but also "*pure Thought*" (908) and the very novel itself within her indefinite makeup. Readers inherit her language through the "*yiá*" song of "that bird" (63) full of Darwinian errors of understanding, while Darwin, for his own inconclusiveness, inherits her legacy.

PART THREE

Speciations

CHAPTER SEVEN

A Romance with Darwin
in the Evolutionary *Noche*
of Alejandro Sawa

Building on the theoretical, scientific-feminist, and historical foundations of part 1, the three chapters of part 2 engaged discrete components of Darwinian sexual selection—the players, the mechanics, and the outcomes—so as to read them anew through literature. In each case, close attention to Darwin's own voice from *The Descent* gave rise to original inquiries into the relationship between his theory and its praxis in the sexual politics of Spain during the late nineteenth century. The realist novels of Picón, Clarín, and Galdós captured this seldom recognized but ever-present aspect of evolutionism through their representation of courtship and, in particular, concerns over the patriarchal power dynamics governing women's choice. Specific instantiations brought to light unanticipated facets of Darwin's thought, and together they illuminated the reach of the indeterminism bound up in his science.

Thus, with each telling it became ever more evident that this indeterminism cannot be separated from questions of community. No doubt, this side of the "extremely complex affair" (*The Descent,* 1:296) has to do with Darwin's inconsistencies and uncertainties, but as we have seen, there are other complicating factors. Constants in the Darwinian model like conscience, language, and the imagination imbue humankind and evolutionary portrayals of it with an unfinished character, an "indefinite amount of fluctuating variability" (*The Descent,* 1:114) as it were, and therefore the novelistic analogues up to this point correspond to historical circumstance only insofar as both the science and the fiction exhibit like plasticity. In other words, to get back to the theoretical frame I establish in chapter 1, the very notion of "real" reciprocity between literature and science is about how we read the realist movement, which was an aesthetic approach to reality held together by "pure possibility" and "historical contingencies" as outlined in my earlier chapters. It is a way of reading centered on the dynamism of the coupling and is ethical to the extent that the search, premised on questions of social justice like women's rights, involves history *in the making*. This is the kind of scholarship Edward Said has in mind when calling for interdisciplinary studies that move literature beyond its "isolated paddock" toward a greater awareness of the "stake in historical and political effectiveness" novels and other texts, like *The Descent*, can be seen to have had once appreciated in tandem.[1]

In the introduction, I mentioned that Bert Bender explains his study of Darwinian sexual selection and American fiction as one concerned with the influence of the former on the latter. What I left out is that the book as a whole bypasses the feminist dimension of the problem as he poses it. By contrast, I cannot see the relationship between the theory and realist representation in any other light, given the sociopolitical stakes of courtship at the time. Sexual selection among men and women has always been about much more than reproductive success; it involves power. Never fixed, the social conditions (historical context) and aesthetic responses (adaptations) remain open-ended. Constant change need not equate to progress as improvement, but it very well might. It requires, instead, that knowledge occur in the questioning through an interdisciplinary optic that brings different forms of cultural production into contact in a setting that makes intelligible the material consequence of their union. Understanding an indeterminate Darwin through literature, therefore, is about understanding both better. But for the union to be meaningful, the second step, naturally, is to make the intersection *mean* something. The chapters of "Adaptations" have begun this process, fashioning a less predictable Darwin, but this is not enough. The space created up to this point, as it happens, allows sexual selection to spill over into issues assumed to lie even further outside its purview.

With a writer like Alejandro Sawa (1862–1909), the bleak fatalism of his novels makes reading for the same sort of openness much more difficult. At the level of content, there is no similar space to maneuver. Sawa's obsession with the evil that lurks behind every corner of society, especially in his novel *Noche* (1888), communicates in its closure a very clear message about all that is wrong with the world. He might therefore be a more limited (and limiting) author than many of his contemporaries, and maybe in this instance history, which has all but forgotten Sawa, got it right, though a recent biography by Amelina Correa Ramón shows how his personal story complicates the oblivion that today surrounds him.[2] In any event, what interests me most about Sawa is not whether his novels are masterpieces, which I hazard to say they are not, but rather why it is that he can be made representative of "deterministic" Darwinism in its most realized form. This association, in fact, between Darwin and Sawa is where this chapter originated. Knowing what I know about the indefinite conclusions of Darwin and the change inherent in evolutionism, the paradox came to center on, in no uncertain terms, the indeterminism of model determinism. For this, I had to reorient myself toward the form, rather than the content, of Sawa's social critiques.

Yet this critical turn did not make the task any easier, and this chapter requires some patience as my argument unfolds. Several critical voices come into play, but their inclusion is not haphazard. Their positions involve important historical and terminological distinctions and thus are interwoven in such a way so as to move my argument ever closer to the stakes of the paradox just described. Darwin's theory of evolution, as history now tells us, turned the world on its head because it revealed an amoral, non-teleological universe ruled by self-preservation rather than a benevolent God. Voices spoke out in condemnation of this vision, and in the past century and a half many have attempted to reclaim our humanity, from scientific elaborations of mutual aid following Peter Kropotkin to faith-based creationism in the schools and proponents of intelligent design to those in today's academic community like Francisco J. Ayala and Kenneth R. Miller who have sought to assuage our concerns about Darwin and the divine with hard facts about the biological world.[3] Likewise, the literary naturalism that emerged in the late nineteenth century across Europe, spearheaded by Émile Zola and his French compatriots, endured many of the same charges as those leveled at Darwin for their novelistic representations of an indifferent, atheistic Nature characterized by materialist fatalism. They proclaimed themselves "experimental moralists" insofar as they examined the effects of social ills on human subjects, but the reputation they earned from depictions of prostitution, murder, and lechery was anything but moral. It should not surprise us, then, that the two often appear in tandem, with Darwin as the figurehead of a specious determinism that characterized the novel in his wake.

Nevertheless, as has become increasingly clear, the historical association between Darwin and this literary movement misrepresents the former and oversimplifies the latter. On the one hand, a reduction of evolution to gross materialism negates the ethical agency central to Darwinian thought in *The Descent*, and on the other, readings of the environment operative in these novels as merely mechanistic highlight again and again, at the level of authorial intent, little more than transparent social critiques of self-interest or the hypocrisy of a culture indifferent to the plight of certain sectors of the population. However, the form of this same novel, as an evolutionary structure of Darwinian sexual selection, remains unaddressed. Were perceptions to be corrected according to form, evolution, without becoming theistic, would look far more moral than this amoral (and hence immoral) reputation of evolutionism suggests. Indeed, Darwin's "entangled bank" of adaptation and change as described at the end of *Origin* mirrors the way we draw meaning from circumstance in literature following *The Descent*, and the reading of circumstance through the "ideology of form" is therefore paramount.[4]

To get to this point, however, requires several smaller, interrelated arguments. We must take account of theoretical reflections on romance and realism, sex in the novel, and, ultimately, how truth instructs the human heart. Moreover, we must not lose sight of Spain, whose literary history is also in many ways one of gender and nation, for there we find that the pessimism of Sawa offers a curious anchor to this inquiry. Of the writers most committed to the movement and one whose painful life typified the unjust world he depicted, Sawa was also in many respects a romantic idealist, which *Noche*, his last published novel, does everything it can to hide. In this work, a biological vision of corrupted sexual selection heightens the bestial impulses of male characters while martyring their female victims. It is, in effect, the darkest night of the rather sunny continuity between man and animals that Darwin paints in *The Descent*, and, consequently, it is the last place one might think to find the "love and sympathy" (1:86) that foreground the Darwinian vision of "civilised life" (2:338).

TAKING JERICHO

When speaking of *Don Quijote*, José Ortega y Gassett says it must be taken just as Jericho, "in wide circles."[5] In effect, across national traditions the problem posed by the novel is one of containment. A hybrid genre, the novel displays compositional heterogeneity, and because of an inherent plasticity, many have theorized both on its capacity to resist fixity and the difficulties posed by its subgenres. Among the prevailing voices, Georg Lukács considers the form to be one of "dissonance"; Mikhail Bakhtin speaks of the novel as a "zone of contact"; and Northrop Frye believes in a process of "displacement" from myth.[6] Courtship, by contrast, does not factor in or alongside these discussions of hybridization as the central issue of novelistic form, though there is no shortage of criticism on the thematic importance of courtship at the level of content in the novel. Still, to overlook courtship in its capacity to structure so many novels of the late nineteenth century is to miss the greater synergy between realism and Darwinian sexual selection at a moment of social transition characterized by growing concern about the civil status and rights of women. It follows then that an integration of these two fundamental aspects of the novel, hybridization and courtship, should be our first task if we are to rewrite the Darwin-determinism pairing in terms of sexual selection and with respect to ideology.

Indeed, novelistic qualities evocative of evolutionary theory—descriptions of animalism, heredity, struggle for life, and the like—trace back to Darwin with specious straightforwardness. Pura Fernández, to give just one example in the context of Spain, takes up "radical naturalism" in "The Application of a Theoretical Ideology: Positivist Determinism and Darwinism" and, like most critics concerned with the novel of the late nineteenth century, maintains that "the characters of the radical naturalists resemble victims who wander about in search of their destructive end, of the 'fatal law' that is carried out unforgivingly."[7] But no "Darwinian" character would ever "wander about" in search of his or her "destructive end"; on the contrary, the opposite is true. Defined in this inaccurate way with respect to Darwin, naturalism proves the most immoral extreme of realism, as an aesthetic subordinate to an amoral science. Stripped of free will, characters are no longer responsible for or in control of their own actions, and with the ethics of representation questioned as such, Darwin's evolutionism threatens human virtue.

Moreover, the naturalist treatment of sex, and above all of prostitution, trumps all other threatening themes in the novels of the period. Working to understand the fascination, Fernández argues that in the "sociological documents" of naturalism the "social question" becomes a "sexual question," and Nil Santiáñez for his part stipulates that "naturalist novels present prostitution as the symbol of a decadent society in a state of disintegration."[8] One need only recall the scandal caused by Zola's protagonist in *Nana* (1880) or complement *el darwinismo* with Cesare Lombroso's writings on the innate promiscuity of the female population, for example, to understand the social potency of such a mixture.[9] In truth, a transformation of "vital *eros*" into "black *eros*," Fernández explains,[10] becomes possible (and even common) in the literature after Darwin, and it is the dichotomy of these forms of *eros*, one in the romantic direction of sentimental idealism and the other toward deterministic materialism, that brings our attention back to the wider panorama of novel theory.

What Fernández is really talking about with her dichotomization of *eros* recalls the more recognizable bifurcation of romance and realism that has shaped literary criticism in one way or another since the late eighteenth century, if not earlier. In fact, questions about the compromised verisimilitude of chivalric novels started to be raised in the Renaissance, when implausibility and idealism were in lockstep; the visionary Spanish humanist Juan de Valdés, for example, laments in his *Diálogo de la lengua* (1533) the "stories wrapped up in thousands of lying errors,"[11] like the fourteenth-century chivalric *Amadís de Gaula*. Closer to the present, Northrop Frye elaborates a continuum for literature of all Western traditions: "Myth . . . is one extreme of literary design; naturalism is the other, and in between lies the whole area of romance, using that term to mean . . . the tendency to displace myth in a human direction and yet, in contrast to 'realism,' to conventionalize content in an idealized direction."[12] According to Frye, for the past several centuries, movement along the continuum has occurred in two directions, "romantic" and "realistic," beginning perhaps in the twelfth century when romance aligned most fully with idealization and culminating in the fatalistic naturalism at the end of the nineteenth century.[13]

Though courtship plays no part in Frye's spectrum, if we turn to Erich Auerbach we find that his curious position on the early modern period ties back to Frye in important ways. In "The Knight Sets Forth" from *Mimesis*, Auerbach explains the courtly romance and the "knightly ideal" to stem from love: "Love in the courtly romances is already . . . the immediate occasion for deeds of valor."[14] The love plot of these romances runs in a predictable fashion, as a "fictitious order of events in which the most significant actions are performed primarily for the sake of a lady's favor" (141). Love thus privileged causes a conceptual shift, according to Auerbach, that sends the progression of realism (not romance) on a detrimental detour: "Courtly culture was decidedly unfavorable to the development of a literary art which should apprehend reality in its full breadth and depth" (142). Moreover, these origins of the courtship plot, tainted by such idealism and the fantasy inherent in the imaginary chivalric hero, pose a serious problem for later structural developments in the novel. Stunted by the limitations of sequential adventures, the nascent novel of the eighteenth century lacks a coherent plotline, for being unable to transcend these "deeds" and the disconnectedness of their episodic form.

With respect to this problem of coherence, Ian Watt believes that Samuel Richardson's *Pamela* (1740) provided the answer to Auerbach's quandary for reasons contrary to Auerbach's own stated position, since Richardson addressed "the major formal problems . . . by basing his novels on a single action, a courtship."[15] In fact, through the epistolary form, Richardson was able to achieve unity from within the courtship dynamic itself, that is, from the inside. Watt defines courtship as a "single action" and thus echoes Aristotle's elevation of plot over character in the *Poetics*. This turnabout has much to tell us. As the crux of romance, courtship undermines realism for Auerbach, while it provides Watt with the mechanism that makes the iconic medium of realism, the nineteenth-century novel, possible.

It is important to understand, though, that this juxtaposition of the views of Auerbach and Watt with regard to courtship in the context of Frye's continuum is more than simply a theoretical exercise toward an elucidation of the aesthetic consequences of mixed literary modes. Recent feminist criticism concerned with the romance-realism dichotomy, in general, and the Spanish nineteenth-century novel, in particular, has shown that traditional definitions of realism as "an absolute denial of the principle of idealism" carry profound ideological implications.[16] Historically, the many manifestations of Spanish romanticism when taken as a totality explain a great deal about literature after the Revolution of 1868 and, as consequence, risk being overshadowed in their own right.[17] Holding a privileged place both in the academy and beyond, the realist novel, as far as the Spanish canon is now concerned, represents the iconic locus of convergence between these diverse romantic strains, foreign models, and autochthonous innovations in these years of political upheaval and those of the Restoration in the decades following.

However, to place Spanish romanticism in the service of realism as a less "realized" precursor, tacit in the above tendency, is no less problematic than to assume that the novel did not exist in Spain before 1868. For it was Benito Pérez Galdós himself who first declared "we have no novel" in his now often cited essay from 1870, "Observaciones sobre la novela contemporánea en España," which decried excesses of fantasy and a literary market gorging itself on romantic serial novels of foreign origin.[18] Whether he is to blame or not, such a contention has led to implicit and explicit suppositions that often generalize the literary production of pre-1868 Spain under the umbrella of the gendered poetics of the *folletín*, characterized by the stock plots of courtly love found in earlier romances. The salient traits of melodrama—characters of good and evil, happy endings, action over description, implausible instances of peripety, imagination over observation, and, often, supernatural interventions—then eclipse the actual, much more multifaceted production of the period. The historical consequence is that the *romance* of Spanish romanticism comes to be aligned with idealism, which carries associations with sentimentality and subjectivity and, in turn, translates to what patriarchal culture has deemed "feminine." A critical schism takes place, and juxtaposed to this ideological delineation of the feminine-romantic, a host of masculine-realist contraries emerges, including determinism, materialism, objectivity, naturalism, and the like. Hence, though one may take issue with Frye's story of origins, his continuum has a lot to do with courtship and, in important ways, underwrites this strand of sociopolitical discourse on nineteenth-century literature, Spanish or otherwise, still very much ongoing among today's scholars.

Though sure to provoke for being itself an oversimplification, my sketch of the politicized climate coloring these critical conversations is meant to illustrate crossover. The intent, in other words, is neither to take issue with the above adumbration nor to argue for its legitimacy. Rather, at this point it is enough to recognize the existence of such a consensus in current scholarship concerned with the period. Indeed, the "gendering of poetics,"[19] what I believe to be the other face of Frye's continuum, has led many to reexamine and reconfigure the representational directions of the nineteenth century in various traditions. For example, writing on George Sand and ideal-ism, Naomi Schor describes a specious division of literary labor, with mimesis as man's work and women writers as unable to see the world without rose-colored glasses. More troublesome than the hierarchy of aesthetic value that emerges from this paradigm in favor of the "(vir-ile) depiction of the horrors of unembellished nature" (44), accord-ing to Schor, is woman's relationship to the truth that women are, literally, unable to see because of their temperament. She also states that "reading the romance is perhaps the most prevalent expression of feminine idealism" in popular culture (32), which highlights the link I aim to establish and later unravel between the two in the context of my own argument.

Likewise, Margaret Cohen calls attention to the "*intraliterary dynamics*" at play in the codification of competing forms of the novel with the emergence of realism in nineteenth-century France, and principally between the realist and the sentimental social nov-els.[20] Cohen maintains the "hostile takeover" of sentimental codes on the part of male authors like Stendhal and Balzac (who were models for later Spanish realists); the operation unfolds in a twofold man-ner: "aggressive campaigns to masculinize the novel in realist poet-ics as well as polemics and the pervasive gendering of sentimentality as feminine" (14). Finally, Laurie Langbauer, who sees woman and romance as "inextricably intertwined," argues against the male novel order, since romance and women have become the scapegoats in a patriarchal construction of history meant to maintain such order.[21] She finds Watt's "rise of the novel" to carry with it a pervasive gender bias and believes that literary history itself is nothing more than an oedipal plot intent on discarding romance, the mother figure, to sup-plant it with the novel father. In this way, both novels and patriarchy construct history so as "to put an end to it" (61), and no distinction of romance and the realist novel is possible that does not blur the two.[22] In sum, though these two literary modes may be different in degree rather than in kind, with neither intrinsically what it has been made to appear in relation to sex, the sexual politics, as these critics aim to show, devalue romance and, by extension, women.

In the case of Spain, Alda Blanco points out a similar (albeit pos-terior) sequence of events along the same lines as Cohen's argument, while emphasizing nationalism and misogyny in her own elaboration of Schor's views on the decanonization of idealism and the associa-tions between femininity and literary decadence.[23] The idea that the

realist novel arrived late to Spain, promulgated in the past by pre-
eminent Hispanists like Marcelino Menéndez Pelayo and José Mon-
tesinos and long since refuted, traces back to the persistent notion
that romantic fiction, reduced to courtly romance and the stock plots
of popular serial novels, was intended for a female audience, making women to blame for a Peninsular delay in the aesthetic "maturation" that had already occurred in other European literary traditions
with respect to the novel. These are the gendered echoes of Galdós's
own opinions on frivolous escapism versus serious observation and
the bane of dependence on foreign models. Canon formation contributed to the construction of Spanishness, and since nation-building
went hand in hand with the realist novel, Blanco argues that "paramount to this nationalist novelistic project was the retrieval and recir-
culation of the traditional idea of 'lo castizo' which came to function
in the discourse as the symbolic representation of 'masculinity' in
opposition to the 'femininity' of imitation and sentimental writing"
(133). Likewise, Wadda C. Ríos-Font postulates that the nineteenth-
century Spanish canon, as it stands today, hides the fact that before
1868 "the serial novel was not an extracanonical form subordinate
or oppositional to other, already prestigious and 'canonized' novels
but, simply, the novel. Men and women writers shared in the development of the form."[24] Finally, given nineteenth-century demograph-
ics, literacy rates, and the personal libraries of prominent Spanish
men, it is doubtful, according to Elisa Martí-López, that the majority
readership of the *folletines* was female.[25] These positions show some
ways a dichotomization of the romance-realist modalities has shaped
critiques on gender and genre, in general, and in the context of nineteenth-century Spain, in particular. The approach brings Frye and
other theorists, namely, Auerbach and Watt, together with those who
draw out, in one way or another, the "gendering of poetics" latent in
their claims.

TRUE IN MATTER

The Spanish term *romance* carries with it a long and complicated
past. Both Donald L. Shaw and Russell P. Sebold have illustrated,
however, that the Spanish conception of *romance*, in its purest form
and as it was understood by most Spaniards in the nineteenth century, did not diverge in any measurable degree from the connotations of the English "romance" in the broader European context.[26] In

Spain during the early decades of the nineteenth century, romanticism was seen as an alternative to the rigid norms of classicism and, in accord with the views of A. W. Schlegel and F. W. J. Schelling, traced back to medieval Christianity and the chivalric ideal. Shaw notes the chronology of the many transformations of the term (*románico, romancista, romanesco, romancesco, romántico*) and underscores two shortcomings on the part of the Fernandine critics (1814–34), the earliest school of Spanish thinkers to theorize on the question. First, the "failure to associate romanticism with a specifically contemporary *Weltanschauung* . . . to distinguish between the old romantics such as Shakespeare and Calderón and the new romantics such as Byron," limited their appreciation of innovation in literary technique and theme.[27] Second, the mistakenly nationalistic notion that romanticism was "something indigenous to Spain and pre-eminently Spanish," stemming from Spanish as a romance language and an admiration for Calderón, made all Christian-era literature romantic and thus rendered "the definition of romanticism so vague as to be virtually meaningless" (349). Though these ideas were eventually corrected, in such a way so as to align Spanish romanticism beginning with José Cadalso (1741–1782) from the late eighteenth century onward with the broader European movement, they persisted nonetheless under various guises well into the twentieth century. In the final analysis, Spanish romantic literature, for Shaw, centers on "the realization of the love-ideal" (358), as a carryover from the medieval chivalric romances or *novelas caballerescas*. He finds this tendency in the works of romantics in the early nineteenth century and the same idealism in the melodramatic romanticism prevalent in Spain by the middle of the nineteenth century.

Sebold builds on Shaw by pointing out that considerable confusion arose from the very fact that Spain, in contrast to England, had long used the term *novela* to refer to a piece of prose fiction (even if, until the nineteenth century, most often connoting a "short" piece of prose fiction). Any adoption, therefore, of the English word "romance," as it was being used in the eighteenth century to describe what would later be replaced by "novel," seemed unnecessary, not to mention unpatriotic, to Spanish romantics. To prove *romance* and *novela* to be synonymous, however, Sebold takes a line of argumentation that resists easy reconciliation with the romanticism-idealism match. He understands romanticism to be a by-product of the empiricism of John Locke and Isaac Newton; founded on an observational and sensorial relationship with Nature, romanticism was construed by eighteenth-century Spanish writers, like Gaspar Melchor de Jovellanos (1744–1811), as something opposed to idealism. Consequently, any clear-cut correlation between romance and romanticism, for Sebold, is misleading, because while the former of these describes the idealism of the medieval chivalric novel, it negates the naturalism of the latter.

Nevertheless, Sebold concedes that by the second half of the nineteenth century there is little difference between English "romance" and Spanish *novela*, for both trace back to the lying truth of fiction, fantasy, and the improbable adventure plots of the *libros de caballerías*. This return to the original Spanish meaning of *romance*, which by the seventeenth century had been divorced from the popular medieval ballad or *romancero* and wed to chivalric narrations like *Amadís de Gaula*, means that Spanish *romanticismo*, from Sebold's perspective, could more aptly be called "*novelesquismo*" or "*novelisticismo*."[28] The coupling of "*novela romántica*" is therefore redundant in Spanish, and yet because the pairing captures realism (*novela*) and romance (*romántica*), the nomenclature reveals in a fortuitous way "the double nature of the genre."[29] Central to Sebold's articulation of the nineteenth-century Spanish *romance*, that is, *novela*, are melodrama and chivalric idealism, yet unlike Shaw, he takes no account of "the realization of the love-ideal."[30] Therefore, while this account corrects the misperception that terminological issues prohibit discussion of the Spanish *novela* as English "romance," it is important to point out that Sebold bypasses the generic importance of courtship in his reflections on what he sees as *novelisticismo*.

So, why does it matter that Spanish *novela* and English "romance" mean the same thing at this moment in history when both were at the early stages of what would ultimately become the novel across national traditions? One connection between the two is that the English romance was, thanks to Sir Walter Scott, a model for Spain's *novela romántica*. As it happens, this romance shows something of the same hybridization at issue in the theorizing of Lukács, Bakhtin, and Frye, but this should not surprise us, since early theories juxtapose romance to "real history," the precursor to realism. Scott in his "Essay on Romance" remarks that "romance and real history have the same common origin. It is the aim of the former to maintain as long as possible the mask of veracity . . . and [novels] may be termed either romantic histories, or historical romances, according to the proportion in which their truth is debased by fiction, or their fiction mingled with truth."[31] Here, fiction compromises truth. The truth of history, though, for Scott and his contemporaries (and to the surprise of many of today's readers), stems not from objective observation and hard facts but instead from "human nature" (88), that is, what we might be imagined to do in a given set of circumstances.

Indeed, the task of writing true histories (i.e., histories that are not morally false) for Alessandro Manzoni, the Italian contemporary of Scott, requires a penetration of the motives behind actions, over the actions themselves, as the only way to know the individual, and thus the causal relationship between events.[32] This recalls Ortega's "ungraspable" individual from chapter 1. History abounds in transgressions that appear to contradict character or foil the desires of those who seek to make infallible heroes out of mortal men (and women); to critics who would suggest, though, that the tragedy be wiped away, the treason and assassination in *Il Conte di Carmagnola* (1820), for example, Manzoni explains:

> And yet, the Venetian senate did it [ordered the death of Carmagnola, their friend and benefactor]; and they had motives for doing it; the knowledge of those motives is of great interest . . . because it is very interesting to know the true thoughts for which men reach the point of committing a great injustice; it is from this knowledge that profound emotions of terror and pity can be born. . . . So, where can I find these motives? Only in history. Only there can I discover the true character of the men and of the epoch that I want to represent. (117)

With this explanation, we are starting to move closer to the ways the dire circumstances of an unjust world, as will come to define novels by writers like Sawa in the late nineteenth century, can also be indeterminate and moral. Real history provides the material substance for romance, for "fiction mingled with truth" as Scott says, but only if one knows how to read that history. And the truth of fiction, it follows, depends on dispassionate interpretation of the motives of the individual, whether these be of the Venetian senators in the case of Manzoni or the fallen women who define so many novels after *The Descent*.

Yet there is an ironic twist, for reading real history in the way Scott and Manzoni outline is to make it romance. Without question, modern theorists of history, like Hayden White, have shown romance to be best understood as a different type of history, rather than as its contrary,[33] but the concerns of Scott and Manzoni reflect those of even today's historians (and contemporary writers of historical fiction). In a little known essay titled "Of History and Romance" (1797), William Godwin addresses the relationship between the two modalities in a way that prefigures the concerns realists would have about determinism a century later, which critics continue to perpetuate with vagaries about the "traces of romanticism" in realism.[34] Instead of asking whether or not history is true or false, Godwin speaks of motives and the individual in terms of instruction (457–61). Because facts alone are an insufficient "skeleton of history," the successful historian must capture "secret thoughts" and craft "ingenious and instructive inventions" (462). However, as such, history becomes "little better than romance under a graver name" (463). The writer of romance, in contrast to the historian, enjoys the freedom to generalize and express his views so as "to impress the heart and improve the faculties of his reader" (464). Indeed, nothing could be more natural than the human proclivity to seek the "reality of romance" (466), since this is where virtue resides.

But given that the "objective" history of facts disfigures the character of the individual, in a beautiful reversal, the writer of romance becomes the only writer of "real history" (466). Determinism, though, proves part of the bargain: "True [moral] history consists in a delineation of consistent, human character, in a display of the manner in which such a character acts under successive circumstances, in showing how character increases and assimilates new substances to its own, and how it decays, together with the catastrophe into which by its own gravity it naturally declines" (466). This sounds a lot like Zola in his prologue to *Thérèse Raquin* (1867), where he claims his novel to be "the study of temperament and of the profound modifications of an organism through the influence of environment and circumstances."[35] But no sooner does Godwin make this stand, that is, behavior *determined* by circumstance, he backtracks that "to write romance is a task too great for the powers of man" ("Of History and Romance," 466), because the chain of circumstance is infinitely complex, making "secret thoughts" impenetrable. Whether in history or romance, the best that can be hoped for is a unified depiction of events as they unfold, for there is "no reason to suppose . . . that what is true in matter is false in morals" (467). Indeed, in a surprising turn, *moral truth* defines determinism, for man "is propelled to act by necessary causes and irresistible motives."[36] So if truth is moral, and morality is matter, and virtue, the ideal, it follows that the fatalism of circumstance *redeems* the individual, at the same time that it instructively shows the errors of mankind.

Godwin's reconciliation of romance and realism, or rather "real history," prefigures the moralism integral to the novel in the late nineteenth century as propounded by the authors themselves and so often denied by their detractors. No doubt, the meaning of romance changes over time, and its connotations for Scott, Manzoni, and Godwin differ from those of the term's modern usage. Yet to pair romance with subjective invention and imagination, while making the realist novel analogous to "real history" as objective and impartial, lessens the discrepancies. The realism of romance, despite its formal linkages to individual character as inseparable from material causality, still leaves Darwinian evolutionism tangential to the moral truth espoused by a writer like Sawa in his depiction of an immoral world, for the form of both, each in this case subsumed by determinism, remains at odds with itself. That is to say, determinism structures moral truth no less than it does the immoral world—this apparent paradox is the key to my corrective reading of the Darwin-determinism pairing.

Consequently, to reconcile this apparent contradiction, it is necessary to posit the real history of romance as dialectical. Michael McKeon sees the origins of the English novel, so influential for Spain, in just such a light, as "a structure of 'reversal' in which change takes place as the generation of difference from similarity, of opposition from identity."[37] One such reversal, enabling a dialectical synthesis that Scott blurs in his juxtaposition of fiction to truth, transpires with the transition from romance to realism: "The novel ceased to be fundamentally opposed to romance once the theory of realism had mastered . . . the basic lesson that fiction might be compatible with truth. This was a lesson romance had always known. And yet the terms in which it could now once again become intelligible were the terms of a complex theory of affective response that had no equivalent [form]."[38] But changes in "affective response," the reactions the novel causes as we recognize the truth value of its narrative form, the resultant pathos described by Manzoni, evolve temporally because they cannot be divorced from the material: "The inescapable materiality of works of art is . . . the irreplaceable materialization of kinds of experience. . . . To write in different ways is to live in different ways."[39] After Darwin, the novel looks different because writers, like Alejandro Sawa, "live in different ways," confronted by the imperceptible biological forces driving behavior and hence dedicated to "the irreplaceable materialization" of real social relations as dictated by the unfathomable operation of non-teleological evolution. In sum, virtue, if present at all, must be found where it cannot be seen.

READING THE NATURE OF CIRCUMSTANCE

Alejandro Sawa's life is inseparable from the art it produced.[40] Born in Seville of a Greek father and an Andalusian mother, Sawa inherited an outsider's identity that would define his mythic self-perception and follow him to a bitter death on the margins of Spanish society. While still a young boy, he moved with his family to Málaga and attended a seminary there until his condemnation of the Church as an adolescent. This experience contributed to the fierce anticlericalism characteristic of his fiction and journalism. In 1885, Sawa left southern Spain for Madrid in hopes of making a name for himself as a writer. During his five years in the capital, he published most of his novels, including *La mujer de todo el mundo* (1885), *Crimen legal* (1886), *Declaración de un vencido* (1887), and *Noche* (1888), but his bohemian existence remained one of abject poverty and scandal. By 1890, Sawa had moved to Paris, where he worked at a publishing house as a translator, most notably of works by the brothers Goncourt. Six years later, he returned to Madrid and became an editor and contributor for important Spanish periodicals of the day, including *El País*, *España*, and *El Liberal*. Nevertheless, the move back to Spain also brought a dramatic deterioration in Sawa's health, physical and psychological. By 1906, he was blind, mad, and in a state of financial ruin, which led to severed ties with even his most loyal supporters. Sawa chronicled the experience of these years in *Iluminaciones en la sombra*, published posthumously in 1910, and is today most remembered (if at all) for his tumultuous friendship with Rubén Darío and as the inspiration for Max Estrella in Ramón María del Valle-Inclán's landmark modernist drama *Luces de bohemia* (1920).[41]

From the hellish conflagration of the vile countess at the conclusion of *La mujer de todo el mundo* to the adulterous husband in *Crimen legal* who "murders" his unfit wife by intentionally impregnating her, Sawa's fatalism culminates in the disturbing degeneration of the González family of *Noche*, which shares something in this respect with Giovanni Verga's *I Malavoglia* (1881).[42] The difference, though, is that the distanced optic of Verga's verism makes of Lia, the young sister who ultimately turns to prostitution, an abstraction. Her representation, like that of the evils that befall the Malavoglia family as a whole, is impressionistic and impersonal. By contrast, the life of Lola constitutes the first half of Sawa's novel and could not be more magnified. Naive and pious as a child, she becomes curious about carnal sin under the sexual innuendos of her perverted confessor, Don Gregorio. Shortly thereafter, a handsome playboy seduces her at a ball, convinces her to run away with him, and leaves her dishonored in a remote part of town. Meanwhile, Don Gregorio, made privy to the details, suffers days of delirium for not having been the one to deflower her, and when she shows up on his doorstep in a state of desperation, he rapes her and throws her to the street. Disowned by her father, Lola survives as a prostitute and, by the (shorter and less realized) second half of the novel, disappears completely, as a montage of subplots depicts the total social collapse of the family.

The bestiality of *Noche* exploits Darwin's principle of continuity between man and animals in *The Descent*. The novel's patriarch, Don Francisco, proves "a bull, as capable of the work as of the rage," whose lineage and Catholic indoctrination compromise his cultural "adaptation."[43] The Church, in fact, interferes with his psychosexual maturation, as he comes to equate women with sin, and the narrator's voice apostrophizes on the subject of those "young organisms" who, perverted by chastity, "never serve to fertilize any woman's womb" (97). Darwin might call this the "senseless practice of celibacy" (*The Descent*, 1:96). Don Francisco's wife, Dolores, suffers as a "slave" in the marriage because of her "powerful animality" in terms of reproductive ability and "tame" disposition (*Noche*, 99). She exemplifies "the animal soul," which is nothing more than "the accumulation of instincts" and, as such, represents "a female . . . exactly like all of those of her species, in that she had mammary glands in her breasts and a urinary genital organ designed for conception under her womb" (99). With respect to their domestic life in the years just after marriage, and especially regarding sexual intercourse, the narrator reflects that "the struggle for life is not only that of the street but also of the home, next to the crib where the firstborn sleeps" (100). However, once "the personality of the wife" has been "suppressed," there is no longer "struggle" at the González home, for "like all inferior animals," Don Francisco knows how to procreate: "He swelled the belly of his wife with the seed of conception five times in ten years" (100). Together Don Francisco and Dolores have "the same strange fecundity as insects" (101). Such sexualized animalism runs throughout Sawa's *Noche*.

The tale turns blackest, however, on the rain-soaked morning when Lola arrives at the house of her confessor, Don Gregorio, in a confused state of remorse after being defiled by Galán. So as to be left alone with her, the sinister priest excuses his maid and displays a degree of bestiality unprecedented in Spanish literature. The scene begins as "a drama in a clearing, like that committed by a satyr with a virgin in the interior of a forest," and ends with a description of Don Gregorio in the act of sexual perpetration:

> He carried out the work, everything he sought, until all the neces-sary forces for continuing to wallow in its execution were completely depleted. And he reached a state closer to the dissipation of his entire being, than to the great rebirth that he awaited; now without blood in his head, that only moments before had been congested; with palpita-tions and without a firm pulse; his dry tongue seemed to flap against the roof of his mouth; his whole body was soaked, even the cassock, in a cold sweat, sebaceous and sticky, that gushed from him with the fecundity of pus from a recently opened tumor, from all the pores of his body. (169–70)

This is not Tess "sleeping soundly" as a "coarse pattern" is traced over her "beautiful feminine tissue" by Alec d'Urberville in Thomas Hardy's novel of the same period.[44] On the contrary, Lola can only scream "Help!" after this violation (*Noche*, 170). So where in Darwin lurks the novelistic skeleton of Don Gregorio, the satyr-priest, and his rape of a helpless young girl? As the biological catchall for naturalism in the writings of Pura Fernández and so many critics across national traditions who describe determinism of the late nineteenth century alongside Darwin, evolutionism has come to absorb Sawa's perverted scientism. His exaggerated bestiality disturbs, though, because the origins of the degeneration depicted are all too cultural.

Yet Sawa's in-your-face scenes, for all their shock value, over-shadow something deeper. *Noche* begins badly, only to end worse, and the unity of the tragic plot buckles under the weight of multi-ple fatalities. Supplanted by episodic incoherence, courtship becomes virtually illegible. Gorged with calamity after calamity, at a certain point one wonders what formal principle, if any, can inspire (and sup-port) such an indulgent structure. It cannot be the "single action" of plot Watt had in mind when speaking of courtship, but neither is it the "deeds of valor . . . performed primarily for the sake of a lady's favor" described by Auerbach. Multiple apostrophes in Sawa's work speak of the cultural consequences of turning against natural forces like reproduction: "Oh, Mother Nature! Oh, saintly instinct of fecundation of all living species on the planet! You are the only true pleasure that exists on this earth! Who says that male and female reproductive organs are unworthy of painting and of ode, that they do not constitute by themselves the most noble and most sacred part of the human organism?" (*Noche*, 189). Asides cry of the abject futility of faith in humanity and in free will, for social pressures compounded over time override self-realization: "Oh, fatalism, soul of the world! Determinism, law of life!" (203). In Hardy, this would be Tess's people saying among one another, "It was to be" (*Tess of the d'Urbervilles*, 74).

By the end of *Noche*, "night had fallen" (262) over the destiny of every character in the novel not because of Nature, as "naturalism" suggests, but because of its unnatural perversion, if not its total erasure. Therefore, when Catherine Jagoe in the context of works by Galdós talks more broadly about naturalism's "denaturalizing of the culture's feminine ideal," her point is well taken, but the contradiction persists in such a way that the terminology we use to discuss the movement works against us.[45] When naturalism denaturalizes by definition, the nomenclature is at odds with itself. There is another way, however, to see the matter. For Sawa, environment dictates the end of the individual—that is the extent of natural law; but paradoxically, environment does not equal Nature, which operates outside of Culture in this conception. In other words, Nature calibrates social morality as a standard by which humanity, thought to be the evolutionary apex, might be gauged. Sawa's bestiality is, in truth, a Darwinian disfigurement, a trope that leads us astray, for when characters act like animals they forget their "human nature," as both Scott and Darwin understood it.

In other words, Sawa makes us think that Nature is ugly, but what he really shows is how despicable Culture can become when rent from Nature. Through the deaths he represents at every turn, the organic serves as a corrective; as much a producer, or more so, the individual is a biological product of circumstance. These circumstances appear never in isolation but rather in relation to events before and after. A question of Darwinian structure, Sawa's determinism is about how we read this circumstance, just as we have seen with respect to the real history of romance. As Godwin would say, there is "no reason to suppose . . . that what is true in matter is false in morals." Like evolution itself, the syntax is at once sequential and relational, and the moral truth, so imbedded in the "entangled bank" (*Origin*, 489) of narrative, is a *matter* of virtue. The indeterminism resides in the sequencing and relating of these circumstances in their indefinite syntax, and with courtship out of the picture the moral truth of sexual selection is even more apparent for its omission.

THE IDEOLOGY OF FORM

From all that we have now seen, it should be clear that a continuum defined by extremes of romance and realism is misleading, since the two modalities are not polar opposites at all. Rather, they have always needed each other, and yet the truth is that we often speak as if the two were entirely separate, contentious entities. In the case of Sawa, this tendency is alive and well, especially in light of his admiration for the romantics. Amelina Correa Ramón in her recent biography of the author describes the legendary account of Sawa's first trip to Paris in search of his idol Victor Hugo, whose (disputed) kiss led him not to wash for days, and she chronicles the love letters Sawa exchanged with his wife during months of separation, which call to mind the "knightly ideal" set in a different age.[46] Sawa himself resented criticism that found his early novels to be too "romantic," and by *Noche* he was writing in such a way that troubled even his naturalist circle for being over the top. His life and reputation, indeed, often lead to a search for his romanticism for these very reasons. Correa says of *La mujer de todo el mundo* that "the imprint of past romanticism is still very visible," and Jean-Claude Mbarga in his critical introduction to *Noche* remarks that "to define the literary trajectory of Sawa, one can say that he is this: a writer who in his novelistic stage utilizes features from naturalism and romanticism."[47] These commentaries echo more commonplace theoretical postulations on realism, Spanish or otherwise. Biruté Ciplijauskaité, for one, claims that "romanticism can be present in a realist work, whether as an assimilated technique, or as a theme for critiquing it, or as a caricature by means of which one parodies both the theme and the technique. . . . While in France, Germany, England, literary movements conform to a chronological sequence, in Spain a superposition/imbrication occurs."[48] Though I find these critiques problematic (and Ciplijauskaité's patently wrong) for the ways they make it seem as if romanticism could somehow be located and extracted like a malignant growth from realism, I also recognize that in the shadow of their claims lurks the dichotomization delineated by Frye.

The trick then to speaking about Darwin in this context is to recognize his pairing with these novels as valid, but not in the ways we have been led to believe by critics like Fernández and so many others. The first step toward this conclusion requires that we transcend the continuum set forth by Frye, while at the same time keeping it in view because of the ideological questions it envelopes with respect to gender, genre, and nation. Frye's polarization leads us to see after all, once we account for courtship, the connection among realism, sexual selection, and the state. But we have not yet managed to free ourselves from the terminology we have inherited, which limits the way we can talk about the dark *eros* of Sawa's *Noche* or any other comparable novelistic variation aimed at dissolving the love-ideal. Even if we accept that reading circumstance can instruct us in the virtue of an unjust world, it remains to be clarified why the deterministic form is itself moral for this very reason. Fredric Jameson's theory of the political unconscious provides one means by which evolution can elucidate the implications without the discursive polarization characteristic of Frye and those in his wake. However, usage of Jameson requires substitutions (not allegorical equivalencies). Early in his argument, he states "that history is not a text, not a narrative, master or otherwise, but that, as an absent cause, it is inaccessible to us except in textual form, and that our approach to it and to the Real itself necessarily passes through its prior textualization, its narrativization in the political unconscious."[49] He might just as well have said, though, that Nature is an absent cause, accessible to us only in textual form, as our approach to the Real passes through its prior textualization, its narrativization in the evolutionary unconscious. In other words, it is true that "naturalism denaturalizes," for in wiping away its own truths it cannot do otherwise.

Our humanity, our human nature written by the "absent cause" of an evolutionary Nature, tells us that the Real is not inert. Indeed, as Jameson writes, Nature acts as a "system of *relationships*" (36), and evolution serves, dialectically, the end of "mediation" between the "work of art and its social ground" (39). In this way, difference, as between romance and realism, acts as a "relational concept" rather than as a static "inventory of unrelated diversity" (41), as in Mbarga's claims to the effect that Sawa's fiction "utilizes features from naturalism and romanticism" (introduction to *Noche*, 29). This "relational concept" of Jameson also harkens back to McKeon's dialectic between romance and realism. It follows then that "the ideal of logical closure," which in the predominant critical frame of Sawa's *Noche* (and all naturalism, for that matter) amounts to "determinism = Darwinism," can now be "an indispensable instrument for revealing those logical and ideological centers a particular historical text fails to realize, or on the contrary seeks desperately to repress" (Jameson, *The Political Unconscious*, 49). *Noche*, as an aesthetic "interference" (56) between two codependent levels—the biological and the social—amounts to "a symbolic mediation on the destiny of community" (70). So, though Jameson might call the "perspectives of Marxism . . . necessary preconditions for adequate literary comprehension" (75), "Darwinism" would be better suited. Indeed, Jameson's "the ideology of form" (98) in "Darwinian determinism" hides the truth that "the inexorable form of events," what Jameson calls "the experience of Necessity" (102), rather than History, is Nature.

Along with Lola, the experience of this Necessity in *Noche* can best be perceived in her sister, Paca. Both are martyrs, but whereas Lola suffers the rape by Don Gregorio and falls into the shadows of prostitution, Paca knows her destitute parents must eat. Consequently, she sacrifices herself to their care, earning a pittance as a seamstress and sleeping on a board without sheets until death intervenes. Her final days bring reflection and feeble rebellion; Paca died "without having lived. She had vegetated, her organism had functioned for twenty-eight years day after day, but with the life of a plant, and at times, like that of a stone, that does not move from where it is placed" (*Noche*, 218). According to the narrator, the fate of Paca, albeit analogous to that of a plant or stone, is unnatural because inanimate, inhuman. It is the Real in its ideological narrativization made inert for a reason, to tell us something about Nature and Necessity. Through the removal of courtship, of the choice and individual will inherent in sexual selection as explicated by Darwin in *The Descent*, the opposite destinies of these sisters speak in silent terms of the "ideology of form." Of course, the plots of many novels from the nineteenth century, before and after, turn on events unrelated to courtship. *Noche* differs from these in that its two female protagonists spiral down, degenerate into a prostitute and a vegetable, because of the absence. The invisibility, the social obliteration of sexual selection, and the determinism itself together constitute the form of events. Yet because Lola and Paca at the same time are "naturalist" representations of Sawa's ideological agenda, the lack of courtship, that is, his refutation of idealism functions as a cultural equivalent to the negation of

Darwinian sexual selection, as the "symbolic mediation on the destiny of community." Without regenerative procreation there can be no life, and still these sisters, as victims of circumstance, escape blame because the very form allows real history to be read as romance. The love-ideal is a present absence. The motives, and hence character, of Lola and Paca are never in question, something Godwin would call an "instructional" turnabout in the interest of moral virtue.

A MORE SYMPATHETIC DARWIN

When people speak today about the study of narrative through the lens of evolution, they forget that among critics concerned with naturalism Darwin has always been the theoretical bedrock, though with only a partial understanding of his science. However, the Darwinism-determinism platform, although useful for an appreciation of authorial intent (Sawa's orientation, for example), proves insufficient for the very same reason. The author-centered approach remains little more than a gloss of both. That is, *Noche* is Darwinian, but not for the reasons the author or we might have thought. Speaking of those who have sought to problematize the Spanish nineteenth-century canon, Hazel Gold rightly stresses that "they point to dislocations, slippages, and contradictions at precisely the level of structure and language as proof of the ways in which the ruling ideologies of texts, their authors, and society at large may be involved in a high-stakes game of concealment and self-betrayal."[50] Since Darwin already holds a place in the Spanish canon and its criticism, as the conceptual frame for determinism, what lacks is a *conceptual* understanding of what he is doing there, other than provoking authors like Alejandro Sawa to kill off their characters, especially those that are female, one by one in gruesome detail (which gives nothing more than the *frame*).

To get to the "concealment and self-betrayal," we need to scrutinize from within, at the level of the form of events, if we are to discover the ideology at work. Let us first recall what Eve Kosofsky Sedgwick says about rape and its representation; it will be rape "*to her* and to all the forces in her culture that produce and circulate powerful meanings."[51] Herein lies the volatility of "the signifying relation of sex to power" (10) in ideological terms. Thinking of Darwin's often referenced image of the "entangled bank" in *Origin*, although "red in tooth and claw" as likened to Tennyson's famous verse, it also offers a sublime moment of Nature teeming with life.[52] Any syntactic comparison, therefore, between this vital image and naturalist realism where fatalism and degeneration reign supreme might seem misguided. It must be noted, first, that "entangled" signifies relational and, then, admitted that mechanistic (amoral/immoral) causality follows in public perception. Hence, Darwin's legacy, like that of the literary "determinism" he unwittingly birthed at the end of the nineteenth century according to the critical consensus, stands far from the moral truth of idealism, where the good are rewarded and the evil punished. However, in something akin to a Godwinian turn, the association of idealism with the courtship of romance rescues both Darwin and the realists, since romance remains the modality that structures readings of circumstance and character in real history, even when it cannot be seen. In this way, Sawa's *Noche* bears, or rather hides, a particular narrative truth—even an indeterminate evolution can be moral when it comes to questions of the human heart.

At one point in *The Descent*, Darwin says that the very existence of community should be an indication that we have an instinctive "impulse" toward "love and sympathy" (1:86), passed down to us from our earliest progenitors. Indeed, this sympathy, which is part and parcel of sexual selection, underwrites the social instincts, "serving as the primary impulse and guide" for the "general happiness of mankind" (1:98), and is among the noblest virtues of our humanity (1:101). This Darwin, no doubt, sounds a lot different from the one we met at the outset of this chapter, whose amoral worldview was responsible for the perceived immorality of novels in his wake. Instead, from Godwin to Jameson, we discover that it is in our nature to seek the reality of romance, out of Necessity, in the quest for the virtue of humanity. When it is nowhere to be found, as in Sawa's dire tale, our "affective response" (McKeon, "Prose Fiction," 263), those "emotions of terror and pity" (Manzoni, "Lettera a Monsieur Chauvet," 117), will tell us it should be there, and this misgiving might just be enough to "to impress the heart and improve the faculties" (Godwin, "Of History and Romance," 464) toward greater sympathy, for the good of the community. George Eliot would call this vision of "Darwinian determinism" a rejection of "sympathy readymade" in preference for the "raw material" that provokes indeterminate change.[53] In the dark of *Noche*, I can read no truer romance with Darwin than this.

CHAPTER EIGHT

The Religious *Descent*
of Armando Palacio Valdés

As Darwin works through sexual selection in *The Descent*, he takes due measure of primary factors and conjectures on everything from language to race. We must forgive him, then, if he fails to consider what might happen to his model should Christ enter the fray. Yet, since the Middle Ages, in countries steeped in Catholicism nubile women have taken nuptials with the Redeemer, and in Spain, where the amorous *Song of Songs* and the legacy of Santa Teresa de Jesús, the most iconic *sponsa Christi*, color the religious identity of a nation, this heavenly Bridegroom has proven a real catch. Likewise, no discussion of the plasticity of sexual selection in the cultural realm would be complete without attention to the confessor turned suitor and the troubling power relations of penitence, in light of the history of solicitation cases during the Inquisition and in the second half of the nineteenth century the wave of Spanish novels concerned with the influence of deviant priests on their impressionable female flock. Indeed, to tease out these phenomena in tandem, to wed Science and Religion according to sex, we must look for Darwin where least expected and turn to fiction that explores the interplay of this most peculiar betrothal and the seductive allure of sinful disclosure.

Following the 1868 revolution, the Spanish novel became ever more empirical in its artistic precepts at the same time that it reflected to an ever-greater degree the ideological fissure between Science and Religion.[1] A political powder keg, Darwin's works took center stage in public debates and the print culture as incendiary associations rather than his own words fanned the polemical fervor surrounding *el darwinismo*.

In chapter 3, I discussed some of the problems with his translations but did not extend my coverage to the context of the Church. As for these translations, there was, though, much that added fuel to the fire. For example, Darwin's controversial French translator, Clémence Royer, played a catalytic role when stating in her 1862 introduction to the earliest edition of *Origin* to be disseminated on the Peninsula: "It is necessary to choose between a quite categorical yes and no [progress (Darwin's science) or Religion], and whoever declares himself for one is against the other."[2] Carl Vogt's prologue to the 1872 French translation of *The Descent* raised ire less for its hyperbolic content than for Vogt's personal notoriety as a scientist made famous for stating that "Science said, down with Religion."[3] Finally, the popularity of the 1875 Spanish edition of John William Draper's *History of the Conflict between Religion and Science* intensified this entire climate.

From this polarized landscape in its real-world sexual manifestations, Armando Palacio Valdés (1853–1938) drew his literary inspiration. Palacio Valdés was in his own lifetime one of the most famous Spanish writers, a prominent cultural critic, and a close collaborator with José del Perojo and Manuel de la Revilla, the primary proponents of Darwin in Spain. Having published more than twenty widely read novels, all of which were reprinted several times, he was rivaled within Spain only by Benito Pérez Galdós and beyond was hailed as one of the world's greatest novelists, his writings having been translated into more than ten different languages and included in many student textbooks across the globe.[4] Yet his fleeting popularity, coupled with his own self-effacement and later dismissals as a second-rate entertainer by renowned Hispanists like Donald L. Shaw, has led some to question the merit of his works.[5] Others, though, laud the acumen of Palacio Valdés with respect to the secularization of Spanish society, perverse semantic domains, naturalist psychopathology, and the spiritual crises that prefigure Spanish modernism.[6] For my part, I believe that the melodramatic quality of his novels gives a transparency of moral absolutes, at the same time that it masks a search for something still sacred in a post-Enlightenment world.[7] The unambiguous virtues upheld by melodrama stem from a complex impulse to push through the surface of the real toward the true, moral realm of experience. Ultimately, though, wherever one falls on Palacio Valdés's writing, when it comes to the treatment of the spiritual marriage plot and the eroticism of the confessor-confessant relationship, no other writer treats sexual selection as he does.

As this chapter will show, Palacio Valdés makes clear the ideological indeterminacy of Darwinian sexual selection in the not-so-clear ways his novels position Science against the Church. This is the religious "*Descent*" of his writing, and on the surface such an anticlerical stance feels progressive in its historical context. A new scientifically enlightened liberalism aims to supplant the ruling orthodoxy of Catholicism and many of the traditions it upholds. However, this platform, akin to the political essays of Manuel de la Revilla on *la cuestión de la mujer* from chapter 3, merely provides a front for the author's conservatism when it comes to the role of women. Palacio Valdés, in effect, positions naturalized sexual selection, that is, the sexual selection of Darwin's evolutionary science in *The Descent*, against perversions of the Church that impede real reproduction, like mystical nuptials and celibate priests, as a means to uphold the status quo of patriarchy in service of the domestic ideal.

In *Marta y María* (1883), the opposed ends of two sisters exemplify this tactic. While one might read María's rejection of a prearranged marriage in favor of the divine Bridegroom as a reappropriation of her rightful selector status, it is too divorced from the material world for that view to be endorsed on evolutionary grounds. By contrast, Marta passively chooses Ricardo at the novel's conclusion and promises to be the perfect, subservient wife in a heart-warming finale that masks the very type of subjugation that troubled Darwin in *The Descent*, albeit in a less recognizable form. Likewise, Father Gil, the priest-protagonist of *La fe* (1892), lets his faith interfere with what it means to be a man in the Darwinian model; rejects the advances of an overly eager Obdulia, whose false accusations later lead to his incarceration; and ends by lying to himself about the saving grace of divine (as opposed to natural) law. But such synopses capture neither the nuances nor the persuasiveness of these novels. Science and Religion are indeed about sex, but sexual selection in the realism of Palacio Valdés provides an unanticipated answer for why. The Darwinian dynamic proves malleable enough to be at once progressive and oppressive when clouded by the supernatural in a world of sex where God should, in theory, have no place.

PLOTTING MYSTICAL NUPTIALS

With *Marta y María*, a novel in which "all the fundamental facts . . . really happened" according to the author's prologue, the worldly and otherworldly matrimonies of two sisters tap the ideological reach of sexual selection in ways Darwin never thought to imagine.[8] In effect, to make marriage to Christ a literal reality, as Palacio Valdés does, transposes the nineteenth-century antagonism between Science and Religion to the courtship dynamic. Female choice, the guiding tenet of Darwin's theory, in the hands of the narcissistic María acts as a caution to readers against the passive imagination, where the facts become unreal for their very fabrication. Her self-absorption and ultimate retreat from the world of men represent a threat to the established community. Conversely, her younger sibling, Marta, proves to be of "scientifically" sound character for both her pragmatism and quiet deference to her father and to her future husband. She becomes the household nun, just as her sister enters a convent in earnest, and as a devoted wife and daughter, she offers an industrious alternative to the sterile María, as one who elects (by being elected) to live governed by reason in the best interest of her family.

María is a blonde, blue-eyed sixteen-year-old of fragile constitution, who finds herself engaged by circumstance to the sentimental Ricardo, an orphaned marquis, since both his deceased mother and public opinion would have it that they "were declared husband and wife shortly after birth" (68). However, in the days leading up to the wedding María rebuffs Ricardo's impassioned advances with contempt, and as her mood swings manipulate his affections, it becomes clear that her heart belongs to another. In private, scantily clothed adultery fantasies with Jesus, she repents the sins she never commits with Ricardo, the betrayals of her Lord's unequaled love, for which she must be punished. On one occasion, María begs that a bewildered maid flagellate her; on another, she experiences the ecstasy of an orgasmic trance under the Redeemer's proposal for her hand; and, finally, after having been apprehended for aiding and abetting a failed Absolutist conspiracy in the name of her Beloved, she becomes "the new wife of Jesus Christ" (258) in a perverse wedding ceremony. Ricardo, in the meantime, must accept that María has found his "substitute" in the one "crowned with thorns" (91).

On the bright side, though, María has a sister. Just two years younger, a pubescent Marta provides a backdrop of contrast against which Ricardo cannot help but ponder the domestic possibilities. Nicknamed "the little round one" (137) for her bewitching stoutness, she is fair with jet-black hair and eyes complemented by a steady, serene demeanor. One day, seeing her in the kitchen kneading dough with sleeves rolled up, Ricardo reflects: "These arms announced a woman in full possession of all the telling charms, of all the pleasing curves of her sex: they were the white, soft arms of a fleshy virgin, firm and robust like the arms of a young maid, they could just as well serve as model for a statue as for making a bed like no other" (73). Her attractiveness is measured by his domestic needs. A (biblical) motif throughout the novel, Marta then feeds Ricardo, serving him as her sister never would. An attraction takes root between the two, but true to the ideal of abnegation she embodies, Marta represses her heart and watches as Ricardo suffers utter disillusionment in his love for her sister. It is not until the final scene that Nature at last rights itself. Exhausted and melancholic, Ricardo dreams that María is in reality Marta. He awakes certain of a stolen kiss, sees through her feigned modesty, and calls forthwith to her father to ask for her hand. As the three cry with joy, Marta inquires, "Will you eat with us today, Ricardo?" to which he replies, "Yes, my precious," falling to his knees and kissing her hands, "I will eat today, and tomorrow, and the day after tomorrow . . . and forever . . ." (276). To be sure, she "hid her face anew against the paternal breast" of her father, for her heart was "so full of happiness!" (276).

To gloss the storyline, nevertheless, oversimplifies what is in truth a singular elaboration by Palacio Valdés of courtship, the marriage plot, and Christ in a post-Darwin world. In other words, while knowing the events might allow us to make inferences about the author's ideological agenda, from his measured anticlericalism to the patriarchal apotheosis of the husband in the domestic sphere, an overview of the sort overlooks the particulars of the peculiar. To move from the *what* to the *how* with respect to María's mystical nuptials requires that we focus on the process, especially if her spiritual marriage to Christ is to be understood in the material terms of Darwinian sexual selection. Indeed, the religious as it is manifest in a social critique of individualist fanaticism remains also at once scientific when framed in this way, yet María's rejection of Ricardo is by no means a typical case study of the laws of male-male combat and female choice. The author makes his choice clear, but María's is embedded in the bizarre "path to perfection" (88) she traverses en route to a twisted vainglory that undermines a dynamic directed, in Darwin's theory, toward variation via reproduction. To this end, the "vivid imagination" and its role in the "strange acts" of María's "secret and saintly fantasies" (89) represent a nexus of realist experimentation on Science and Religion with respect to sex.

In the prologue to the first edition, Palacio Valdés relates that María's character was inspired by an image he found in a popular periodical of his day. It depicted the distress of onlookers, most notably of a mother, as a young girl took her vows to enter a convent. The illustration reminds him of so many cases he has known like hers, not from distant history but rather from his own times. He wants to understand the forces behind these cases and hopes that his readers will probe the causes for themselves:

> I felt myself moved before that scene, admirably interpreted by the artist, and as a natural consequence I was besieged by various recollections and no shortage of reflections tied to that very subject, and I thought that it deserved further study. It was not something ancient, remote, that might only serve as a topic for the research of the historian, but rather of a most curious and interesting occurrence that was taking place before our very own eyes. The enthusiasm, the impassioned raptures, the intoxication and even mania of those souls, at once innocent and ardent, that find no means to quench the thirst that devours them and to calm the restlessness that martyrs them in the market of the world; they look for medicine for its evil in the mystery of the cloister. These souls seemed to me a worthwhile theme for the contemporary novelist to treat and I offer it with due respect for the public's consideration. (ii–iii)

This is what he means by "all the fundamental facts . . . really happened" (i). The question then is not whether the social ill decried by Palacio Valdés is about sex but rather why sex, in the real cases here recalled and that of María, is about religion. In other words, one must wonder what it is about the Church that has given rise to this particular manifestation, or rather deviation, of sexual selection.

Her character and its trajectory are a first step. Like so many (anti) heroines of nineteenth-century Spanish fiction, María embodies a female Don Quixote of sorts, given that her readings take hold of her mind. In "happy times," María's "favorite recreation" was to devour novels of "the primitive romantic school" (44–46), from Walter Scott to medieval chivalric tales to gothic horrors, and to better live these realities, she beseeches her father for permission to install herself in a relic of his estate, a stone tower overlooking the sea, where she envisions her perch a lighthouse and idealizes trials of chastity upon the arrival of warrior suitors and exotic travelers from far-off lands. It does not take long, however, for her to exhaust these fictions, and in their stead she turns to Santa Teresa, whose erotic mysticism and self-deprecation ignite a new, heightened subjectivity. Robert T. Petersson, writing on divine love, also characterizes this impulse as a Cervantine truth, since she measures herself according to the object of her devotion.[9] María's maid praises her character and is the first to learn the effect: "Hush, Genoveva, be quiet, don't say that; I am nothing more than a wretched sinner, much more wretched than you think. . . . I am a very bad girl, Genoveva, I am a very bad girl!" (*Marta y María*, 52–53). The guilt translates to devotion, yet in confessions to Him she "thought not about her sins, but rather how she should tell them" (56). Note the aesthetic impulse here, narrative as a form of Darwinian ornamentation that the female suitor assumes to woo her divine Love. As such, in addition to Santa Teresa, her semantic models include Santa Isabel, Santa Catalina, Santa Gertrudis, Santa Eulalia, Santa Mónica, and "some others" (87), for it is her "desire to imitate them" (89), all the "heroic souls" (88).

These imitations matter for the sex described and the outcome. The first occurs on a dark night in the tower when María's "body was nervous" (94) just before bed. She turns to her maid and asks for a recitation of her favorite passage from Santa Isabel, in which "the young and innocent princess . . . in a room adjacent to where she slept with her husband, asked that her maids give her a severe lashing, returning afterwards to his side more content and agreeable than ever" (94). María yearns to follow the example of the one "who spent the whole night awake with Jesus, the husband of her soul" (94), and thus implores a dumbstruck Genoveva to help. She disrobes and with a "jovial tone" (97) whispers in her maid's ear, "You must whip hard, Genovita, because that is how I have promised it to God" (98). Aghast, the maid complies and the performance unfolds:

> One breathed in the room an atmosphere of mystery and absorption that enraptured María and penetrated her in an intoxicating pleasure. Her beautiful body, naked, shook each time the straps of the whip crossed over it with a pain that was not without sensual delight. She pressed her forehead against the feet of the Redeemer, breathing anxiously and with certain oppression, and felt in her temples blood beat with singular violence, while the golden, delicate hairs of her nape stood up imperceptibly in response to the impulse of emotion that overpowered them. At times her lips, pale and trembling, would say in a soft voice: Keep going, keep going! (99)

The sight of blood mortifies poor Genoveva, and she drops the whip and throws her arms around María, who consoles her saying that, really, the flagellation did not hurt a bit.

Writing on this particular scene, Beth Wietelmann Bauer believes that Palacio Valdés moves beyond traditional concepts of good and evil in order to explore "the deeper, primitive motives of human behavior."[10] This position, I would offer, falls under the broader reflections of René Girard in *Violence and the Sacred* when he says of transfiguration that primordial difference "directs all religious thought toward victims [in this case, woman] that, thanks to their nature and sacrificial preparation, are neither divisive nor trivial victims."[11] Implicit for both arguments here is the religious identity of women, "neither divisive nor trivial victims" in the community in relation to sexual power dynamics, and the inherited sin behind María's masochism explains in part her ritualistic purging as a vestige of the earlier cultures Bauer and Girard describe. In other words, woman's self-mutilation says a lot about her society and its history. Yet while allusions to conditioned actions made to appear instinctual in this way provide a pseudo-anthropological answer, what remains unexplained is the supernatural Redeemer image upon which María and those like her channel their reproductive impulses. Though the shock value of flagellation is high, we cannot approach the Darwinian laws of sexual selection, that is, how science underwrites religion in these instances, without thinking of her erotic torture as one in a series of sexual "strange acts" undertaken toward mystical nuptials with an immaterial Christ.

The second imitation, an ecstatic trance, complicates the picture on these grounds. An afternoon when María finds herself "prostrated before the image of Jesus" (*Marta y María*, 123), she falls into a semiconscious state, "a celestial faint" (124), and feels herself being caressed in an encounter of coy seduction, which delivers a reversal of Darwinian gender roles akin to Darwin's own reversals in *The Descent*. Christ the suitor has turned selector coquette. As María calls out to her timid Lover, "the Husband yielded now to the voice of His wife. . . . He was close, she felt Him at her side and lost herself in craving to see Him, but He did not show Himself, nor surrender Himself to her tender and amorous entreaties . . . in order to whet her appetite . . . the divine Spouse kept her in enraptured suspense, arousing more and more her desire" (128). Then, at the moment of her desperation, He appears, and she begs, "My Jesus, will you permit your servant to put her lips on your divine person?" (130). Needless to say, in the medieval tower that evening, "silent, enshrouded in darkness" as it was, one could hear the sound of passionate kisses "for a long time" (131). Indeed, their tryst speaks to the "imaginary quality of reality" in realism that seeks to make intelligible these real-world cases in the context of community.[12]

As for the outcome of this unusual form of sexual selection, Ricardo stands little chance against such a rival. A letter arrives one day from María that reads, "Before renouncing the world forever I must tell you that I have absolutely no complaint against your conduct toward me. . . . I would consider myself very fortunate calling myself your wife, if it were not for the fact that I know myself to be much more so being the wife of Christ" (*Marta y María*, 248). Indeed, hers is the happy ending of a marriage plot worthy of any novel: "Jesus . . . would not forget Himself in the arms of His wife" (250–51); "it was her day [for as she said] 'God blesses me by calling me to be His wife'" (251); at which, "the new bride of Jesus Christ smiled" (258); for "the wife of the Lord could be at peace" (260); and "'Don't you know that María is getting married?' 'Who is she going to marry?' 'Jesus Christ, come see the wedding'" (271). But in the town "an extraordinary agitation reigned" (253), as the residents ask themselves, "Wasn't the wedding already arranged with the marquis?" (253). A popular romance is rewritten as someone in the plaza gossips, "I know that her father got furious when he found out and tried to dissuade her in every way possible," to which a sardonic youth scoffs, "Come on, then she's marrying Jesus Christ against her family's wishes?" (255). Nothing could be more absurd.

THE FACTS ABOUT DIVINE SEX

The history behind Christ as Bridegroom is long and convoluted.[13] It can be traced, in part, back to the inclusion of *Song of Songs* in the Old Testament and the various allegorical interpretations of this out-of-place love poem in which a young woman addresses her absent lover in anticipation of his return. Early readings explain this amorous couple as the special relationship between God (the Bridegroom) and the Jewish Nation (the Bride), and later Christian exegeses substitute this pairing for Christ and the Church. There is no doubt, however, about the impact *Song of Songs* had on mysticism and other theological writings, especially in Spain. It was both central to the tradition, referenced or appropriated time and again in the sixteenth and seventeenth centuries, and a constant preoccupation of the Church, which sought to circumvent the potentially "misleading" sexual language. At some point, perhaps in the writings of San Juan de la Cruz, "Bridegroom" and "Spouse" became interchangeable monikers, and the scandalous imprisonment of Fray Luis de León for his sixteenth-century translation of *Song of Songs* from Hebrew to the vulgate stands as a well-known marker in Spain's cultural history.

It would be a mistake, though, to think that only mystical writings and those connected with the *Song of Songs* feature the Bridegroom; this sexualized encounter also has a patriarchal history that crisscrosses with the Church and recalls many of the feminist issues raised in the earlier chapters of this study. Juan Luis Vives, the influential Spanish humanist, made the Bridegroom instrumental for his counsel to virgins in *Instrucción de la mujer cristiana* [*De institutione feminae christianae*] (1524). There Vives says that all virgins are wed to Christ, who will tell them at the gates of Heaven, "If you do not know the good of virginity, you are not my wife."[14] The message is explicit, yet not at all clear: "Now you see, my daughter, how your Husband desires that all of you be his: in body and soul. . . . Know that the safeguard of your virginity will be priceless, if to the purity of your body you add that of a chaste spirit and if you close the body and the spirit together, putting those locks on them that no one can open except your Husband who has the keys" (37). Again, the ambivalence stems from the play between body and soul. Though we might imagine a privileging of the latter, Vives emphasizes the carnal dimension of this sexualized relationship.

Hence, in light of such history the question of whether this betrothal is about sex resurfaces, because if it is not, then sexual selection is moot. Sarah Salih, for one, argues that the sexual in mysticism is not self-evident. She finds instead a natural slippage between the carnal and the spiritual, given that sex and religion "are not now and were not then discrete realms of discourse or of experience."[15] Similarly, Nelson Pike, who concedes that mystical language is "not merely figurative," also believes that the bridal metaphor is used simply because it works; in his words, it shows "the dignity and beauty of the passionate and sensuous elements of human life."[16] Yet his explication of mystical "full union" seems to approximate something else:

> In the sexual embrace, the bride is typically covered by her mate. She is then enwrapped by him and submerged beneath him. He penetrates her as well—he saturates her with his issue [whatever that is]. Her sensations are various. She smells his breath and hears his breathing and sweet whispers. But the love act is most importantly associated

with its massive tactile element. She feels her mate in contact with the outside of her body. She also feels him on the inside . . . the female is the receiver of the action. The male initiates and sustains the act—her action is reaction. (77)

This certainly sounds like a literal instance of sexual selection according to the active-passive bifurcation. Nevertheless, for a figure like Santa Teresa, the complicating factors are many, and it is not my intention to challenge Salih and Pike or add my voice to the ongoing critical conversation in this way. I will say, however, that in the case of Palacio Valdés we can assume, at the very least, a blurring of the theological and the pathological, so in vogue in the late nineteenth century, and, more to the point, a cynical irony with respect to the sincerity of María. In other words, her behavior differs from her saintly models, since it is mediated by history and narrative until real sex motives supplant those of salvation. In sum, sexual selection is by no means moot.

Yet to showcase sexual selection to make it intelligible in the context of my broader argument about an indeterminate Darwin requires an elaboration of the context behind María's case. There are a couple of options. Under the social pressures of an arranged marriage to Ricardo, a mediocre mate who fails to measure up to her romantic fantasies of idealized love, María employs a strategy of empowerment through the rhetoric of femininity similar to what Alison Weber describes in her study of Santa Teresa.[17] María's affected modesty and what Weber might call her "obfuscations" subvert patriarchal power relations, as she gains agency by operating from within certain codified gender expectations in an appeal to a higher authority. That is to say, she reclaims the selector status Darwin attributes to the female in nature. At the same time, however, it is important, as Weber notes, that "the *sponsa Christi* was not just a literary motif but rather a psychic reality for Teresa" (114), since such a reality broaches dangerous questions of sex and eroticism in the sacred sphere—from the Inquisition's response to Fray Luis de León's translation of *Song of Songs* as "differing hardly at all from the love poems of Ovid" (trial transcript quoted in Weber, 118) to affidavits of witnesses at orgiastic scenes of "Christ's brides" (121) to the Bridegroom's own seductive penetration of Santa Teresa in her *El castillo interior* (1577).

Simone de Beauvoir, for her part, does not equivocate; patriarchy and religion represent a united front. A woman who is denied human love by circumstances and turns to God, whether because she is disappointed or overparticular, will always find a man, for the two are analogous. In the redemption of her femininity, Heaven becomes her narcissistic mirror, and she tortures her flesh in order to lay claim to a body that has belonged since birth to Man-God, thus dethroning him through her own humiliation. With this role reversal, she asserts herself as selected, rather than selector, in a disassociation from the world, and hence we come to see the crucified God, her sacrificial double, as an unreality. In this way, she acts both as selector and selected in her sexual relationship with the divine.[18]

My sense is that, regarding María, the type of analysis Weber and Beauvoir provide is right. As complement, though, we might also look for synthesis with her sister, Marta, in the "facts" Palacio Valdés sets forth. The etymology of the word "fact" traces to the verb "to do" or "to make," as the English "factory" and "manufacture" still show; only in the seventeenth century did it come to mean an authentic, observed truth in opposition to a fiction or fabrication. Lorraine Daston, who sees Science as a creative enterprise in ways similar to those I introduce in chapter 1, uses this etymology to establish an epistemological distinction between passive imagination, which amounts to unchecked, incommunicable individualism—as characterizes the "scientific" explanations of fantastical phenomena, like animal magnetism—and active imagination, which controlled by reason is also communal, like the invention necessary for advances in mathematics or mechanics.[19] Both are claimed to be rooted in facts, but historically only the latter endures as scientific for being objectively replicative. This juxtaposition on the part of Daston is useful because it can be transposed to María, whose mystical truths are ineffable, and Marta, whose thought remains social and material. The passive imagination (of María) contrives an actual though impossible marriage to Christ through sexual selection, whereas the active imagination (of Marta) takes Ricardo to be the reasonable, pragmatic path to righteousness in the collective reality. Hence, as regards the facts about sex and Christ, deeper issues of community begin to come into view and with them cracks in the united front of patriarchy and the Church.

Speaking on the varieties of religious experience, William James says that "the recesses of feeling, the darker, blinder strata of character, are the only places in the world in which we catch real fact in the making."[20] This assertion has much to do with the social reach of faith and natural tendencies toward "over-belief," but does not endorse the passive imagination in the ways Daston likens it to the "fictions that begin to operate as realities."[21] Rather, James's view of religion here is pragmatic, almost utilitarian, and at the same time, for the ways religion serves as "a postulator of new facts,"[22] it is also reasoned and hence appears on the scientific side of Daston's active imagination. I see this foray into the writings of Daston and James, two quite different thinkers from two quite different periods, as a way to marry Science and Religion and then divorce them in the context of a novel in which "all the fundamental facts . . . really happened" (*Marta y María*, i), the empirical cornerstone of realism that Palacio Valdés articulates in his prologue. For the author to redeem Ricardo over the Redeemer Himself through marriage to Marta, who chooses him for utilitarian reasons—namely, reproduction—amounts to a postulation of "new facts" on the part of Palacio Valdés.

In other words, with *Marta y María* Palacio Valdés fabricates the real, proclaiming at the outset: "I have tried to the best of my ability to position myself from a relatively indifferent point of view (knowing that there is no such thing) and to study the subject with the clearheadedness of a physiologist" (iv). This gets us back to what I said in chapter 1 about the "clinical study" undertaken by the brothers Goncourt with *Germinie Lacerteux*. The science of sexual selection serves as the pragmatic religion of Palacio Valdés, in a Jamesian way, since for a realist like him it is only reasonable, that is, natural, that the female sex, in this case, the heroine Marta, should use her active (collective) imagination to passively choose the husband who "will eat today, and tomorrow, and the day after tomorrow . . . and forever . . . " (*Marta y María*, 276), lest she be an egoist like her sister in the ways Daston maintains. So, in terms of male-male combat, Ricardo versus Christ becomes a secondary rivalry that the author uses to distract us. The heavenly Bridegroom's real combatant is the author himself, who stands in for patriarchy and has a vested interest in supplanting the convent with the home.

The Church-chastity coupling of an early writer like Vives for Palacio Valdés in the late nineteenth century means something quite different. Mating is a science meant to ensure the domestic ideal. By manipulating the pressures of sexual selection, intruding and possessing nubile females, Religion represents a threat to patriarchy instead of acting as its ally, as one might assume from its role in keeping women chaste and subservient. Palacio Valdés intervenes on behalf of his concerned (male) public and from a "progressive" point of view challenges the Order, only to restore it in the end on the husband's (rather than the Husband's) own terms. To be sure, Science-versus-Religion has always been about ideology, and now it is clear why sex matters. *Marta y María* shows that the two do not always come to be pitted against each other in the sort of banal anticlerical opposition so prevalent in the nineteenth century. Since sexual selection infiltrates even the sacred sphere, it need not subvert (or uphold) from the outside, and it is this indeterminate inside presence that makes its operation all the more difficult to delineate and hence all the more ideologically effective.

CONFESSIONS OF SEXUAL SALVATION

The other place to look for God and sex is the confessional. Three parallel histories tell the tale. The first details the medieval transition from public to private penitence punctuated by the Lateran Council of 1215 and regulated practices with parish priests, through the mandated sacrament as dictated by the Council of Trent (1545–63), to the Counter-Reformation of the Catholic Church and the ecclesiastical power play behind the institutionalization of the confessor as the necessary mediator with God. The second history, then, gives a sordid account of the sexual solicitation cases and other abuses between confessor and confessant as documented in penitence handbooks and recorded by the trials of the Inquisition, which sought to curb corruption and strengthen the Church from the sixteenth through the eighteenth centuries. Last, there is the third, the cultural history one finds in the "confessing animal" Michel Foucault says we have all become or the "new sense of selfhood" that Peter Brooks sets forth in his writings on confession as the point of overlap between the legal and the literary.[23]

Colored by all three histories is Palacio Valdés's novel titled *La fe* (1892), one of numerous nineteenth-century Spanish works concerned with the confessor figure and published after Jules Michelet's anticlerical blockbuster *Le Prête, la femme et la famille* (1845). Though Palacio Valdés admits in his prologue to *La fe* that there are those who aspire to priesthood simply to have more access to women, he is quick to make clear that his well-intentioned protagonist, Father Gil, is not of such stock. A "spiritual friendship" develops between this provincial priest and the young Obdulia, who spurred on by the desire to win over her confessor "excelled in the invention of various ways to torture her delicate body."[24] This unexpected intimacy begins to trouble Gil, and when Obdulia finds that their once fervent bond has begun to cool, she announces her plan to enter a convent. For Gil, this is happy news, but there is nothing simple about how to carry out her decision. Either he must help her escape a tyrannical father, the moral thing to do, or she will set off to reach the convent alone, which could compromise her virtue should anyone take advantage of a vulnerable female traveler without escort. The plan she contrives strikes Gil as nothing less than a scandalous elopement—a hired coach, a night train, short stays at secluded rural inns, and abundant luggage just in case of an unforeseen illness or "who knows!" (249)—but he rebukes himself for doubting her propriety.

Still, if the mystical nuptials of *Marta y María* left some doubt about real sex, in this novel there can be no question. Just before their departure, Obdulia finds herself alone in Gil's room, caresses a soiled neckband from his habit, and pauses for a stolen orgasmic moment on his bed. The next day she and Gil find themselves together at dawn making their way in a coach across the muddy countryside. They say a scintillating Our Father in unison to break the silence, and then to lighten Gil's somber mood, Obdulia takes out some food and says: "I'm going to set the table." Moving toward his lap, she tells him, "Keep your legs still, because I need them," and with no utensils either, "We're pious, right? We'll eat with our fingers" (255). Cheering up a bit, he asks her whether it is out of humility "or because it tastes better that way," which prompts her to respond: "You, Sir, are my confessor and I can't tell you a lie. I like it much better this way. . . . It is one of the few dirty things I like. . . . I'm taking off my gloves right this minute . . . you care for me and will savor it more passing through my hands. . . . What a silly girl I am!" (255). Indeed, from one page to the next, profanation of the sacred fuels the sexual attraction through the perversion of these mating games.

Finally at the inn, Gil heeds calls for assistance and enters Obdulia's room only to find her scantily dressed with eyes full of tears. She has a confession to make, which her confessor promises he will be glad to hear in the nearest church. No such luck. The *cat is out of the bag*, to use what Brooks calls now common parlance in legalistic discussions of confession.[25] Obdulia reveals her secret—she loves her confessor "more than salvation" (*La fe*, 267). Gil panics, "as pale as a corpse, with fear painted on his eyes," and runs out into the forest. When he returns, the inn is in a state of frenzy over what has transpired with his young companion. She needs immediate medical attention but, once resuscitated, seizes the moment. Prostrate on her bed, alone with Gil, and too weak to speak, she asks that her confessor lean over to hear her last words, and doing so, he is caught: "All of a sudden, in an unforeseen assault, the devout young girl took her bare arms from underneath the covers, threw them around his neck, pulling his face to hers with uncommon strength, and gave him a prolonged, frenetic kiss on the lips, and then another and another" (270). He faints and then recovers only to see her unconscious and half naked on the floor by his side. At that very moment, her father and his cronies arrive. Gil is humiliated, slapped by the real father in a parodic honor scene, and eventually imprisoned for attempted rape by her false testimony.

SALACIOUS SOLICITATIONS

The logical place to locate Science-versus-Religion in *La fe* is in the atheism espoused by Don Álvaro, a townsman whom Gil hopes to convert. For all intents and purposes, he is a token, one-dimensional character whose reasoned views and seductive books tempt the faith of the parish priest. But while his role might be recognizable and secondary in this way, it does not tell us anything about the role of sex in the Science-versus-Religion schema his voice serves to balance. For this, we must set aside the all too obvious purpose of his atheism for the plot and instead look to his seemingly less important articulation of sexual selection in Darwinian terms: "All animals are born with defenses for the struggle in the combat of life, some have teeth, others have claws, others have horns, others have wings to flee . . . man is the only animal without means of defense. . . . Within the universe is hidden an astute force, perverse, that compels us . . . we are necessary and it requires that we reproduce ourselves" (104). What underlies the struggle Don Álvaro has in mind here, though, is not the signature *struggle for life* of the hapless individual up against an indifferent Nature but rather the "perverse" relationship between men and women with respect to reproduction. Far from unimportant, the argument he takes to his deathbed, that "love is nothing more than a ploy of Nature" (228), frames the book as a whole.

Palacio Valdés, instead of removing the Church from what would otherwise appear a Godless dynamic, puts the sacred front and center. This stratagem works because Darwinian sexual selection in its articulation is not so far off from standard theological understandings of sex and the Church. An authority on the codification of penitence in the Middle Ages, Pierre J. Payer postulates that if the Church had had the language, it might have decreed: "Sex is a natural, impersonal biological force with an inherent teleological orientation to the conservation of the species."[26] The difference with Darwin resides in the Church's moral ideal of creation in the name of God. In brief, sexual pleasure, though a concomitant of intercourse, could not become an end in itself without also resulting in sin, for the lustful appetite between men and women, according to the Church, is animalistic and therefore a threat to reason and, by extension, the (heterosexual) institution of monogamous marriage as dictated by God.

For sexual selection in *The Descent*, a variable like ornamentation interests Darwin far more than the pleasures of coitus, a factor he never broaches, and sin is altogether foreign to his thinking on the matter, which derives from and details more about animals and insects than humans. Yet in the modern Christian era, history shows Darwin to have been shortsighted in these respects and attests to the ways sexual selection, rather than a static dynamic of universal, unchanging laws, bends according to social circumstance. It is thus at once synchronic and diachronic, an indeterminate constant of our nature that is shaped by and participates in the shaping of culture over time. The Council of Trent marked solicitation as a serious threat to the Catholic Church, and the Counter-Reformation, in response to Martin Luther's rejection of the priest's role in penitence, was keen to tighten the reins through the codification of practices such as Communion and regimentation of the ecclesiastic hierarchy. Consequently, the sixteenth and seventeenth centuries witnessed a dramatic rise in the popularity of confession, which went from being a yearly to daily obligation and became indispensable for the sacrament of penitence.

Writing on sexuality in the confessional, the historian Stephen Haliczer chronicles "a certain feminization of Roman Catholicism" at this time as a rise in Marian devotions like the festival of Our Lady of Conception attracted an overwhelming majority of devoted female penitents who came from all socioeconomic classes, given a particular type of newfound equality premised on the private virtue of the individual.[27] At the same time, however, there was a crackdown against confessors living in concubinage with multiple pious virgins, or *virgines subintroductae* ("live-in virgins"), which had long been an accepted practice, and the Inquisition became the primary enforcer of punishment for the abuses of lewd clergy, as transgressions both inside and outside the confessional increased at an alarming rate, from simple acts of favoritism toward selected *beatas* to suggestive language, fondling, consensual intercourse, mutual masturbation, sexual bribery, and rape, to name the most common, in the hundreds of Spanish cases brought to light by both Haliczer and Adelina Sarrión Mora, whose archival research shows how such legal proceedings can give a voice to the otherwise silent history of these women.[28] Novels with deviant priests who use their power to take advantage of their unsuspecting female confessants are the norm of the period, and classics like Benito Pérez Galdós's *La familia de León Roch* (1878) and Clarín's *La Regenta* (1884–85), as well as less mainstream works like Eduardo López Bago's *El confessionario* (1885), reflect in varying degrees the public perception of these dangers of the confessional at the end of the nineteenth century.[29]

One reason for choosing Palacio Valdés, though, is that he is not the norm. But, to be clear, Obdulia is not simply an erotic invention on the part of the author cooked up to satisfy his own fantasies or political agenda—anticlerical, misogynist, or otherwise. True to the realism of the age, her character is both historical and verisimilar. There were women like Obdulia, for no comprehensive history of solicitation that I have seen is without mention of female penitents who courted their confessors. In addition to showing that almost 40 percent of women solicited by priests greeted advances "warmly," Haliczer also points to numerous cases in which "women even took an aggressive role and actively sought sexual favors from their confessors" (*Sexuality in the Confessional*, 122). He claims that these examples defy the stereotype of female penitent passivity found in literature. Hence, what Haliczer recounts and Palacio Valdés illustrates can best be described in Darwinian terms as a dynamic characterized by a female suitor in pursuit of a male selector.

Yet the pious confessor in these cases is far from being the Victorian gentleman Darwin describes who rarely surveys his potential wives with the same care he takes in selecting his horses. When Obdulia says to Gil, "I wish you were more severe . . . that you would punish me harder . . . that you might even hit me so that I could really show you my submission" (*La fe*, 260), she in her own way calls him out for being cowardly and soft. Through erotic displacement, she wants this Father to treat her like her own abusive father. To elucidate similar phenomena, Haliczer details cases of laywomen who

were denied free choice in marriage and experienced sexual dissatisfaction with the husbands chosen for them by their fathers, as well as
examples of frustrated widows, naive poor girls, single women kept
under lock and key by social conventions, women prone to hysterical
fits who request medical "treatments" from their spiritual doctors,
and the economic distress of female penitents in need of the financial favors of clergy (*Sexuality in the Confessional*, 122–48). Other
factors include the effect of popular priests on young females, thrill
seekers in small towns who became obsessed with their confessors
simply for the rush of intrigue, and a process of Freudian transference
in which the power imbalance, heightened by the confessor as father
figure, could "make for a potent aphrodisiac" (137). Looking to Latin
America during the colonial period, Jorge René González Marmolejo
finds cases of women who feigned illness in order to tempt their confessors, like one who asked to be undressed for an examination or
another who pretended to faint, and it seems that the men of God
who were seduced into transgression by these tactics could not resist
the temptation: "Evidently, the body of a woman prostrate in bed,
perhaps scantily clad and most certainly in a state of weakness, could
very well awaken the carnal appetite of the priest."[30] Any one of such
accounts could be taken as historical evidence of the originality and
acumen Palacio Valdés shows in the realism of *La fe*. Obdulia is that
same woman of feigned illness and prostrate in bed, even though she
fails to awaken the "carnal appetite" of Gil.

GUILTY AS CHARGED

The question then becomes why Palacio Valdés might choose to be in-
verisimilar with Gil's response. None of the above histories or hypoth-
eses about "aggressive" female penitents explains the seductive nature
of confession in terms of sexual selection. The examples given, though
confirming the realism of Obdulia's representation, are little more than
case studies in the factors involved. They do, however, make a meaningful start toward connection between sex and confession. By turning
the tables, Palacio Valdés becomes the exception to what had become a
commonplace perception in the late nineteenth century about perverse
priests, as exemplified in the frequent cartoons of lewd confessors in
the popular periodical *El Motín*. His novel departs from those of his
anticlerical contemporaries with a shift in focus from a straightforward
power imbalance (the unsavory priest who abuses his position over a

submissive female penitent) to the erotic allure of what it means to tell (and listen to) the dark secrets of sex.[31]

Sarrión Mora, after her detailed analysis of solicitation cases in Spain, finds confession to be the fundamental method for formation of individual subjectivity, which is framed by the sexual transgressions between men and women. In her view, conscience is the "number one objective" of the Church confessional, and there would be no conscience without confession.[32] An exaggeration no doubt, but her point is well taken. Moreover, celibate priests, whose only knowledge of sex comes from the handbooks of sexual science (written by other priests), must probe this conscience through subtle, suggestive methods of questioning aimed at revelations about carnal desire, that is, acts of sinful pleasure either committed or considered—a line of interrogation that inspired female penitents to imagine and behave in ways that might not otherwise have crossed their minds. Naturally, of course, they then would have to confess these thoughts, all of which has led to a general consensus in the wake of Foucault that confession does not translate to sexual repression.

For various reasons, Foucault's thinking on confession has cast a wide shadow on virtually all writings on penitence following his *History of Sexuality*. Most enduring is his contention in "*Scientia Sexualis*" that the obligation to conceal sex "was but another aspect of the duty to admit it."[33] This presupposition leads him to conjoin truth and sex in such a way that the former becomes a medium for the latter. The speech act is paramount to his understanding of this relationship, in that confession is always a discursive practice—just as María thought more about how to tell her sins than the actual sins in *Marta y María*—but it also has as much to do with subjectivity. In "Sexuality and Power," a conference paper now included in a volume of Foucault's writings on religion and culture, he maintains that confession opens the interior, as a "technique of taking conscience," by making one aware of oneself, which he argues, like Sarrión Mora, is the essential contribution of Christianity.[34] Confession functions as a mechanism of power and control, but also a "mechanism of knowledge [*savoir*]" (126) of the self. Seduced by this knowledge, Obdulia recognizes the power that comes with it and inverts the power dynamic between confessor and confessant by subverting it on selection terms with her "confession" of sexual desire at the inn. In this way, I think it accurate to say that "confession may simply be a trope of (mis)understanding,"[35] since the utterance appropriates the discursive structure in order to undermine its very authority. Indeed, as much as confession is about power, it is also about the subject's belief in the rule of law, and when Obdulia's recourse to natural law fails her, that is, her conviction in the totalizing force of sexual selection as Darwin understood it, of the irresistible attraction of her flesh, she makes recourse instead to the law of the State, which in the conclusion to *La fe* comes to supplant the Law of the Church through the secular confessional of the court during Gil's trial.

After the incident at the inn, Obdulia admitted to her father that she was to blame, that the whole thing had been her idea, and a reluctant public still appalled by the affair greets her explanation with halfhearted acceptance. Yet, as if to mirror so many of the solicitation cases brought before the Inquisition, Gil's enemies pounce. Don Narciso, a rival priest, begins to confess Obdulia and persuades her to change her story. Still obsessed with her fallen confessor, however, she resists such a betrayal and fueled by romantic imagination makes an unannounced visit to his apartment one night to reclaim him. But her surprise attack fails as she is rejected outright by a now hard-hearted Gil. Alone in the street after being swiftly shown to the door under a shower of insults from his maid, a disillusioned Obdulia feels the sting of wounded pride and resolves to get her revenge. In a symbolic switch, she makes a false confession to her actual father, Osuna, who promises to punish Gil to the fullest extent of the law.[36]

A few nights later, the town judge comes to arrest Gil, who up until this moment had been a judge of a different sort in his own right. After some time in jail, he is called before the court and sits through the testimonies of multiple character witnesses out to show that "priests are . . . men just like the rest" (*La fe*, 297). Then Obdulia takes the stand, "like an actress of the first order" (307), and to the laughs and murmurings of the public, she tells how in the weeks leading up to the incident her confessor had wanted to "prolong" (309) the sessions. This persuasive doubletalk, Obdulia's "diabolical talent" (309), is complemented by the prosecuting attorney, who paints Gil as "a despicable hypocrite, secretly feeding shameful passions" (311). Gil, though, *confesses* his innocence in a statement of just a few words, putting himself in God's hands, to which he is told: "That's all fine; in the future God will judge you; for the moment, you will be judged by men" (313). The court's sentence puts him away for almost fifteen years.

With this conclusion, Palacio Valdés carries confession through to its end, from the cloister to the courtroom, from the private to the public, as the point of intersection between the religious and the legal realms. This overlap, so ingrained in culture and literature, prompts Peter Brooks to explore the contradictions of confession, which he sees as at once the most authentic and most suspicious of acts. Once institutionalized by the Lateran Council in the early thirteenth century, confession marks the origin of "the proto-modern self," given the ever more complex psychological elaborations that were to follow in the arts.[37] Others, like Foucault, speak of this turning point in terms of heightened subjectivity. In light of the "strange production of confessional discourse" (148) described by Brooks, we must also bear in mind that what instigates a confession often produces dubious pronouncements saturated with "confused, imagistic language" (148) because of the "transvaluation of values" (151) that can occur during custodial interrogation. Obdulia's change of heart and duplicitous speech with Father Narciso and with her own father, Osuna, both her custodians after Gil, would be an example of just such an inversion. Moreover, the return to the confessional, reset in the courtroom, represents a return to and mockery of communal judgment (if not an instance of its very savvy). Gil confesses his innocence, but as the prosecuting attorney confirms for the public, he will forever be more man than priest in the eyes of the town. Hence, the charge of sexual misconduct presumes Gil's guilt as a priest, since as a man in a Darwinian world denial of carnal impulse functions a priori as a false confession.

In effect, the jury and those in the courtroom appeal to the Darwinian laws of sexual selection in order to reach the verdict, which makes me believe that sex is what Brooks too hastily passes over. Confession is the point of crossover between the legal and the religious spheres, as well as the impetus behind so much of what we read, from contemporary memoirs to works like Thomas De Quincey's *Confessions of an English Opium-Eater* (1821) and Ippolito Nievo's *Confessioni d'un italiano* (1867), but sex underwrites these confessions, how they are made and heard. Brooks does, though, begin and end his study with Bill Clinton's denial of having had "sexual relations" with Monica Lewinsky, and to open chapter 4 he quotes James Joyce speaking as Stephen Dedalus about the allure of secret knowledge from "the lips of women and of girls" (from *A Portrait of the Artist as a Young Man*, quoted in Brooks, *Troubling Confessions*, 88). But the latter of these illustrations only serves as a transition to psychoanalysis in the study, which in turn brings Brooks back to the

Church. In my view, we would do well to pause longer on these particular words from Joyce and even more so on Freud's astonishment at hearing his mentor Josef Breuer confess a limited meaning of *alcôve* as simply "a marriage-bed," for "he [Breuer] failed to realize how extraordinary the *matter* of his statement" (Freud, "On the History of the Psycho-analytic Movement," quoted in Brooks, 89) really was. The point here is how much the confession hides rather than reveals, especially as regards sex.

Similarly, Palacio Valdés in *La fe* is out to show that the world is not what it seems. During Gil's trial, the "facts" of his escapade with Obdulia are set forth to *prove* what never happened. And in the novel's final scene, a distinguished physician together with a lawyer known for his studies of the penal system visit Gil's cell to ask him a few questions and take measurements of his body, face, and head "with the obstinate insistence of someone who is going to buy an animal" (*La fe*, 320). Spreading his arms out for this scientific examination, Gil makes the shape of a cross, and his two guests exchange a knowing look about his sexual guilt. The next day in the local paper an article titled "A Visit to Father Gil" reads: "The physiognomy of Father Gil offers absolutely all the traits that the school of positivist criminology assigns as particular to *rapists and libertines*; that is: a protruding outer ear, set well back, an intense gaze, delicate features (with the exception of the jaw), straight hair, soft skin, long hands and an altogether rather effeminate appearance" (321). Indeed, the author closes with this cynical bit of Lombrosian relief as a way to caution his readers to be wary of Science, of life reduced to pure matter, of untrustworthy facts. Gil finds consolation in his faith.

Yet this ready-made reading is questionable. For against this penal background we cannot help but suspect that the world might be exactly what it seems. That is to say, false confessions have very real consequences; the lies of fiction hold indirect truths about the material world. Though an incarcerated Gil rejects the life of the senses, moving himself to the darkest corner of his cell and liberating himself from being "a slave to time and necessity" (318), his confinement is a tale of "how extraordinary the *matter*" of confession is. Alone, the excommunicated father confesses to himself: "I have the conscience of my freedom" (318); however, a clear conscience is an oxymoron. If confession has taught us anything, it is the truth that there can be no interior without transgression, without an exterior, and as for the Church, sexual selection is of paramount importance. Gil's spiritual withdrawal from the world, therefore, is the confessional impulse at the extreme, what Brooks describes as the "sterile, passive, self-satisfied complicity" (*Troubling Confessions*, 166) that shackles humanity to the law, in this case, God's Law.

In other words, I believe that what Palacio Valdés really has in mind is a warning against the spiritual tyranny that contradicts the natural laws of evolution. He worries over an inwardness whence life ceases to be life at all. The irony then is that the "altogether rather effeminate appearance" of Gil literally translates in Darwinian terms to not being man enough, that is, too much priest, for sexual selection gone awry in *La fe* is meant to show the "perverse" struggle of the confessor-confessant relationship, which Palacio Valdés knows must always and never be about sex. Hence, when Gil whispers to himself from the shadows of his four stone walls, "I am emancipated" (*La fe*, 318), a strange "transvaluation of values" has occurred, prompted by circumstance and cloaked in the reality of faith in false confessions. Darwin remains ever present, because "an astute force . . . requires that we reproduce ourselves" (*La fe*, 104), but we cannot understand the indeterminism of his theory as it relates to women's material repression (not the absence of sexual repression as Foucault understood it) until its indefinite role in Science-versus-Religion comes into view through the fiction of Palacio Valdés.

In both *Marta y María* and *La fe*, the author manages multivalent messages thanks to the open-endedness of his subject matter. María is an unsympathetic character, but she is also the product of a prevailing power structure that denies her agency, so that even when she does make a choice, the Bridegroom and the cloister negate real reproduction. This sequence of events, from the perspective of Palacio Valdés, points to a social ill, and the science of naturalized sexual selection makes this critique of the Church possible. At the same time, however, the alternative ending of Marta's character reminds us that the very same science need not be progressive, as the patriarchal (as opposed to religious) order is restored through the "pragmatism" of domesticity. Likewise, on face value, *La fe* appears to promote transcendence of the carnal; the last laugh, after all, is aimed at Science. Yet, with confession in the mix, the "complex affair" (*The Descent*, 1:296) of sexual selection becomes a lot more complicated, and so, too, does the author's message. Gil finds himself "emancipated" in his cell, and this says something about the false confessions and the sex of Religion as well. The community of the courtroom can rewrite sexual selection as it sees fit, because in the Darwinian model there must be space enough to correct the lies of a confessor incapable of being honest with himself about his own reproductive nature. In other words, the ultimate authority, for this *matter*, is a fluid Science that can encompass but need not endorse the Religion of sex when the status quo is at stake. These are the many faces of the ideological *Descent* of Armando Palacio Valdés.

CHAPTER NINE

Emilia Pardo Bazán, Reproduction, and Change

Inconsistencies, contradictions, complete unknowns, choice, and the change born from indeterminate "nicks of time" between every action—sexual selection is hardly as algorithmic as Darwinian evolutionism has more broadly been described.[1] In fact, the most "dangerous idea" is to forget these unresolved qualities in the face of sexual politics during the decades following *The Descent* in Spain and elsewhere. The preceding chapters thus stand as something of a prologue to the writings of Emilia Pardo Bazán for the ways they foreground what her position on the matter of female choice has to say about the stakes of the theory in its historical context. Many of her works could, no doubt, be introduced here, given the particular relevance of each to the facets of sexual selection discussed up to this point. *Insolación* (1889), for example, situates two suitors, Gabriel Pardo and Diego Pacheco, in a complex triangle framed by the desires of a female protagonist, Asís Taboada, whose selection scaffolds a tale of curious conquest with racial and nationalist undertones. Likewise, for those who know *Dulce Dueño* (1911), this late novel is sure to bring to mind my exploration of mysticism and confession in the novels of Armando Palacio Valdés from chapter 8. With no shortage of attention to her own role in the courtship power dynamic, Lina Mascareñas narrates her rejection of three potential mates whose ideological embodiments both allegorize and catalyze her ultimate renunciation of the external world. Finally institutionalized and having given herself in body and mind to her divine lover, Dulce Dueño, she finds certain peace ("And I am happy. I am where

He wants me to be") in a resolution that disquiets our reading in equal measure.[2]

This depth is but one reason why I make a point in the introduction of describing Pardo Bazán, who was a vocal proponent of women's rights, as the bookend to my thinking on sexual selection. She is the only woman writer here included, and her visible engagement with Darwin and issues of social justice alike brings a culminating perspective to this study. Darwin emphasized "Duty!" (*The Descent*, 1:70), but he overlooked the costs involved in the reproductive practices he sought to understand. Men and women do not share an equal burden at the various stages of parental investment, and Pardo Bazán brought attention to this imbalance as amplified in the cultural context of "maternal sacrifice" and community welfare. These are problematic corollaries to Darwin's theory that must be taken into account.

Moreover, it is also the case that today questions about Pardo Bazán's fiction elicit questions about her feminism. The issue is less about the degree to which her novels conform to her theoretical writings on naturalism in favor of what her life and politics say about the movement for women's emancipation at the end of the nineteenth century.[3] Still, matters of genre remain integral to readings of alternative models for Spanish womanhood in Pardo Bazán, that is, of models that break with the traditional role of the domestic angel. In the 1890s, Pardo Bazán published two novels, *Doña Milagros* (1894) and *Memorias de un solterón* (1896), as complementary pieces in a series titled *Adán y Eva (Ciclo)*, and together they capture the tensions that went along with being a woman writer intent upon reform in a culture where any *literata* was perceived as a threat to the status quo of male dominance.[4] To clarify, as a Spanish woman writer Pardo Bazán is singular for her novelistic consideration of Darwin's science during this particular period. Hence, in many respects the matters of genre that still matter most for readings of Pardo Bazán have to do with misgivings about the perceived influence of "evolutionary determinism" on her realism as it circumscribes female agency in a society defined by sexual inequalities.

Consequently, these novels, for their lack of closure on feminist issues, also have a lot to reveal about Darwin's theory. *Doña Milagros* tells the story of an incompetent father, Benicio Neira, and the demise of a household that collapses under the weight of his loveless marriage to Ilda, who dies from the reproductive toll of eighteen pregnancies, twelve surviving offspring, and a deep resentment for her husband's loss of patrimony. Doña Milagros, her counterpart and neighbor, is the childless wife of a retired army major and offers salvation to Benicio through her innate maternal virtue, which he idolizes to the point of giving her the twins Ilda delivers just before dying from the strains of labor. The sequel, *Memorias de un solterón*, then charts the transformation of a self-satisfied bachelor, Mauro Pareja, as his sympathies for the Neira family lead to love with the bookish, "ugly ducking" daughter of their clan, Feíta, who rejects his initial marriage proposal only to offer her own based on mutual respect and motivated by a sense of obligation to family.

In the context of these plots, feminist critiques return to three principal subversions on the part of Pardo Bazán: (1) inversions of sexuality, namely, of a "feminine" Benicio and a "masculine" Feíta; (2) usurpation of patriarchal authority through first-person narrations of the respective male protagonists, Benicio and Mauro; and (3) the emancipatory terms of the concluding marriage contract between Mauro and Feíta. Yet, while the texts do bear out such claims, these same readings often overlook, downplay, or reject the more problematic conformism of Pardo Bazán's conclusions. Doña Milagros, a paragon of idealized femininity in the mold of *la mujer virtuosa*, becomes a surrogate mother made heroine, while Feíta, by marrying Mauro, renounces her own aspirations in an apparently defeatist exchange of self-sacrifice.[5] Both cases cause discomfort, for either these aspects signal capitulations to patriarchy or else they are interpreted so as not to appear concessions at all. With the former, the author's personal history and feminist writings on women's emancipation make it difficult, if not impossible, to maintain this type of disharmony between her novels and coetaneous political essays written in support of civil rights, employment, and education for women. With the latter, there is the risk that expectations about Pardo Bazán's own ideological position might skew what the novels permit.

Another paradoxical logic, though, grants the possibility that Pardo Bazán's conciliations, rather than being negated, act as subversions.[6] In other words, what feels least feminist about these novels need not be so at all. Pardo Bazán's vision for modern Spanish womanhood, which she adumbrates in "La mujer española" (1890) and "Una opinión sobre la mujer" (1892), among other articles, takes measure of Spain's patriarchy in unique ways, namely, via a transnational, self-conscious perspective informed by Darwinian deductions whereby natural selection for Spanish females, *struggle for life*, morphs into one of materialist sexual selection, *trapping a husband*.[7] Hence, the issues that emerge surrounding women's emancipation in Spain at the end of the nineteenth century translate to those of more contemporary feminist debates on reproductive labor and domesticity within capitalism, whether from a Marxist perspective or otherwise. The fate of Ilda from *Doña Milagros*, determined by Spain's marriage contract and her wageless labor of no apparent use-value in the pro-creation of eleven daughters and a deadbeat son, calls into question the ideology of love that frames the ending exchange between Beni-cio and Doña Milagros. Likewise, the family structure defined by the duties assigned to wives for the good of civilization paints Feíta and *her* choice at the end of *Memorias de un solterón* in a light far less beautiful than has been the preference of those who elect to see her character's transformation in an ironic juxtaposition to her name.[8] All of this is to say that Darwinian sexual selection in its sociopoliti-cal praxis at the time was by no means clear-cut. For women, once *struggle for life* translated to *trapping a husband* a host of other uncomfortable questions were raised about self-interest and a science that seemed to be much more about economics than about love in the realm of culture.

PARDO BAZÁN AND SEXUAL SELECTION

At the end of the nineteenth century, transnational engagement height-ened Pardo Bazán's political activism. Originally written for the Brit-ish *Fortnightly Review* and reprinted a year later in Spain, her essay "The Spanish Woman" (1889) ("La mujer española" [1890]) entreats the reader to assume the objective distance and self-awareness of an outsider looking in when taking measure of Spanish women and their social circumstance. Moving beyond Spain's borders, Pardo Bazán car-ries out a comparative illustration of a national history defined by sex-ist hypocrisy, while at the same time drawing attention to problematic correlations between gender and class. In her assessment of marriage, she understands "naturalized" sexual inequality under the law as a cul-tural distortion of what can only be described, in Darwinian terms, as a situation in which the "search for a husband" has become "the only form of *struggle for life* possible for women."[9] As consequence, Spanish women have become resigned to their very subjugation:

> This somber and dire pessimism that locks up half of humankind [women] in an iron circle of immobility . . . is tied to another error

no less important with respect to women: the error of affirming that a woman's role corresponds to the reproductive functions of the species, that it determines and limits all remaining functions of her human activity, taking away from her destiny all individual significance, and leaving her nothing more than that which is relevant to the destiny of men. (75)

The connection between Darwin and women's issues is in no way arbitrary. Moreover, Pardo Bazán's denunciation of the limitations inherent in the patriarchal construction of women in terms of reproduction echoes what John Stuart Mill censures in *The Subjection of Women* (1869), which she extolled in the Spanish press and published in translation in her collection of works for women in these same years.[10] Mill rejects the supposition that the ideal character of women—submissive self-abnegation with all affections directed toward the husband and children—is innate; sexual attractiveness according to these characteristics is a perverse cultural construction intended to maintain male dominance. Yet Pardo Bazán should not be misconstrued so as to appear in complete opposition to the maternal idolatry Mill bemoans; she makes no such renunciation. Nature in her essay stands apart in sanctified autonomy, for "motherhood is the masterpiece of natural instinct, not only of the human species, but also of all the animal species; motherhood and nature are one and the same" ("La mujer española," 81). That is to say, even while Pardo Bazán takes issue with the social expectations that define women as nothing more than wombs, she upholds the very biological determinism that enables such oppression.

Contradictions, in fact, color Pardo Bazán's life and work. She was a devout Catholic, and her religious views often temper her radicalism or, as in the case of her arguments against Darwin in "Reflexiones científicas contra el darwinismo" (1877), provoke a discomforting rejection of ideas that she believed posed a threat to the Church.[11] This double-edged quality, so apparent in her fiction, between reformism and conservatism complicates reconciliation of her position on the subject of marriage in the context of women's emancipation.[12] As is well known from her personal history, Pardo Bazán married at a young age only to later defy Spanish custom by obtaining a divorce; thus, she knew firsthand the rights women forfeited in contracted matrimony. She also understood the bleak social realities for single women in a culture that barred their access to education and employment. It is not surprising, therefore, that Pardo Bazán, who remained very much current and informed on Darwin's publications, would incorporate (and question) the theory of sexual selection in her political writings on marriage, given that reproduction (still believed to be women's sole purpose) is the mechanism by which natural variation is achieved through such selection.

For example, in her essay "Una opinión sobre la mujer," Pardo Bazán recognizes the operation of sexual selection, while dismissing its determinism with respect to either sex:

> Sexual attraction, the source of conjugal unions, and the reproductive instinct, the law of nature that imposes procreation for the sake of future generations, have been, are, and will be a very powerful impulse for human actions—human actions, understand this well, of males and females, that make up humanity—; but they are not the only impulse nor the only end of rational beings nor must they be taken in any circumstance as a negation or necessary limitation on other impulses and noble ends, whether social, artistic, political, scientific, religious, or even on the exercise of unquestionable individual freedom.[13]

Though Darwin postulates continuity between animals and humans in *The Descent*, Pardo Bazán believes sexual selection—albeit the natural bedrock for marriage in the realm of culture—stops short of supplanting the sacrosanct agency of the individual. Indeed, the "exercise of unquestionable individual freedom," especially with respect to gender relations, or what Mill calls the "freedom of individual choice" in modern society, will become the cornerstone of Pardo Bazán's theoretical writings on Spanish realism in *La cuestión palpitante* (1883) as she seeks to distance herself from her naturalist contemporaries.[14]

MOTHERHOOD AND NATURE ARE (NOT) ONE AND THE SAME

The tension between the physical exigencies of reproduction and the lofty ideals of motherhood plays out in *Doña Milagros* according to the ideological critique of sexual selection Pardo Bazán proffers in the above essays. The narrator, Benicio Neira, takes a no-nonsense approach to "honest conjugal happiness," believing that "just as the bird seeks his mate and nest, nothing could be more natural than that man look for a female companion and home."[15] He seeks out this companion beyond the reach of social change, in a timeless medieval village where a "grim and frightful" (584) tower of feudal lords still reigns, and after the first year of matrimony, his wife, Ilduara, becomes that tower in Benicio's eyes because of her icy disposition and stonelike appearance. Hardship and anger soon plague the Neira home, as the firstborn son dies in a tragic fall and familial disputes over finances fester. Still, along with six failed pregnancies, nine girls and a son are born, which together make Ilda nothing more than a "spent organism" (591) and burden the household with debt and cramped quarters. Then, twenty-nine years after their first child, Ilda delivers again, this time identical twin girls, increasing the total to twelve Neira children and bringing their moribund mother to the point of no return.

At this point, Doña Milagros makes her first appearance in the novel and in the stairwell strikes Benicio as "a very pleasing object to contemplate" (611). With Ilda absent from the scene in fragile postpartum recovery, Doña Milagros usurps the maternal role: "One would have thought that the major's wife had given birth to and raised at least half a dozen children. She handled that gelatinous mass with incomparable agility, and swaddled it as if she had done nothing else in her life" (617). Through the gaze of Benicio, Pardo Bazán emphasizes that the responses of Doña Milagros come naturally, through an innate capacity for rearing newborns. She was "in her element" (618) and thus becomes the domestic double of the failed Ilda, who cannot sustain the resentment she experiences from such intrusions. Benicio recalls with horror her dying words: "I heard her renounce her maternity, curse the work that dignified her in my eyes, and crush me with a vicious and inhuman hatred" (634). To Benicio's disbelief, Ilda disavows "in a matter of minutes an entire life consecrated to duty and conjugal love" (634), for the bitter costs of reproductive labor. Doña Milagros eventually sets out to relocate in Barcelona with her husband, and during the farewell, Benicio presents her with Ilda's twins, who he recounts were "the two beings for whom and in whom we [he and Doña Milagros] had loved each other" (776). The gesture, which "entertains the provocative proposition that reproduction and nurturing may, indeed, be separate functions," as Elizabeth J. Ordóñez asserts,[16] points to the very sort of "noble ends" Pardo Bazán privileges in her feminists essays concerned with sexual selection, and, at the same time, Benicio's "exercise of individual freedom" rights an indifferent Nature, which otherwise would have left Doña Milagros, the personification of motherhood, childless.

Nevertheless, to apotheosize maternal virtue at the expense of reproductive labor, which Pardo Bazán makes not simply a "separate function" of womanhood but also one that is degraded through the grim characterization of Ilda, results in a problematic concession to the patriarchal ideal, and all the more so because it purports, through the eyes of Benicio and framed by the author's own political writings, to offer a "progressive" refutation of domestic exploitation in favor of an ideology of maternal love. In other words, Benicio leaves us with Doña Milagros, "the incarnation of feminine *goodness*" (*Doña Milagros*, 766), while making Ilda, whose tragic end his own ideology of wifely duty effects, a silent backdrop of villainy. Thus, in a troublesome turnabout, Pardo Bazán denaturalizes reproduction, which in fact she aligns with determinism in "Una opinión sobre la mujer," just as she elevates motherhood to "the masterpiece of natural instinct." Hence, the political dimension of the text is a clear-cut opposition between Doña Milagros and Ilda transposed to an alternative model for gender relations in the interest of greater sexual equality—maternal virtue over mere breeding—and thus remains an oversimplification that promotes only a specious subversion on feminist grounds. It shows nothing progressive about Pardo Bazán or, for that matter, Darwin.

THE REPRODUCTIVE LABOR OF REALISM

To the credit of both, however, the case is far more complex. Pardo Bazán's use of Benicio as narrator creates a subtext that we as readers piece together out of his "male gaze" as projected by a feminist author. Noting that in her many first-person narrations Pardo Bazán rarely employs a female narrator, Joyce Tolliver calls attention to the ways a male narrative voice allows Pardo Bazán to undermine the very same masculinity that she, as a turn-of-the-century woman writer, appropriated in order to distance herself from the much maligned moralism of the female literary tradition.[17] Likewise, Beth Wietelmann Bauer argues that first-person male narrators serve a twofold purpose in Pardo Bazán, at once granting male authority to her works while discrediting "the reliability, power, and dignity of their respective voices."[18] These assertions about a polyvalent narrative voice, whether in terms of reliability or authority, raise important questions about where and how we search for meaning in Pardo Bazán's fiction. Maurice Hemingway, who discusses *Doña Milagros* and *Memorias de un solterón* at length in his often-referenced study on Pardo Bazán, posits that these two novels reflect the culmination of a progression toward greater psychological depth in her writing.[19] However, his conclusion that at Ilda's death "we cannot but feel for Benicio" (122) falls short. If we grant an unprecedented psychology to these works, as Hemingway would have it, we should be keen to draw out not what Benicio's speech reveals about his own mind but instead what it attempts to veil of the patriarchal culture for which he acts as spokesman.

The silence that accompanies Ilda's departure from the text offers emptiness charged with signification, the resolution of which requires an analysis of her fate in relation to reproductive labor and Benicio's idealizations of Doña Milagros. To this end, a telling moment comes when Feíta, in mourning over her mother's death, confronts her father with doubts about salvation, asking him whether or not Ilda will make it to Heaven. He is perplexed, and when he demands to know why she would even ask, she responds, "Because our dear mom, in my opinion, committed suicide" (*Doña Milagros*, 643). There are many ways, Feíta explains, to kill oneself, and in this case the choice to die was conscious. Benicio recounts his reaction to Feíta's words: "I did not answer, and the girl, guessing that the thought made me sad, also remained hushed, lowering her eyes, from which a lucid teardrop fell" (644). In the context of Spanish culture, this tacit recognition on the part of the narrator signals the dire state of gender relations in general and women's oppression in particular. As critique, it also repositions Pardo Bazán's broader critical agenda, shifting focus from the felicitous spiritual union of Benicio and Doña Milagros back to the hand both had in Ilda's self-destructive tendencies. Furthermore, Doña Milagros's own worldview, as later explicated to Benicio, assumes new resonance, when she reminds him that all the misfortunes and unhappiness we endure are because of the opposite sex, that "when you see an Adam or an Eve near death . . . it is because of an Adam or an Eve" (679). Thus, Pardo Bazán's use of *Adán y Eva (Ciclo)* as the title for her series points to much more than the "noble ends" of Benicio's final gesture. The closure written by Ilda's husband and narrator belies the reproductive costs.

As a result, Pardo Bazán is at her best when she grants us subtle, psychological access to Benicio as Ilda's Adam, for in this way she undermines *his* closure. Though Ilda might be reduced to a grotesque parody of the traditional Spanish wife or a one-dimensional tool for the characterization of Benicio, she need not be.[20] Rather, just as patriarchal norms mask the female experience in works by Pardo

Bazán with male narrators, these norms at the same time constitute such experience. Language in her novels becomes synonymous with what contemporary feminists like Julia Kristeva will come to see in Lacanian terms as the Law of the Father.[21] To categorize this novel as idealist or spiritualist, as Nelly Clèmessy and others have done with Pardo Bazán's later fiction, is to invert what the author in reality delivers—commentary on the tendency of human beings, male and female alike, to see the world through an optic of symbolic distortion.[22] This can be a good thing, as we saw Cassirer intimate in the first chapter of this study, but not always. When Benicio compares his wife with his saintly neighbor, his reflections mingle with a piece of colored glasswork he espies in the hall: "And in front of the gilded glass, the task [i.e., speaking openly to Doña Milagros about Ilda's ire] seemed to me not only easy but pleasing, because I relished the idea of confessing my troubles of the heart to that very kind woman, who would pity and console me to no end. But passing in front of the blue glass, melancholic and afflicted, all the difficulties of the undertaking came back to me" (*Doña Milagros*, 627). Trite as his metaphoric thinking may be, the angel-monster dichotomy his gaze constructs, which in the nineteenth century manifests itself in idols of perversity and madwomen in the attic, amounts to a figurative refraction of the plight of women in Pardo Bazán's historical circumstance.[23]

Though her plot in the hands of Benicio appears to reinforce the opposition, Pardo-Bazán as author undercuts the angel-monster dichotomy. If we follow the imagery of the glass, we discover that her critique has to do as much with what Benicio sees as with what he overlooks. Baffled by the doctor's diagnosis that Argos, one of the Neira daughters, has fallen in love with a priest for lack of socially acceptable alternatives, like education and employment, Benicio exclaims that all women should do nothing more than what his mother did: "A lot of sewing . . . a lot of praying . . . at home . . . and loving her husband and children" (*Doña Milagros*, 703). Following this declaration, he reflects: "When I expressed these sound opinions, it seemed to me that the shadow of Ilduara, irritated and exhausted, livid with color, crossed in front of the blue glass of the hall. . . . And above the yellow candle, as if bathed in golden light, appeared Doña Milagros" (703). Benicio projects their dissimilarity, as his patriarchal culture upholds it. Hence, the most "provocative proposition" about *Doña Milagros* is not that reproduction and motherhood are "separate functions," as Ordóñez maintains, but rather that the sexual politics in these very

decades makes them so. And though this interpretation would seem
to run counter to Pardo Bazán's own remarks in her political essays, a
dissonance of the sort need not be the case. She says that "motherhood
and nature are one and the same," which might likewise read "Doña
Milagros and Ilda are one and the same." It is not a trivial detail that
Benicio's metaphors materialize in the hall, the space between the two
women, a corridor where they converge in the psychological prism of
his mind, and neither is it mere happenstance that identical twin girls
fuse the two women in a symbolic union at the end.

The ontological capacity of metaphor, what Jacques Derrida speaks
of in terms of *différance* for that which at once *is and is not*,[24] enables
Pardo Bazán to unite Ilda and Doña Milagros as she explores the
sociopolitical praxis of Darwinian sexual selection through a transposition of reproductive labor to questions of capitalism and the State.
Indeed, this novel represents a fictional precursor to contemporary
feminist theory on women's work in the domestic sphere. The State
relies on the unpaid services of women for its very survival by means
of sexual divisions of labor that transcend borders and class.[25] It is in
this vein that the problematic relationship between women and the
modern nation-state also translates to issues of subjectivity. Women
once made tropes uphold nationalist agendas via the perpetuation of
categories that grant agency to some while making others into spectacle.[26] As consequence, those who theorize on reproductive labor from
a Marxist-feminist perspective must often qualify their positions with
respect to women and class. To equate the housewife with a household serf is to emphasize that though gender may be incongruous with
class, it in fact plays a significant role in the processes behind class
structures, such as the production, appropriation, and distribution of
surplus labor.[27] Nancy C. M. Hartsock in her approach to a feminist
historical materialism sets aside "the important differences among
women" in order to construct a simplified model of exchange value.[28]
Women's reproductive labor and its appropriation by men, for Hart-
stock, make sexual exploitation comparable to that of the proletariat.
Distinctions, however, emerge once reproduction is understood as a
"unity with nature" and motherhood is seen as a "complex relational
nexus" (297). Her work has been used by Lou Charnon-Deutsch and
others who have written on the novel and nineteenth-century Spanish women writers, including Pardo Bazán, as a means to equate both
liberation strategies and coping mechanisms with these notions of an
intersubjective feminine experience.[29]

Nevertheless, though such concerns over reproductive labor and patriarchy echo much of what *Doña Milagros* anticipates, they do not allow us to move Ilda beyond arguments of essence, biological determinism, and the Eurocentric view of capitalism, which orthodox Marxism sees in strict terms of wage labor relations. To grasp the last words on Ilda's lips, the renunciation of her maternity and conjugal enslavement, requires a fuller appreciation of nonwage labor exploitation. In the wake of Rosa Luxemburg and others, Maria Mies explains that procreation and other wifely duties, because naturalized, do not correspond to productive work under the patriarchal conditions of capitalism.[30] It is clear then that a sexual division of labor is not simply a state in which men do certain tasks and women others, but rather it masks an asymmetrical relationship of dominance. Locating the institutionalization of men-women relations in the universalized and ahistoric concept of the family, Mies asserts that labor "can only be productive in the sense of producing surplus value as long as it can tap, extract, exploit, and appropriate labour which is spent in the *production of life*, or *subsistence production* [italics original] which is largely non-wage labour mainly done by women" (47). In this way, the production of life, which yields use value, becomes productive labor, and since it is subsistence production, the basis of capitalism, it transcends the family to the realm of global structures of accumulation. Women, like Ilda, are reduced to "breeders of children" (63); looking for someone to bear and raise his own progeny, Benicio travels outside of civilization, lays claim to her, and colonizes her body, in what Gilles Deleuze and Félix Guattari understand as desire's "deterritorialization" of an inhabited concept.[31] That is, Pardo Bazán's text exposes, even if in an inchoate form, the interrelatedness of housewifization and colonization that Mies emphasizes (*Patriarchy and Accumulation*, 110). Benicio manages Ilda as his property, held in check by the ideology of reproduction and, above all, the marriage contract.

As consequence, this concern with the disagreeable, secondary plot of Ilda, instead of the edifying union between Benicio and Doña Milagros, bridges Pardo Bazán's fiction and contemporary feminist theory on reproductive labor and the domestic sphere. Ilda's reality, through the eyes of Benicio, signals a complex critique of the status quo, once she is seen to be the patriarchal double of Doña Milagros rather than her villainous contrary. In other words, where Ilda's killing off has been the norm, literally and figuratively, it is instead possible to reconcile these women in a coming together of resemblance. The marriage contract, from its origins as treated by Friedrich Engels in *The Origin of the Family, Private Property, and the State* (1891) to the particular case of nineteenth-century Spain, provides a material and historical foundation to questions of women's subjugation; in the economic interest of the gendered State, at the level of its very subsistence, the marriage contract serves, along with limited access to education and employment, to maintain an asymmetrical, hierarchal sexual division of labor. Mill considered it the last remaining lawful bondage, and Engels associated it with the overthrow of mother-right, "*the world historical defeat of the female sex* [italics original]," and the subsequent "open or concealed domestic slavery of the wife."[32] These postulations on the material connection between marriage and subjugation highlight the economic and civil implications of this cultural institution for women with respect to the reproductive exigencies of sexual selection in the social sphere.[33]

Darwin factors in this theoretical and historical panorama for various reasons. For one, he ends *The Descent* saying, "I would as soon be descended from that heroic little monkey . . . as from a savage who . . . treats his wives like slaves" (2:404–5). This declaration decries in explicit terms the "open" subjugation of women. Yet Darwin seems much less explicit about the "concealed domestic slavery of the wife." He takes pains to show that "in civilised nations women have free or almost free choice" and notes as well that "their choice is largely influenced by the social position and wealth of the men" (2:356). But then he turns right around and attributes the selector status to men. The transposition from *struggle for life* to *trapping a husband* never materializes outright, though it is implicit in what he says about "the social position and wealth of the men." Moreover, "free or almost free choice" could not be a more important hesitation. He wavers precisely because the choice is not free, and "almost free" therefore means not free at all, which is not that far off from the "passive" qualifier used on other occasions. Hence, what Pardo Bazán shows us about sexual selection as Darwin struggled to understand it is how the dynamic intertwines with the material forces inseparable from its praxis within the patriarchal state apparatus. In the process, she also comes to reveal the full magnitude of Darwin's relative silence on one type of (savage) subjugation and not the (civil) other.

UGLY CHOICES

So, what type of choice and, more important, what type of change can Darwinian sexual selection deliver in a society of "domestic slavery" where women find themselves "almost free" and yet not free at all because of the ideological stakes superimposed on the reproductive ends of the very same dynamic? Pardo Bazán offers an uncomfortable answer with *Memorias de un solterón*, her sequel to *Dona Milagros*. For most readers, the two works have little in common other than the characters. In truth, these novels complement one another within the frame of the author's own feminist agenda, given that the marriage contract in its historical context reveals what Feíta's decision accommodates when she resigns herself to marrying Mauro at the end of the second. In other words, as she comes to "carry the cross" of her sex,[34] Feíta is not the paragon of measured emancipation or, as some have argued, a model for prudent compromise and a precursor to the radical feminism of the decades to come but rather the face of ugly necessity in her own times, for her frustrated attempts at self-determination reveal the cultural determinism that scripts her limited opportunities.

Mauro Pareja, the narrator of *Memorias de un solterón*, is a friend of Benicio Neira. In his thirties, he prides himself on a worldview at odds with marriage, which he believes reflects self-interest and propels us toward the dire Malthusian predictions on population. In fact, this "greatest enemy of the reality of marriage" (795) sees in the Neira family all the evils of the institution and its hold on society. His ironic inclination, therefore, is to marry one of Benicio's many daughters, knowing that unless husbands are found for them they and their father will be lost. Such a resolution brings him to reflect on Feíta, who catches his attention as a "wise savage" (827). She, in turn, befriends him and in disregard for public opinion visits him at his apartment unannounced. It is not long before Mauro facilitates her desires for greater freedom by giving her a key to the library of his building. This gesture awakens uncertain feelings in him; his inner reactions toward this "*marimacho*" (865), or manly woman, confuse him; her presence in the bookroom leaves him powerless "to repress an intense chill, a kind of mysterious horror that does not come from the person hidden by darkness, but rather from the *unknown*, from an apprehension without object, almost supernatural . . ." (864; italics original). As it happens, he finds himself in love (with possible undertones of narcissism, emasculation, and even repressed homo-sexuality), while she also transforms, using her newfound empower-ment to justify more attention to her appearance and his expectations of femininity.

The emotions Mauro experiences, however, signal something for-bidden, fueled by, of all things, *the rights of women* (869; ital-ics original), though no doubt eased by the fact that Feíta goes from looking like "an altar boy or a page" to a bewitching young lady in full possession of "all the charm and seductive presence of woman in her most tender maidenhood, as an April in bloom" (867). She adopts what had been his own outlook of individualism, saying, "I live for myself, for myself" (871), and thus becomes "the new woman, the dawn of a society different from that of today" (888). Nevertheless, he questions "this foolish and impossible emancipation" (908) and chides her for aspiring "to abandon the domestic home" (908) and her family. It is not until she comes to him in need of money, though, that Mauro really loses control (or, rather, gains it). He gallantly offers to give her all his cash and belongings if it will help her strike out on her own. In this frame of reference, which Mauro reads as a history of his own personal growth, he no longer knows himself: "I had barely spo-ken these decisive words [his 'yes!' to her entreaties], when it crossed my mind that they had been pronounced by another, an unknown person that was there, inside of me, taking hold of my innermost being, but who was not me, but rather my antagonist" (919). No sur-prise, this "antagonist," the one ready to turn his back on manly self-interest for a woman, wins out, and all of the ebullient confusion culminates in a moment of high drama, when Mauro must choose between friendship and marriage.

With his mind set on making an honest woman of Feíta, Mauro gives his pitch for marriage, which she, who aspires only "to be free" (923), rejects outright. Faced with the prospect of failure, Mauro must renegotiate the terms. He rationalizes that in a culture opposed to her freedom, a husband is her only hope for survival:

> Feíta, . . . the woman who tries to emancipate herself, like you
> are trying to do, will only find rocks and thorns in her path that
> bloody . . . her heart. . . . All the novelties that are floating around
> in your little revolutionary head . . . will be great in other European
> countries or the New World . . . but this is today. . . . How miserable
> you will be if you persist in swimming upstream! . . . Think about it,
> my girl . . . my crazy little girl . . . I'm offering you liberty . . . within

duty . . . and with love as a bonus. . . . It seems to me that there can
be no reason to turn that down. What do you say? (925)

Her response, "Because I want to walk the path of thorns" (925),
throws him into a state of desperation; in a farewell laced with double
meaning, she tells him thanks anyway, "Pareja" (926), no need to ac-
company her home, for as she says, "I know the house" (926).[35]

Nevertheless, the novel cannot so easily let go of this match made
in fiction, and by the conclusion we discover that following the death
of Feíta's father Benicio, with the Neira household spiraling toward
utter economic and moral disarray, Mauro and Feíta together take
full control of the situation, he as "counselor, director, and judge"
(961) and she as a mother-figure whom "the family obeyed . . . without questioning" (962). As it turns out, she never ended up leaving
after all; the narrator recounts in a subtle aside: "And Feíta? . . . Feíta!
I imagine that no one will have doubted that the independent one
stayed . . . her grand trip was never spoken about again, not a
chance!" (961). In fact, she answers his next proposal with these decisive words: "I never wanted to marry. You know that. I dreamed of
freedom, and of something that to me seemed the ideal. Things have
worked out in a far different way. Duty and Family (in capital letters,
my friend Mauro) have fallen on me . . . and, how heavy they are! I
declare myself defeated . . . I need someone to help me carry the cross
. . ." (963). Mauro understands well, and his good fortune makes him
think that he should write a sequel—the memoirs of a married man.
Pardo Bazán, though, never followed through with such a project,
which she might have thought impossible from the moment she put
these words on Mauro's lips, for what could be less interesting than
culturally scripted domestic bliss. It is the ugly choice of sexual selection in a world of "Duty and Family" that concerns us most.

THE DILEMMA OF MODERN SPANISH WOMANHOOD

With the exception of Maryellen Bieder, who sees Feíta's choice as a
clear-cut capitulation,[36] the majority of critics find a new model for
equality in *Memorias de un solterón*. For example, Beth Wietelmann
Bauer calls it "a blueprint for the modern woman and for enlightened marriage between equals"; Mary Lee Bretz maintains that "as
a feminist novel" it promotes "social change at the same time that it
displays literary change"; and Lou Charnon-Deutsch equates Feíta's
"awareness of her responsibility to others" with "female maturity"

and "an ethic of care that she, and obviously Pardo Bazán, interpreted as a positive development."[37] I am not so sure that Pardo Bazán "obviously" read the denouement in this light (or Feíta, for that matter), but nevertheless, since authorial intent remains both elusive and secondary to the text (though by no means irrelevant), we must again be reminded of the either-or dilemma of these approaches. Either the novel ends in a concession to patriarchy, in which case it is not subversive, or Feíta's union with Mauro and maternal role are emancipatory, in which case it is. With both interpretations, we are often told of the historical realities that Feíta (and Pardo Bazán) faced, as Mauro himself underscores, and of the conservatism of the author, who never rejected marriage as a socio-sacred institution. That is to say, though Pardo Bazán might have wished otherwise, it is argued that as author she elects for the safest route, "a tactical retreat" from an unrealistic utopia, in order not to upset a readership still skeptical about women's emancipation.[38]

Yet in *La mujer española*, it is Pardo Bazán who asserts that the housewife is antithetical to human progress. Plus, to contend that Mauro is "willed into becoming what the female subject, Fe Neira, requires in order to be substantiated and validated as a subject" borders on a dangerous sublimation of what is most disquieting about the text, namely, Mauro's supervision of this same outcome.[39] One need only look back to book 5 of Jean-Jacques Rousseau's *Émile* (1762) to appreciate the sexism of these compensations with respect to women's will: "She [woman] ought to reign in the home . . . by getting herself commanded to do what she wants to do."[40] Or, as Harold Bloom says of Kate in Shakespeare's *The Taming of the Shrew* (1593–94), she teaches the art of her own will by "advising women how to rule absolutely while feigning obedience."[41] It is, after all, Mauro who ends up the victor, with "Duty and Family" (*Memorias de un solterón*, 963) in capital letters in his corner. He authors himself as the voice of reason, the commonsense figure who was right all along: "And Feíta? . . . her grand trip was never spoken about again, not a chance!" (961). Thus, his memoirs can be seen to have "substantiated and validated" *him* as subject and the patriarchy that his careful rhetoric safeguards.

However, an alternative reading of Feíta's choice allows us to move beyond an opposition between frustrated aspirations and new models of equality. Rather than an either-or scenario, what Pardo Bazán achieves in *Memorias de un solterón* requires that we recognize the ways an accommodation like Feíta's decision to "carry the cross" (963) of her gender can be far more subversive than an outright dismissal. In other words, I do not believe that her conclusion reflects a "tactical retreat"; the novel could have ended in many ways, including with Feíta's initial rejection of Mauro. On the contrary, Pardo Bazán's moral truth, made manifest in her social critique, lies in the reality of the ugly necessity she represents through Mauro's psychology, and Feíta's very name speaks to the nature of the ugly (Feíta) faith (Fe) her "new woman" ultimately places in the self-sacrifice of Old World, patriarchal tradition. In this way, Pardo Bazán's political essays on women's emancipation in the frame of sexual selection can be reconciled with the message her fiction promoted during these same years.

Together, Pardo Bazán's *Doña Milagros* and *Memorias de un solterón* show that "almost free" choice subverts to the degree that it reflects the culture that engenders it. Yet, while Ilda speaks to the economic and ideological impetus behind the status quo, it is the latter of these two novels that captures the paradox of Darwin's oxymoronic law. For in *Memorias de un solterón*, Pardo Bazán labors to reproduce modern Spanish womanhood with a "heavy" (963) dose of realism. She does so, though, according to a deterministic worldview, the "Duty and Family" (963) that script Feíta's fate, which gainsays her own best intentions as author. Indeed, in her theoretical treatise on French naturalism, *La cuestión palpitante* (1883), Pardo Bazán separates herself from those who "subjugate thought and passion to the same laws that cause a stone to fall," in favor of a more balanced aesthetic able to harmonize matter and the imagination.[42] In the case of Feíta, however, we should not be blind to such a fall or "subjugate thought and passion" to the patriarchal laws behind it. For when it comes to sexual selection, a complex psychology underwrites the ineluctable cycle of Adam and Eve as one of return and reinvention. Expulsion from paradise is painted in the material terms of its ugly history.

Of the most astute remarks to be found in Pardo Bazán's aforementioned treatise of *reflexiones científicas* against Darwin is her rhetorical admission, which she intends as a slight, that Darwinism "will be everything one wants it to be, except simple and open to our understanding."[43] In truth, she understood quite a bit. The essay, however, buries sexual selection, which will later come to be the least simple aspect of her fiction as far as Darwin is concerned, under a barrage of the most persistent charges against Darwin's more polemical theories of natural selection and descent, like his inability to explain the origin of life or the lack of intermediary species as proof of ongoing evolution or questions of heredity with respect to primitive cultures. In fact, several lengthy commentaries on race, differentiation, and progeny notwithstanding, the two references in which Pardo Bazán targets sexual selection most explicitly are her affirmation that the phenomenon is no trivial matter but rather the essential key to life (553) and her emphasis on the imagination as our only recourse to envisioning the past changes in humankind and those to come (557). In the context of both, though, she remains certain of one thing—the recognition that we have always been and will forever be imperfect, no matter how progressive we believe ourselves to be (564).

Consequently, though written almost twenty years before the two novels treated in this chapter, "Reflexiones científicas contra el darwinismo" offers a fascinating window into Pardo Bazán's perception of Darwin, and it is no small irony that the insights we can glean from it about her reservations originate in her most confident arguments against evolutionism. For example, because Darwin's science is forever open-ended (538, 569), she claims that the most interesting direction in which to take the theory, as far as its unintended implications, would be "the study of the moral, social, and political consequences" (539) of natural laws defined by change, which no doubt would lead to outcomes very different from what his many enthusiasts believe. Likewise, she grants certain validity to these same tenets of plasticity in the interest of self-preservation and reproduction, saying that when "external influences" take hold the individual changes as need be to meet environmental challenges and thus "ensure offspring and existence" (551). Yet all of this in her eyes does little more than lead to the conclusion that "Darwinism is a novel" (567), that is, fiction, a fantasy. In light of her life's work and the social currency that fantasy holds for reimagining the world, my sense is that she never let go of this idea.

It follows, then, that Pardo Bazán's Darwinism will indeed be, to a certain degree, "everything one wants it to be, except simple and open to our understanding" (548). This is a good thing, for alternative readings emerge out of such inconclusiveness. For instance, the simple answer to the novels treated in this chapter would be the superimposition of Mill's ideal partnership of two cultivated faculties on the marriage of Feíta and Mauro or on the love between Doña Milagros and Benicio. Yet, to see nothing but roses, that is, to be satisfied with bold steps forward given the times, is to circumvent the more meaningful contradictions of Pardo Bazán's fiction, political beliefs, and engagement with Darwin's own theory. To complicate the question is to frame her vision of "almost free" choice in its internal inconsistencies. In effect, Feíta's voluntary submission is nothing if not a transposition at the level of the individual of what Rousseau outlines in broader strokes when proclaiming that

> it becomes manifestly false to assert that individuals make any real renunciation by the social contract; indeed, as a result of the contract they find themselves in a situation preferable in real terms to that which prevailed before; instead of an alienation, they have profitably exchanged an uncertain and precarious life for a better and more secure one; they have exchanged natural independence for freedom, the power to injure others for the enjoyment of their own security; they have exchanged their own strength which others might overcome for a right which the social union makes invincible.[44]

As we have seen, in the context of Darwin's science Pardo Bazán understands adaptation to "external influences" in a similar light, as a submission in the interest of existence. Nonetheless, scholars of Rousseau know his contract to be in fundamental disharmony with his larger philosophical platform at the moment when he says that "conscience never deceives us" in book 4 of *Émile* and elsewhere. In these instances, what he has in mind reflects the infallible, innate principle of justice of the individual, whereas in *The Social Contract* it is made clear that "the public conscience . . . is the arbiter of just and unjust."[45] In this latter case, we are forced, so to speak, by the general will of the community to be free, in a model in which freedom is choosing to live under someone else's rules.

Darwin, for his part, opens the third chapter of *The Descent* by citing Immanuel Kant's exclamation of "Duty!" as a way to broach his own discussion of "moral sense or conscience," saying that it is "summed up in that short but imperious word *ought*, so full of high significance" (1:70; italics original). He then goes on to construct an analogy between human society and a bee colony, to suggest what life might look like were we not to be in some measure innately moral: "There can hardly be a doubt that our unmarried females would, like the worker-bees, think it a sacred duty to kill their brothers, and mothers would strive to kill their fertile daughters; and no one would think of interfering" (1:73). But reflecting on our own evolution, Darwin does not see things this way, "for each individual would have an inward sense of possessing certain stronger or more enduring instincts . . . so that there would often be a struggle as to which impulse should be followed" (1:73). This "inward monitor" (1:73) is "retained from an extremely remote period" (1:85) in which a bond was felt among our earliest progenitors. Hence, the general will assumes a privileged place in Darwin's theory: "Consequently man would be greatly influenced by the wishes, approbation, and blame of his fellow-men, as expressed by their gestures and language" (1:86). Yet over time, as self-command and reasoning mature, we come to appreciate the justice of the judgments of others and "may then say, I am the supreme judge of my own conduct" (1:86), even in the face of a community that may or may not approve of our actions. The individual will can be trusted above all else because, having been groomed by the collective, it literally has reason on its side, above any public sentiment unreasonably resistant to change.

Not exactly. If contradiction has become a recurrent theme over the course of this study, here at the end Darwin again gives more of the same. He concludes the section with the sort of wavering that we have seen to be characteristic of his thought:

> It is obvious that every one may with an easy conscience gratify his own desires, if they do not interfere with his social instincts, that is with the good of others; but in order to be quite free from self-reproach, or at least of anxiety, it is almost necessary for him to avoid the disapprobation, whether reasonable or not, of his fellow men. Nor must he break through the fixed habits of his life, especially if these are supported by reason; for if he does, he will assuredly feel dissatisfaction. (1:92–93)

Reading these lines, we might recall Feíta's closing words to Mauro: "I never wanted to marry. You know that. I dreamed of freedom" (*Memorias de un solterón*, 963). This is by no means the freedom of Rousseau's social contract, of voluntary submission to the public will, and asking Mauro to help her "carry the cross" of "Duty and Family" hardly sounds like the partnership Mill has in mind. Her words ring more like the self-abnegation both decry. In fact, it is safe to say that Feíta and her readers "assuredly feel dissatisfaction," as Darwin would say, with this ending. The only one who does not appear the least bit dissatisfied is Mauro, which is none too telling. As consequence, it is "almost necessary" to call *Doña Milagros* and *Memorias de un solterón* subversive, for the ways Pardo Bazán's manipulations of passive choice, so central to Darwinian sexual selection and the power dynamics of her day, trouble the conscience. It is also, therefore, reasonable to assume that *The Descent* might be subversive in this way as well.

Conclusion

The Imperfect Science of Conscience

The novels of Pardo Bazán revealed a key truth about the indeterminate Darwin this study as a whole aims to show. The progressive potential of the theory of sexual selection lies in its unresolved tensions. Because something like "almost free" choice for women of "civilised nations" (*The Descent*, 2:356) leads to more questions than answers, its sociopolitical praxis with respect to reproduction and the marriage contract raises concerns about the welfare of the community. Self-interest and self-sacrifice once conflated through the survival strategy of *trapping a husband* appear equally ugly. The struggle becomes perverse. In this way, courtship remains a contest, but for reasons other than those Darwin imagined. The constitutive components have morphed over the course of my explorations with ever more complex reflections on the collective and a Nature of change. Lingering difficulties tied to the latter therefore prompt a last look at the social consequence of the silence surrounding sexual selection, the present absence with which this book began.

It might be said of Darwinian sexual selection that to be successful, that is, lucky in love, one must remember to take the back stairs. This sense indeed figures in the writing of Jacinto Octavio Picón, whose inversions informed my earlier discussions of suitor-selector reversals, and in his peculiar short story, "Los favores de Fortuna" (1895), such subversion becomes a literal reality, though the tale itself is allegorical.[1] Of the protagonist, Fortuna, there can be no doubt, "her love blinds . . . making some grovel, and others go crazy" (135). Nevertheless, in keeping with the times she has given up her "goddess sanctuary" for "the boudoir of a courtesan" (136). Three suitors compete for her favor: "Carlos Tizona, a young man of extraordinary courage, for whom the best answer was the sword; the doctor Infolio, who without being old looked it for having studied so much; and one so-called Lepe, the last offspring of a proverbial family line, according to the records" (138). All of them have talent, the first capable of anything, the second meticulous in every respect, and the third never missing a beat; to be sure, "if the traits of all three came together in one, he would easily make himself the king of the world" (138). Valor, hard work, and wit—together these men personify the perfect mate.

By chance, the rivals meet one day and decide to set off on different paths in search of Fortuna. Years later, after countless trials and tribulations, all three arrive at her palace at the same moment. The narrator explains: "Tizona, seeing the iron gates shut, at the risk of killing himself, scaled in through a window; Infolio, placing himself before the entrance said such admirable things, both in his own and a foreign tongue, that the doors opened up by themselves to let him pass; and it was then that Lepe astutely slipped in" (142). Minutes later, they come together in the foyer to Fortuna's bedroom, where from behind the door "sounded the unequaled explosion of a real smooch, and no sooner did it end than out sauntered a shrimp of a man—insignificant, unsightly, and vulgar—who with a triumphant air came toward them cracking his knuckles and caressing his beard" (143). Needless to say, there is total panic and confusion among the other three now miserable suitors, as aghast they shout in unison: "Profanation! Who are you? How did you get in here?" (143). The flippant reply, which could not have been made "with more haughtiness," strikes a bitter chord, for the message of this inferior intruder is as blunt as it is disconcerting: "I am Perico Mediano, and I came up by way of the service stairs" (144). Nothing, it seems, could be more unexpected and yet so natural as to be matter of fact for this average ladies man.[2]

In the context of such an outcome, we might recall that the indeterminacy of natural law served as our point of departure for how Darwin has been misunderstood with respect to cultural production in Spain and elsewhere. Darwinism as determinism traces back to the nineteenth-century political defamation of evolutionary science at the moment when Darwin's theories were thought to pose a threat to the establishment, but his Spanish history is, likewise, literally of epic consequence. In the hands of José Ortega y Gasset, Darwin lands on the receiving end of a blow that would come to frame his legacy:

> The natural sciences based on determinism conquered the field of biology in the early years of the last century. Darwin believed he had managed to imprison life . . . within the confines of physical necessity. Life descends to nothing more than mere matter, physiology to mechanics . . . there is no liberty . . . adaptation is submission and renunciation. Darwin sweeps heroes from the face of the earth.[3]

In this articulation, Darwin's science is the beginning of the end of humanity, of all that is noble in the *struggle for life*. The struggle, though, is what Ortega y Gasset overlooks in our shared evolutionary past; he writes off Darwin by making him the bane of existence and the death knell for the creative spirit. For Ortega y Gasset, heroism amounts to the act of willing, "the heroic act may be found . . . in a real act of will" (392), and this will, what moves the individual to tragedy for want of self, has no place in the Darwinian world, irrespective of sex.

Nothing could be further from the truth. For all that "Los favores de Fortuna" might have in common with Picón's novels, Fortuna stays in her boudoir, as a mythic and cynical abstraction of the social ills of the nineteenth century that had come to distort the dynamics of sexual selection. This was not the fortune of Picón's other protagonists or of those in the novels selected for analysis throughout this study, and regarding Darwinian sexual selection in its sociopolitical praxis, the conquest by Perico Mediano would be no laughing matter for society at large. As chapter 9 showed, an indefinite relationship exists among female choice, conscience, and community that extends to the very realm of action itself, where the will operates in the public sphere. Yet conscience, when understood in its now accepted usage as reflection as opposed to instinct, brings with it ties to inaction, that is, to the Nietzschean notion of "bad conscience" in its alignment with guilt.[4] A problematic gulf therefore separates the will of the struggle from the conscience of community in Darwin's model when set in this light. Without a means to bring the two together, an oppositional antagonism defines the relationship, and we are left with only a partial appreciation of his message. This tension thus presents a serious issue because it misrepresents a number of important evolutionary principles outlined by Darwin in *The Descent* and, in the case of female choice, positions agency contrary to the moral sense of social instincts. The disharmony then has real-world, political implications for those of the "weaker sex" who are led to believe that Nature would have them know their place—that life for women is unchanging, that their *struggle for life* in terms of self-determination and equal rights was somehow shameful, a threat to the collective well-being.

However, evolution runs counter to this type of oppressive stasis on various levels, the most obvious being that change is the fundamental constant of its operation. Reconciliation is hence necessary for Darwin's model on these terms, even if it is by no means readily apparent. In *La scienza nuova* (1725), Giambattista Vico declared that those "who do not know what is true of things take care to hold fast to what is certain, so that, if they cannot satisfy their intellects by knowledge [*scienza*], their wills at least may rest on conscience [*coscienza*]."[5] The opposition Vico poses between intellect and will employs "conscience" in its etymological sense of "with knowledge," or what otherwise would be the intuition. In a world of circumstance, of things whose true nature can never be known, where infallible "Truth" remains an impossibility, when all else has been stripped away, we act in deference to the criteria we already possess, what is innate within us, our "conscience." Here, it is not the guilt of Nietzschean inaction, sin, and all the rest, but rather the opposite. Agency comes out of intuition and self-awareness.

By recalling Vico in this way, whose sociological writings were as eccentric as they were profound, we locate conscience in a primordial territory foreign to the intellect and divorced from its modern epistemological offshoots of reason and empiricism. Or so it appears. A broad aim for this inquiry has been to marry literature and science in such a way so as to show how each might help us understand the other, where neither enjoys more claim to Truth and both work in tandem to reveal that thought transcends our disciplinary thinking when discoveries are imagined before they are made. At a pivotal moment in history when the above separation between intellect and intuition began to first take full root, John Locke and William Blake became a contentious couple whose relationship still embodies in many ways the greater rift between science and literature I delineate and seek to question in chapter 1. Hence, they provide an unorthodox yet useful turn at this stage for revealing why Ortega's reduction of realism to mechanistic determinism and evolutionism to submissive fatalism remains fallacious, especially as concerns the ideological offshoots of biological essentialism detailed in chapter 2.

For situated on opposite poles of the conceptual universe, Locke and Blake, as observation versus imagination, disagree on the grounds by which individuation occurs, with their divergence on the possibility of innate ideas.[6] In Locke's building-block model of the individual as a tabula rasa who acquires knowledge one piece at a time through experience, there is no place for inborn certainties. In response, Blake thinks otherwise, as is clear from his annotation to Joshua Reynolds's *Discourse III*: "Knowledge of Ideal Beauty. is Not to be Acquired It is Born with us Innate Ideas. are in Every Man Born with him. they are <truly> Himself. The Man who says that we have No Innate Ideas must be a Fool & Knave. Having no Con-Science <or Innate Science>."[7] Blake views conscience not in terms of inaction or as the property of "culture's norms,"[8] that is, in conflict with subjective imagination and vitalism, which is the most common understanding today in the wake of Friedrich Nietzsche, but rather as the inborn, certain knowledge that directs us toward, among other things, the beautiful.

Yet Locke, too, has his moments, and his mechanistic Mind must burn on something. He imagines this generator to be "*Power*," or that which allows for "the consideration of any Idea," and he names this impulse the "*Will* . . . the Source from whence all Action proceeds."[9] To approximate the reach of this power, Locke speaks best for himself: "My right Hand writes, whilst my left Hand is still: What causes rest in one, and motion in the other? Nothing but my Will, a Thought of my Mind . . . Explain this, and make it intelligible, and then the next step will be to understand Creation" (4.10.19). This is important—the intellect cannot contain creation. As a result, Lockean "*Rational Knowledge*" must give ground to "*Intuitive Knowledge*," which is "certain, beyond all Doubt, and needs no Probation, nor can have any; this being the highest of all Humane Certainty" (4.17.14). We can therefore revise Vico without letting go of him and, in so doing, wed Blake and Locke and, by extension, literature and science in the abstract. The individual does not make recourse to "conscience" for want of "science," that is, certain knowledge; rather, the latter is embedded within the former. It is not a question of alternatives, one or the other, because conscience would be impossible without science; there can be no certainties without such innate Truth and with respect to ideal beauty.

To carry over from Locke then and with an eye toward the ugly realities of realism we have seen in the preceding chapters regarding choice, my "intuitive knowledge" tells me that the best way to come full circle is to perceive an arch. This study began with Plato, whose reflections on the civil dimension of procreation prepared us for where we might take Darwinian sexual selection and the hurdles of history we might face. Nevertheless, Plato was concerned far more with love than advantageous breeding, and in the *Symposium*, where the virtues of amorous relations between men, between women, and between men and women are set forth, he treats the subject in ways we never see in Darwin, whose focus on heterosexual mating (not love) guided his thinking and, for this reason, my discussion of the courtship plot in relation to his laws of sexual selection. Love is a factor, though, in Darwin's model and without question is one that colors the nineteenth-century novel. In this light, I think it worth returning to Plato and some of his most transcendent ideas about the matter. Diotima, the lone female interlocutor in this dialogue, believes that "Love is neither beautiful nor good" but rather something in between: "He is tough and shriveled and shoeless and homeless, always lying on the dirt without a bed, sleeping at people's doorsteps and in roadsides under the sky . . . he is brave, impetuous, and intense . . . through all his life, a genius with enchantments, potions, and clever pleadings."[10] As such, what Love wants is "reproduction," the object of *ta erōtika*, or the art of love. We are all of us pregnant with ideas and because of our mortal nature we struggle to live forever through the birth of that which will always be at once both the same and different, what Diotima calls "birth in beauty" (206e). This constant change creates a life in which knowledge passes away and returns: "What is departing and aging leaves behind something new, something such as it had been" (207e). Hence, we seek beauty in that which we would beget, though we might, at times, have to resort to ugly means for noble ends. At the highest stage of Love, we will be interested no longer in mere images of virtue but rather in the beauty of virtuous knowledge.

At this point, Diotima's speech is interrupted by the arrival of the drunken Alcibiades, who says of his lover Socrates: "If you were to listen to his arguments, at first they'd strike you as totally ridiculous; they're clothed in words as coarse as the hides worn by the most vulgar satyrs" (221e). It is only when we "go behind their surface" that we "realize that no other arguments make any sense" (222a). Faced with a reality of "concealed domestic slavery" (Engels, *The Origin of the Family, Private Property, and the State*, 65), its social contradictions, and a "complex affair" (*The Descent*, 1:296) made distasteful for its materialist and ideological perversions, the realists showcased the surface in order to reach the virtuous knowledge of the other side at a deeper level of "affective response" (McKeon, "Prose Fiction," 263). Or, to put it another way, they, too, shared Eliot's preference for "raw material" over "sympathy ready-made" ("The Natural History of German Life," in *Essays of George Eliot*, 230). The intent of these authors was not to "beget in anything ugly" (*Symposium*, 209b), which Plato held to be impossible, but rather as Benito Pérez Galdós maintained when speaking of the novel at the end of the nineteenth century: "If we correct ourselves, so much the better; but if not, our art has fulfilled its mission, and we will always have before us that eternal mirror to reflect and safeguard our ugliness" ("Observaciones sobre la novela," 116).[11] Like his contemporaries, Galdós understood realism as reproduction, not the "totally ridiculous" representations "clothed in words as coarse as the hides worn by the most vulgar satyrs." We saw firsthand the troubling lessons that could come out of such a satyr in the dark *noche* of Alejandro Sawa, whose depraved priest Don Gregorio raped the young Lola like "a satyr with a virgin in the interior of a forest" after she had been seduced and abandoned to the streets.

No, to find the beauty in Darwinian sexual selection as construed in these novels we must confront the ugly realities they sought to convey and approach them as if reading in translation, from behind the Galdosian "mirror" that realism never truly was. We must also understand, as did Pardo Bazán, that such reproduction will always be an imperfect science. A master of similar unseen truths, Cervantes brings both facets of the process as understood by Galdós and Pardo Bazán together on a single front. Having arrived in Barcelona, Don Quixote finds himself in a printer's shop and strikes up a conversation about translation, which he imagines to be rather like looking at a tapestry "on the wrong side, because even though you can make out the figures, they're partially hidden behind this thread and that thread, and you can't ever see them as clearly and with all the detail you can find on the right side."[12] The hard part, however, comes at the moment we accept that the "right side" is a confusion from the outset because of "this thread and that thread." I conceive of the reciprocity between literature and science in this way, the truth of which "is not the colors we see, but rather the subtle vibration of the ether that we do not see."[13] Don Quixote pointed out, as consolation, that we might occupy ourselves "with worse and even less profitable things"

(Cervantes, *Don Quijote*, 682). The novel's obsession with courtship at this moment in Spanish history is testimony to both the confusion of sexual selection and its resultant sociopolitical importance. An imperfect science, it will be as blurred as the wrong side of the tapestry and equally jumbled on the right side. Whether we think of science through literature or the reverse, the act is one of translation because the constitutive threads make for the long-standing historical distinctions between the two and their equally demonstrable cultural intertwinement.

Still, it would appear that conscience, *being with knowledge*, can have no origin other than self, Ortega's "ungraspable" individual, which amounts to a conception of inborn science that seems to leave community in the lurch—a tension not unlike the one with which this conclusion began. Darwin, though, points out that the self is always social, and the "social instincts" in *The Descent* give rise to a "moral sense" that underwrites "conscience" in his evolutionism (1:71–103). Moreover, if evolution, which is temporal, leaves us with one thing, it is the con-science that *being* is *becoming*. Our intuition makes plain, because we will even toward tragedy, that no self is given. We continue to run up against the "stone wall" of natural laws,[14] but we do so by choice, with the intuition that to run in such a way, to struggle, is not shameful or unnatural but rather an inalienable right. The paradox of this Darwinian ontology cannot help but be metaphorical; in the Derridean spaces of *différance* in between what is and is not, we like our species are defined by differentiation.[15] Likewise, we realize ourselves in language, which Darwin believed to originate in sexual selection, and evolution makes clear that we are as much products as producers of our environments. That is why "Nature" can be seen, as in chapter 7, to calibrate our social morality as something other than and rhetorically aligned with the social environment. Material change is a matter of will, and *mater* heroism, even if driven by the *mater*nal impulses of reproduction, need not be incompatible with evolutionism, as Ortega would have it.

Yet without the poets, we would find this virtuous knowledge about change lost on us, since we would be unable to see the symbiotic relationship between the will and community in Darwin's thought. It is the charge of literature to give us the backside of the tapestry, from which the partially hidden figures prompt our own reproductions, the beauty of birth out of the ugly reality that so often surrounds us. In *L'èra nuova* (1899), Giovanni Pascoli laments that scientific advances in the nineteenth century have done nothing to better the moral state of man, but rather the opposite.[16] To right the ship, he claims that we need remember one thing, that the poets, among whom I include the Spanish novelists, are the only ones who can "make conscience from science" (117). This formula is a profound inversion of what Vico maintains, for in this case the will must respond to that "true knowledge" which remains no longer absent but rather omnipresent. From Pascoli's perspective, Science now says to Poetry: "I have worked, but not you, and all the good that should have been born from my work has not been, and what is more, bad things have come to pass that should not have, because you have not cooperated with me. . . . I set the table with truth, but you have not nourished the souls. I cannot do everything by myself" (117). The point here is well taken; the poets have a social role to play. Literature in its own right is by no means divorced from the material world or opposed to science, and neither is it pure invention. Nor is science about hard facts alone. But such eagerness for reciprocity between the two also reveals that Pascoli, a voice of cultural crisis, lacks the distance that he advocates for with his own writing to appreciate the fruits of poetry gathered from science and, in particular, from evolutionism.

With a technical "reproduction" of Spanish verse, Charles Baudelaire, as poet, writes about "Mary perfectly" in *Les Fleurs du mal* (1857): "Madonna, mistress, out of my distress / I'd like to raise an altar in the depths . . . within your sobbing Heart, your streaming Heart."[17] This closing echo reverberates with the significance of the tragedy it sounds, the social unrest set in motion by increasingly visible reservations about "woman" as a masculine, patriarchal construction of contradiction in the nineteenth century. Hence, this particular instance of poetry serves as a point of transition toward closure in my conclusion, for it begs attention to what motivates action, calling for emphasis on those forces of (r)evolution that surface from relationships characterized by a restrictive imbalance of power held in place by convention, that is, the masculine construction that at once also decries, intuitively, the "sobbing Heart" of which Baudelaire wrote. In evolutionary terms of sexual selection, there could be nothing less natural or more problematic than woman made "Madonna" and "mistress" in the same breath. Choice is negated a priori for both.

Indeed, it is therefore conceivable with respect to the willed forces of change that Darwin cannot be understood absent a fantastical prehistory in which humankind, as described by Italo Svevo, always knew itself to be unfinished because of an inborn restlessness. In a state of subservience to the great woolly mammoth, whose size and other attributes proved advantageous, we begrudgingly adapted to an existence of parasitism. It was only a matter of time, however, before the mammoth, as master, became complacent aided by our presence and began to do nothing more than sleep and eat. Svevo explains: "For the Mammoth the service of the little man became so important that the beast felt the necessity of his presence as much as of the trees in which he lived, of the plains over which he roamed, and even of the air he breathed."[18] Nevertheless, in spite of not needing to defend ourselves, our minds never stopped contemplating, our spirit never stood still, and as consequence we at last rebelled in a monumental overthrow of this mammoth, having "freely applied all that we had learned in slavery" (833) to achieve a new state of autonomy.

This peculiar vision of transcendent, evolutionary disquiet under the shadow of the mammoth offers a certain comfort. As much as we look back, our collective becoming is about tomorrow, and in a world of mammoth unrest, this tomorrow is a *matter* of action. Spinoza posits that the impulse to action originates in *conatus*, which is an action of the mind in the form of judgment that operates according to an intuitive knowledge of timeless and necessary relations. In this context, it is important to stress that no one "neglects to seek what is useful to himself, i.e., to preserve his being, unless he is overcome by causes which are external to him and contrary to his nature."[19] Indeed, one should be fearful of "hidden external causes" that might cause the individual by the necessity of his (or her) own nature to endeavor not to exist (242). Spanish women (like the characters of Cristeta, Juanita, Ana, Isidora, Jacinta, Fortunata, Lola, Paca, María, Obdulia, Ilda, Feíta, and so many others) in the late nineteenth century found themselves living various degrees of contrariness for a host of "hidden external causes," and courtship under discriminatory gender, economic, and class conditions was foremost among them. Virginia Woolf, for her part, once said of the angelic paragon of abnegation to which women had become beholden, "Had I not killed her she would have killed me."[20] Given such *struggle for life* in response to being "changed into another form" (Spinoza, *Ethics*, 242) contrary to self, I can think of no heroism more Darwinian.

Consequently, it has now been made clear that with judgment about action there must be room for choice in both. Humankind, as we have understood since Augustine, is unique for being the only species that knows it possesses reason by means of reason. In other words, knowledge is, in this sense, produced by self-perception. Beyond such knowledge, one finds free will, but it too has limits. For, though we might will ourselves to live—getting up each morning and carrying out the routine of subsistence—we do not will our conditions in the same way. The shape of these conditions depends on the real autonomy of the actors, on their endowed claim to voluntary movement (physical or metaphysical), which represents the highest stage of our humanity in Augustine's view.[21] Along separate but related lines, Darwin said that all women should enjoy "free or almost free choice" (*The Descent*, 2:356). Women in countries like Spain in the nineteenth century were free to marry, but seldom to choose. This limited autonomy might reflect the foundational Darwinian law of female "passive choice" in its purest, most oxymoronic form, but as an alternative, I would contend from all that we have seen up to this point—the multifaceted guises of sexual selection and Darwin's own uncertainties, qualifications, vacillations, and outright contradictions—that our collective judgment will intuit otherwise. What "limited autonomy" really conveys in the face of such "hidden external causes" is that the autonomy is not there but is there to be had. For again, the subversive potential of sexual selection lies in its unresolved tensions: "The precise manner in which sexual selection acts is to a certain extent uncertain" (*The Descent*, 1:259).

The cultural praxis of this evolutionary theory at the end of the nineteenth century appeared to *determine* that women should be domestic angels, slaves to their husbands and political nonentities in the larger patriarchal structure. Yet the Darwinian "conscience" behind the "social instincts" haunted the collective will with a different conception of identity founded on original principles of self-determination. Innate knowledge of ideal beauty must, in its very conception, reject the oppression of women, but to find this virtue, realism took the ugliest route, making evident the deeper social implications of so many hapless individuals unlucky in love. This contradiction carries over to our fascination with the curious moralism of the movement, that is, what we hope to learn from the blurred certainties these novels reproduce anew. The works of this period describe just the sort of reality we should not want to see—prostitution, adultery, depravity, and the like—while we relish every detail whether to point out what was wrong with the world in which they were written or to superimpose on them any number of our own fantasies. No doubt, as Augustine reminds us, conscience is self-perception, the consciousness that choice is the common good of all who think and the one to which our collective will must cleave. In Blake, it is the inborn science that directs us to the beautiful; in Plato, virtuous knowledge; and in Darwin, the certainty that "conscience . . . affords the strongest argument for educating and stimulating in all possible ways the intellectual faculties of every human being" (*The Descent*, 2:393), women included.

In sum, Clarín was one who looked at his culture and in its contortion saw the plight of women to emanate from, among other sources, *La perfecta casada*, the canonical conduct book for wives written by Fray Luis de León in the sixteenth century. In a response of contraries, he left us with two short stories, "La perfecta casada" and "La imperfecta casada." The first recounts the tale of a man who commits suicide because his wife is so angelic. The narrator explains the reaction of the courtroom at her trial after the judge reads the husband's last words, "I'm killing myself because I can't stand my wife," from a letter written just before his death: "The good sense of the public at large, knowing the qualities of the virtuous woman, told them that the man had gone mad from absolute domestic bliss. Only in such a way could the absurdity of *killing oneself for not being able to endure the perfect wife* be explained [italics original]."[22] The second story, a sketch of the "imperfect" wife, relates the thoughts of a middle-aged woman who, after going to the theater by herself under the disillusionment of a failed marriage, comes to see that having lost all her charm she is to blame for things. At home again, alone, she rebukes herself for not loving her husband: "And the unhappy woman thought, while she stayed up waiting for her absent husband, who was perhaps at an orgy: 'My God! My God! True virtue is so divine, Heaven so above me, that sometimes the two seem to me to be dreams, illusory because unattainable.'"[23] These stories make evident why sexual selection is such a meaningful point of intersection between literature and science at this moment in history. An indeterminate Darwin illuminates change where choice cannot be explained, where only intuitive knowledge grasps the virtue of reality gone awry.

NOTES

INTRODUCTION

1. Plato, *Complete Works*, ed. John M. Cooper (Indianapolis: Hackett, 1997). All works referenced in this opening paragraph come from this edition with the corresponding line numbers for the passages cited as: *Statesman*, 311b; *Theages*, 121b; *Laws*, 6.783e; *Republic*, 5.459e, 5.460a.

2. Bert Bender, *The Descent of Love: Darwin and the Theory of Sexual Selection in American Fiction, 1871–1926* (Philadelphia: University of Pennsylvania Press, 1996).

3. Fredric Jameson, *The Political Unconscious: Narrative as a Socially Symbolic Act* (Ithaca, N.Y.: Cornell University Press, 1981), 40.

4. Joseph Carroll, *Literary Darwinism: Evolution, Human Nature, and Literature* (New York: Routledge, 2004).

5. David Barash and Nanelle Barash, *Madame Bovary's Ovaries: A Darwinian Look at Literature* (New York: Delacorte, 2005).

6. José Ortega y Gasset, *Meditaciones del Quijote*, vol. 1 of *Obras completas* (Madrid: Revista de Occidente, 1961), 400. Unless otherwise noted or indicated in the list of works cited, all translations throughout this study are my own.

7. Émile Zola, "The Experimental Novel," in *Documents of Modern Literary Realism*, ed. George J. Becker (Princeton, N.J.: Princeton University Press, 1963), 177.

8. Adrian Desmond and James Moore, *Darwin* (New York: Warner Books, 1991).

9. René Girard, *Deceit, Desire, and the Novel: Self and Other in Literary Structure*, trans. Yvonne Freccero (Baltimore: Johns Hopkins University Press, 1965); Eve Kosofsky Sedgwick, *Between Men: English Literature and Male Homosocial Desire* (New York: Columbia University Press, 1985).

10. Harriet S. Turner, "Family Ties and Tyrannies: A Reassessment of Jacinta," *Hispanic Review* 51 (1983): 1–22.

11. Gillian Beer, *Darwin's Plots: Evolutionary Narrative in Darwin, George Eliot, and Nineteenth-Century Fiction* (Cambridge: Cambridge University Press, 2000).

12. Eve-Marie Engels and Thomas Glick, eds., *The Reception of Charles Darwin in Europe*, 2 vols. (London: Continuum, 2009); Jerry Hoeg and Kevin Larsen, eds., *Interdisciplinary Essays on Darwinism in Hispanic Literature and Film: The Intersection of Science and the Humanities* (New York: Mellen, 2009).

13. Sedgwick, *Between Men*, 16.

14. David Damrosch, *What Is World Literature?* (Princeton, N.J.: Princeton University Press, 2003).

15. William Flesch, *Comeuppance: Costly Signaling, Altruistic Punishment, and Other Biological Components of Fiction* (Cambridge, Mass.: Harvard University Press, 2007); Laura Otis, *Membranes: Metaphors of Invasion in Nineteenth-Century Literature, Science, and Politics* (Baltimore: Johns Hopkins University Press, 1999).

CHAPTER I. THE VERY NOTION OF "REAL" RECIPROCITY BETWEEN LITERATURE AND SCIENCE

1. An early history of studies and professional organizations concerned with literature and science is provided by Stuart Peterfreund, ed., *Literature and Science: Theory and Practice* (Boston: Northeastern University Press, 1990), 3–13. Other book-length studies on science and literature include John H. Cartwright and Brian Baker, *Literature and Science: Social Impact and Interaction* (Santa Barbara, Calif.: ABC-CLIO, 2005); John Christie and Sally Shuttleworth, eds., *Nature Transfigured: Science and Literature, 1700–1900* (Manchester: Manchester University Press, 1989); Tess Cosslett, *The "Scientific Movement" and Victorian Literature* (Sussex: Harvester, 1982); N. Katherine Hayles, *Chaos and Order: Complex Dynamics in Literature and Science* (Chicago: University of Chicago Press, 1991); L. J. Jordanova, ed., *Languages of Nature: Critical Essays on Science and Literature* (New Brunswick, N.J.: Rutgers University Press, 1986); George Levine, ed., *One Culture: Essays in Science and Literature* (Madison: University of Wisconsin Press, 1987); and Peter Morton, *The Vital Science: Biology and the Literary Imagination, 1860–1900* (London: Allen and Unwin, 1984).

2. The nomenclature here and in the following paragraphs, of "humanists" (constructivists) and "empiricists" (essentialists), originates in the discourse under investigation; these are not casual descriptors. Therefore, though these dichotomies might be false, they are not empty. Rather than dismiss the terminology it inherits, this study aims to draw out the internal contradictions of such oppositions in an effort to reveal the double-edged nature of the issues at stake.

3. Jordanova, *Languages of Nature*, 15; George Levine, "One Culture: Science and Literature," in Levine, *One Culture*, 3.

4. Gillian Beer, "Problems of Description in the Language of Discovery," in Levine, *One Culture*, 56.

5. James Bono, "Science, Discourse, and Literature: The Role/Rule of Metaphor in Science," in Peterfreund, *Literature and Science*, 59–90.

6. Stephen Alter, *Darwinism and the Linguistic Image: Language, Race, and Natural Theology in the Nineteenth Century* (Baltimore: Johns Hopkins University Press, 1999); Robert M. Young, *Darwin's Metaphor: Nature's Place in Victorian Culture* (Cambridge: Cambridge University Press, 1985).

7. Bono, "Science, Discourse, and Literature," 82.

8. Susan Merrill Squier, *Liminal Lives: Imagining the Human at the Frontiers of Biomedicine* (Durham, N.C.: Duke University Press, 2004), 16, 44–47. Squier frames her usage(s) of "science" in terms of Bruno Latour's "technoscience": "all the elements tied to the scientific contents no matter how dirty, unexpected or foreign they seem." Latour, *Pandora's Hope: Essays on the Reality of Science Studies* (Cambridge, Mass.: Harvard University Press, 1999), 174, quoted in Squier, *Liminal Lives*, 3. Latour himself speaks at length on the "two-culture debate" in *Pandora's Hope*. There he elaborates on the institutional divide between the sciences and the humanities: "But where does the two-culture debate itself originate? In a division of labor between the two sides of the campus. One camp deems the sciences accurate only when they have been purged of any contamination by subjectivity, politics, or passion; the other camp, spread out much more widely, deems humanity, morality, subjectivity, or rights worthwhile only when they have been protected from any contact with science, technology, and objectivity" (18).

9. Beer, "Darwin's Myths," in *Darwin's Plots*, 97–136.

10. Joseph Carroll, *Evolution and Literary Theory* (Columbia: University of Missouri Press, 1995), 81. Vitriol characterizes Carroll's concluding remarks: "If my polemical contentions are basically right, a very large proportion of the work in critical theory that has been done in the past twenty years will prove to be not merely obsolete but essentially void. It cannot be regarded as an earlier phase of a developing discipline, with all the honor due antecedents and ancestors. It is essentially a wrong turn, a dead end, a misconceived enterprise, a repository of delusions and wasted efforts" (468). He further reprimands Levine, Bono, and Beer and several others (74–81) and digresses in ways that show the potential dangers of a "Darwinian" discourse gone astray. On homosexuality: "One can plausibly speculate that the theory ["poststructuralism"] lends itself to certain elementary functions within the psychological economy of homosexual life" (*Evolution and Literary Theory*, 166), where in his praise of John Bowlby and rejection of others, he implicitly affirms homosexuality to be "a dysfunction in the organization of complex psychophysiological systems" (167); his characterization of the humanities: "The conceptual shift that takes place when moving from the Darwinian social sciences to the humanities can be likened to the technological shift that takes place when traveling from the United States or Europe to a country in the Third World. While traveling in space, one also moves backward in time" (*Literary Darwinism*, x); and the stakes of his agenda, the toppling of "the mainstream literary establishment (exemplified by the Modern Language Association)" as if it were the "collapse of the Soviet Union" (*Literary Darwinism*, xi).

11. Carroll, *Evolution and Literary Theory*, 1–3, 77, 223, 95. Once applied, however, this approach boils down to concepts "neither hard to understand

nor difficult to use [for Carroll, presumably]" (*Literary Darwinism*, 187), like point of view, theme, tone, and formal organization, and Carroll models these with an unremarkable reading of *Pride and Prejudice* that concludes that "sex and property, family or kin relations, parenting, social relations, and cognitive power—those are the central concerns of the book" (*Literary Darwinism*, 212). What he fails to explain is why one might use Darwin to show these "concerns," pointed out so often in far more interesting ways, by the very same "poststructuralists" he positions himself against. For an appreciation of the sociobiology of Edward O. Wilson, see *Sociobiology: The New Synthesis* (Cambridge, Mass.: Harvard University Press, 1975) and *On Human Nature* (Cambridge, Mass.: Harvard University Press, 1978). Other recent undertakings along this line of "empirical" inquiry include the essays from Jonathan Gottschall and David Sloan Wilson, eds., *The Literary Animal: Evolution and the Nature of Narrative* (Evanston, Ill.: Northwestern University Press, 2005). Carroll also gives his own overview of contributors to Darwinian social science, sociobiology, and epistemologically grounded literary criticism both in his introduction to and in chapter 6 of *Literary Darwinism*.

12. Carroll, *Evolution and Literary Theory*, 468.

13. Benedetto Croce, *Estetica come scienza dell'espressione e linguistica generale (teoria e storia)*, ed. Giuseppe Galasso (Milan: Adelphi, 1990), 6.

14. Beer, *Darwin's Plots*, xxv, 46.

15. George Levine, *Darwin and the Novelists: Patterns of Science in Victorian Literature* (Cambridge, Mass.: Harvard University Press, 1988), 9–10.

16. Ernst Cassirer, *An Essay on Man: An Introduction to a Philosophy of Human Culture* (New Haven, Conn.: Yale University Press, 1944), 21.

17. Jacques Rancière, *The Names of History: On the Poetics of Knowledge*, trans. Hassan Melehy (Minneapolis: University of Minnesota Press, 1994), 1.

18. Hayden White, *Metahistory: The Historical Imagination in Nineteenth-Century Europe* (Baltimore: Johns Hopkins University Press, 1973), 3.

19. Tony Bennett, *Outside Literature* (London: Routledge, 1990), 50.

20. Gilles Deleuze and Félix Guattari, *Anti-Oedipus: Capitalism and Schizophrenia* (New York: Viking, 1972).

21. Bennett, *Outside Literature*, 53.

22. Ibid., 77.

23. John Frow, *Marxism and Literary History* (Cambridge, Mass.: Harvard University Press, 1986), 103.

24. Ibid., 104.

25. Stephen Jay Gould, *Ever since Darwin: Reflections in Natural History* (New York: Norton, 1977).

26. Frow, *Marxism and Literary History*, 105.

27. Ralph Cohen, "Genre Theory, Literary History, and Historical Change," in *Theoretical Issues in Literary History*, ed. David Perkins (Cambridge, Mass.: Harvard University Press, 1991), 90.

28. Bennett, *Outside Literature*, 112.

29. Edward Said, *The World, the Text, and the Critic* (Cambridge, Mass.: Harvard University Press, 1983), 225.

30. Hippolyte Adolphe Taine, *History of English Literature*, trans. Henry Van Laun (New York: Colonial, 1900), 1:13; Ferdinand Brunetière, *Le roman naturaliste* (Paris: Calmann Lévy, 1896), 3.

31. Owen Chadwick, *The Secularization of the European Mind in the Nineteenth Century* (Cambridge: Cambridge University Press, 1975), 241.

32. Erich Auerbach, *Mimesis: The Representation of Reality in Western Literature*, trans. Willard R. Trask (Princeton, N.J.: Princeton University Press, 2003).

33. Edmond and Jules de Goncourt, "On True Novels," in Becker, *Documents of Modern Literary Realism*, 117–19.

34. David Baguley discusses the historical distinction, and more frequent conflation, of realism and naturalism in *Naturalist Fiction: The Entropic Vision* (Cambridge: Cambridge University Press, 1990), 40–70. Despite the differences privileged by Baguley, I believe these two terms to be interchangeable in essence, while granting that their very existence makes absolute equivalence impossible from a linguistic/historical standpoint. My use also allows me to cite Baguley on occasion, as I do, regarding the importance of science in the novel of the late nineteenth century, which I think he rightly emphasizes though wrongly assigns in particular ways to naturalism alone. One objective of the present chapter is to provide a working definition of "realism" that will address any concerns about nomenclature from the outset, that is, why I call the novels treated throughout this study "realist" as opposed to "naturalist" or use both terms together on occasion or even, as in the case of chapter 7, speak of the "naturalist" novel as in certain measure a subgenre of broader nineteenth-century realism.

35. Zola, "The Experimental Novel," in Becker, *Documents of Modern Literary Realism*, 167.

36. For fuller appreciation of Pardo Bazán's position and chapter 9 of the present study, in which I discuss the debate surrounding her critical writings and the ways Darwin shaped her thinking, see Emilia Pardo Bazán, *La cuestión palpitante*, ed. José Manuel González Herrán (Barcelona: Anthropos, 1989).

37. Baguley, *Naturalist Fiction*, 61.

38. Mikhail Bakhtin, *The Dialogic Imagination: Four Essays*, ed. Michael Holquist, trans. Caryl Emerson and Michael Holquist (Austin: University of Texas Press, 1981), 353, 358, 360, 388–89.

39. Michael McKeon, ed., *Theory of the Novel: A Historical Approach* (Baltimore: Johns Hopkins University Press, 2000), 356. Including Bakhtin among his "grand theorists" of the novel, McKeon explains that all three (the other two being Georg Lukács and José Ortega y Gasset) understood novelistic realism as dialectical amalgam of distance ("empirical objectivity") and mediation ("self-conscious reflexivity"). This observation provokes a significant transition in McKeon's own theoretical trajectory, from which I draw, toward the generic "science" of the realist novel to the very epistemology of novelistic realism.

40. Marshall Brown, "The Logic of Realism: A Hegelian Approach," *PMLA* 96 (1981): 231.

41. J. Hillis Miller, *The Form of Victorian Fiction: Thackeray, Dickens, Trollope, George Eliot, Meredith, and Hardy* (Notre Dame, Ind.: University of Notre Dame Press, 1968), 35–36.

42. Ibid., 45.

43. See note 39 on McKeon.

44. Alan Rauch, *Useful Knowledge: The Victorians, Morality, and the March of Intellect* (Durham, N.C.: Duke University Press, 2001), 2, 12.

45. Richard Rorty, *Philosophy and the Mirror of Nature* (Princeton, N.J.: Princeton University Press, 1979), 337.

46. Thomas S. Kuhn, *The Structure of Scientific Revolutions* (Chicago: University of Chicago Press, 1962), 24–25, 52.

47. Gould, *Ever since Darwin*, 201.

48. Peter J. Bowler, *The Non-Darwinian Revolution: Reinterpreting a Historical Myth* (Baltimore: Johns Hopkins University Press, 1988), 195.

49. Ernst Mayr, "The Nature of the Darwinian Revolution," *Science* 176 (1972): 987.

50. Steven Shapin, *The Scientific Revolution* (Chicago: University of Chicago Press, 1996), 10; Gregory Radick, "Is the Theory of Natural Selection Independent of Its History?" in *The Cambridge Companion to Darwin*, ed. Jonathan Hodge and Gregory Radick (Cambridge: Cambridge University Press, 2003), 163.

51. Diane B. Paul, "Darwin, Social Darwinism, and Eugenics," in Hodge and Radick, *Cambridge Companion to Darwin*, 237.

52. David C. Lindberg, *The Beginnings of Western Science: The European Scientific Tradition in Philosophical, Religious, and Institutional Context, 600 B.C. to A.D. 1450* (Chicago: University of Chicago Press, 1992), 3.

53. José Ortega y Gasset, "Asamblea para el progreso de las ciencias," in *Obras completas*, 1:102.

54. José Ortega y Gasset, "Galileísmo de la historia," in *En torno a Galileo*, vol. 5 of *Obras completas*, 15.

55. Ortega y Gasset, "Asamblea," 1:101.

56. Becker, introduction to *Documents of Modern Literary Realism*, 6.

CHAPTER 2. THE POWER DYNAMICS
OF SEXUAL SELECTION

1. Janet Sayers, *Biological Politics: Feminist and Anti-Feminist Perspectives* (London: Tavistock, 1982), 2.

2. Alys Weinbaum, *Wayward Reproductions: Genealogies of Race and Nation in Transatlantic Modern Thought* (Durham, N.C.: Duke University Press, 2004), 148.

3. Michel Foucault, *The History of Sexuality*, vol. 1, *An Introduction*, trans. Robert Hurley (New York: Random House, 1978).

4. Charles Darwin, *On the Origin of Species* (Cambridge, Mass.: Harvard University Press, 2001), 88.

5. Charles Darwin, *The Descent of Man, and Selection in Relation to Sex*, with an introduction by John Tyler Bonner and Robert M. May (Princeton,

N.J.: Princeton University Press, 1981). This centennial edition provides a facsimile of the 1871 first English edition, which appears divided in two volumes, with the second of these divided in two parts. For simplicity, since separate, yet consecutive, pagination is used in each of the two principle volumes contained in this single edition, when citing in the text of my study with parenthetical reference I will indicate the corresponding volume number before giving page numbers.

6. Evelleen Richards, "Darwin and the Descent of Woman," in *Darwin*, ed. Philip Appleman (1983; repr., New York: Norton, 2001), 434–44.

7. Paul Civello, "Evolutionary Feminism, Popular Romance, and Frank Norris's 'Man's Woman,'" *Studies in American Fiction* 24 (1996): 24.

8. Lawrence Birken, "Darwin and Gender," *Proteus* 6 (1989): 24, 28.

9. David Garlock, "Entangled Genders: Plasticity, Indeterminacy, and Constructs of Sexuality in Darwin and Hardy," *Dickens Study Annual* 27 (1998): 291.

10. Richard R. Yeo would characterize this shift as an affirmation of the "hypothetico-deductive method," the "new orthodoxy" of the late nineteenth century, defined by "speculative leaps and intuition" prompted by the scientific "imagination." From his "Scientific Method and the Rhetoric of Science in Britain, 1830–1917," in *The Politics and Rhetoric of Scientific Method: Historical Studies*, ed. John A. Schuster and Richard R. Yeo (Dordrecht, Holland: Reidel, 1986), 259–98.

11. Levine, *Darwin and the Novelists*, 104.

12. John R. Durant, "The Ascent of Nature in Darwin's *Descent of Man*," in *The Darwinian Heritage*, ed. David Kohn (Princeton, N.J.: Princeton University Press, 1985), 291, 302.

13. In arguing that "science is a rhetorical enterprise, centered on persuasion," Alan Gross explains the means by which the persuasive quality of science comes about: "The objectivity of scientific prose is a carefully crafted rhetorical invention, a nonrational appeal to the authority of reason; scientific reports are the product of verbal choices designed to capitalize on the attractiveness of an enterprise that embodies a convenient myth, a myth in which, apparently, reason has subjugated the passions. But the disciplined denial of emotion in science is only a tribute to our passionate investment in its method and goals." Moreover, to these ends scientific argumentation is arranged logically with the inventions of classical rhetoric, "comparison, cause, definition," and enhanced by style. Alan Gross, *The Rhetoric of Science* (Cambridge, Mass.: Harvard University Press, 1990), 6, 9.

14. Helena Cronin, *The Ant and the Peacock: Altruism and Sexual Selection from Darwin to Today* (Cambridge: Cambridge University Press, 1991).

15. M. B. Andersson, *Sexual Selection* (Princeton, N.J.: Princeton University Press, 1994).

16. Wilson, *On Human Nature*, 128.

17. Richard Dawkins, *The Selfish Gene* (Oxford: Oxford University Press, 2006), 146.

18. Evelyn Shaw and Joan Darling, *Female Strategies* (New York: Walker, 1985).

19. Sue V. Rosser, *Biology and Feminism: A Dynamic Interaction* (New York: Twayne, 1992), 59.

20. Zuleyma Tang-Martínez, "The Curious Courtship of Sociobiology and Feminism: A Case of Irreconcilable Differences," in *Feminism and Evolutionary Biology: Boundaries, Intersections, and Frontiers*, ed. Patricia Adair Gowaty (New York: Chapman and Hall, 1997), 118.

21. Kate Millett, *Sexual Politics* (Garden City, N.Y.: Doubleday, 1970).

22. It is important to qualify the notion of "biological determinism" from the perspective of feminists working in the field of biology. For a practicing scientist like Helen H. Lambert, whose laboratory efforts center on sexual differentiation, development, and behavior in nonhuman vertebrates, such nomenclature begs revision: "The notion that 'innate' factors, such as genes or hormones, influence human behavior is often called (usually pejoratively) 'biological determinism.' To equate biological with intrinsic, inflexible, or programmed is an unfortunate misuse of the term biological. Behavior is itself a biological phenomenon, an interaction between organism and environment." Helen H. Lambert, "Biology and Equality: A Perspective on Sex Differences," in *Sex and Scientific Inquiry*, ed. Sandra Harding and Jean F. O'Barr (Chicago: University of Chicago Press, 1975), 132. Lambert objects to those feminists who seek to abolish sex differences on the grounds that biological differentiation provokes sexual discrimination against women. She admits that biological differences "are often regarded as more reasonable bases for unequal social rewards than are differences that result from variations in the environment, which are held to have more of a claim to compensatory special treatment" (142). Yet because "biological and social causation of difference involves manifold practical difficulties" (142), it is ineffective for feminists (and Millett would be included here) to argue over whether "sex differences are socially or biologically caused" (144). Lambert sees this question as "unanswerable" and, moreover, counterproductive (144). From her perspective, if observed sex differences, like pregnancy, are "incompatible with important aspects of social equality, we should argue for compensatory measures, independent of biological causation" (145). Lambert's push for social change through the redefinition of an infamous concept like "biological determinism" demonstrates again how terminology propels the discourse surrounding science and sex.

23. Evelyn Fox Keller, *Reflections on Gender and Science* (New Haven, Conn.: Yale University Press, 1985), 8, 71.

24. Sandra Harding, *The Science Question in Feminism* (Ithaca, N.Y.: Cornell University Press, 1986), 57, 56.

25. Elisabeth Anne Lloyd, "Pre-theoretical Assumptions in Evolutionary Explanations of Female Sexuality," in *Feminism and Science*, ed. Evelyn Fox Keller and Helen E. Longino (Oxford: Oxford University Press, 1996), 91.

26. For more on sexuality in the nineteenth century, see Peter Gay, *The Bourgeois Experience: Victoria to Freud*, vol. 1 of *Education of the Senses* (New York: Norton, 1984). Also useful in this context is Thomas Laqueur's *Making Sex: Body and Gender from the Greeks to Freud* (Cambridge, Mass.: Harvard University Press, 1990), where a cultural history is provided

for sexual dimorphism along with an argument for understanding the challenges to established notions of differentiation that emerged in the nineteenth century.

27. Stephen Heath, *The Sexual Fix* (London: Macmillan, 1982), 25.

28. Cesare Lombroso and Guglielmo Ferrero, *Criminal Woman, the Prostitute, and the Normal Woman*, trans. Nicole Hahn Rafter and Mary Gibson (Durham, N.C.: Duke University Press, 2004); Charlotte Perkins Gilman, *Herland* (New York: Pantheon, 1979).

29. See Civello, "Evolutionary Feminism," 23–44.

30. Weinbaum, *Wayward Reproductions*, 150.

31. Ibid., 153.

32. Simone de Beauvoir, *The Second Sex* (New York: Knopf, 1976), xviii.

33. Luce Irigaray, *This Sex Which Is Not One* (Ithaca, N.Y.: Cornell University Press, 1985), 180.

34. Maria Mies, *Patriarchy and Accumulation on a World Scale: Women in the International Division of Labour* (London: Zed, 1986), 48.

35. Beer, *Darwin's Plots*, 198.

36. Nancy Armstrong, *Desire and Domestic Fiction: A Political History of the Novel* (Oxford: Oxford University Press, 1987), 222.

37. The use of "plot" here should be understood in Aristotelian terms, as the "imitation of an action that is serious and also, as having magnitude, complete in itself." *De Poetica*, in *The Basic Works of Aristotle*, ed. Richard McKeon (New York: Modern Library, 2001), 1449b24–25. Though in this particular instance, Aristotle is speaking of Greek dramatic tragedy, he later transposes this definition of plot to his considerations of epic poetry, which he understands to be narrative. It is therefore an accepted practice, as evidenced by the widespread application of Aristotle's writings to critical theory concerned with various genres, to extend his theories beyond the dramatic form, while also keeping in mind that narrative by most is understood to be dramatic, that is, performative because of point of view.

38. Cynthia Eagle Russet, *Sexual Science: The Victorian Construction of Womanhood* (Cambridge, Mass.: Harvard University Press, 1989), 101.

39. Patricia Adair Gowaty, "Introduction: Darwinian Feminists and Feminist Evolutionists," in Gowaty, *Feminism and Evolutionary Biology*, 13.

40. Elizabeth Grosz, *Time Travels: Feminism, Nature, Power* (Durham, N.C.: Duke University Press, 2005), 52.

CHAPTER 3. TRANSLATIONS, TRANSLATORS, AND THE
SEXUAL POLITICS OF SEXUAL SELECTION IN SPAIN

1. The notion that moral indignation at the perceived determinism of natural selection resulted in a pervasive disregard for what Darwin says about sexual selection, deemed less serious because it focused on reproduction rather than survival, explains to a degree the imbalance of attention given to the two theories. Moreover, most historians of science underscore that scientists of all nations more or less ignored sexual selection until the early twentieth century. Nevertheless, such rationalizations stop short of

resolving, for example, how *Anthropos: Boletín de Información y Documentación*, a respected journal of science and culture in the Hispanic world, could publish under the direction of the eminent biologist Faustino Cordón an entire volume in 1982 dedicated to Darwin on the centennial of his death, complete with a forty-page chronological bibliography of all publications in Spanish related to Darwin's works from 1859 through 1982, without a single reference to sexual selection. The same holds true for authoritative historical studies on *el darwinismo*, namely, those of Thomas Glick and Diego Núñez, which also contain comprehensive bibliographies as well as anthologized periodical articles and conference proceedings. See Faustino Cordón, ed., "El darwinismo en España: En el 1er centenario de la muerte de Charles Darwin (1882–1982); Aportación innovadora de Faustino Cordón a la teoría evolucionista," special issue, *Anthropos: Boletín de Información y Documentación*, nos. 16–17 (1982); Thomas Glick, *Darwin en España* (Barcelona: Península, 1982); Glick, "Spain," in *The Comparative Reception of Darwinism*, ed. Thomas Glick (Austin: University of Texas Press, 1972), 307–45; and Diego Núñez, *El darwinismo en España* (Madrid: Castalia, 1969). In a more recent look at Darwin in nineteenth-century Spain, Dale J. Pratt uncovers strategies for the signification of science in literature of the period, in *Signs of Science: Literature, Science, and Spanish Modernity since 1868* (West Lafayette, Ind.: Purdue University Press, 2001).

2. Glick, "Spain," 343; Núñez, *El darwinismo*, 8.

3. Núñez, *El darwinismo*, 9.

4. Charles Darwin, *De l'origine des espèces, ou des lois du progrès chez les êtres organisés*, 1st ed., trans. and with a preface by Clémence Royer (Paris: Guillaumin and V. Masson, 1862); Darwin, *De l'origine des espèces, ou des lois de la transformation des êtres organisés*, 3rd ed., trans. and with a preface by Clémence Royer (Paris: Guillaumin and V. Masson, 1870).

5. Robert E. Stebbins, "France," in Glick, *Comparative Reception of Darwinism*, 126–27. Yvette Conry also gives a historical overview of Darwin's nineteenth-century reception in France in *L'introduction du Darwinisme en France au XIXe siècle* (Paris: Librairie Philosophique, 1974).

6. Stebbins, "France," 127.

7. Charles Darwin, *La descendance de l'homme et la sélection sexuelle*, 1st ed., trans. Jean-Jacques Moulinié, with a preface by Carl Vogt (Paris: Reinwald, 1872).

8. Ibid., xv.

9. The following selections juxtapose a few key passages from the 1872 Moulinié translation and Darwin's 1871 first English edition of *The Descent*; the page numbers correspond to each as indicated: "L'homme a plus de puissance de corps et d'esprit que la femme, et dans la vie sauvage il la tient dans un état d'assujettissement beaucoup plus abject que ne le font les mâles de toute autre espèce; il n'est donc pas surprenant qu'il ait acquis la puissance de sélection" (2:390); in Darwin, "Man is more powerful in body and mind than woman, and in the savage state he keeps her in a far more abject state of bondage than does the male of any other animal; therefore it is not surprising that he should have gained the power of selection" (2:371).

/ "Les idées émises ici sur le rôle que la sélection sexuelle a joué dans l'histoire de l'homme, manquent de précision scientifique" (2:403); in Darwin, "The views here advanced, on the part which sexual selection has played in the history of man, want scientific precision" (2:383). / "L'admission du principe de la sélection sexuelle conduit à la conclusion remarquable, que le système cérébral règle non-seulement la plupart des fonctions actuelles du corps, mais a indirectement influencé le développement progressif de diverses conformations corporelles et de certaines qualités mentales. Le courage, le caractère belliqueux, la persévérance, la force et la grandeur du corps, les armes de tous genres, les organes musicaux, vocaux et instrumentaux, les couleurs vives, les raies, les marques et appendices d'ornementation ont sous l'influence de l'amour ou de la jalousie, par l'appréciation du beau dans le son, la couleur ou la forme, et par l'exercice d'un choix, facultés de l'esprit qui dépendent évidemment du développement du système cérébral" (2:423); in Darwin, "He who admits the principle of sexual selection will be led to the remarkable conclusion that the cerebral system not only regulates most of the existing functions of the body, but has indirectly influenced the progressive development of various bodily structures and of certain mental qualities. Courage, pugnacity, perseverance, strength and size of body, weapons of all kinds, musical organs, both vocal and instrumental, bright colours, stripes and marks, and ornamental appendages, have all been indirectly gained by the one sex or the other, through the influence of love and jealousy, through the appreciation of the beautiful in sound, colour or form, and through the exertion of a choice; and these powers of the mind manifestly depend on the development of the cerebral system" (2:402).

10. Charles Darwin, *El origen del hombre: La selección natural y la sexual (primera versión española)*, trans. and with an introduction by [Joaquim Bartrina] (Barcelona: Renaixensa, 1876). For more on Bartrina and this translation, see J. A. Zabalbeascoa, "El primer traductor de Charles R. Darwin en España," *Filología Moderna* 8 (1968): 269–75.

11. Charles Darwin, *Origen de las especies por selección natural: O resumen de las leyes de transformación de los seres organizados (con dos prefacios de Madame Clemencia Royer)*, trans. anon., Biblioteca social, histórica y filosófica (Madrid: Jacobo María Luengo, 1872).

12. Charles Darwin, *Origen de las especies: Por medio de la selección natural ó la conservación de las razas favorecidas en la lucha por la existencia*, trans. Enrique Godínez (Madrid: José de Rojas, 1873).

13. These conjectures, however, remain unverified, and neither Godínez nor Perojo makes any reference to an earlier translation in their letters to Darwin included in the preface to their 1877 edition of *Origin*, which they herald as the first translation (authorized or otherwise) of Darwin in Spanish.

14. Charles Darwin, *Origen de las especies por medio de la selección natural ó la conservación de las razas favorecidas en la lucha por la existencia*, trans. Enrique Godínez (Madrid: Perojo, 1877).

15. These letters, dated 1876–77, speak of a translation "in progress," a detail which complicates the hypothesis that Godínez had already completed (and published with "José de Rojas") the translation in 1873 (note 12 above).

And, if aware of Bartrina's pirate translation of *The Descent* a year earlier, one might surmise that Perojo included these letters for purposes of posterity, in competition to be remembered as the first to bring Darwin to print in Spanish, as is the case made by Zabalbeascoa.

16. See note 10 above.

17. Zabalbeascoa, "El primer traductor de Charles R. Darwin en España," 272.

18. Bartrina, translation and introduction to Darwin's *El origen del hombre*, v.

19. An important note of qualification appears under the appendix title with regard to Bartrina's source: "The following pithy extract from the Darwinian theory of sexual selection, we take, largely supplementing it and introducing variations, from the learned French writer, Edmund Perier, who has studied at length the modern transformist theories" (ibid., 281). I have not been able to locate this referenced source however.

20. Charles Darwin, *La descendencia del hombre y la selección en relación al sexo*, trans. José del Perojo and Enrique Camps (Madrid: Administración de la Revista de Medicina y Cirugía Prácticas [Rivadeneyra], 1885).

21. This change could reflect a subtle corrective on the part of Spanish editors up to the present to minimize the possibility that one might insinuate from Darwin's original title that man descended (i.e., is a "lower" form) from his simian predecessors; even in English his title disorients for its play on "descent," with the idea that man has "descended" toward a more evolved state. Still more telling, in his introduction to the 2006 edition of *El origen del hombre* distributed worldwide by Biblioteca Edaf, the Hispanic world's authority on evolutionary biology, Faustino Cordón, strangely refers to the text as *La ascendencia del hombre*, a translation of the title apparently of his own invention that does not appear in any published edition. See Charles Darwin, *El origen del hombre*, ed. Faustino Cordón (Madrid: Edaf, 2006), 14. Also, although I have found no record of the number of copies printed of the 1885 Perojo-Camps translation or of the actual extent of its dissemination, in the third appendix of Thomas Glick's study, *Darwin en España* (Barcelona: Península, 1982), an account of the personal library of Baltasar Champsaur, a lawyer in the Canary Islands in the late nineteenth century, shows that even a nonspecialist, outside Madrid, could acquire this translation soon after it went into publication, though we must also keep in mind that these islands were an important port for the international commerce of the day. Finally, unlike the 1872 French edition from Moulinié, the Perojo-Camps translation uses the 1874 second English edition of *The Descent*, which differs from the 1871 original, today considered the authoritative version.

22. Darwin, *La descendencia del hombre*. This short preface to Perojo and Camps's 1885 translation appears without pagination.

23. Josep Roca i Roca, *Memoria biográfica de Joaquim María Bartrina y d'Aixemús* (Barcelona: Ajuntament Constitucional de Barcelona, 1916), 18–19. This source provides me with the biographical information on Bartrina and corresponding citations for this portion of my discussion.

24. Bartrina's unfinished book projects (all titles translated here from Catalan) from the time of his death paint a picture of his belief in knowledge as interdisciplinary: "America before Columbus"; "Spanish Gypsies: An Anthropological Study"; "Echoes of Latium (Verses in Latin)"; "Funeral Anthology (The Problem of Death and Its Manifestations across Time and in Diverse Peoples)"; "Complaints of the Soul (Inscriptions Found in Prisons)"; "History of the Seven Capital Sins in Spain"; "The Theater and Actors in Spain"; "Paganism in the Spanish People"; "Physics of the Soul (Psychological Essay)"; "The Feeling of Color"; "The Life of Mary"; and "Notes on Some Notes of *The Quixote*."

25. A group of Spanish historians have published a critical anthology on Perojo that includes a well-researched biographical introduction in addition to a representative selection of his many publications. Until this study, the only academic resource on Perojo was an unpublished dissertation held on microfilm at the Universidad Autónoma de Madrid for research purposes only. In fact, the collaborators of the 2003 anthology on Perojo spend the better part of the first few pages of their introduction explaining why Perojo presents such a challenge, the primary reason being the lack of reliable sources. However, they also make clear, as the biographical sketch given in this chapter shows (a summary of portions from their introduction), that Perojo merits attention as a key figure in the history of modern Spain. See *Artículos filosóficos y políticos de José del Perojo (1875–1908)*, ed. María Dolores Díaz Regadera, Fernando Hermida de Blas, José Luis Mora, Diego Núñez, and Pedro Ribas (Madrid: Universidad Autónoma de Madrid, 2003).

26. Ibid., 26.

27. Ibid., 29.

28. Also noteworthy is the political-literary contact Perojo maintained with Benito Pérez Galdós in these same years.

29. As Perojo's views in "La raza negra" from *La Opinión* (1886) demonstrate:

It is no longer possible to maintain illusions about the black race:
the sad decadence in which the United States has fallen, and the
shameful spectacle that Haiti offers, amply prove that, left to its
own inclinations, this race will be led more by the pulls of its savage
temperament than by those of civilization and progress. Only for
a very short time has this race enjoyed the rights and privileges in
towns civilized by the white race, and despite such a brief span, the
black race has not delayed in showing how rooted the retrograded
instincts of savagery are in their breasts. In gigantic steps, this race
regresses toward barbarism, as if upon seeing itself free, the more
freely also do its rooted traditions spring forth, before contained by
the passion of the cultured society on which they depended. One
would say that their ancient memories acquire new vigor, and that
captivated by the love of their barbarous past, this race laments the
environment in which it finds itself, within such an atmosphere it
cannot live, as if it were suffering from a strange nostalgia, from
the nostalgia of barbarism. . . . The black race is not just a dis-
turbed race, the locus of immorality and corruption, from which it

is to be understood that the first precaution that must be followed is a prudent separation from its mephitic action, but rather it is a strange race, a foreign race. (Perojo, *Artículos filosóficos y políticos*, 175–78)

30. These articles are, in chronological order of publication: Antonio María Fabié, "Exámen del materialismo moderno," *Revista Europea* 3, no. 43 (December 20, 1874): 225–29; Elme Marie Caro, "La democracia ante la moral del porvenir: Las nuevas teorías acerca del derecho natural" [*Revue de Deux Mondes*], trans. anon., *Revista Europea* 6, no. 95 (December 19, 1875): 253–64; Eduard von Hartmann, "La filosofía pesimista" [*Westminster Review*], trans. [R. M.], *Revista Contemporánea* 1, no. 5 (February 15, 1876): 93–112; Hartmann, "Ernesto Häckel" [*Deutsche Rundschau*], trans. anon., *Revista Europea* 7, no. 106 (March 5, 1876): 7–15; A. Torres-Solanot, "Filosofía novísima: El universalismo de A. Pezzani," *Revista Europea* 7, no. 122 (June 25, 1876): 656–66; Elme Marie Caro, "La moral sin metafísica" [*Edinburgh Review*], trans. Armando Palacio Valdés, *Revista Europea* 8, no. 143 (November 19, 1876): 641–49; Pedro Estassen, "Contribución al estudio de la evolución de las instituciones religiosas o materiales para llegar a la síntesis transformista de las instituciones humanas: La religiosidad en los animales," *Revista Contemporánea* 13, no. 1 (January 15, 1878): 62–74; Ernst Haeckel, "Teorías evolutivas de Lyell y de Darwin," trans. Claudio Cuveiro, *Revista Europea* 12, no. 233 (August 11, 1878): 174–83; Haeckel, "La selección natural verificada por la lucha por la existencia, la división del trabajo, y el progreso," trans. Claudio Cuveiro, *Revista Europea* 12, no. 238 (September 15, 1878): 334–44; Haeckel, "Emigración y distribución de los organismos: La corología y la edad glacial de la tierra," trans. Claudio Cuveiro, *Revista Europea* 12, no. 242 (October 13, 1878): 467–76; L. Carrau, "El darwinismo y la moral," *Revista Europea* 13, no. 257 (January 26, 1879): 97–99; Joaquín Sánchez de Toca, "La doctrina de la evolución de las modernas escuelas científicas," pts. 1 and 2, *Revista Contemporánea* 21, no. 1 (May 15, 1879): 55–91, and 21, no. 3 (June 15, 1879): 273–303; and Cran Allen, "Un adversario de la evolución," trans. anon., *Revista Contemporánea* 21, no. 4 (June 30, 1879): 474–79. Bibliographical information for the sources I include in this section of my discussion corresponds to the publication details provided here unless otherwise indicated.

31. Charles Darwin, *La descendance de l'homme et la sélection sexuelle*, 2nd ed., trans. Jean-Jacques Moulinié, ed. Edmond Barbier, with a preface by Carl Vogt (Paris: Reinwald, 1873).

32. Sánchez de Toca, "La doctrina de la evolución," pt. 2:275.

33. Jo Labanyi, *Gender and Modernization in the Spanish Realist Novel* (Oxford: Oxford University Press, 2000), 32.

34. Excellent studies on *la cuestión de la mujer* include Theresa Ann Smith, *The Emerging Female Citizen: Gender and Enlightenment in Spain*, Studies on the History of Society and Culture (Berkeley: University of California Press, 2006); Margarita Nelken, *La condición social de la mujer en España* (Madrid: CVS, 1975); Geraldine Scanlon, *La polémica feminista en la España contemporánea (1868–1974)* (Madrid: Siglo XXI, 1976); and Gloria Sole Romeo, *La*

instrucción de la mujer en la Restauración: La Asociación para la Enseñanza de la Mujer (Madrid: Universidad Complutense de Madrid, 1990).

35. Manuel de la Revilla, "La emancipación de la mujer," pts. 1 and 2, *Revista Contemporánea* 30, no. 12 (1878): 447–63; 30, no. 1 (1879): 162–81. See also the introduction to *Obras completas: Manuel de la Revilla*, ed. Fernando Hermida de Blas, José Luis Mora García, Diego Núñez, and Pedro Ribas, 3 vols. (Madrid: Universidad Autónoma de Madrid, 2006); and Carlos García Barrón, *Vida, obra y pensamiento de Manuel de la Revilla* (Madrid: Turanzas, 1987), 109, as quoted here.

36. Labanyi, *Gender and Modernization*, 53.

37. Leopoldo Alas [Clarín], "El amor y la economía," in *Clarín político: Leopoldo Alas (Clarín), periodista, frente a la problemática política y social de la España de su tiempo (1875–1901) Estudio y Antología*, ed. Yvan Lissorgues (Toulouse: Institut d'Etudes Hispaniques et Hispano-Américaines, 1980), 1:126–31.

38. The Spanish here, "*el novio inconsciente* [italics original]," defies easy translation. The choice of "boyfriend" or "fiancé" for "*novio*" becomes awkward over the course of the essay, though *pretendiente* in Spanish would be closer to the English "suitor," and "suitor of the unconscious" seems a better fit than "the unconscious suitor," which brings to mind images of a lover who has lost consciousness. However, while the former of these solutions speaks to a courting of the desires of the female heart (i.e., what Clarín paints as her "unconscious"), the latter option does in fact make sense later in the essay as Clarín talks about this same suitor as an idealist dreamer detached from reality (i.e., not conscious of the material world).

39. Clarín's model here, I think, can be simplified to competition (individual) versus altruism (species).

40. A case in point is his attack on women writers, ironically from the very same year, in Leopoldo Alas (Clarín), "Las literatas" (1879), in *Clarín político*, 1:231–35.

41. Santiago Ramón y Cajal, "Sobre el amor y las mujeres," from *Charlas de café*, in *Obras literarias completas* (Madrid: Aguilar, 1947), 954–93.

42. In a memoir from 1887 composed of sketches of the most visible orators from Madrid at the time, Armando Palacio Valdés, then secretary of the Division of Moral and Political Sciences at the Ateneo of Madrid, writes in his prologue:

> The most arduous and interesting problems are debated in this cultured society; but one must observe the, at first glance, strange phenomenon, that all of its discussions, previously announced on a concrete theme, come precipitously to arrive at a purely theological or political issue. Strongly impressed by these singular currents that in no time always carry the topic to its dissolution, I tried to inquire about the cause, and not putting great stock in the judgment of my own poor reason, I looked for some sort of answer from the most learned participants. The majority were inclined to believe nobly, that the transcendence of such topics, the irresistible attraction that they exert on the spirit in these critical times and their

contemporary relevance, above all in our Spain, where at the present hour theology and politics go about supremely mingled, explain in large part the wanderings of our thought. The minority and with the worst intention, wanted to see in such a phenomenon clear proof of our inability to penetrate with profound and delicate analysis a determined point of science. Our readers will opt between the two contrary theories, though from my point of view it would not be difficult to find elements of truth in both. What is certain from all of this, as I say, is that discussions move forward in complete and general disorder. Each participant, without worrying in the least about the issue to be discussed, a true castaway in these stormy sessions, weaves as best he can a speech and entrusts to Providence the conviction of his listeners. I doubt that a country exists in the world where they talk as much and as well as in Spain, but certain I find myself that nowhere do they get less from so much oratory. This comes from the fact that the form, the artistic aspect of Spanish oratory, absorbs and enslaves its scientific base, which one finds exquisitely veiled, but veiled in the end, by the beautiful adornments of an unchecked rhetoric. In no other country more than in Spain, in order to appeal to the National representatives for a vote on a brandy tax will the orator be brought to a story, floating on a sea of rippled waves, of primitive pelagic devices, the monotheism of the Semitic race or the paintings of Correggio. Spanish orators do not create works of science but works of art, and as artists they should be judged. (Armando Palacio Valdés, "Los oradores del Ateneo," in *Obras completas* [Madrid: Victoriano Suárez, 1908], 11:ix–xiii)

For more on Spain's "discussing society," see Raymond Carr, *Spain, 1808–1975* (Oxford: Oxford University Press, 1982), 207.

CHAPTER 4. SUITORS AND SELECTORS— JACINTO OCTAVIO PICÓN

1. Rorty, *Philosophy and the Mirror of Nature*, 384.
2. Noël Valis, "Figura femenina y escritura en la España finisecular," in *¿Qué es el modernismo? Nueva encuesta, nuevas lecturas*, ed. Richard Cardwell and Bernard McGuirk (Boulder, Colo.: Society of Spanish and Spanish-American Studies, 1993), 107.
3. Hazel Gold, "'Ni soltera, ni viuda, ni casada': Negación y exclusión en las novelas femeninas de Jacinto Octavio Picón," *Ideologies and Literature: Journal of Hispanic and Lusophone Discourse Analysis* 4, no. 17 (1983): 65, 68.
4. Ángeles Ezama Gil, "El profeminismo en los cuentos de Picón," in *Actas del IX Simposio de la Sociedad Española de Literatura General y Comparada*, ed. Túa Blesa et al. (Saragossa: Universided de Zaragoza, 1994), 1:176.
5. George Bernard Shaw, *Man and Superman* (London: Penguin, 2000), 13.

6. Albert Camus, *The Myth of Sisyphus and Other Essays*, trans. Justin O'Brien (New York: Vintage, 1991), 75.

7. The relationship between song and sexual selection, especially with respect to Darwin's conjectures on the origin of language, is discussed at greater length in chapter 5, where I treat the rivalries and rituals in novels by Leopoldo Alas (Clarín).

8. It is important to reiterate, however, that today's science understands sexual selection to be subordinate to natural selection, as one of the two mechanisms (the other being environmental constraints) by which natural selection is achieved. In chapter 2 of the present study I explore the possibility of limitless variations with respect to sexual selection, as well as the ways Darwin's case for variable males and static females translates to sexual politics when transposed to culture. In chapter 3, I show this to be the point where Joaquim Bartrina, the first translator of Darwin to Spanish, conflates natural and sexual selection.

9. Durant, "Ascent of Nature in Darwin's *Descent of Man*," 291.

10. Gregorio Marañón, "Don Juan," in *Cinco ensayos sobre don Juan* (Santiago, Chile: Cultura, 1937), 27.

11. Mercedes Sáenz-Alonso, *Don Juan y el donjuanismo* (Madrid: Guadarrama, 1969), 10.

12. Ibid., 34.

13. Søren Kierkegaard, *Either/Or*, ed. and trans. Howard V. Hong and Edna H. Hong, Kierkegaard's Writings, 3 (Princeton, N.J.: Princeton University Press, 1987), 1:92, 87–135.

14. Camus, *The Myth of Sisyphus and Other Essays*, 69.

15. Shaw, *Man and Superman*, 10.

16. Jacinto Octavio Picón, *Juan Vulgar*, in *Obras completas* (Madrid: Renacimiento, 1918), vol. 6.

17. María del Pilar Sinués de Marco, *El ángel del hogar: Estudios morales acerca de la mujer* (Madrid: Española de Nieto, 1862), 245.

18. Bridget Aldaraca, *El ángel del hogar: Galdós and the Ideology of Domesticity in Spain* (Chapel Hill: University of North Carolina, Department of Romance Languages, 1991), 28. Though of religious orientation, one of the earliest conceptions of *el ángel del hogar* comes from Fray Luis de León's *La perfecta casada* (*The Perfect Wife*; 1583), in which the law of the Father translates to subservience to the husband.

19. Scanlon, *La polémica feminista*, 60.

20. Bram Dijkstra, *Idols of Perversity: Fantasies of Feminine Evil in Fin-de-Siècle Culture* (New York: Oxford University Press, 1986), 17, 120.

21. See chapter 2.

22. *Dulce y sabrosa* is one of two works by Picón, the other being *La hijastra del amor*, that have been published as critical editions, and likewise, it is the only one of his novels available in English translation. Jacinto Octavio Picón, *Sweet and Delectable*, trans. Robert M. Fedorchek (Lewisburg, Pa.: Bucknell University Press, 2000); Picón, *La hijastra del amor*, ed. Noël Valis (Barcelona: Promociones y Publicaciones Universitarias, 1990). For the purposes of the present study, all translations are my own from Picón, *Dulce y sabrosa*, ed.

Gonzalo Sobejano (Madrid: Cátedra, 1990), with pagination corresponding accordingly and in consultation with the Fedorchek translation.

23. Picón, *Dulce y sabrosa*, 72. Of Darwin's many conjectures in *The Descent* on the purpose for the often extravagant pinchers of male beetles, which no one found to be well adapted for male-male combat, was the supposition that in addition to pure ornamentation they were evolved to grasp and hold the female.

24. Ezama Gil, "El profeminismo en los cuentos de Picón," 1:176.

25. This novel is the only one of my study not published in the nineteenth century; however, my justification is that in addition to reflecting well the broader corpus of Picón, who was very much a product of and participant in the Spanish realist movement, *Juanita Tenorio* is an ideal fit to my case for reversals in Darwinian sexual selection.

26. Elena Soriano, *El donjuanismo femenino* (Barcelona: Península, 2000), 170.

27. Osvaldo Orico, *Don Juan o el vicio de amar* (Madrid: Estados, 1950), 37.

28. J. W. Smeed, *Don Juan: Variations on a Theme* (London: Routledge, 1990), 104. Psychoanalysis and Darwinian evolutionism are not such an odd couple as one might suppose. While it is true that the former treats the mind and the latter, matter (if this were to be a tenable dichotomy, which it is not), both rely on foundations of imperceptible forces from an unknowable past driving behavior, to give just one example of how the two converge in their most general makeup. Alys Weinbaum chooses somatic manifestations like hysteria for her point of intersection between the two in her last chapter, "Sexual Selection and the Birth of Psychoanalysis," from her study *Wayward Reproductions*. Noyles B. Livingston III looks at narrative crossovers in "Darwin, Nietzsche, and Freud: The Evolutionary Link between Biology, Philosophy, and Psychology," *Journal of Evolutionary Psychology* 15 (1994): 176–83.

29. Otto Rank, *The Don Juan Legend*, trans. and ed. David G. Winter (Princeton, N.J.: Princeton University Press, 1975), 95.

30. Jacinto Octavio Picón, *Juanita Tenorio*, vol. 3 of *Obras completas* (Madrid: Renacimiento, 1922), 13. My references to the novel throughout this chapter come from this edition.

31. Irigaray, *This Sex Which Is Not One*, 180.

32. James Mandrell, *Don Juan and the Point of Honor: Seduction, Patriarchal Society, and Literary Tradition* (University Park, Pa.: Penn State University Press, 1992), 128.

33. Américo Castro, prologue to *Cinco ensayos sobre Don Juan*, 15.

34. Noël Valis, *The Novels of Jacinto Octavio Picón* (Lewisburg, Pa.: Bucknell University Press, 1986), 187.

35. Georges Gendarme de Bévotte, *La légende de Don Juan: Son évolution dans la littérature des origines au romantisme* (Geneva: Slatkine, 1993), 11.

36. José Ortega y Gasset, "Las dos ironías, o Sócrates y Don Juan," in *Obras completas* (Madrid: Taurus, 2004), 3:593.

37. José Lasaga Medina, *Las metamorfosis del seductor: Ensayo sobre el mito de Don Juan* (Madrid: Síntesis, 2004), 135.

38. Arthur Schopenhauer, "Metafísica del amor sexual," in *El mundo como voluntad y representación*, trans. Pilar López de Santa María (Madrid: Trotta, 2005), 2:620.

39. Giacomo Casanova, *History of My Life*, trans. Willard R. Trask, 2 vols. (Baltimore: Johns Hopkins University Press, 1997).

40. Kierkegaard, *Either/Or*, 1:90.

41. Jacinto Octavio Picón, "La prudente," in *Novelitas* (Madrid: La España, 1892), 12, 21.

42. Jacinto Octavio Picón, "Divorcio moral," in *Mujeres*, vol. 4 of *Obras completas* (Madrid: Renacimiento, 1916), 251.

43. Casanova, *History of My Life*, 1:26.

CHAPTER 5. RIVALRIES AND RITUALS—
LEOPOLDO ALAS (CLARÍN)

1. For a general discussion of irony in Clarín, see Joseph Schraibman and Leda Carazzola, "Hacia una interpretación de la ironía en *La Regenta* de Clarín," in *Studies in Honor of José Rubia Barcia*, ed. Roberta Johnson and Paul C. Smith (Lincoln, Neb.: Society of Spanish and Spanish-American Studies, 1982), 175–86. For more specific claims about irony as the distinguishing characteristic of Clarín's writing, see Carolyn Richmond, "En torno al vacío: La mujer, idea hecha carne de ficción, en *La Regenta* de Clarín," in *Realismo y naturalismo en España en la segunda mitad del siglo XIX*, ed. Yvan Lissorgues (Barcelona: Anthropos, 1988), 341–67; and Richmond, "*Su único hijo*," in *Romanticismo y realismo*, ed. Iris M. Zavala, vol. 5 of *Historia y crítica de la literatura española*, ed. Francisco Rico (Barcelona: Editorial Crítica, 1982), 598–601. For commentary on Clarín's use of irony to undermine the State and Church, see Frances W. Weber, "Ideología y parodia religiosa en *La Regenta*," in *Clarín y La Regenta*, ed. Sergio Beser (Barcelona: Ariel, 1982), 117–36. In studies on role-playing and gender ambivalence in Clarín considerable overlap occurs, and discussion is often framed by the challenges posed by irony. For further reading, see Beth Wietelmann Bauer, "Something Lost: Translation, Transaction, and Travesty in Clarín's *Su único hijo*," *Revista Hispánica Moderna* 48 (1995): 92–105; Frank Durand, "Structure and the Drama of Role-Playing in *La Regenta*," in *"Malevolent Insemination" and Other Essays on Clarín*, ed. Noël Valis (Ann Arbor: University of Michigan, Department of Romance Languages, 1990), 141–54; Ricardo Krauel, "Rasgos victimarios y persecución: Los estereotipos de la homofobia," in *Voces desde el silencio: Heterologías genérico-sexuales en la narrativa española moderna (1875–1975)* (Madrid: Libertarias, 2001), 31–48; Jo Labanyi, "Pathologizing the Bodily Economy: Alas's *La Regenta* (1884–1885)," in *Gender and Modernization*, 209–68; Roberto G. Sánchez, "Teatro e intimidad en *Su único hijo*: Un aspecto de la modernidad de Clarín," *Insula* 27 (1972): 3, 12; Sánchez, "The Presence of the Theater and 'The Consciousness of Theater' in Clarín's

La Regenta," *Hispanic Review* 37 (1969): 491–509; Alison Sinclair, "The Force of Parental Presence in *La Regenta,*" and Abigail Lee Six, "Mothers' Voices and Medusas' Eyes: Clarín's Construction of Gender in *Su único hijo,*" in *Culture and Gender in Nineteenth-Century Spain,* ed. Lou Charnon-Deutsch and Jo Labanyi (Oxford: Clarendon, 1995), 182–98, 199–215; and Noël Valis, "*Su único hijo,*" in *The Decadent Vision in Leopoldo Alas: A Study of* La Regenta *and* Su único hijo (Baton Rouge: Louisiana State University Press, 1981), 107–90.

2. In support of Darwin's historical influence on Clarín, *La Regenta*'s editor, Juan Oleza, affirms in a note to the novel that Clarín was a self-declared Darwinian and partisan to the Darwinian ideas espoused by his brother at a conference in 1887. See Leopoldo Alas (Clarín), *La Regenta,* ed. Juan Oleza, 2 vols. (Madrid: Cátedra, 1994), 1:168n44. All susequent references to *La Regenta* throughout this chapter come from this edition. A discussion of Clarín and Darwin can also be found in Pratt, *Signs of Science,* 65–80. For Clarín with respect to Darwinian sexual selection, see my discussion in chapter 3 on Leopoldo Alas, "El amor y la economía." An additional resource is the lecture by Genaro Alas, *El darwinismo: Conferencias pronunciadas en el Casino de Oviedo en los días 25 de febrero, 4 y 11 de marzo de 1887,* ed. Francisco Gar-cía Sarría (Exeter: University of Exeter Press, 1978). The lecture was published in *Revista de Asturias* in the years between *La Regenta* and *Su único hijo.*

3. Elizabeth Grosz, *The Nick of Time: Politics, Evolution, and the Untimely* (Durham, N.C.: Duke University Press, 2004), 77. There have been some very interesting recent studies on music with relevance to sexual selection, among them, Daniel J. Levitin, *This Is Your Brain on Music: The Science of a Human Obsession* (New York: Plume, 2006); and Oliver Sacks, *Musicophilia: Tales of Music and the Brain* (New York: Knopf, 2007).

4. Alas, *La Regenta,* 1:352 (Ronzal); 1:364 (Vegallana); 2:96 (theatergoers).

5. Sedgwick, *Between Men.*

6. René Girard, *Violence and the Sacred,* trans. Patrick Gregory (Baltimore: Johns Hopkins University Press, 1979), 148.

7. Girard, *Deceit,* 17.

8. Sedgwick, *Between Men,* 21.

9. Girard, *Violence,* 148, and *Deceit,* 16.

10. Denise DuPont argues that in *La Regenta* the identity of the text's internal primary author is at stake in the power struggle over language among Álvaro, Fermín, and Ana. She concludes that Ana, as the true author of events, is a victim not of the males who seek to control her but rather of her own self-seduction. See Denise DuPont, "*La Regenta* and the Hegemony of the Female Author," in *Realism as Resistance: Romanticism and Authorship in Galdós, Clarín, and Baroja* (Lewisburg, Pa.: Bucknell University Press, 2006), 173–220.

11. In chapter 8, I treat at length the relationship between confession and sexual selection in novels by Armando Palacio Valdés.

12. Stendhal (Marie-Henri Beyle), *Love* (London: Penguin, 1957), 83.

13. Tony Tanner, *Adultery in the Novel: Contract and Transgression* (Baltimore: Johns Hopkins University Press, 1979), 377.

14. Peter Brooks, *Reading for the Plot: Design and Intention in Narrative* (New York: Knopf, 1984), 37.

15. Sedgwick, *Between Men*, 14–15.

16. Brooks, *Reading for the Plot*, 54, 61.

17. For more on desire along these lines, see Georges Bataille, *Death and Sensuality: A Study of Eroticism and the Taboo* (New York: Arno, 1977), "innerness of the desire," 29–39; Julia Kristeva, *Desire in Language: A Semiotic Approach to Literature and Art* (New York: Columbia University Press, 1980), "desire as an objective," 116–17; and Deleuze and Guattari, *Anti-Oedipus*, "deterritorialization" and "the social machine is identical with the desiring-machine," 145–53.

18. Sedgwick, *Between Men*, 15.

19. Selected studies on ritual include Catherine Bell, *Ritual Theory, Ritual Practice* (New York: Oxford University Press, 1992); Maurice Bloch, *Ritual, History, and Power: Selected Papers in Anthropology* (London: Athlone, 1989); Max Gluckman, ed., *Essays on the Ritual of Social Relations* (Manchester: Manchester University Press, 1962); Don Handelman and Galina Lindquist, eds., *Ritual in Its Own Right: Exploring the Dynamics of Transformation* (New York: Berghahn, 2004); Claude Lévi-Strauss, *The Savage Mind* (Chicago: University of Chicago Press, 1966); Lévi-Strauss, *The Naked Man*, vol. 4 of *Mythologiques* (Chicago: University of Chicago Press, 1981); Henry Pernet, *Ritual Masks: Deceptions and Revelations* (Columbia: University of South Carolina Press, 1992); Mario Perniola, *Ritual Thinking: Sexuality, Death, World* (New York: Humanity Books, 2001); and Roy A. Rappaport, *Ritual and Religion in the Making of Humanity* (Cambridge: Cambridge University Press, 1999).

20. Bell, *Ritual Theory*, 14–19.

21. Rappaport, *Ritual and Religion*, 24, 37.

22. Lévi-Strauss, *The Savage Mind*, 32.

23. Lévi-Strauss, *The Naked Man*, 681.

24. In my conclusion to this study as a whole, I examine precisely this issue of "inaction" as I work through the different understandings of conscience.

25. Don Handelman, "Introduction: Why Ritual in Its Own Right? How So?" in Handelman and Lindquist, *Ritual in Its Own Right*, 27.

26. Bruce Kapferer, "Ritual Dynamics and Virtual Practice: Beyond Representation and Meaning," in Handelman and Lindquist, *Ritual in Its Own Right*, 42.

27. With his usage of "habitus," Kapferer here is drawing on the fluid model for understanding oppositions used by Pierre Bourdieu in *Outline of a Theory of Practice* (Cambridge: Cambridge University Press, 1977).

28. Krauel, *Voces desde el silencio*, 32.

29. Labanyi, *Gender and Modernization*, 224.

30. Valis, *The Decadent Vision*, 173; Six, "Mothers' Voices and Medusas' Eyes," 199; Bauer, "Something Lost," 93; Sánchez, "Teatro e intimidad," 12.

31. Richmond, "En torno al vacío," 355.

32. Handelman, "Introduction: Why Ritual in Its Own Right?" 17.

33. Ibid., 19–21.

34. Leopoldo Alas (Clarín), *Su único hijo*, ed. Carolyn Richmond (Madrid: Espasa-Calpe, 1979), 4. All subsequent references come from this edition.

35. Kapferer, "Ritual Dynamics and Virtual Practice," 51.

36. Handelman, "Introduction: Why Ritual in Its Own Right?" 27.

37. Gay, *The Bourgeois Experience*, 193.

38. Søren Kierkegaard, *The Concept of Irony, with Continual Reference to Socrates*, ed. and trans. Howard V. Hong and Edna H. Hong, *Kierkegaard's Writings* (Princeton, N.J.: Princeton University Press, 1989), 247.

39. George Meredith, prelude to *The Egoist*, ed. Robert M. Adams (New York: Norton, 1979), 3.

40. George Bernard Shaw, "Ideals and Idealists," in Becker, *Documents of Modern Literary Realism*, 123.

41. Gary Handwerk, *Irony and Ethics in Narrative: From Schlegel to Lacan* (New Haven, Conn.: Yale University Press, 1985), 2.

42. Grosz, *The Nick of Time*, 23.

43. Nil Santiáñez, *Investigaciones literarias: Modernidad, historia de la literatura y modernismos* (Barcelona: Editorial Crítica, 2002).

44. Ibid., 355.

45. Ludwig Wittgenstein, "A Lecture on Ethics," *Philosophical Review* 74 (1965): 3–12.

46. Ibid., 12. Emmanuel Lévinas, *Ethics and Infinity: Conversations with Philippe Nemo*, trans. Richard A. Cohen (Pittsburgh: Duquesne University Press, 1985). Also relevant to the discussion of language here, as well as with respect to De Pas's articulation of "your rival" and Bonifacio's final proclamation, is the work of Jacques Lacan on the ethics of desire and the act of naming in *The Seminar of Jacques Lacan*, bk. 1, *Freud's Papers on Technique, 1953–1954*, ed. Jacques-Alain Miller, trans. John Forrester (New York: Norton, 1991), and *The Seminar of Jacques Lacan*, bk. 7, *The Ethics of Psychoanalysis, 1959–1960*, ed. Jacques-Alain Miller, trans. Dennis Porter (New York: Norton, 1997).

CHAPTER 6. HEIRS AND ERRORS—BENITO PÉREZ GALDÓS

1. Jim Endersby explains the history and subtleties of this theory in "Darwin on Generation, Pangenesis, and Sexual Selection," in Hodge and Radick, *Cambridge Companion to Darwin*, 69–91.

2. See Michael A. Schnepf, "History to Fiction: The Political Background of Galdós' *La desheredada*," *Letras Peninsulares* 4 (1991): 295–306; Wifredo de Ràfols, "From Institution to Prostitution: Bureaumania and the Homeless Heroine in *La desheredada*," *Anales Galdosianos* 37 (2002): 69–87; Ignacio-Javier López, *Realismo y ficción: La desheredada de Galdós y la novela de su tiempo* (Barcelona: Promociones y Publicaciones Universitarias, 1989); Emma Martinell, "Isidora Rufete (La desheredada), a través del entorno inanimado," *Letras de Deusto* 16 (1986): 107–22; María del Carmen Porrúa, "La función de la ambigüedad en la protagonista de *La*

desheredada de Galdós," *Filología* 20 (1985): 139–51; and Monroe Z. Hafter, "Galdós' Presentation of Isidora in *La desheredada*," *Modern Philology* 60 (1962): 22–30.

3. Benito Pérez Galdós, *La desheredada*, ed. Germán Gullón (Madrid: Cátedra, 2000), 503. All subsequent references to the novel throughout this chapter come from this edition.

4. Benito Pérez Galdós, *Fortunata y Jacinta* (Madrid: Hernando, 1979). All subsequent references to the novel throughout this chapter come from this edition.

5. The mid-nineteenth-century establishment of the state asylum of Leganés, "el Manicomio Modelo," located not far from the capital, became a visible marker of social ills (and the victims) in Spain, and it is in this context, along with being a site of medicine and madness, that the institution often factors in Galdós's writings. It substitutes both for Spain as a nation during the upheaval of the Restoration and for the imaginary escapism that echoed in the nation's Cervantine consciousness. Michael A. Schnepf discusses Leganés and Galdós in "Galdós's Madhouse: Notes on the Socio-political and Medical Background to Leganés in *La desheredada*," *Letras Peninsulares* 17 (2004): 345–60. More on pathology in Galdós, the history of Leganés, and mental illness in nineteenth-century Spain can be found in George H. Allison and Joan Connelly Ullman, "Galdós as Psychiatrist in *Fortunata y Jacinta*," *Anales galdosianos* 9 (1974): 7–36; Allison and Ullman, "The Intuitive Psychoanalytic Perspective of Galdós in *Fortunata and Jacinta*," *International Journal of Psycho-Analysis* 55 (1974): 333–43; Fernando Alvarez-Uría, *Miserables y locos: Medicina mental y orden social en la España del siglo XIX* (Barcelona: Tusquets Editores, 1983); Francisco Javier Buqueras, *La asistencia psiquiátrica y la sanidad militar española en el siglo XIX* (Barcelona: Espaxs Publicaciones Medicas, 1992); Manuel Delgado Criado, "Los primeros años del manicomio modelo de Leganés (1852–1871)," *Asclepio* 38 (1986): 273–97; and Julián Espinosa Iborra, *La asistencia psiquiátrica en la España del siglo XIX* (Valencia: Cátedra e Instituto de Historia de la Medicina, 1966). It is also important to note that in the later decades other influential writings on degeneration, like Max Nordau's *Degeneration* (1892), were beginning to circulate in Spain. Pompeyo Gener's *Literaturas malsanas: Estudios de patología literaria contemporánea* (Madrid: F. Fé, 1894) offers an excellent example of Nordau's influence.

6. See chapter 7 of the present study for a fuller elaboration of Darwinian sympathy and annotated information on Kropotkin's life and publications.

7. T. E. Bell, *Galdós and Darwin* (Rochester, N.Y.: Tamesis, 2006). An account of the holdings in Galdós's personal library, which contained various editions of Darwin, is given by H. Chonon Berkowitz in *La biblioteca de Benito Pérez Galdós: Catálogo razonado* (Las Palmas, Canaries: El Museo Canario, 1951).

8. Pérez Galdós, *La desheredada*, 130.

9. My contention here is that Isidora's case represents a female version of what Sigmund Freud describes in "Family Romances," in *The Standard Edition of the Complete Psychological Works of Sigmund Freud*, ed. and trans.

James Strachey, with Anna Freud, Alix Strachey, and Alan Tyson (London: Hogarth, 1959), 9:235–42.

10. Arnold Weinstein, *A Scream Goes through the House: What Literature Teaches Us about Life* (New York: Random House, 2003), 378, 382.

11. There is an intentional conflation here between what Darwin says of "civilised life" and Labanyi's remarks on Spain's "civil society" in *Gender and Modernization*, 53.

12. Elizabeth Amann, "Metaphor, Metonymy, and Inheritance: Representing Revolution in Galdós's *La desheredada*," *Revista de Estudios Hispánicos* 37 (2003): 437–62.

13. Catherine Jaffe, "Mothers and Orphans in *La desheredada*," *Confluencia: Revista Hispánica de Cultura y Literatura* 5 (1990): 27–38; Eamonn Rodgers, "Galdós' *La desheredada* and Naturalism," *Bulletin of Hispanic Studies* 45 (1968): 285–98.

14. Frank Durand, "The Reality of Illusion: *La desheredada*," *Modern Language Notes* 89 (1974): 201.

15. Stephanie Sieburth, "Enlightenment, Mass Culture, and Madness: The Dialectic of Modernity in *La desheredada*," in *A Sesquicentennial Tribute to Galdós, 1843–1993*, ed. Linda M. Willem (Newark, Del.: Juan de la Cuesta, 1993), 33.

16. Stephanie Sieburth, *Inventing High and Low: Literature, Mass Culture, and Uneven Modernity in Spain* (Durham, N.C.: Duke University Press, 1994), 98.

17. Also recalled here through these references is my discussion of Bennett, *Outside Literature*, 77.

18. Benito Pérez Galdós, "La sociedad presente como materia novelable," in *Ensayos de crítica literaria de Benito Pérez Galdós*, ed. Laureano Bonet (Barcelona: Península, 1990), 163.

19. As is well known, Darwin himself experienced misgivings, and controversy, for his own marriage to his first cousin Emma.

20. Turner, "Family Ties and Tyrannies."

21. Geoffrey Ribbans, *Conflicts and Conciliations: The Evolution of Galdós's* Fortunata y Jacinta (West Lafayette, Ind.: Purdue University Press, 1997), 109.

22. Demetrio Estébanez Calderón, "Naturaleza y sociedad: Claves para una interpretación de *Fortunata y Jacinta*," in *Textos y contextos de Galdós: Actos del Simposio Centenario de* Fortunata y Jacinta, ed. John W. Kronik and Harriet S. Turner (Madrid: Castalia, 1994), 82.

23. Harriet S. Turner, "The Realist Novel," in *The Cambridge Companion to the Spanish Novel from 1600 to the Present*, ed. Harriet S. Turner and Adelaida López de Martínez (Cambridge: Cambridge University Press, 2003), 88–89.

24. John W. Kronik, "Feijoo and the Fabrication of Fortunata," in *Conflicting Realities: Four Readings of a Chapter by Pérez Galdós (*Fortunata y Jacinta, Part III, Chapter IV)*, ed. Peter B. Goldman (London: Tamesis, 1984), 72.

25. Smith, *Emerging Female Citizen*.

26. With his three orders, Jacques Lacan offers a psychoanalytic model of the Symbolic and the Imaginary and the Real in *The Seminar of Jacques Lacan*, bk. 2, *The Ego in Freud's Theory and in the Technique of Psychoanalysis, 1954–1955*, ed. Jacques-Alain Miller, trans. Sylvana Tomaselli (New York: Norton, 1991), and *The Seminar of Jacques Lacan*, bk. 3, *The Psychoses, 1955–1956*, ed. Jacques-Alain Miller, trans. Russell Grigg (New York: Norton, 1997). Kronik never invokes Lacan, and the choice of "symbolic" and "imaginary" in this discussion of his reading is my own.

27. Pedro Calderón de la Barca, *La vida es sueño*, ed. José María García Martín (Madrid: Castalia, 1984), 162.

28. Darwin, *On the Origin of Species*, 489.

29. Pérez Galdós, "La sociedad presente," 162.

CHAPTER 7. A ROMANCE WITH DARWIN IN THE EVOLUTIONARY *NOCHE* OF ALEJANDRO SAWA

1. The references here point back to my discussion at the end of chapter 1 where I draw on Said, *The World, the Text, and the Critic*, 225.

2. Amelina Correa Ramón, *Alejandro Sawa: Luces de bohemia* (Seville: Fundación José Manuel Lara, 2008).

3. Peter Kropotkin (1842–1921), a Russian geographer and zoologist imprisoned for his anarchistic activism, offered mutual aid in *Mutual Aid: A Factor of Evolution* (1902) (Washington, D.C.: Counterpoint, 2001), which privileged cooperation over competition, as a counter theory to social Darwinism's "survival of the fittest" creed. As for Ayala and Miller, on scientific ground they both advocate for reconciliation in their respective works, *Darwin's Gift to Science and Religion* (Washington, D.C.: John Henry Press, 2007) and *Finding Darwin's God: A Scientist's Search for Common Ground* (New York: Harper Perennial, 2000), and each, I suspect, falls short on the questions that really matter, using conversational rhetoric to skirt doctrinal issues of salvation and the hereafter in deference to sacrosanct, personal faith.

4. Jameson, *The Political Unconscious*, 98.

5. Ortega y Gasset, *Meditaciones*, 327.

6. Georg Lukács, *The Theory of the Novel*, trans. Anna Bostock (Cambridge, Mass.: MIT Press, 1971), 72; Bakhtin, *Dialogic Imagination*, 346; Northrop Frye, *Anatomy of Criticism: Four Essays* (Princeton, N.J.: Princeton University Press, 1990), 137.

7. Pura Fernández, *Eduardo López Bago y el naturalismo radical: La novela y el mercado literario en el siglo XIX* (Amsterdam: Rodopi, 1995), 109, 114. Similarly, Yvan Lissorgues also posits a "radical" strain of Spanish naturalism in "El naturalismo radical: Eduardo López Bago (y Alejandro Sawa)," in Lissorgues, *Realismo y naturalismo en España*, 237–56. Nil Santiáñez, however, argues against critics like Fernández and Lissorgues, who seek to distinguish "radical" naturalists (among them, Alejandro Sawa, Eduardo López Bago, and Remigio Vega Armentero) from their more "moderate" mainstream contemporaries (including, Benito Pérez Galdós, Leopoldo

290 Notes to Chapter 7

Alas [Clarín], and Emilia Pardo Bazán). For a treatment of Spanish naturalism and reassessment of its influence on modernism, see Nil Santiáñez, "Las consecuencias del naturalismo," in Santiáñez, *Investigaciones literarias*, 207–44.

8. Fernández, *Eduardo López Bago y el naturalismo radical*, 230; Santiáñez, *Investigaciones literarias*, 225.

9. Gilbert Paolini uses Zola and Lombroso as his point of reference for a concise reading of *Noche* in "*Noche*, novela de Alejandro Sawa en el ambiente científico de la década de 1880," *Boletín de la Biblioteca Menéndez Pelayo* 60 (1984): 321–38. In *La donna criminale, la prostituta e la donna normale* (1893), Lombroso appropriates Darwin in all sorts of inappropriate ways as he makes his case for the biological inferiority of women and their tendencies toward depravity. For a recent translation with an excellent introduction on the cultural stakes of his pseudoscience, see Lombroso and Ferrero, *Criminal Woman, the Prostitute, and the Normal Woman*.

10. Fernández, *Eduardo López Bago y el naturalismo radical*, 231.

11. Juan de Valdés, *Diálogo de la lengua*, ed. Juan M. Lope Blanch (Madrid: Editorial Castalia, 1969), 6.

12. Frye, *Anatomy of Criticism*, 136–37.

13. Northrop Frye, *The Secular Scripture: A Study of the Structure of Romance* (Cambridge, Mass.: Harvard University Press, 1976), 37.

14. Auerbach, *Mimesis*, 137.

15. Ian Watt, *The Rise of the Novel: Studies in Defoe, Richardson, and Fielding* (Berkeley: University of California Press, 1974), 135.

16. The cited position here is that of Becker, *Documents of Modern Literary Realism*, 34–35. Furthermore, scholarship that investigates the two faces of Spanish literature is now a well-established critical community characterized by its feminist agenda and shared theoretical orientation. For an appreciation of the issues at stake in diverse readings of a split culture, often along gender lines, see Alicia G. Andreu, *Galdós y la literatura popular* (Madrid: Sociedad General Española, 1982); Lou Charnon-Deutsch, *Gender and Representation: Women in Spanish Realist Fiction* (Amsterdam: John Benjamins, 1990); Charnon-Deutsch and Labanyi, *Culture and Gender in Nineteenth-Century Spain*; DuPont, *Realism as Resistance*; Hazel Gold, *The Reframing of Realism: Galdós and the Discourses of the Nineteenth-Century Spanish Novel* (Durham, N.C.: Duke University Press, 1993); Catherine Jagoe, *Ambiguous Angels: Gender in the Novels of Galdós* (Berkeley: University of California Press, 1994); Elisa Martí-López, *Borrowed Words: Translation, Imitation, and the Making of the Nineteenth-Century Novel in Spain* (Lewisburg, Pa.: Bucknell University Press, 2002); Wadda C. Ríos-Font, *The Canon and the Archive: Configuring Literature in Modern Spain* (Lewisburg, Pa.: Bucknell University Press, 2004); and Sieburth, *Inventing High and Low*. Also, Catherine Jagoe, Alda Blanco, and Cristina Enríquez de Salamanca provide an indispensable critical anthology of Spanish nineteenth-century writings by and about women in *La mujer en los discursos de género: Textos y contextos en el siglo XIX* (Barcelona: Icaria, 1998).

17. The oversimplification I am describing here in terms of gender obfuscates what was in fact a very complex Romantic movement in Spain, characterized by the early contributions of José de Espronceda (1808–1843) and Mariano José de Larra (1809–1837); the lyricism of Gustavo Adolfo Bécquer (1837–1870); the theater of Ángel de Saavedra, duque de Rivas (1791–1865), and José Zorrilla (1817–1893); the novels and poetry of women writers like Cecilia Böhl de Faber (Fernán Caballero) (1796–1877), Ángela Grassi (1823–1883), Faustina Sáez de Melgar (1834–1895), Rosalía de Castro (1837–1885), and María del Pilar Sinués de Marco (1835–1893); the popular serial novels of Wenceslao Ayguals de Izco (1801–1873) and Manuel Fernández y González (1821–1888); and the *costumbrismo* of Ramón de Mesonero Romanos (1803–1882). Leonardo Romero Tobar provides a useful overview of the period in *Panorama crítico del romanticismo español* (Madrid: Castalia, 1994).

18. Benito Pérez Galdós, "Observaciones sobre la novela contemporánea en España," in *Ensayos de crítica literaria de Benito Pérez Galdós*, 105.

19. Naomi Schor, *George Sand and Idealism* (New York: Columbia University Press, 1993), 43.

20. Margaret Cohen, *The Sentimental Education of the Novel* (Princeton, N.J.: Princeton University Press, 1999), 4–9.

21. Laurie Langbauer, *Women and Romance: The Consolations of Gender in the English Novel* (Ithaca, N.Y.: Cornell University Press, 1990), 1.

22. It is necessary to note, in the context of this chapter, that Langbauer treats Watt, Frye, and Jameson, all central to my own argument, at the outset of her study. In piecing through her position, which I find dated and with no real alternative to the histories she rejects, it seems the collective guilt of these critics lies in their status quo associations between women and romance, and courtship as understood by Watt does nothing more than maintain differences between men and women, which belies his own contradictions as romance and novel continually collapse on each other over the course of his exposition.

23. Alda Blanco, "Gender and National Identity: The Novel in Nineteenth-Century Spanish Literary History," in Charnon-Deutsch and Labanyi, *Culture and Gender in Nineteenth-Century Spain*, 120–36.

24. Ríos-Font, *The Canon and the Archive*, 43.

25. Martí-López, *Borrowed Words*.

26. Russell P. Sebold, *La novela romántica en España: Entre libro de caballerías y novela moderna* (Salamanca: Universidad de Salamanca, 2002); Sebold, *Trayectoria del romanticismo español* (Barcelona: Crítica, 1983); Donald L. Shaw, "Spain / Romántico—Romanticismo—Romancesco—Romancista—Romántico," in *"Romantic" and Its Cognates / The European History of a Word*, ed. Hans Eichner (Toronto: University of Toronto Press, 1972), 341–71.

27. Shaw, "Spain / Romántico," 349.

28. Sebold, *Trayectoria del romanticismo español*, 161.

29. Sebold, *La novela romántica*, 22.

30. In fact, courtship does not even appear in the four principal romantic plots Sebold identifies (*La novela romántica*, 40), despite its structural importance for the romantic novels he treats in the same study.

31. Walter Scott, "Essay on Romance," in *Essays on Chivalry, Romance, and the Drama* (London: Frederick Warne, 1942), 67.

32. Alessandro Manzoni, "Lettera a Monsieur Chauvet sull'unità di tempo e di luogo nella tragedia," in *Scritti di teoria letteraria* (Milan: Biblioteca Universale Rizzoli, 1981), 53–154.

33. White, *Metahistory*.

34. William Godwin, "Of History and Romance," in *Political and Philosophical Writings*, ed. Pamela Clemit, 5 vols. (London: Pickering and Chatto, 1993), reprinted in *Caleb Williams*, by William Godwin, ed. Gary Handwerk and A. A. Markley (Ontario: Broadview, 2000), 453–67. Page references are to the reprinted essay.

35. Émile Zola, *Thérèse Raquin*, ed. Leonard Tancock (London: Penguin, 1962), 7.

36. William Godwin, *Enquiry concerning Political Justice and Its Influence on General Virtue and Happiness* (1793), reprinted in Godwin, *Caleb Williams*, 490.

37. Michael McKeon, *The Origins of the English Novel, 1600–1740* (Baltimore: Johns Hopkins University Press, 1987), 420.

38. Michael McKeon, "Prose Fiction: Great Britain," in *The Eighteenth Century*, ed. H. B. Nisbet and Claude Rawson, vol. 4 of *The Cambridge History of Literary Criticism* (New York: Cambridge University Press, 1997), 263.

39. Raymond Williams, *Marxism and Literature* (Oxford: Oxford University Press, 1977), 162, 205.

40. Unlike Clarín, Galdós, and even Picón, Sawa has been all but erased from Spain's cultural history, despite recent attempts to resurrect his biography and contributions. More on Sawa can be found in Amelina Correa Ramón's authoratative biography, *Alejandro Sawa: Luces de bohemia*, and her earlier study, *Alejandro Sawa y el naturalismo literario* (Granada: Universidad de Granada, 1993), 17–55; see also Allen W. Phillips, *Alejandro Sawa: Mito y realidad* (Madrid: Turner, 1976), 13–157; and Iris M. Zavala, ed., "Estudio Preliminar," in *Iluminaciones en la sombra*, by Alejandro Sawa (Madrid: Alhambra, 1977), 3–54.

41. Reprints and critical editions of Sawa's novels include *Declaración de un vencido / Criadero de curas*, ed. Francisco Gutiérrez Carbajo (Madrid: Biblioteca de Autores Españoles, 1999); *Iluminaciones en la sombra*, edited by Zavala; *La mujer de todo el mundo*, facsimile (Madrid: Moreno-Ávila, 1988); and *Noche*, ed. Jean-Claude Mbarga (Madrid: Libertarias/Prodhufi, 2001). All subsequent references to *Noche* throughout this chapter come from this edition.

42. Giovanni Verga, *I Malavoglia* (Verona: Mondadori, 1990).

43. Sawa, *Noche*, 94, 96.

44. Thomas Hardy, *Tess of the d'Urbervilles* (London: Penguin, 2003), 73.

45. Jagoe, *Ambiguous Angels*, 10.

46. Correa Ramón, *Alejandro Sawa: Luces de bohemia*.

47. Ibid., 78; Jean-Claude Mbarga, introduction to *Noche*, 29.

48. Birute Ciplijauskaité, "El romanticismo como hipotexto en el realismo," in Lissorgues, *Realismo y naturalismo en España*, 92.

49. Jameson, *The Political Unconscious*, 35.

50. Gold, *Reframing of Realism*, 182.

51. Sedgwick, *Between Men*, 10.

52. Though written before the publication of Darwin's *Origin*, Lord Tennyson's famous verses from *In Memorium A.H.H.* (1844), which read "Who trusted God was love indeed / And love Creation's final law / Tho' Nature red in tooth and claw / With ravine, shriek'd against his creed," decry an indifferent Nature and, because of their evolutionary resonance, are often used to invoke the heartless dimension of Darwin's science. See Alfred Tennyson, *A Collection of Poems by Alfred Tennyson*, selected and with introduction by Christopher Ricks (New York: Doubleday, 1972), 357.

53. George Eliot, "The Natural History of German Life," in *Essays of George Eliot*, ed. Thomas Pinney (New York: Columbia University Press, 1963), 270.

CHAPTER 8. THE RELIGIOUS *DESCENT* OF ARMANDO PALACIO VALDÉS

1. Selected accounts of the contentious relationship between science and religion in Spain in the nineteenth and twentieth centuries include Joan Connelly Ullman, *The Tragic Week: A Study of Anticlericalism in Spain, 1875–1912* (Cambridge, Mass.: Harvard University Press, 1968); Francisco Pelayo López, "Ciencia y religión en España durante el siglo XIX," *Asclepio* 40 (1988): 187–206; and the anthology of Ernesto and Enrique García Camarero, eds., *La polémica de la ciencia española* (Madrid: Alianza, 1970).

2. Royer, preface to Darwin, *De l'origine des espèces* (1862), lxxi.

3. Chadwick, *The Secularization of the European Mind*, 175.

4. Brian J. Dendle, *Spain's Forgotten Novelist: Armando Palacio Valdés (1853–1938)* (Lewisburg, Pa.: Bucknell University Press, 1995), 13.

5. Donald L. Shaw, *A Literary History of Spain: The Nineteenth Century* (London: Ernest Benn, 1972), 128–30.

6. Respectively, these include Santiáñez, *Investigaciones literarias*; Beth Wietelmann Bauer, "*Marta y María*: Romanticismo y misticismo en Palacio Valdés," in *Estudios sobre Armando Palacio Valdés*, ed. Brian J. Dendle and Stephen Miller, Ottawa Hispanic Studies 14 (Ottawa: Dovehouse, 1993), 24–35; Gilbert Paolini, "La psicopatología en la literatura italo-española: D'Annunzio y Palacio Valdés," in *The Two Hesperias: Literary Studies in Honor of Joseph G. Fucilla on the Occasion of His 80th Birthday*, ed. Americo Bugliani (Madrid: Turanzas, 1978), 275–90; and Peter Bly, "*La fe*: Palacio Valdés Looks Back to Alas and Forward to Unamuno," *Romance Quarterly* 35 (1988): 339–46.

7. My use of melodrama here should be understood according to what Peter Brooks says about the high-stakes drama of reality in *The Melodramatic Imagination: Balzac, Henry James, Melodrama, and the Mode of Excess* (New York: Columbia University Press, 1985).

8. Armando Palacio Valdés, *Marta y María* (Madrid: Espasa-Calpe, 1974), i. All subsequent references to the novel throughout this chapter come from this edition.

9. Robert T. Petersson, *The Art of Ecstasy: Teresa, Bernini, and Crashaw* (New York: Atheneum, 1970), 6.

10. Bauer, "*Marta y María*," 29.

11. Girard, *Violence and the Sacred*, 273.

12. With "imaginary quality of reality," I am here recalling my discussion in chapter 1 of J. Hillis Miller, *The Form of Victorian Fiction*, 35.

13. Nelson Pike, whose work I paraphrase here, gives a more thorough account of this history in "God as Lover and Mother," from *Mystic Union: An Essay in the Phenomenology of Mysticism* (Ithaca, N.Y.: Cornell University Press, 1992), 66–86.

14. Juan Luis Vives, *Libro llamado instrucción de la mujer cristiana*, trans. Juan Justiniano (Madrid: Signo, 1936), 37.

15. Sarah Salih, "When Is a Bosom Not a Bosom?" in *Medieval Virginities*, ed. Anke Bernau, Ruth Evans, and Sarah Salih (Toronto: University of Toronto Press, 2003), 26.

16. Pike, *Mystic Union*, 86.

17. Alison Weber, *Teresa of Avila and the Rhetoric of Femininity* (Princeton, N.J.: Princeton University Press, 1990), 14.

18. Beauvoir, *The Second Sex*, 670–78.

19. Lorraine Daston, "Fear and Loathing of the Imagination in Science," in *Science in Culture*, ed. Peter Galison, Stephen R. Graubard, and Everett Mendelsohn (London: Transaction, 2001), 76–88.

20. William James, *The Varieties of Religious Experience: A Study in Human Nature* (New York: University Books, 1963), 501.

21. Ibid., 518; Daston, "Fear and Loathing," 77.

22. James, *Varieties of Religious Experience*, 518.

23. Michel Foucault, *Religion and Culture*, ed. Jeremy R. Carrette (New York: Routledge, 1999), 59; Peter Brooks, *Troubling Confessions: Speaking Guilt in Law and Literature* (Chicago: University of Chicago Press, 2000), 97.

24. Armando Palacio Valdés, *La fe* (Madrid: Librería de Victoriano Suárez, 1926), 59, 60. All subsequent references to the novel throughout this chapter come from this edition.

25. Brooks, *Troubling Confessions*, 144–71.

26. Pierre J. Payer, *The Bridling of Desire: Views of Sex in the Later Middle Ages* (Toronto: University of Toronto Press, 1993), 179.

27. Stephen Haliczer, *Sexuality in the Confessional: A Sacrament Profaned* (Oxford: Oxford University Press, 1996), 33.

28. Adelina Sarrión Mora, *Sexualidad y confesión: La solicitación ante el Tribunal del Santo Oficio (siglos XVI–XIX)* (Madrid: Alianza, 1994).

29. For a more comprehensive treatment of this theme in these works and popular culture, see Haliczer's chapter "Solicitation and Confession in the Anticlerical Imagination," in *Sexuality in the Confessional*, 183–203.

30. Jorge René González Marmolejo, "Confesores y mujeres en el obispado de Puebla, siglo XVIII," in *El placer de pecar y el afán de normar: Seminario de historia de las mentalidades*, ed. Joaquín Mortiz (Mexico City: Instituto Nacional de Antropología e Historia, 1987), 155–56.

31. It is true, as we saw in chapter 5, that Ana Ozores in *La Regenta* fantasizes about her confessor Fermín de Pas as a peculiar sort of rival suitor of Don Álvaro Mesías, but as I've shown, once this rivalry evolves into a full-blown reality the mere possibility of actual consummation with De Pas horrifies Ana. By contrast, Obdulia goes to great lengths in order to have sexual relations with Gil, and thus confession in *La fe* has a more direct relevance to sexual selection than in Clarín's grand novel, where I choose to foreground the importance of rivalries and rituals in the courtship dynamic.

32. Sarrión Mora, *Sexualidad y confesión*, 37.

33. Foucault, *The History of Sexuality*, 1:17–73.

34. Foucault, *Religion and Culture*, 126.

35. Jeremy Tambling, *Confession: Sexuality, Sin, the Subject* (Manchester: Manchester University Press, 1990), 206.

36. It is worth noting, to show the subtle irony of Palacio Valdés, that both Osuna and Narciso were actual historical figures persecuted by the Inquisition, the former for having written against confessional practices and the latter for solicitation. I have found the novels by Palacio Valdés to be replete with nuanced historical and biblical allusions of this sort, many of which I am sure have escaped me (and would no doubt have escaped most of his readers). These details, however, show that his writing, in the spirit of the realist age, is every bit as researched as the now more well-regarded works of his contemporaries. *Marta y María* is a further case in point, from the seemingly insignificant fact that Magdalene, with whom María is identified by her second name, derives from "tower," like María's dwelling, to the deeper transposition of Marta's preparation of meals for Ricardo, just as Martha feeds Christ in the New Testament, to give only a couple of examples of this symbolic, double-edged side to Palacio Valdés's fiction.

37. Brooks, *Troubling Confessions*, 96.

CHAPTER 9. EMILIA PARDO BAZÁN, REPRODUCTION, AND CHANGE

1. Here I am contrasting the indeterminacy of evolutionism that Elizabeth Grosz privileges in *The Nick of Time* with Daniel Dennett's *Darwin's Dangerous Idea: Evolution and the Meaning of Life* (New York: Simon and Schuster, 1995).

2. Emilia Pardo Bazán, *Dulce Dueño*, ed. Marina Mayoral (Madrid: Editorial Castalia, 1989), 287.

3. Joyce Tolliver points out that

until recently, Pardo Bazán criticism has focused insistently on the question of naturalism in this author's fiction. The question asked by critics, over and over again, about each work they discussed was

'How naturalistic is it?' Usually the answer represented some variety of 'Not as naturalistic as Zola' or 'More naturalistic than what she proposes in *La cuestión palpitante*.' . . . Pardo Bazán criticism, then, was characterized by an insistence on considering only a small portion of her immense oeuvre, and on viewing these works through a very narrow optic that placed them primarily in their relation to the works of Zola or to those of other Spanish male writers showing naturalistic tendencies. (Joyce Tolliver, introduction to *Cigar Smoke and Violet Water: Gendered Discourse in the Stories of Emilia Pardo Bazán* [Lewisburg, Pa.: Bucknell University Press, 1998], 20)

For more on this historical trajectory in the context of gender, see Mary Lee Bretz, *Voices, Silences, and Echoes: A Theory of the Essays and the Critical Reception of Naturalism in Spain* (London: Tamesis, 1992). Though Tolliver mentions no names, selected studies of critics who ask the same question "over and over again," as she frames it, could include Mariano Baquero Goyanes, *La novela naturalista española: Emilia Pardo Bazán* (Murcia: Universidad de Murcia, 1986); Fernando J. Barroso, *El naturalismo en la Pardo Bazán* (Madrid: Playor, 1973); M. Gordon Brown, "La condesa de Pardo Bazán y el naturalismo," *Hispania* 31, no. 2 (1948): 152–56; Francisco Caudet, "La querella naturalista: España contra Francia," *Ojancano* 2 (1989): 3–16; Gifford Davis, "Catholicism and Naturalism: Pardo Bazán's Reply to Zola," *Modern Language Notes* 90, no. 2 (1975): 282–87; José Manuel González Herrán, "Emilia Pardo Bazán y el naturalismo," *Ínsula* 44 (1989): 17–18; Maurice Hemingway, "Emilia Pardo Bazán: Narrative Strategies and the Critique of Naturalism," in *Naturalism in the European Novel: New Critical Perspectives*, ed. Brian Nelson (New York: Berg, 1992), 135–50; Hemingway, "Naturalism and Decadence in Zola's *La Faute de l'abbé Mouret* and Pardo Bazán's *La madre naturaleza*," *Revue de Litterature Comparee* 61, no. 1 (1987): 31–46; Mariano López-Sanz, *Naturalismo y espiritualismo en la novelística de Galdós y Pardo Bazán* (Madrid: Pliegos, 1985); and Ruth A. Schmidt, "Emilia Pardo Bazán's Retrospective View of Naturalism: Thirty Years after *La cuestión palpitante*," in *Papers on Romance Literary Relations*, ed. Hugh H. Chapman (University Park, Pa.: Penn State University Press, 1979), 29–42.

4. Studies that typify the broader shift in focus from naturalist to feminist issues in the writings of Pardo Bazán include Beth Wietelmann Bauer, "Narrative Cross-Dressing: Emilia Pardo Bazán in *Memorias de un solterón*," *Hispania* 77, no. 1 (1994): 23–30; Maryellen Bieder, "Capitulation: Marriage, Not Freedom; A Study of Emilia Pardo Bazán's *Memorias de un solterón* and Galdós' *Tristana*," *Symposium* 30, no. 2 (1976): 93–109; Bieder, "En-gendering Strategies of Authority: Emilia Pardo Bazán and the Novel," in *Cultural and Historical Grounding for Hispanic and Luso-Brazilian Feminist Literary Criticism*, ed. Hernán Vidal (Minneapolis: Institute for the Study of Ideologies and Literature, 1989), 473–96; Mary Lee Bretz, "Text and Intertext in Emilia Pardo Bazán's *Memorias de un solterón*," *Symposium* 43, no. 2 (1989): 83–94; Lou Charnon-Deutsch, "Feíta's Decision: Pardo Bazán's Exploration of Female Identity in *Memorias de un solterón*," *Discurso* 11, no. 1 (1993): 25–50; Charnon-Deutsch,

Narratives of Desire: Nineteenth-Century Spanish Fiction by Women (University Park, Pa.: Penn State University Press, 1994), 151–85; Nelly Clèmessy, *Emilia Pardo Bazán como novelista (de la teoría a la práctica)*, trans. Irene Gambra, 2 vols. (Madrid: Fundación Universitaria Española, 1981); Mary E. Giles, "Feminism and the Feminine in Emilia Pardo Bazán's Novels," *Hispania* 63, no. 2 (1980): 356–67; Elizabeth J. Ordóñez, "Gender Woes: Refiguring Familial Spheres in Pardo Bazán's *Doña Milagros*," *Hispanic Journal* 20, no. 2 (1999): 311–25; Ordóñez, "Revising Realism: Pardo Bazán's *Memorias de un solterón* in Light of Galdós's *Tristana* and John Stuart Mill," in *In the Feminine Mode: Essays on Hispanic Women Writers*, ed. Noël Valis and Carol Maier (Lewisburg, Pa.: Bucknell University Press, 1990), 146–63; and Robin Ragan, "Gossip, Gender, and Genre in *Memorias de un solterón* by Emilia Pardo Bazán," *Romance Languages Annual* 7 (1995): 597–603.

5. In the context of the nineteenth-century Spanish literary market and the popular novel, Alicia G. Andreu gives a comprehensive discussion of *la mujer virtuosa*, the Spanish ideal for the bourgeois woman in whom resignation and abnegation are the principal attributes, in *Galdós y la literatura popular*, 71–92. It should be noted, however, that Doña Milagros pretends such an identity in the eyes of Ilda and several of her daughters because of her history, as a childless Andalusian woman of humble origins who married up with respect to class status.

6. This chapter acknowledges cautions against searches for subversion in Pardo Bazán that, as Charnon-Deutsch points out (*Narratives of Desire*, 16), fail to appreciate the contradictions of novels by women concerned with domesticity, and yet, in accord with Tolliver's assertion that "part of the meaning her [Pardo Bazán's] words carried then, and still carry today, lies in the fact that they were indeed the words of a woman, and of a self-avowed 'radical feminist'" (*Cigar Smoke*, 174–75), I take subversion as a given and move beyond the identification of contradictions toward their resolution.

7. These essays are included in Emilia Pardo Bazán, *La mujer española y otros artículos feministas*, ed. Leda Schiavo (Madrid: Editora Nacional, 1976), which is the source for my references to them throughout this chapter. It should also be noted that discussion of female self-interest in terms of marriage surfaced well before Charles Darwin, in works like Daniel Defoe's *Conjugal Lewdness, or Matrimonial Whoredom: A Treatise concerning the Use and Abuse of the Marriage Bed* (Menston, England: Scolar, 1970) from 1727. The difference, though, is that by the late nineteenth century, as is the case with Pardo Bazán, outright condemnation and/or satiric ridicule of wives so judged had been substituted for a distinctly Darwinian understanding of, and hence tacit tolerance for, misguided motivations in matrimony, which came to say more about social ills and limitations on women's self-determination than about the character of the individuals in question. In other words, materialist motivations on the part of women seeking to marry could be excused biologically in terms of maternal instinct and self-preservation, that is, providing for offspring and oneself in the face of an indifferent Nature (or rather, Culture) characterized by inequalities.

8. *Feíta*, a Spanish diminutive of the name *Fe* (Faith), is also a play on the feminine form of the adjective *fea* (ugly), and Pardo Bazán, according to contemporary criticism, uses this name in an ironic way, to call attention to the elevated character of her heroine, as opposed to the way nineteenth-century Spain would have labeled her.

9. Emilia Pardo Bazán "La mujer española," in *La mujer española y otros artículos feministas*, 50.

10. Pardo Bazán's article titled "John Stuart Mill," which first appeared in her own periodical *Nuevo Teatro Crítico* (vol. 2, no. 17 [1892]), later provided the prologue to the translation of *The Subjection of Women* (*La esclavitud femenina*) in her collection of works for women, *Biblioteca de la mujer*, volume 2. This essay on Mill, like others under discussion here, also appears in Pardo Bazán, *La mujer española y otros artículos feministas*, 113–34.

11. In "Reflexiones científicas contra el darwinismo" (1877), which predates the 1885 authorized Spanish edition of *The Descent*, Pardo Bazán demonstrates a sophisticated understanding of some of the most problematic portions of Darwin's *On the Origin of Species* in her qualified refutation of the theory of natural selection, though it is also important to note that in this treatise she appears to be informed by and concerned with those most frequently associated with Darwin, like Haeckel, Spencer, Vogt, and De Quatrefages, among many others, as much as with Darwin himself. See Emilia Pardo Bazán, "Reflexiones científicas contra el darwinismo," in *Obras completas*, ed. Federico Carlos Sáinz de Robles (Madrid: Aguilar, 1973), 3:557–70.

12. Susan Kirkpatrick offers a pithy discussion of the widespread conservatism of Spanish women writers in the nineteenth century in her chapter "The Female Tradition in Nineteenth-Century Spanish Literature," in Vidal, *Cultural and Historical Grounding for Hispanic and Luso-Brazilian Feminist Literary Criticism*, 343–70.

13. Emilia Pardo Bazán, "Una opinión sobre la mujer," in *La mujer española y otros artículos feministas*, 159.

14. John Stuart Mill, *The Subjection of Women* (Ontario: Broadview, 2000), 25.

15. Emilia Pardo Bazán, *Doña Milagros*, in *Obras completas*, ed. Darío Villanueva and José Manuel González Herrán (Madrid: Castro, 1999), 3:584. All subsequent references to this novel throughout this chapter come from this edition.

16. Ordóñez, "Gender Woes," 317.

17. Tolliver, *Cigar Smoke*, 90–92.

18. Bauer, "Narrative Cross-Dressing," 25.

19. Maurice Hemingway, *Emilia Pardo Bazán: The Making of a Novelist* (Cambridge: Cambridge University Press, 1983), 15.

20. Bieder, "En-gendering Strategies of Authority," 480; Hemingway, *Emilia Pardo Bazán*, 121.

21. Kristeva, *Desire in Language*.

22. Clèmessy, *Emilia Pardo Bazán como novelista*.

23. See Dijkstra, *Idols of Perversity*; and Sandra Gilbert and Susan Gubar, *The Madwoman in the Attic: The Woman Writer and the Nineteenth-Century Literary Imagination* (New Haven, Conn.: Yale University Press, 1979).

24. Jacques Derrida, *Of Grammatology*, trans. Gayatri Chakravorty Spivak (Baltimore: Johns Hopkins University Press, 1974).

25. Jan Jindy Pettman, "Women, Gender, and the State," in *Worlding Women: A Feminist International Politics* (New York: Routledge, 1996), 5–15.

26. Caren Kaplan, Norma Alarcón, and Minoo Moallem, eds., *Between Woman and Nation: Nationalisms, Transnational Feminisms, and the State* (Durham, N.C.: Duke University Press, 1999), 1–16.

27. Harriet Fraad, Stephen A. Resnick, and Richard D. Wolff, *Bringing It All Back Home: Class, Gender, and Power in the Modern Household* (London: Pluto, 1994), 1–41.

28. Nancy C. M. Hartsock, "The Feminist Standpoint: Toward a Specifically Feminist Historical Materialism," in *Feminist Theory Reader: Local and Global Perspectives*, ed. Carole R. McCann and Seung-Kyung Kim (New York: Routledge, 2003), 294.

29. Charnon-Deutsch, *Narratives of Desire*.

30. Mies, *Patriarchy and Accumulation*.

31. Deleuze and Guattari, *Anti-Oedipus*, 145–53.

32. Friedrich Engels, *The Origin of the Family, Private Property, and the State in the Light of the Researches of Lewis H. Morgan* (New York: International, 1942), 50, 65.

33. Jo Labanyi underscores that women in Spain in the later decades of the nineteenth century remained outside civil society because, in being denied certain public rights like political participation, they lacked full citizenship. In this light, she calls attention to the fact that the 1870 Civil Marriage Law, which shifted marriage from a sacred Church bond to a secular State contract, brought new awareness to the issue of full civil rights for women, since any contract of the like was to be predicated on such rights (*Gender and Modernization*, 53).

34. Emilia Pardo Bazán, *Memorias de un solterón*, in *Obras completas* (1999), 3:963. All subsequent references to this novel throughout this chapter come from this edition.

35. Mauro's last name, *Pareja*, in Spanish signifies either "romantic partner" or, better still in the context of Pardo Bazán's novel, "(married) couple."

36. Bieder, "Capitulation: Marriage, Not Freedom."

37. Bauer, "Narrative Cross-Dressing," 23; Bretz, "Text and Intertext," 92; Charnon-Deutsch, "Feíta's Decision," 38.

38. Charnon-Deutsch, *Narratives of Desire*, 153.

39. Ibid.

40. Jean-Jacques Rousseau, *Émile, or On Education*, ed. Allan Bloom (New York: Basic, 1979), 408.

41. Harold Bloom, *Shakespeare: The Invention of the Human* (New York: Riverhead, 1998), 33.

42. Pardo Bazán, *La cuestión palpitante*, 150.

43. Pardo Bazán, "Reflexiones científicas contra el darwinismo," 548.

44. Jean-Jacques Rousseau, *The Social Contract*, ed. Maurice Cranston (London: Penguin, 1968), 77.

45. Ibid., 39.

CONCLUSION

1. Jacinto Octavio Picón, "Los favores de Fortuna," in *Cuentos de mi tiempo* (Madrid: Fortanet, 1895), 135-44. All references to this story that follow are from this edition.

2. True to the allegorical bent of this narration, "Fortuna" is not the only name imbued with double meaning. "Tizona" was the celebrated sword of Spain's great epic hero El Cid; "Infolio" literally means "book" of uncommon size; in allusion to Don Pedro de Lepe, a famous fifteenth-century bishop, "Lepe" is used in Spanish colloquialisms like "to know more than Lepe (saber más que Lepe)" to describe someone keen and in the know; and with respect to naming, "Perico Mediano" proves the richest of them all, in that "Perico" can signify various things, from "parakeet" to "ladies man" (and almost everything in between), while "Mediano" denotes how "average" this individual really is.

3. Ortega y Gasset, *Meditaciones*, 400.

4. Friedrich Nietzsche, *The Birth of Tragedy / The Genealogy of Morals*, trans. Francis Golffing (New York: Anchor, 1956), 189–230.

5. Giambattista Vico, *La scienza nuova* (Milan: Biblioteca Universale Rizzoli, 1998), 177–78. Though Thomas Goddard Bergin and Max Harold Fisch translate *coscienza* here as "consciousness" (*The New Science* [Ithaca, N.Y.: Cornell University Press, 1968], 63), I believe that "conscience" captures better the sense that Vico intends, namely, that in the absence of any criterion of absolute truth the will resorts to something other than the intellect, what I understand and discuss in this conclusion as innate ideas or intuition, not what Vico's French contemporary Nicolas Malebranche (1638–1715) would view as the world of opinion and custom (as Paolo Rossi holds in his edition of *La scienza nuova*). For a more comparative study of Vico and Malebranche, see Paolo Fabiani, *La filosofia dell'immaginazione in Vico e Malebranche* (Florence: Università di Firenze, 2002).

6. Of the many commentaries specifically concerned with the relationship between Locke and Blake, the best known is Northrop Frye's "The Case against Locke," in *Fearful Symmetry* (Princeton, N.J.: Princeton University Press, 1947), 11–36.

7. *The Complete Poetry and Prose of William Blake*, ed. David Erdman (New York: Anchor, 1988), 648. When citing Blake's annotations I maintain the original punctuation.

8. Philip M. Weinstein, *The Semantics of Desire: Changing Models of Identity from Dickens to Joyce* (Princeton, N.J.: Princeton University Press, 1984), 8.

9. John Locke, *An Essay concerning Human Understanding*, ed. Peter H. Nidditch (Oxford: Clarendon, 1975), 2.21.5, 2.22.11. Citations are by book, chapter, and section.

10. Plato, *Symposium*, ed. Alexander Nehamas and Paul Woodruff (Indianapolis: Hackett, 1989), 201e, 201d.

11. The citations of this paragraph appear elsewhere at key moments throughout my study and therefore are provided here in parenthetical reference as a means to showcase more explicitly how they might now be interwoven in this final reflection.

12. Miguel de Cervantes, *The History of That Ingenious Gentleman Don Quijote de La Mancha*, trans. Burton Raffel (New York: Norton: 1995), 682.

13. Ortega y Gasset, "Asamblea," 1:101. See my earlier discussion of this passage in the concluding pages of chapter 1.

14. Fyodor Dostoevsky, *Notes from Underground*, trans. Michael R. Katz (New York: Norton, 1989), 5.

15. Derrida, *Of Grammatology*.

16. Giovanni Pascoli, *L'èra nuova: Pensieri e discorsi* (Milan: EGEA, 1994).

17. Charles Baudelaire, *The Flowers of Evil* (Oxford: Oxford University Press, 1993), 119.

18. Italo Svevo, "L'uomo e la teoria darwiniana," in *Zeno*, ed. Mario Lavagetto (Turin: Einaudi, 1987), 832.

19. Benedict de Spinoza, *Ethics*, ed. and trans. G. H. R. Parkinson (Oxford: Oxford University Press, 2000), 241.

20. Virginia Woolf, *Killing the Angel in the House: Seven Essays* (London: Penguin, 1995), 4.

21. Augustine, *On Free Choice of the Will*, ed. Thomas Williams (Indianapolis: Hackett, 1993).

22. Leopoldo Alas (Clarín), "La perfecta casada," in *Relatos sueltos y narraciones incompletas*, vol. 3 of *Obras completas*, ed. Santos Sanz Villanueva (Madrid: Castro, 2003), 671.

23. Leopoldo Alas (Clarín), "La imperfecta casada," in *Cuentos morales*, vol. 2 of *Obras completas*, ed. Santos Sanz Villanueva (Madrid: Castro, 1995), 612.

Alas, Genaro. *El darwinismo: Conferencias pronunciadas en el Casino de Oviedo en los días 25 de febrero, 4 y 11 de marzo de 1887.* Ed. Francisco García Sarría. Exeter: University of Exeter Press, 1978.

Alas, Leopoldo [Clarín]. "El amor y la economía." 1879. In *Clarín político: Leopoldo Alas (Clarín), periodista, frente a la problemática política y social de la España de su tiempo (1875–1901)—Estudio y Antología.* Ed. Yvan Lissorgues. Vol. 1. Toulouse: Institut d'Etudes Hispaniques et Hispano-Américaines, 1980. 126–31.

———. "La imperfecta casada." In *Cuentos morales.* 1896. Vol. 2 of *Obras completas.* Ed. Santos Sanz Villanueva. Madrid: Castro, 1995. 607–12.

———. "Las literatas." 1879. In *Clarín político: Leopoldo Alas (Clarín), periodista, frente a la problemática política y social de la España de su tiempo (1875–1901) Estudio y Antología.* Ed. Yvan Lissorgues. Vol. 1. Barcelona: Lumen, 1989. 231–35.

———. "La perfecta casada." N.d. In *Relatos sueltos y narraciones incompletas.* Vol. 3 of *Obras completas.* Ed. Santos Sanz Villanueva. Madrid: Castro, 2003. 669–72.

———. *La Regenta.* 1884–85. Ed. Juan Oleza. 2 vols. Madrid: Cátedra, 1994.

———. *Su único hijo.* 1890. Ed. Carolyn Richmond. Madrid: Espasa-Calpe, 1979.

Aldaraca, Bridget. *El ángel del hogar: Galdós and the Ideology of Domesticity in Spain.* Chapel Hill: University of North Carolina, Department of Romance Languages, 1991.

Allen, Cran. "Un adversario de la evolución." Trans. anon. *Revista Contemporánea* 21, no. 4 (June 30, 1879): 474–79.

Allison, George H., and Joan Connelly Ullman. "Galdós as Psychiatrist in *Fortunata y Jacinta.*" *Anales galdosianos* 9 (1974): 7–36.

———. "The Intuitive Psychoanalytic Perspective of Galdós in *Fortunata and Jacinta*." *International Journal of Psycho-Analysis* 55 (1974): 333–43.

Alter, Stephen. *Darwinism and the Linguistic Image: Language, Race, and Natural Theology in the Nineteenth Century.* Baltimore: Johns Hopkins University Press, 1999.

Alvarez-Uría, Fernando. *Miserables y locos: Medicina mental y orden social en la España del siglo XIX.* Barcelona: Tusquets Editores, 1983.

Amann, Elizabeth. "Metaphor, Metonymy, and Inheritance: Representing Revolution in Galdós's *La desheredada*." *Revista de Estudios Hispánicos* 37 (2003): 437–62.

Andersson, M. B. *Sexual Selection.* Princeton, N.J.: Princeton University Press, 1994.

Andreu, Alicia G. *Galdós y la literatura popular.* Madrid: Sociedad General Española, 1982.

Aristotle. *De Poetica.* In *The Basic Works of Aristotle.* Ed. Richard McKeon. New York: Modern Library, 2001.

Armstrong, Nancy. *Desire and Domestic Fiction: A Political History of the Novel.* Oxford: Oxford University Press, 1987.

Auerbach, Erich. *Mimesis: The Representation of Reality in Western Literature.* Trans. Willard R. Trask. Princeton, N.J.: Princeton University Press, 2003.

Augustine. *On Free Choice of the Will.* Ed. Thomas Williams. Indianapolis: Hackett, 1993.

Ayala, Francisco J. *Darwin's Gift to Science and Religion.* Washington, D.C.: John Henry Press, 2007.

Baguley, David. *Naturalist Fiction: The Entropic Vision.* Cambridge: Cambridge University Press, 1990.

Bakhtin, Mikhail. *The Dialogic Imagination: Four Essays.* Ed. Michael Holquist. Trans. Caryl Emerson and Michael Holquist. Austin: University of Texas Press, 1981.

Baquero Goyanes, Mariano. *La novela naturalista española: Emilia Pardo Bazán.* Murcia: Universidad de Murcia, 1986.

Barash, David, and Nanelle Barash. *Madame Bovary's Ovaries: A Darwinian Look at Literature.* New York: Delacorte, 2005.

Barroso, Fernando J. *El naturalismo en la Pardo Bazán.* Madrid: Playor, 1973.

Bataille, Georges. *Death and Sensuality: A Study of Eroticism and the Taboo.* New York: Arno, 1977.

Baudelaire, Charles. *The Flowers of Evil.* 1857. Oxford: Oxford University Press, 1993.

Bauer, Beth Wietelmann. "*Marta y María*: Romanticismo y misticismo en Palacio Valdés." In *Estudios sobre Armando Palacio Valdés*. Ed. Brian J. Dendle and Stephen Miller. Ottawa Hispanic Studies 14. Ottawa: Dovehouse, 1993. 24–35.

———. "Narrative Cross-Dressing: Emilia Pardo Bazán in *Memorias de un solterón*." *Hispania* 77, no. 1 (1994): 23–30.

———."Something Lost: Translation, Transaction, and Travesty in Clarín's *Su único hijo*." *Revista Hispánica Moderna* 48 (1995): 92–105.

Beauvoir, Simone de. *The Second Sex*. New York: Knopf, 1976.

Becker, George J., ed. *Documents of Modern Literary Realism*. Princeton, N.J.: Princeton University Press, 1963.

Beer, Gillian. *Darwin's Plots: Evolutionary Narrative in Darwin, George Eliot, and Nineteenth-Century Fiction*. Cambridge: Cambridge University Press, 2000.

———. "Problems of Description in the Language of Discovery." In *One Culture: Essays in Science and Literature*. Ed. George Levine. Madison: University of Wisconsin Press, 1987. 35–58.

Bell, Catherine. *Ritual Theory, Ritual Practice*. New York: Oxford University Press, 1992.

Bell, T. E. *Galdós and Darwin*. Rochester, N.Y.: Tamesis, 2006.

Bender, Bert. *The Descent of Love: Darwin and the Theory of Sexual Selection in American Fiction, 1871–1926*. Philadelphia: University of Pennsylvania Press, 1996.

Bennett, Tony. *Outside Literature*. London: Routledge, 1990.

Berkowitz, H. Chonon. *La biblioteca de Benito Pérez Galdós: Catálogo razonado*. Las Palmas, Canaries: El Museo Canario, 1951.

Bieder, Maryellen. "Capitulation: Marriage, Not Freedom; A Study of Emilia Pardo Bazán's *Memorias de un solterón* and Galdós' *Tristana*." *Symposium* 30, no. 2 (1976): 93–109.

———. "En-gendering Strategies of Authority: Emilia Pardo Bazán and the Novel." In *Cultural and Historical Grounding for Hispanic and Luso-Brazilian Feminist Literary Criticism*. Ed. Hernán Vidal. Minneapolis: Institute for the Study of Ideologies and Literature, 1989. 173–96.

Birken, Lawrence. "Darwin and Gender." *Proteus* 6 (1989): 24–29.

Blake, William. *The Complete Poetry and Prose of William Blake*. Ed. David Erdman. New York: Anchor, 1988.

Blanco, Alda. "Gender and National Identity: The Novel in Nineteenth-Century Spanish Literary History." In *Culture and Gender in Nineteenth-Century Spain*. Ed. Lou Charnon-Deutsch and Jo Labanyi. Oxford: Clarendon, 1995. 120–36.

Bloch, Maurice. *Ritual, History, and Power: Selected Papers in Anthropology.* London: Athlone, 1989.

Bloom, Harold. *Shakespeare: The Invention of the Human.* New York: Riverhead, 1998.

Bly, Peter. "*La fe*: Palacio Valdés Looks Back to Alas and Forward to Unamuno." *Romance Quarterly* 35 (1988): 339–46.

Bono, James. "Science, Discourse, and Literature: The Role/Rule of Metaphor in Science." In *Literature and Science: Theory and Practice.* Ed. Stuart Peterfreund. Boston: Northeastern University Press, 1990. 59–90.

Bourdieu, Pierre. *Outline of a Theory of Practice.* Cambridge: Cambridge University Press, 1977.

Bowler, Peter J. *The Non-Darwinian Revolution: Reinterpreting a Historical Myth.* Baltimore: Johns Hopkins University Press, 1988.

Bretz, Mary Lee. "Text and Intertext in Emilia Pardo Bazán's *Memorias de un solterón.*" *Symposium* 43, no. 2 (1989): 83–94.

———. *Voices, Silences, and Echoes: A Theory of the Essays and the Critical Reception of Naturalism in Spain.* London: Tamesis, 1992.

Brontë, Emily. *Wuthering Heights.* 1847. Ed. Richard J. Dunn. New York: Norton, 2002.

Brooks, Peter. *The Melodramatic Imagination: Balzac, Henry James, Melodrama, and the Mode of Excess.* New York: Columbia University Press, 1985.

———. *Reading for the Plot: Design and Intention in Narrative.* New York: Knopf, 1984.

———. *Troubling Confessions: Speaking Guilt in Law and Literature.* Chicago: University of Chicago Press, 2000.

Brown, M. Gordon. "La condesa de Pardo Bazán y el naturalismo." *Hispania* 31, no. 2 (1948): 152–56.

Brown, Marshall. "The Logic of Realism: A Hegelian Approach." *PMLA* 96 (1981): 224–41.

Brunetière, Ferdinand. *Le roman naturaliste.* Paris: Calmann Lévy, 1896.

Buqueras, Francisco Javier. *La asistencia psiquiátrica y la sanidad militar española en el siglo XIX.* Barcelona: Espaxs Publicaciones Medicas, 1992.

Calderón de la Barca, Pedro. *La vida es sueño.* Ed. José María García Martín. Madrid: Castalia, 1984.

Camus, Albert. *The Myth of Sisyphus and Other Essays.* Trans. Justin O'Brien. New York: Vintage, 1991.

Caro, Elme Marie. "La democracia ante la moral del porvenir: Las nuevas teorías acerca del derecho natural." [*Revue de Deux Mondes.*] Trans. anon. *Revista Europea* 6, no. 95 (December 19, 1875): 253–64.

———. "La moral sin metafísica." [*Edinburgh Review.*] Trans. Armando Palacio Valdés. *Revista Europea* 8, no. 143 (November 19, 1876): 641–49.

Carr, Raymond. *Spain, 1808–1975*. Oxford: Oxford University Press, 1982.

Carrau, L. "El darwinismo y la moral." *Revista Europea* 13, no. 257 (January 26, 1879): 97–99.

Carroll, Joseph. *Evolution and Literary Theory*. Columbia: University of Missouri Press, 1995.

———. *Literary Darwinism: Evolution, Human Nature, and Literature*. New York: Routledge, 2004.

Cartwright, John H., and Brian Baker. *Literature and Science: Social Impact and Interaction*. Santa Barbara, Calif.: ABC-CLIO, 2005.

Casanova, Giacomo. *History of My Life*. 1794. Trans. Willard R. Trask. 2 vols. Baltimore: Johns Hopkins University Press, 1997.

Cassirer, Ernst. *An Essay on Man: An Introduction to a Philosophy of Human Culture*. New Haven, Conn.: Yale University Press, 1944.

Castro, Américo. Prologue to *Cinco ensayos sobre Don Juan*. Santiago, Chile: Cultura, 1937. 1–24.

Caudet, Francisco. "La querella naturalista: España contra Francia." *Ojancano* 2 (1989): 3–16.

Cervantes, Miguel de. *The History of That Ingenious Gentleman Don Quijote de La Mancha*. Trans. Burton Raffel. New York: Norton: 1995.

Chadwick, Owen. *The Secularization of the European Mind in the Nineteenth Century*. Cambridge: Cambridge University Press, 1975.

Charnon-Deutsch, Lou. "Feíta's Decision: Pardo Bazán's Exploration of Female Identity in *Memorias de un solterón.*" *Discurso* 11, no. 1 (1993): 25–50.

———. *Gender and Representation: Women in Spanish Realist Fiction*. Amsterdam: John Benjamins, 1990.

———. *Narratives of Desire: Nineteenth-Century Spanish Fiction by Women*. University Park, Pa.: Penn State University Press, 1994.

Charnon-Deutsch, Lou, and Jo Labanyi, eds. *Culture and Gender in Nineteenth-Century Spain*. Oxford: Clarendon, 1995.

Christie, John, and Sally Shuttleworth, eds. *Nature Transfigured: Science and Literature, 1700–1900*. Manchester: Manchester University Press, 1989.

Cinco ensayos sobre Don Juan. Santiago, Chile: Cultura, 1937.

Ciplijauskaité, Birute. "El romanticismo como hipotexto en el realismo." In *Realismo y naturalismo en España en la segunda mitad del siglo XIX*. Ed. Yvan Lissorgues. Barcelona: Antropos, 1988. 90–98.

Civello, Paul. "Evolutionary Feminism, Popular Romance, and Frank Norris's 'Man's Woman.'" *Studies in American Fiction* 24 (1996): 23–44.

Clèmessy, Nelly. *Emilia Pardo Bazán como novelista (de la teoría a la práctica)*. Trans. Irene Gambra. 2 vols. Madrid: Fundación Universitaria Española, 1981.

Cohen, Margaret. *The Sentimental Education of the Novel*. Princeton, N.J.: Princeton University Press, 1999.

Cohen, Ralph. "Genre Theory, Literary History, and Historical Change." In *Theoretical Issues in Literary History*. Ed. David Perkins. Cambridge, Mass.: Harvard University Press, 1991. 85–113.

Conry, Yvette. *L'introduction du Darwinisme en France au XIXe siècle*. Paris: Librairie Philosophique, 1974.

Cordón, Faustino, ed. "El darwinismo en España: En el 1er centenario de la muerte de Charles Darwin (1882–1982); Aportación innovadora de Faustino Cordón a la teoría evolucionista." Special issue, *Anthropos: Boletín de Información y Documentación*, nos. 16–17 (1982).

Correa Ramón, Amelina. *Alejandro Sawa: Luces de bohemia*. Seville: Fundación José Manuel Lara, 2008.

———. *Alejandro Sawa y el naturalismo literario*. Granada: Universidad de Granada, 1993.

Cosslett, Tess. *The "Scientific Movement" and Victorian Literature*. Sussex: Harvester, 1982.

Croce, Benedetto. *Estetica come scienza dell'espressione e linguistica generale (teoria e storia)*. Ed. Giuseppe Galasso. Milan: Adelphi, 1990.

Cronin, Helena. *The Ant and the Peacock: Altruism and Sexual Selection from Darwin to Today*. Cambridge: Cambridge University Press, 1991.

Damrosch, David. *What Is World Literature?* Princeton, N.J.: Princeton University Press, 2003.

D'Annunzio, Gabriele. *Trionfo della morte*. 1894. Milan: Mondadori, 1983.

Darwin, Charles. *De l'origine des espèces, ou des lois du progrès chez les êtres organisés*. Trans. and with preface by Clémence Royer. Paris: Guillaumin and V. Masson, 1862.

———. *La descendance de l'homme et la sélection sexuelle*. Trans. Jean-Jacques Moulinié. Preface by Carl Vogt. Paris: Reinwald, 1872.

———. *La descendencia del hombre y la selección en relación al sexo*. Trans. José del Perojo and Enrique Camps. Madrid: Administración de la Revista de Medicina y Cirugía Prácticas (Rivadeneyra), 1885.

———. *The Descent of Man, and Selection in Relation to Sex*. 1871. Introduction by John Tyler Bonner and Robert M. May. Princeton, N.J.: Princeton University Press, 1981.

———. *On the Origin of Species*. 1859. Cambridge, Mass.: Harvard University Press, 2001.

————. *Origen de las especies: Por medio de la selección natural ó la con-servación de las razas favorecidas en la lucha por la existencia*. Trans. Enrique Godínez. Madrid: José de Rojas, 1873.

————. *Origen de las especies por medio de la selección natural ó la conser-vación de las razas favorecidas en la lucha por la existencia*. Trans. Enri-que Godínez. Madrid: Perojo, 1877.

————. *Origen de las especies por selección natural: O resumen de las leyes de transformación de los seres organizados (con dos prefacios de Madame Clemencia Royer)*. Trans. anon. Biblioteca social, histórica y filosófica. Madrid: Jacobo María Luengo, 1872.

————. *El origen del hombre: La selección natural y la sexual (primera ver-sión española)*. Trans. and with an introduction by [Joaquim Bartrina]. Barcelona: Renaixensa, 1876.

————. *El origen del hombre y la selección en relación al sexo*. Introduction by Faustino Cordón. Madrid: Edaf, 2006.

Daston, Lorraine. "Fear and Loathing of the Imagination in Science." In *Science in Culture*. Ed. Peter Galison, Stephen R. Graubard, and Everett Mendelsohn. London: Transaction, 2001. 73–95.

Davis, Gifford. "Catholicism and Naturalism: Pardo Bazán's Reply to Zola." *Modern Language Notes* 90, no. 2 (1975): 282–87.

Dawkins, Richard. *The Selfish Gene*. Oxford: Oxford University Press, 2006.

Defoe, Daniel. *Conjugal Lewdness, or Matrimonial Whoredom: A Treatise concerning the Use and Abuse of the Marriage Bed*. 1727. Menston, Eng-land: Scolar, 1970.

Deleuze, Gilles, and Félix Guattari. *Anti-Oedipus: Capitalism and Schizo-phrenia*. New York: Viking, 1972.

Delgado Criado, Manuel. "Los primeros años del manicomio modelo de Leganés (1852–1871)." *Asclepio* 38 (1986): 273–97.

Dendle, Brian J. *Spain's Forgotten Novelist: Armando Palacio Valdés (1853–1938)*. Lewisburg, Pa.: Bucknell University Press, 1995.

Dennett, Daniel. *Darwin's Dangerous Idea: Evolution and the Meaning of Life*. New York: Simon and Schuster, 1995.

De Quincey, Thomas. *Confessions of an English Opium-Eater*. 1821. Lon-don: Penguin, 2003.

Derrida, Jacques. *Of Grammatology*. Trans. Gayatri Chakravorty Spivak. Baltimore: Johns Hopkins University Press, 1974.

Desmond, Adrian, and James Moore. *Darwin*. New York: Warner Books, 1991.

Dijkstra, Bram. *Idols of Perversity: Fantasies of Feminine Evil in Fin-de-Siècle Culture*. New York: Oxford University Press, 1986.

Dostoevsky, Fyodor. *Notes from Underground.* Trans. Michael R. Katz. New York: Norton, 1989.

DuPont, Denise. *Realism as Resistance: Romanticism and Authorship in Galdós, Clarín, and Baroja.* Lewisburg, Pa.: Bucknell University Press, 2006. 173–220.

Durand, Frank. "The Reality of Illusion: *La desheredada.*" *Modern Language Notes* 89 (1974): 191–201.

———. "Structure and the Drama of Role-Playing in *La Regenta.*" In *"Malevolent Insemination" and Other Essays on Clarín.* Ed. Noël Valis. Ann Arbor: University of Michigan, Department of Romance Languages, 1990. 141–54.

Durant, John R. "The Ascent of Nature in Darwin's *Descent of Man.*" In *The Darwinian Heritage.* Ed. David Kohn. Princeton, N.J.: Princeton University Press, 1985. 283–306.

Eliot, George. "The Natural History of German Life." 1856. In *Essays of George Eliot.* Ed. Thomas Pinney. New York: Columbia University Press, 1963. 266-99.

Endersby, Jim. "Darwin on Generation, Pangenesis, and Sexual Selection." In *The Cambridge Companion to Darwin.* Ed. Jonathan Hodge and Gregory Radick. Cambridge: Cambridge University Press, 2003. 69–91.

Engels, Eve-Marie, and Thomas Glick, eds. *The Reception of Charles Darwin in Europe.* 2 vols. London: Continuum, 2009.

Engels, Friedrich. *The Origin of the Family, Private Property, and the State in the Light of the Researches of Lewis H. Morgan.* 1891. New York: International, 1942.

Espinosa Iborra, Julián. *La asistencia psiquiátrica en la España del siglo XIX.* Valencia: Cátedra e Instituto de Historia de la Medicina, 1966.

Estassen, Pedro. "Contribución al estudio de la evolución de las instituciones religiosas o materiales para llegar a la síntesis transformista de las instituciones humanas: La religiosidad en los animales." *Revista Contemporánea* 13, no. 1 (January 15, 1878): 62–74.

Estébanez Calderón, Demetrio. "Naturaleza y sociedad: Claves para una interpretación de *Fortunata y Jacinta.*" In *Textos y contextos de Galdós: Actos del Simposio Centenario de* Fortunata y Jacinta. Ed. John W. Kronik and Harriet S. Turner. Madrid: Castalia, 1994. 81–90.

Ezama Gil, Ángeles. "El profeminismo en los cuentos de Picón." In *Actas del IX Simposio de la Sociedad Española de Literatura General y Comparada.* Vol. 1. Ed. Túa Blesa et al. Saragossa: Universidad de Zaragoza, 1994. 171–78.

Fabiani, Paolo. *La filosofia dell'immaginazione in Vico e Malebranche.* Florence: Università di Firenze, 2002.

Fabié, Antonio María. "Exámen del materialismo moderno." *Revista Europea* 3, no. 43 (December 20, 1874): 225–29.

Fernández, Pura. *Eduardo López Bago y el naturalismo radical: La novela y el mercado literario en el siglo XIX*. Amsterdam: Rodopi, 1995.

Fisher, R. A. *The Genetical Theory of Natural Selection*. 1915. Oxford: Oxford University Press, 1999.

Flesch, William. *Comeuppance: Costly Signaling, Altruistic Punishment, and Other Biological Components of Fiction*. Cambridge, Mass.: Harvard University Press, 2007.

Fontane, Theodor. *Effi Briest*. 1896. Ed. Hugh Rorrison and Helen Chambers. London: Penguin, 2001.

Foucault, Michel. *The History of Sexuality*. Vol. 1, *An Introduction*. Trans. Robert Hurley. New York: Random House, 1978.

———. *Religion and Culture*. Ed. Jeremy R. Carrette. New York: Routledge, 1999.

Fraad, Harriet, Stephen A. Resnick, and Richard D. Wolff. *Bringing It All Back Home: Class, Gender, and Power in the Modern Household*. London: Pluto, 1994.

Freud, Sigmund. "Family Romances." 1909. In *The Standard Edition of the Complete Psychological Works of Sigmund Freud*. Vol. 9. Ed. and trans. James Strachey, with Anna Freud, Alix Strachey, and Alan Tyson. London: Hogarth, 1959. 235–42.

Frow, John. *Marxism and Literary History*. Cambridge, Mass.: Harvard University Press, 1986.

Frye, Northrop. *Anatomy of Criticism: Four Essays*. Princeton, N.J.: Princeton University Press, 1990.

———. *Fearful Symmetry*. Princeton, N.J.: Princeton University Press, 1947.

———. *The Secular Scripture: A Study of the Structure of Romance*. Cambridge, Mass.: Harvard University Press, 1976.

García Barrón, Carlos. *Vida, obra y pensamiento de Manuel de la Revilla*. Madrid: Turanzas, 1987.

García Camarero, Ernesto, and Enrique García Camarero. *La polémica de la ciencia espanola*. Madrid: Alianza, 1970.

Garlock, David. "Entangled Genders: Plasticity, Indeterminacy, and Constructs of Sexuality in Darwin and Hardy." *Dickens Study Annual* 27 (1998): 287–305.

Gay, Peter. *The Bourgeois Experience: Victoria to Freud*. Vol. 1 of *Education of the Senses*. New York: Norton, 1984.

Gendarme de Bévotte, Georges. *La légende de Don Juan: Son évolution dans la littérature des origines au romantisme*. Geneva: Slatkine, 1993.

Gener, Pompeyo. *Literaturas malsanas: Estudios de patología literaria contemporánea.* Madrid: F. Fé, 1894.

Gilbert, Sandra, and Susan Gubar. *The Madwoman in the Attic: The Woman Writer and the Nineteenth-Century Literary Imagination.* New Haven, Conn.: Yale University Press, 1979.

Giles, Mary E. "Feminism and the Feminine in Emilia Pardo Bazán's Novels." *Hispania* 63, no. 2 (1980): 356–67.

Gilman, Charlotte Perkins. *Herland.* New York: Pantheon, 1979.

Girard, René. *Deceit, Desire, and the Novel: Self and Other in Literary Structure.* Trans. Yvonne Freccero. Baltimore: Johns Hopkins University Press, 1965.

———. *Violence and the Sacred.* Trans. Patrick Gregory. Baltimore: Johns Hopkins University Press, 1979.

Glick, Thomas. *Darwin en España.* Barcelona: Península, 1982.

———. "Spain." In *The Comparative Reception of Darwinism.* Ed. Thomas Glick. Austin: University of Texas Press, 1972. 307–45.

Gluckman, Max, ed. *Essays on the Ritual of Social Relations.* Manchester: Manchester University Press, 1962.

Godwin, William. *Enquiry concerning Political Justice and Its Influence on General Virtue and Happiness.* 1793. Reprinted in *Caleb Williams.* By William Godwin. Ed. Gary Handwerk and A. A. Markley. Ontario: Broadview, 2000. 483–97.

———. "Of History and Romance." 1797. In *Political and Philosophical Writings.* Ed. Pamela Clemit. 5 vols. London: Pickering and Chatto, 1993. Reprinted in *Caleb Williams.* By William Godwin. Ed. Gary Handwerk and A. A. Markley. Ontario: Broadview, 2000. 453–67. Page references are to the reprinted essay.

Gold, Hazel. "'Ni soltera, ni viuda, ni casada': Negación y exclusión en las novelas femeninas de Jacinto Octavio Picón." *Ideologies and Literature: Journal of Hispanic and Lusophone Discourse Analysis* 4, no. 17 (1983): 63–77.

———. *The Reframing of Realism: Galdós and the Discourses of the Nineteenth-Century Spanish Novel.* Durham, N.C.: Duke University Press, 1993.

Goncharov, Ivan. *Oblomov.* 1859. Ed. David Magarshack and Milton Ehre. London: Penguin, 2005.

Goncourt, Edmond de, and Jules de Goncourt. *Germinie Lacerteux.* 1864. Ed. Ernst Boyd. New York: A. A. Knopf, 1922.

———. "On True Novels." 1865. In *Documents of Modern Literary Realism.* Ed. George J. Becker. Princeton, N.J.: Princeton University Press, 1963. 117–19.

González Herrán, José Manuel. "Emilia Pardo Bazán y el naturalismo." *Ínsula* 44 (1989): 17–18.

González Marmolejo, Jorge René. "Confesores y mujeres en el obispado de Puebla, siglo XVIII." In *El placer de pecar y el afán de normar: Seminario de historia de las mentalidades.* Ed. Joaquín Mortiz. Mexico City: Instituto Nacional de Antropología e Historia, 1987. 147–66.

Gottschall, Jonathan, and David Sloan Wilson, eds. *The Literary Animal: Evolution and the Nature of Narrative.* Evanston, Ill.: Northwestern University Press, 2005.

Gould, Stephen Jay. *Ever since Darwin: Reflections in Natural History.* New York: Norton, 1977.

Gowaty, Patricia Adair. "Introduction: Darwinian Feminists and Feminist Evolutionists." In *Feminism and Evolutionary Biology: Boundaries, Intersections, and Frontiers.* Ed. Patricia Adair Gowaty. New York: Chapman and Hall, 1997. 1-19.

Gross, Alan. *The Rhetoric of Science.* Cambridge, Mass.: Harvard University Press, 1990.

Grosz, Elizabeth. *The Nick of Time: Politics, Evolution, and the Untimely.* Durham, N.C.: Duke University Press, 2004.

———. *Time Travels: Feminism, Nature, Power.* Durham, N.C.: Duke University Press, 2005.

Haeckel, Ernst. "Emigración y distribución de los organismos: La corología y la edad glacial de la tierra." Trans. Claudio Cuveiro. *Revista Europea* 12, no. 242 (October 13, 1878): 467–76.

———. "La selección natural verificada por la lucha por la existencia, la división del trabajo, y el progreso." Trans. Claudio Cuveiro. *Revista Europea* 12, no. 238 (September 15, 1878): 334–44.

———. "Teorías evolutivas de Lyell y de Darwin." Trans. Claudio Cuveiro. *Revista Europea* 12, no. 233 (August 11, 1878): 174–83.

Hafter, Monroe Z. "Galdós' Presentation of Isidora in *La desheredada.*" *Modern Philology* 60 (1962): 22–30.

Haliczer, Stephen. *Sexuality in the Confessional: A Sacrament Profaned.* Oxford: Oxford University Press, 1996.

Handelman, Don. "Introduction: Why Ritual in Its Own Right? How So?" In *Ritual in Its Own Right: Exploring the Dynamics of Transformation.* Ed. Don Handelman and Galina Lindquist. New York: Berghahn, 2004. 1–34.

Handwerk, Gary. *Irony and Ethics in Narrative: From Schlegel to Lacan.* New Haven, Conn.: Yale University Press, 1985.

Harding, Sandra. *The Science Question in Feminism.* Ithaca, N.Y.: Cornell University Press, 1986.

Hardy, Thomas. *Tess of the d'Urbervilles.* 1891. London: Penguin, 2003.

Hartmann, Eduard von. "Ernesto Häckel." [*Deutsche Rundschau*.] Trans. anon. *Revista Europea* 7, no. 106 (March 5, 1876): 7–15.

———. "La filosofía pesimista." [*Westminster Review*.] Trans. [R. M.]. *Revista Contemporánea* 1, no. 5 (February 15, 1876): 93–112.

Hartsock, Nancy C. M. "The Feminist Standpoint: Toward a Specifically Feminist Historical Materialism." In *Feminist Theory Reader: Local and Global Perspectives*. Ed. Carole R. McCann and Seung-Kyung Kim. New York: Routledge, 2003. 292–307.

Hayles, N. Katherine. *Chaos and Order: Complex Dynamics in Literature and Science*. Chicago: University of Chicago Press, 1991.

Heath, Stephen. *The Sexual Fix*. London: Macmillan, 1982.

Hemingway, Maurice. "Emilia Pardo Bazán: Narrative Strategies and the Critique of Naturalism." In *Naturalism in the European Novel: New Critical Perspectives*. Ed. Brian Nelson. New York: Berg, 1992. 135–50.

———. *Emilia Pardo Bazán: The Making of a Novelist*. Cambridge: Cambridge University Press, 1983.

———. "Naturalism and Decadence in Zola's *La Faute de l'abbé Mouret* and Pardo Bazán's *La madre naturaleza*." *Revue de Litterature Comparee* 61, no. 1 (1987): 31–46.

Hodge, Jonathan, and Gregory Radick, eds. *The Cambridge Companion to Darwin*. Cambridge: Cambridge University Press, 2003.

Hoeg, Jerry, and Kevin Larsen, eds. *Interdisciplinary Essays on Darwinism in Hispanic Literature and Film: The Intersection of Science and the Humanities*. New York: Mellen, 2009.

Irigaray, Luce. *This Sex Which Is Not One*. Ithaca, N.Y.: Cornell University Press, 1985.

Jaffe, Catherine. "Mothers and Orphans in *La desheredada*." *Confluencia: Revista Hispánica de Cultura y Literatura* 5 (1990): 27–38.

Jagoe, Catherine. *Ambiguous Angels: Gender in the Novels of Galdós*. Berkeley: University of California Press, 1994.

Jagoe, Catherine, Alda Blanco, and Cristina Enríquez de Salamanca, eds. *La mujer en los discursos de género: Textos y contextos en el siglo XIX*. Barcelona: Icaria, 1998.

James, William. *The Varieties of Religious Experience: A Study in Human Nature*. 1902. New York: University Books, 1963.

Jameson, Fredric. *The Political Unconscious: Narrative as a Socially Symbolic Act*. Ithaca, N.Y.: Cornell University Press, 1981.

Jordanova, L. J., ed. *Languages of Nature: Critical Essays on Science and Literature*. New Brunswick, N.J.: Rutgers University Press, 1986.

Kapferer, Bruce. "Ritual Dynamics and Virtual Practice: Beyond Representation and Meaning." In *Ritual in Its Own Right: Exploring the Dynamics of Transformation*. Ed. Don Handelman and Galina Lindquist. New York: Berghahn, 2004. 35–54.

Kaplan, Caren, Norma Alarcón, and Minoo Moallem, eds. *Between Woman and Nation: Nationalisms, Transnational Feminisms, and the State*. Durham, N.C.: Duke University Press, 1999.

Keller, Evelyn Fox. *Reflections on Gender and Science*. New Haven, Conn.: Yale University Press, 1985.

Kierkegaard, Søren. *The Concept of Irony, with Continual Reference to Socrates*. Ed. and trans. Howard V. Hong and Edna H. Hong. Kierkegaard's Writings, 2. Princeton, N.J.: Princeton University Press, 1989.

———. *Either/Or*. Ed. and trans. Howard V. Hong and Edna H. Hong. 2 vols. Kierkegaard's Writings, 3. Princeton, N.J.: Princeton University Press, 1987.

Kirkpatrick, Susan. "The Female Tradition in Nineteenth-Century Spanish Literature." In *Cultural and Historical Grounding for Hispanic and Luso-Brazilian Feminist Literary Criticism*. Ed. Hernán Vidal. Minneapolis: Institute for the Study of Ideologies and Literature, 1989. 343–70.

Krauel, Ricardo. *Voces desde el silencio: Heterologías genérico-sexuales en la narrativa española moderna (1875–1975)*. Barcelona: Libertarias, 2001.

Kristeva, Julia. *Desire in Language: A Semiotic Approach to Literature and Art*. New York: Columbia University Press, 1980.

Kronik, John W. "Feijoo and the Fabrication of Fortunata." In *Conflicting Realities: Four Readings of a Chapter by Pérez Galdós (*Fortunata y Jacinta, *Part III, Chapter IV)*. Ed. Peter B. Goldman. London: Tamesis, 1984. 39–72.

Kropotkin, Peter. *Mutual Aid: A Factor of Evolution*. 1902. Washington, D.C.: Counterpoint, 2001.

Kuhn, Thomas S. *The Structure of Scientific Revolutions*. Chicago: University of Chicago Press, 1962.

Labanyi, Jo. *Gender and Modernization in the Spanish Realist Novel*. Oxford: Oxford University Press, 2000.

Lacan, Jacques. *The Seminar of Jacques Lacan*. Bk. 1, *Freud's Papers on Technique, 1953–1954*. Ed. Jacques-Alain Miller. Trans. John Forrester. New York: Norton, 1991.

———. *The Seminar of Jacques Lacan*. Bk. 2, *The Ego in Freud's Theory and in the Technique of Psychoanalysis, 1954–1955*. Ed. Jacques-Alain Miller. Trans. Sylvana Tomaselli. New York: Norton, 1991.

———. *The Seminar of Jacques Lacan*. Bk. 3, *The Psychoses, 1955–1956*. Ed. Jacques-Alain Miller. Trans. Russell Grigg. New York: Norton, 1997.

──────. *The Seminar of Jacques Lacan*. Bk. 7, *The Ethics of Psychoanalysis, 1959–1960*. Ed. Jacques-Alain Miller. Trans. Dennis Porter. New York: Norton, 1997.

Lambert, Helen H. "Biology and Equality: A Perspective on Sex Differences." In *Sex and Scientific Inquiry*. Ed. Sandra Harding and Jean F. O'Barr. Chicago: University of Chicago Press, 1975. 125–46.

Langbauer, Laurie. *Women and Romance: The Consolations of Gender in the English Novel*. Ithaca, N.Y.: Cornell University Press, 1990.

Laqueur, Thomas. *Making Sex: Body and Gender from the Greeks to Freud*. Cambridge, Mass.: Harvard University Press, 1990.

Lasaga Medina, José. *Las metamorfosis del seductor: Ensayo sobre el mito de Don Juan*. Madrid: Síntesis, 2004.

Latour, Bruno. *Pandora's Hope: Essays on the Reality of Science Studies*. Cambridge, Mass.: Harvard University Press, 1999.

Lévinas, Emmanuel. *Ethics and Infinity: Conversations with Philippe Nemo*. Trans. Richard A. Cohen. Pittsburgh: Duquesne University Press, 1985.

Levine, George. *Darwin and the Novelists: Patterns of Science in Victorian Literature*. Cambridge, Mass.: Harvard University Press, 1988.

──────. "One Culture: Science and Literature." In *One Culture: Essays in Science and Literature*. Ed. George Levine. Madison: University of Wisconsin Press, 1987. 3–34.

Lévi-Strauss, Claude. *The Naked Man*. Vol. 4 of *Mythologiques*. Chicago: Chicago University Press, 1981.

──────. *The Savage Mind*. Chicago: Chicago University Press, 1966.

Levitin, Daniel J. *This Is Your Brain on Music: The Science of a Human Obsession*. New York: Plume, 2006.

Lindberg, David C. *The Beginnings of Western Science: The European Scientific Tradition in Philosophical, Religious, and Institutional Context, 600 B.C. to A.D. 1450*. Chicago: University of Chicago Press, 1992.

Lissorgues, Yvan. "El naturalismo radical: Eduardo López Bago (y Alejandro Sawa)." In *Realismo y naturalismo en España en la segunda mitad del siglo XIX*. Ed. Yvan Lissorgues. Barcelona: Anthropos, 1988. 237–56.

──────, ed. *Realismo y naturalismo en España en la segunda mitad del siglo XIX*. Barcelona: Anthropos, 1988.

Livingston, Noyles B., III. "Darwin, Nietzsche, and Freud: The Evolutionary Link between Biology, Philosophy, and Psychology." *Journal of Evolutionary Psychology* 15 (1994): 176–83.

Lloyd, Elisabeth Anne. "Pre-theoretical Assumptions in Evolutionary Explanations of Female Sexuality." In *Feminism and Science*. Ed. Evelyn Fox Keller and Helen E. Longino. Oxford: Oxford University Press, 1996.

Locke, John. *An Essay concerning Human Understanding*. Ed. Peter H. Nidditch. Oxford: Clarendon, 1975.

Lombroso, Cesare, and Guglielmo Ferrero. *Criminal Woman, the Prostitute, and the Normal Woman*. 1893. Trans. Nicole Hahn Rafter and Mary Gibson. Durham, N.C.: Duke University Press, 2004.

López, Ignacio-Javier. *Realismo y ficción:* La desheredada *de Galdós y la novela de su tiempo*. Barcelona: Promociones y Publicaciones Universitarias, 1989.

López-Sanz, Mariano. *Naturalismo y espiritualismo en la novelística de Galdós y Pardo Bazán*. Madrid: Pliegos, 1985.

Lukács, Georg. *The Theory of the Novel*. Trans. Anna Bostock. Cambridge, Mass.: MIT Press, 1971.

Mandrell, James. *Don Juan and the Point of Honor: Seduction, Patriarchal Society, and Literary Tradition*. University Park, Pa.: Penn State University Press, 1992.

Manzoni, Alessandro. "Lettera a Monsieur Chauvet sull'unità di tempo e di luogo nella tragedia." 1823. In *Scritti di teoria letteraria*. Milan: Biblioteca Universale Rizzoli, 1981. 53–154.

Marañón, Gregorio. "Don Juan." In *Cinco ensayos sobre don Juan*. Santiago, Chile: Cultura, 1937. 25–52.

Martí-López, Elisa. *Borrowed Words: Translation, Imitation, and the Making of the Nineteenth-Century Novel in Spain*. Lewisburg, Pa.: Bucknell University Press, 2002.

Martinell, Emma. "Isidora Rufete (La desheredada), a través del entorno inanimado." *Letras de Deusto* 16 (1986): 107–22.

Maupassant, Guy de. *Bel-Ami*. 1885. Ed. Douglas Parmee. London: Penguin, 1975.

Mayr, Ernst. "The Nature of the Darwinian Revolution." *Science* 176 (1972): 981–89.

Mbarga, Jean-Claude, ed. Introduction to *Noche*. By Alejandro Sawa. Madrid: Libertarias, 2001.

McKeon, Michael. *The Origins of the English Novel, 1600–1740*. Baltimore: Johns Hopkins University Press, 1987.

———. "Prose Fiction: Great Britain." In *The Eighteenth Century*. Ed. H. B. Nisbet and Claude Rawson. Vol. 4 of *The Cambridge History of Literary Criticism*. New York: Cambridge University Press, 1997. 249–63.

———, ed. *Theory of the Novel: A Historical Approach*. Baltimore: Johns Hopkins University Press, 2000.

Meredith, George. Prelude to *The Egoist*. 1879. Ed. Robert M. Adams. New York: Norton, 1979.

Mies, Maria. *Patriarchy and Accumulation on a World Scale: Women in the International Division of Labour.* London: Zed, 1986.

Mill, John Stuart. *The Subjection of Women.* 1869. Ontario: Broadview, 2000.

Miller, J. Hillis. *The Form of Victorian Fiction: Thackeray, Dickens, Trollope, George Eliot, Meredith, and Hardy.* Notre Dame, Ind.: University of Notre Dame Press, 1968.

Miller, Kenneth R. *Finding Darwin's God: A Scientist's Search for Common Ground.* New York: Harper Perennial, 2000.

Millett, Kate. *Sexual Politics.* Garden City, N.Y.: Doubleday, 1970.

Morton, Peter. *The Vital Science: Biology and the Literary Imagination, 1860–1900.* London: Allen and Unwin, 1984.

Nelken, Margarita. *La condición social de la mujer en España.* Madrid: CVS, 1975.

Nietzsche, Friedrich. *The Birth of Tragedy / The Genealogy of Morals.* Trans. Francis Golffing. New York: Anchor, 1956.

Nievo, Ippolito. *Le confessioni d'un italiano.* 1867. Torino: Einaudi, 1946.

Nordau, Max. *Degeneración.* Trans. N. Salmerón y García. Madrid: Librería Fernando Fé, 1892.

Núñez, Diego. *El darwinismo en España.* Madrid: Castalia, 1969.

Ordóñez, Elizabeth J. "Gender Woes: Refiguring Familial Spheres in Pardo Bazán's *Doña Milagros*." *Hispanic Journal* 20, no. 2 (1999): 311–25.

———. "Revising Realism: Pardo Bazán's *Memorias de un solterón* in Light of Galdós's *Tristana* and John Stuart Mill." In *In the Feminine Mode: Essays on Hispanic Women Writers.* Ed. Noël Valis and Carol Maier. Lewisburg, Pa.: Bucknell University Press, 1990. 146–63.

Orico, Osvaldo. *Don Juan o el vicio de amar.* Madrid: Estados, 1950.

Ortega y Gasset, José. "Asamblea para el progreso de las ciencias." 1908. In *Obras completas.* Vol. 1. Madrid: Revista de Occidente, 1961. 99–104.

———. "Las dos ironías, o Sócrates y Don Juan." 1923. In *Obras completas.* Vol. 3. Madrid: Taurus, 2004. 589–93.

———. "Galileísmo de la historia." 1934. In *En torno a Galileo.* Vol. 5 of *Obras completas.* Madrid: Revista de Occidente, 1961. 13–20.

———. *Meditaciones del Quijote.* 1914. Vol. 1 of *Obras completas.* Madrid: Revista de Occidente, 1961. 309–400.

Otis, Laura. *Membranes: Metaphors of Invasion in Nineteenth-Century Literature, Science, and Politics.* Baltimore: Johns Hopkins University Press, 1999.

Palacio Valdés, Armando. *La fe.* 1892. Madrid: Librería de Victoriano Suárez, 1926.

———. *Marta y María.* 1883. Madrid: Espasa-Calpe, 1974.

———. "Los oradores del Ateneo." 1887. In *Obras completas*. Vol. 11. Madrid: Victoriano Suárez, 1908. ix–xiii.

———. Prologue to *Marta y María*. Barcelona: Biblioteca Arte y Letras, 1883.

Paolini, Gilbert. "*Noche*, novela de Alejandro Sawa en el ambiente científico de la década de 1880." *Boletín de la Biblioteca Menéndez Pelayo* 60 (1984): 321–38.

———. "La psicopatología en la literatura italo-española: D'Annunzio y Palacio Valdés." In *The Two Hesperias: Literary Studies in Honor of Joseph G. Fucilla on the Occasion of His 80th Birthday*. Ed. Americo Bugliani. Madrid: Turanzas, 1978. 275–90.

Pardo Bazán, Emilia. *La cuestión palpitante*. 1883. Ed. José Manuel González Herrán. Barcelona: Anthropos, 1989.

———. *Doña Milagros*. 1894. In *Obras completas*. Vol. 3. Ed. Darío Villanueva and José Manuel González Herrán. Madrid: Castro, 1999.

———. *Dulce Dueño*. 1911. Ed. Marina Mayoral. Madrid: Editorial Castalia, 1989.

———. *Memorias de un solterón*. 1896. In *Obras completas*. Vol. 3. Ed. Darío Villanueva and José Manuel González Herrán. Madrid: Castro, 1999.

———. *La mujer española y otros artículos feministas*. Ed. Leda Schiavo. Madrid: Editora Nacional, 1976.

———. "Reflexiones científicas contra el darwinismo." 1877. In *Obras completas*. Vol. 3. Ed. Federico Carlos Sáinz de Robles. Madrid: Aguilar, 1973. 557–70.

Pascoli, Giovanni. *L'èra nuova: Pensieri e discorsi*. 1899. Milan: EGEA, 1994.

Paul, Diane B. "Darwin, Social Darwinism, and Eugenics." In *The Cambridge Companion to Darwin*. Ed. Jonathan Hodge and Gregory Radick. Cambridge: Cambridge University Press, 2003. 214–39.

Payer, Pierre J. *The Bridling of Desire: Views of Sex in the Later Middle Ages*. Toronto: University of Toronto Press, 1993.

———. *Sex and the Penitentials: The Development of a Sexual Code, 550–1150*. Toronto: University of Toronto Press, 1984.

Pelayo López, Francisco. "Ciencia y religión en España durante el siglo XIX." *Asclepio* 40 (1988): 187–206.

Pérez Galdós, Benito. *La desheredada*. 1881. Ed. Germán Gullón. Madrid: Cátedra, 2000.

———. *Fortunata y Jacinta*. 1886–87. Madrid: Hernando, 1979.

———. "Observaciones sobre la novela contemporánea en España." 1870. In

Ensayos de crítica literaria de Benito Pérez Galdós. Ed. Laureano Bonet. Barcelona: Península, 1990. 105–20.

———. "La sociedad presente como materia novelable." 1897. In *Ensayos de crítica literaria de Benito Pérez Galdós.* Ed. Laureano Bonet. Barcelona: Península, 1990. 157–65.

Pernet, Henry. *Ritual Masks: Deceptions and Revelations.* Columbia: University of South Carolina Press, 1992.

Perniola, Mario. *Ritual Thinking: Sexuality, Death, World.* New York: Humanity Books, 2001.

Perojo, José del. *Artículos filosóficos y políticos de José del Perojo (1875–1908).* Ed. María Dolores Díaz Regadera, Fernando Hermida de Blas, José Luis Mora, Diego Núñez, and Pedro Ribas. Madrid: Universidad Autónoma de Madrid, 2003.

Peterfreund, Stuart, ed. *Literature and Science: Theory and Practice.* Boston: Northeastern University Press, 1990.

Petersson, Robert T. *The Art of Ecstasy: Teresa, Bernini, and Crashaw.* New York: Atheneum, 1970.

Pettman, Jan Jindy. "Women, Gender, and the State." In *Worlding Women: A Feminist International Politics.* New York: Routledge, 1996. 5–15.

Phillips, Allen W. *Alejandro Sawa: Mito y realidad.* Madrid: Turner, 1976.

Picón, Jacinto Octavio. *Cuentos de mi tiempo.* Madrid: Fortanet, 1895.

———. *Dulce y sabrosa.* 1891. Ed. Gonzalo Sobejano. Madrid: Cátedra, 1990.

———. *La hijastra del amor.* 1884. Ed. Noël Valis. Barcelona: Promociones y Publicaciones Universitarias, 1990.

———. *Juan Vulgar.* 1885. In *Obras completas.* Vol. 6. Madrid: Renacimiento, 1918.

———. *Juanita Tenorio.* 1910. Vol. 3 of *Obras completas.* Madrid: Renacimiento, 1922.

———. *Mujeres.* Vol. 4 of *Obras completas.* Madrid: Renacimiento, 1916.

———. *Novelitas.* Madrid: La España, 1892.

Pike, Nelson. *Mystic Union: An Essay in the Phenomenology of Mysticism.* Ithaca, N.Y.: Cornell University Press, 1992.

Plato. *Complete Works.* Ed. John M. Cooper. Indianapolis: Hackett, 1997.

———. *Symposium.* Ed. Alexander Nehamas and Paul Woodruff. Indianapolis: Hackett, 1989.

Porrúa, María del Carmen. "La función de la ambigüedad en la protagonista de *La desheredada* de Galdós." *Filología* 20 (1985): 139–51.

Pratt, Dale J. *Signs of Science: Literature, Science, and Spanish Modernity since 1868.* West Lafayette, Ind.: Purdue University Press, 2001.

Radick, Gregory. "Is the Theory of Natural Selection Independent of Its History?" In *The Cambridge Companion to Darwin*. Ed. Jonathan Hodge and Gregory Radick. Cambridge: Cambridge University Press, 2003. 143–67.

Ràfols, Wifredo de. "From Institution to Prostitution: Bureaumania and the Homeless Heroine in *La desheredada*." *Anales Galdosianos* 37 (2002): 69–87.

Ragan, Robin. "Gossip, Gender, and Genre in *Memorias de un solterón* by Emilia Pardo Bazán." *Romance Languages Annual* 7 (1995): 597–603.

Ramón y Cajal, Santiago. "Sobre el amor y las mujeres." From *Charlas de café*. 1908. In *Obras literarias completas*. Madrid: Aguilar, 1947. 954–93.

Rancière, Jacques. *The Names of History: On the Poetics of Knowledge*. Trans. Hassan Melehy. Minneapolis: University of Minnesota Press, 1994.

Rank, Otto. *The Don Juan Legend*. Trans. and ed. David G. Winter. Princeton, N.J.: Princeton University Press, 1975.

Rappaport, Roy A. *Ritual and Religion in the Making of Humanity*. Cambridge: Cambridge University Press, 1999.

[R.A.S.]. "Coloración de los insectos y las flores." *Revista Contemporánea* 56, no. 1 (1885): 25–41.

Rauch, Alan. *Useful Knowledge: The Victorians, Morality, and the March of Intellect*. Durham, N.C.: Duke University Press, 2001.

Revilla, Manuel de la. "La emancipación de la mujer." Pts. 1 and 2. *Revista Contemporánea* 30, no. 12 (1878): 447–63; 30, no. 1 (1879): 162–81.

———. *Obras completas: Manuel de la Revilla*. Ed. Fernando Hermida de Blas, José Luis Mora García, Diego Núñez, and Pedro Ribas. 3 vols. Madrid: Universidad Autónoma de Madrid, 2006.

Ribbans, Geoffrey. *Conflicts and Conciliations: The Evolution of Galdós's Fortunata y Jacinta*. West Lafayette, Ind.: Purdue University Press, 1997.

Richards, Evelleen. "Darwin and the Descent of Woman." 1983. In *Darwin*. Ed. Philip Appleman. New York: Norton, 2001. 434–44.

Richmond, Carolyn. "En torno al vacío: La mujer, idea hecha carne de ficción, en *La Regenta* de Clarín." In *Realismo y naturalismo en España en la segunda mitad del siglo XIX*. Ed. Yvan Lissorgues. Barcelona: Anthropos, 1988. 341–67.

———. "Su único hijo." In *Romanticismo y realismo*. Ed. Iris M. Zavala. Vol. 5 of *Historia y crítica de la literatura española*. Ed. Francisco Rico. Barcelona: Editorial Crítica, 1982. 598–601.

Ríos-Font, Wadda C. *The Canon and the Archive: Configuring Literature in Modern Spain*. Lewisburg, Pa.: Bucknell University Press, 2004.

Roca i Roca, Josep. *Memoria biográfica de Joaquim María Bartrina y d'Aixemús*. Barcelona: Ajuntament Constitucional de Barcelona, 1916.

Rodgers, Eamonn. "Galdós' *La desheredada* and Naturalism." *Bulletin of Hispanic Studies* 45 (1968): 285–98.

Romero Tobar, Leonardo. *Panorama crítico del romanticismo español*. Madrid: Castalia, 1994.

Rorty, Richard. *Philosophy and the Mirror of Nature*. Princeton, N.J.: Princeton University Press, 1979.

Rosser, Sue V. *Biology and Feminism: A Dynamic Interaction*. New York: Twayne, 1992.

Rousseau, Jean-Jacques. *Émile, or On Education*. 1762. Ed. Allan Bloom. New York: Basic, 1979.

———. *The Social Contract*. Ed. Maurice Cranston. London: Penguin, 1968.

Russet, Cynthia Eagle. *Sexual Science: The Victorian Construction of Womanhood*. Cambridge, Mass.: Harvard University Press, 1989.

Sacks, Oliver. *Musicophilia: Tales of Music and the Brain*. New York: Knopf, 2007.

Sáenz-Alonso, Mercedes. *Don Juan y el donjuanismo*. Madrid: Guadarrama, 1969.

Said, Edward. *The World, the Text, and the Critic*. Cambridge, Mass.: Harvard University Press, 1983.

Salih, Sarah. "When Is a Bosom Not a Bosom?" In *Medieval Virginities*. Ed. Anke Bernau, Ruth Evans, and Sarah Salih. Toronto: University of Toronto Press, 2003. 14–32.

Sánchez, Roberto G. "The Presence of the Theater and 'The Consciousness of Theater' in Clarín's *La Regenta*." *Hispanic Review* 37 (1969): 491–509.

———. "Teatro e intimidad en *Su único hijo*: Un aspecto de la modernidad de Clarín." *Insula* 27 (1972): 3, 12.

Sánchez de Toca, Joaquín. "La doctrina de la evolución de las modernas escuelas científicas." Pts. 1 and 2. *Revista Contemporánea* 21, no. 1 (May 15, 1879): 55–91; 21, no. 3 (June 15, 1879): 273–303.

Santiáñez, Nil. *Investigaciones literarias: Modernidad, historia de la literatura y modernismos*. Barcelona: Editorial Crítica, 2002.

Sarrión Mora, Adelina. *Sexualidad y confesión: La solicitación ante el Tribunal del Santo Oficio (siglos XVI–XIX)*. Madrid: Alianza, 1994.

Sawa, Alejandro. *Noche*. 1888. Ed. Jean-Claude Mbarga. Madrid: Libertarias, 2001.

Sayers, Janet. *Biological Politics: Feminist and Anti-Feminist Perspectives*. London: Tavistock, 1982.

Scanlon, Geraldine. *La polémica feminista en la España contemporánea (1868–1974)*. Madrid: Siglo XXI, 1976.

Schmidt, Ruth A. "Emilia Pardo Bazán's Retrospective View of Naturalism: Thirty Years after *La cuestión palpitante*." In *Papers on Romance Literary Relations*. Ed. Hugh H. Chapman. University Park, Pa.: Penn State University Press, 1979. 29–42.

Schnepf, Michael A. "Galdós's Madhouse: Notes on the Socio-political and Medical Background to Leganés in *La desheredada*." *Letras Peninsulares* 17 (2004): 345–60.

———. "History to Fiction: The Political Background of Galdós' *La desheredada*." *Letras Peninsulares* 4 (1991): 295–306.

Schopenhauer, Arthur. "Metafísica del amor sexual." In *El mundo como voluntad y representación*. Trans. Pilar López de Santa María. Vol. 2. Madrid: Trotta, 2005. 584–621.

———. *Pererga and Paralipomena: Short Philosophical Essays*. Vol. 1. Oxford: Oxford University Press, 2001.

Schor, Naomi. *George Sand and Idealism*. New York: Columbia University Press, 1993.

Schraibman, Joseph, and Leda Carazzola. "Hacia una interpretación de la ironía en *La Regenta* de Clarín." In *Studies in Honor of José Rubia Barcia*. Ed. Roberta Johnson and Paul C. Smith. Lincoln, Neb.: Society of Spanish and Spanish-American Studies, 1982. 175–86.

Scott, Walter. "Essay on Romance." 1824. In *Essays on Chivalry, Romance, and the Drama*. London: Frederick Warne, 1942. 65–108.

Sebold, Russell P. *La novela romántica en España: Entre libro de caballerías y novela moderna*. Salamanca: Universidad de Salamanca, 2002.

———. *Trayectoria del romanticismo español*. Barcelona: Editorial Crítica, 1983.

Sedgwick, Eve Kosofsky. *Between Men: English Literature and Male Homosocial Desire*. New York: Columbia University Press, 1985.

Shapin, Steven. *The Scientific Revolution*. Chicago: University of Chicago Press, 1996.

Shaw, Donald L. *A Literary History of Spain: The Nineteenth Century*. London: Ernest Benn, 1972.

———. "Spain / Romántico—Romanticismo—Romancesco—Romancista—Romántico." In *"Romantic" and Its Cognates / The European History of a Word*. Ed. Hans Eichner. Toronto: University of Toronto Press, 1972. 341–71.

Shaw, Evelyn, and Joan Darling. *Female Strategies*. New York: Walker, 1985.

Shaw, George Bernard. "Ideals and Idealists." 1891. In *Documents of Mod-*

ern Literary Realism. Ed. George J. Becker. Princeton, N.J.: Princeton University Press, 1963.

———. *Man and Superman*. 1903. London: Penguin, 2000.

Sieburth, Stephanie. "Enlightenment, Mass Culture, and Madness: The Dialectic of Modernity in *La desheredada*." In *A Sesquicentennial Tribute to Galdós, 1843–1993*. Ed. Linda M. Willem. Newark, Del.: Juan de la Cuesta, 1993. 27-40.

———. *Inventing High and Low: Literature, Mass Culture, and Uneven Modernity in Spain*. Durham, N.C.: Duke University Press, 1994.

Sinclair, Alison. "The Force of Parental Presence in *La Regenta*." In *Culture and Gender in Nineteenth-Century Spain*. Ed. Lou Charnon-Deutsch and Jo Labanyi. Oxford: Clarendon, 1995. 182–98.

Sinués de Marco, María del Pilar. *El ángel del hogar: Estudios morales acerca de la mujer*. Madrid: Española de Nieto, 1862.

Six, Abigail Lee. "Mothers' Voices and Medusas' Eyes: Clarín's Construction of Gender in *Su único hijo*." In *Culture and Gender in Nineteenth-Century Spain*. Ed. Lou Charnon-Deutsch and Jo Labanyi. Oxford: Clarendon, 1995. 199–215.

Smeed, J. W. *Don Juan: Variations on a Theme*. London: Routledge, 1990.

Smith, Theresa Ann. *The Emerging Female Citizen: Gender and Enlightenment in Spain*. Studies on the History of Society and Culture. Berkeley: University of California Press, 2006.

Sole Romeo, Gloria. *La instrucción de la mujer en la Restauración: La Asociación para la Enseñanza de la Mujer*. Madrid: Universidad Complutense de Madrid, 1990.

Soriano, Elena. *El donjuanismo femenino*. Barcelona: Península, 2000.

Spinoza, Benedict de. *Ethics*. Ed. and trans. G. H. R. Parkinson. Oxford: Oxford University Press, 2000.

Squier, Susan Merrill. *Liminal Lives: Imagining the Human at the Frontiers of Biomedicine*. Durham, N.C.: Duke University Press, 2004.

Stebbins, Robert E. "France." In *The Comparative Reception of Darwinism*. Ed. Thomas Glick. Austin: University of Texas Press, 1972. 117–64.

Stendhal [Marie-Henri Beyle]. *Love*. 1822. London: Penguin, 1957.

Stoker, Bram. *Dracula*. 1897. Oxford: Oxford's World Classics, 2011.

Svevo, Italo. "L'uomo e la teoria darwiniana." 1907. In *Zeno*. Ed. Mario Lavagetto. Turin: Einaudi, 1987. 829–33.

Taine, Hippolyte Adolphe. *History of English Literature*. Vol. 1. Trans. Henry Van Laun. New York: Colonial, 1900.

Tambling, Jeremy. *Confession: Sexuality, Sin, the Subject*. Manchester: Manchester University Press, 1990.

Tang-Martínez, Zuleyma. "The Curious Courtship of Sociobiology and Feminism: A Case of Irreconcilable Differences." In *Feminism and Evolutionary Biology: Boundaries, Intersections, and Frontiers.* Ed. Patricia Adair Gowaty. New York: Chapman and Hall, 1997. 116–50.

Tanner, Tony. *Adultery in the Novel: Contract and Transgression.* Baltimore: Johns Hopkins University Press, 1979.

Tennyson, Alfred. *A Collection of Poems by Alfred Tennyson.* Selected and with introduction by Christopher Ricks. New York: Doubleday, 1972.

Tolliver, Joyce. *Cigar Smoke and Violet Water: Gendered Discourse in the Stories of Emilia Pardo Bazán.* Lewisburg, Pa.: Bucknell University Press, 1998.

Torres-Solanot, A. "Filosofía novísima: El universalismo de A. Pezzani." *Revista Europea* 7, no. 122 (June 25, 1876): 656–66.

Turner, Harriet S. "Family Ties and Tyrannies: A Reassessment of Jacinta." *Hispanic Review* 51 (1983): 1–22.

———. "The Realist Novel." In *The Cambridge Companion to the Spanish Novel from 1600 to the Present.* Ed. Harriet S. Turner and Adelaida López de Martínez. Cambridge: Cambridge University Press, 2003. 81–101.

Ullman, Joan Connelly. *The Tragic Week: A Study of Anticlericalism in Spain, 1875–1912.* Cambridge, Mass.: Harvard University Press, 1968.

Valdés, Juan de. *Diálogo de la lengua.* 1533. Ed. Juan M. Lope Blanch. Madrid: Editorial Castalia, 1969.

Valis, Noël. *The Decadent Vision in Leopoldo Alas: A Study of* La Regenta *and* Su único hijo. Baton Rouge: Louisiana State University Press, 1981.

———. "Figura femenina y escritura en la España finisecular." In *¿Qué es el modernismo? Nueva encuesta, nuevas lecturas.* Ed. Richard Cardwell and Bernard McGuirk. Boulder, Colo.: Society of Spanish and Spanish-American Studies, 1993. 103–26.

———. *The Novels of Jacinto Octavio Picón.* Lewisburg, Pa.: Bucknell University Press, 1986.

Verga, Giovanni. *I Malavoglia.* 1881. Verona: Mondadori, 1990.

Vico, Giambattista. *La scienza nuova.* 1725. Milan: Biblioteca Universale Rizzoli, 1998.

Vives, Juan Luis. *Libro llamado instrucción de la mujer cristiana.* 1524. Trans. Juan Justiniano. Madrid: Signo, 1936.

Watt, Ian. *The Rise of the Novel: Studies in Defoe, Richardson, and Fielding.* Berkeley: University of California Press, 1974.

Weber, Alison. *Teresa of Avila and the Rhetoric of Femininity.* Princeton, N.J.: Princeton University Press, 1990.

Weber, Frances W. "Ideología y parodia religiosa en *La Regenta.*" In *Clarín y La Regenta.* Ed. Sergio Beser. Barcelona: Ariel, 1982. 117–36.

Weinbaum, Alys. *Wayward Reproductions: Genealogies of Race and Nation in Transatlantic Modern Thought.* Durham, N.C.: Duke University Press, 2004.

Weinstein, Arnold. *A Scream Goes through the House: What Literature Teaches Us about Life.* New York: Random House, 2003.

Weinstein, Philip M. *The Semantics of Desire: Changing Models of Identity from Dickens to Joyce.* Princeton, N.J.: Princeton University Press, 1984.

White, Hayden. *Figural Realism: Studies in the Mimesis Effect.* Baltimore: Johns Hopkins University Press, 1999.

———. *Metahistory: The Historical Imagination in Nineteenth-Century Europe.* Baltimore: Johns Hopkins University Press, 1973.

Williams, Raymond. *Marxism and Literature.* Oxford: Oxford University Press, 1977.

Wilson, Edward O. *On Human Nature.* Cambridge, Mass.: Harvard University Press, 1978.

———. *Sociobiology: The New Synthesis.* Cambridge, Mass.: Harvard University Press, 1975.

Wittgenstein, Ludwig. "A Lecture on Ethics." *Philosophical Review* 74 (1965): 3–12.

Woolf, Virginia. *Killing the Angel in the House: Seven Essays.* London: Penguin, 1995.

Yeo, Richard R. "Scientific Method and the Rhetoric of Science in Britain, 1830–1917." In *The Politics and Rhetoric of Scientific Method: Historical Studies.* Ed. John A. Schuster and Richard R. Yeo. Dordrecht, Holland: Reidel, 1986. 259–98.

Young, Robert M. *Darwin's Metaphor: Nature's Place in Victorian Culture.* Cambridge: Cambridge University Press, 1985.

Zabalbeascoa, J. A. "El primer traductor de Charles R. Darwin en España." *Filología Moderna* 8 (1968): 269–75.

Zavala, Iris M., ed. "Estudio Preliminar." In *Iluminaciones en la sombra.* By Alejandro Sawa. Madrid: Alhambra, 1977. 3–54.

Zola, Émile. "The Experimental Novel." 1880. In *Documents of Modern Literary Realism.* Ed. George J. Becker. Princeton, N.J.: Princeton University Press, 1963. 162–96.

———. *Nana.* 1880. Ed. George Holden. London: Penguin, 1972.

———. *Thérèse Raquin.* 1867. Ed. Leonard Tancock. London: Penguin, 1962.